WHAT IS EUROPE?

A Dynamic Perspective

Richard Rose
University of Strathclyde
Glasgow, Scotland

■ HarperCollins*CollegePublishers*

Acquisitions Editor: Leo A. W. Wiegman
Project Coordination, Text and Cover Design: York Production Services
Cover Photograph: Courtesy of German Information Center
Art Coordination: York Production Services
Electronic Production Manager: Valerie Zaborski
Manufacturing Manager: Helene G. Landers
Electronic Page Makeup: York Production Services
Printer and Binder: R. R. Donnelley & Sons Company
Cover Printer: The Lehigh Press, Inc.

For permission to use copyrighted material, grateful acknowledgement is made to
the following: David M. Olson, "The Parliaments of New Democracies: the
Experience of Central Europe," in George Kurian, editor, *World Encyclopedia of
Parliaments and Legislatures.* Washington DC: Congressional Quarterly Press; Paul
Lazarsfeld Society, Vienna, *New Democracies Barometer I, II, and III* 1991–1994;
and *The Geography of the European Community,* John Cole and Francis Cole,
Routledge.

What Is Europe? A Dynamic Perspective

Library of Congress Cataloging-in-Publication Data

Rose, Richard
    What is Europe? a dynamic perspective/Richard Rose.
        p.   cm.
    Includes bibliographical references and index.
    ISBN 0-673-98087-1
    1. Europe—Politics and government—1989-   2. Democracy—Europe.
I. Title.
JN12.R63   1996
320.94'09'049—dc20
                                                                95-25903
                                                                       CIP

96 97 98 9 8 7 6 5 4 3 2

Dedicated
to two people

Juan and Rocio Linz

and one principle

Freiheit

CONTENTS

PART IV MAKING PUBLIC POLICIES

PART V INCREASING INTERDEPENDENCE

LIST OF FIGURES

LIST OF TABLES

PREFACE

This book has been more than a half century in the making. My introduction to European politics was following the news about World War II from the security of the United States. Anyone who grows up in wartime, even when a war is an ocean away, cannot be indifferent to place names and events that took the lives of tens of millions of people. As a native of Saint Louis, I was also exposed to the best of German culture, daily broadcasts of Bach, Beethoven, and Brahms on a local Lutheran radio station. This was extended by undergraduate study at Johns Hopkins University, an institution that believed in teaching European civilization from the beginning. There I was introduced to the book that became my guide to Europe from Ravenna onward: Sir Bannister Fletcher's, *A History of Archi- tecture*, a Victorian masterpiece of systematic comparison (Rose, forthcoming).

When I arrived in Europe as a student in 1953, the destruction of World War II was very evident. I saw Russian troops on patrol in Vienna, and celebrated my twenty-first birthday in the only concert house in Munich with a roof that had not been bombed off. In the countryside, the lives of millions were visibly ruled by tradition; this was true of England as it was in Ireland and in Italy south of Eboli.

Initially, my research concentrated upon the small world of Westminster pol- itics, and it was conducted in two very traditional centers, the London School of Economics and Oxford. Writing a book about English politics as a deviant case made me curious about what it left out. I turned to Northern Ireland, which had not resolved historic European conflicts about religion, nationality, and state- hood. Encouraged by Stein Rokkan, I began to undertake systematic comparative analysis of electoral behavior from Scandinavia to the Mediterranean. This gave me an excellent grounding in comparing European social structures; it also intro- duced me to Juan Linz, then a young professor at Columbia and now esteemed on many continents as a scholar with a profound feel for Europe, past and pre- sent, bad and good, and North and South.

Unlike political scientists who specialize in either European or American politics, I have always believed in comparing advanced industrial societies across the Atlantic. In the Watergate era I began systematic research in Washington, lead- ing to books on the presidency in comparative perspective. Research on the growth of government led across Europe and America to Japan, valuable because of its combination of Asian, European, and American attributes.

In no sense is this book a repeat of what I have written before. Nor could it be, given the importance for the whole of Europe of the fall of the Berlin Wall in

1989, and all that follows from that great event. As a guest professor at the Wissenschaftszentrum Berlin in those fateful years, I was able to observe history in the making when the outcome was not known. The circumstances invited deep reflection. The idea for this book came while standing by the Landswehr Canal around the corner from the Stauffenberg monument, waiting for a bus to take me to Rathenau Platz, locations that invoke tragedies of twentieth-century German history from the fall of the Kaiser's *Reich* through the Weimar Republic to the fall of Hitler's Reich.

In undertaking the research drawn on in this book, I have benefited from periods as a guest professor at the Wissenschaftszentrum Berlin, the Central European University, Prague, and a stay at the European University Institute, Florence, supported by the United States Institute of Peace. Participation in the councils of the International Political Science Association when it was actively collaborating with academicians in Communist systems gave me an insight into the old regimes there. Since 1991, I have directed an annual series of sample surveys of mass response to transformation in 15 post-Communist societies of Central and Eastern Europe and the former Soviet Union. In this book I have made particular use of the New Democracies Barometer, a multi-national survey of Central and Eastern European countries conducted annually since 1991 by the Paul Lazarsfeld Society, Vienna, with the aid of grants from the Austrian Ministry of Science & Research and the Austrian National Bank. In each country a nationally representative stratified sample of approximately 1000 respondents is interviewed each year. The author has had the good fortune to be involved from the beginning as the international scientific advisor to the Lazarsfeld Society. The continuing success of the Barometer owes much to the practical vision of Dr. Heinz Kienzl, chair of the society, and to the professional skills and *elan* of Dr. Christian Haerpfer, its scientific director. Materials on change in post-Communist Europe have also been drawn from a research program supported by Dr. Ali Kazancigil, director of the Division for the International Development of Social and Human Sciences, UNESCO. Over the years I have learned much from discussions with officials in many national governments and by acting as a consultant to OECD, the World Bank, and UN agencies.

Appropriately enough, the ideas forming the opening chapters of this book were first articulated in a conference of the Committee on Political Sociology at the University of Mannheim, chaired by Peter Flora and attended by Mattei Dogan, Juan Linz, Marty Lipset, Giovanni Sartori, and other veterans of comparative research. Citations to my co-authored works is evidence that comparative analysis can benefit through collaboration with coauthors from many countries, including Austria, Britain, France, Germany, Ireland, Japan, the United States, and Australia. Helpful comments on specific sections of earlier drafts were received from Attila Agh, Klaus von Beyme, Vernon Bogdanor, Simon Bulmer, Jim Bulpitt, Rudolf Klein, Juan J. Linz, William Maley, Thomas T. Mackie, Andrew Moravcsik, David M. Olson, Edward C. Page, Mark Pollack, Jorgen Rasmussen, Alberta Sbragia, Goran Therborn, and Sir Oliver Wright.

Richard Rose

Introduction

EUROPE: THE CHANGING IDEA OF A CONTINENT

Europe is often referred to as a clear and timeless ideal. Yet there is no agreement about what the idea of Europe symbolizes. It can be invoked as a symbol of war or of peace; of freedom or oppression; of economic dynamism or backwardness; of great achievements in music and art or a passive audience for American television sitcoms.

Geography appears to offer certainty, for the earth's surface alters very slowly. In a geographical sense, Europe is one continent among a number. It definitely excludes North America, Africa, Latin America, and Asia. Yet the boundaries of Europe have never been fixed. Egypt is an older civilization than Greece, and the Greeks regarded Persia not Rome as their rival in civilization and in war. The largest city in Turkey, Istanbul, was the defender of Christianity during the dark ages and crusades. Empires such as Britain and France had colonial outposts on distant continents. Even though England is geographically only 20 miles from France, many English people feel closer to America, Canada, or Australia than to their continental neighbors.

The significance of European geography in peace and war has been fundamentally transformed by modern technology. Whereas World War I was fought on battlefields where soldiers were within rifle shot of each other, World War II introduced aerial warfare. Today, jet planes have reduced travel time between major European centers to less than the time it takes to get to the airport and back. Telecommunications and the spread of English as a common language of international communication enable Europeans to communicate with each other at the touch of a few keys. Today, barriers to communication are not physical; they reflect individual personalities, cultures, and political institutions.

The internal boundaries of Europe have been variable through the centuries, as states have risen, expanded, contracted, or disappeared. The Italian peninsula is a fixed feature of the Mediterranean landscape, but the creation of a unified Italian state did not begin until the middle of the nineteenth century. The downfall of Communism has been followed by the breakup of Czechoslovakia, Yugoslavia, and the Union of Soviet Socialist Republics (USSR). This is in keeping with the historic European pattern of the integration and disintegration of states.

Locating Europe on a map is a test of political values. Where we look depends upon what we are looking for. A philosopher might locate the heart of Europe in Athens, the home of ancient Greek philosophers. But Athens was preem-

1

inent in the distant past; today it is the capital of a small, relatively poor European state. To describe Europe as the heir to the Roman Empire and Christian civilization is to ignore the religious schisms and wars that have torn Christianity during its history. Samuel Huntington (1993) argues that the dividing line today between European or Western civilization and other civilizations is the same as in 1500, the boundary between Western Christianity and Orthodox Christianity and Islam. In the eighteenth century Enlightenment scholars sought to "invent Western Europe and Eastern Europe" by contrasting the two parts of the continent as progressive and backward (Wolff, 1994: 5). To define contemporary Europe as a set of advanced industrial societies, implies that any country that becomes industrialized, such as Korea, thereby becomes "European."

The post-1945 Cold War between the United States and Russia drew a sharp line between Eastern Europe and the West, a term that refers to the United States as well as half of Europe. Cities such as Dresden and Prague, although west of Vienna and Stockholm, were assigned to an alien Eastern Europe. Today, a convinced European federalist might argue that Europe consists of all those countries that belong to or want to become members of the Brussels-based European Union. But doing so would rule out of Europe the nonmember states of Switzerland and Norway.

Any attempt to reduce contemporary Europe to a single idea is bound to fail, for Europeans differ about almost everything imaginable. There are striking differences *between* countries in language, religion, and economic prosperity. The two great wars of this century have been European civil wars, for they were fought between France, Germany, Austria, Italy, and Britain, countries that have always been part of Europe, however defined.

> A common civilization is one thing, political unity is another, and they should not be confused. In fact, relationships among the countries of the West have been marked by division and by particularly bloody internecine conflicts throughout their history. Fratricidal warfare might well be offered as one of the distinguishing characteristics of Western civilization (Harries, 1993: 47).

Even though countries share a commitment to democratic institutions, there are differences in the conduct of free elections.

There are also differences *within* every European country. Income and class, urban and rural, and regional differences are found in every European society. Religious commitment or indifference divides societies too. In the Netherlands differences between Protestants, Catholics, and secular groups have been so strong that the state recognizes separate educational and cultural institutions for each of these three Dutch communities. In a few European countries, such as Switzerland and Belgium, there are major divisions of language.

Berlin is the best symbol of the ambiguities of contemporary Europe. In the eighteenth century it was the capital of a small kingdom, Prussia, ruled by absolute monarchs who prided themselves on being patrons of musicians such as Johann Sebastian Bach and of giants of the Enlightenment such as Voltaire. In the nineteenth century Prussia took the lead in unifying a large number of small territories into a single German state that defeated France in battle in 1870. Berlin was central for the start of the two world wars of the twentieth century. For four decades after 1945 the city was divided between Communist East Berlin and

West Berlin. The city contains museums, opera houses and splendid buildings that are a monument to German culture; it is also the city where the final solution of the Holocaust was planned. The Soviet-built wall that divided East from West Berlin fell in 1989. The reunified Federal Republic of Germany is committed to returning the capital of the country from Bonn to Berlin; it is also committed to strengthening political barriers against the return of the worst of Berlin's past.

WHERE IS EUROPE WHEN?

In political science terms, Europe can be described as the home of the modern state. The modern European state was created in the seventeenth and eighteenth centuries as a "hard" state, legal in form but authoritarian in practice. The French king, Louis XIV, was an absolute monarch, who said: *"L'état, c'est moi"* (I am the state). The monarch's power was not controlled by the nobility, and ordinary subjects had no rights. Bureaucrats enforcing laws and collecting taxes were servants of the king, and acted on his authority. In eighteenth-century Prussia, the king claimed to be an enlightened despot, who promoted the collective good and not just the interests of "mere" individuals. The French Revolution of 1789 beheaded a monarch and created a new type of state, a republic.

From the end of the Napoleonic wars in 1815 to the outbreak of World War I in 1914, institutions of the modern state spread throughout Europe. Nationalism became a potent political force, leading to the creation of Germany and Italy as states incorporating territories formerly divided among many rulers. Industrialization created large cities, changing the way of life of millions who had lived in rural isolation. The population explosion meant there were more mouths to feed, and more soldiers to serve in armies. The transportation revolution moved goods and foodstuffs across the continent and to and from other continents. It also gave armies the capacity to attack swiftly. The idea of democracy became part of the political debate, but in many countries it was regarded as an alien idea. In 1831 Alexis de Tocqueville believed it necessary to travel to the United States in order to observe the workings of a democratic political system.

When Is Europe?

Political changes have dramatically altered the meaning and boundaries of Europe in the twentieth century. In 1900 Europe was a set of *undemocratic multinational empires.* Countries in which control of government depended on the vote of a majority of the adult male population were in a minority, and none gave the vote to women. The rule of law was upheld—but it was a system of law in which the state's authority was far more important than the rights of individuals. Authoritarian regimes were the norm. Democracy was suspect; "popular rule" and "mob rule" were often considered the same.

The pre-1914 states of Europe were multinational. States were not formed to represent people with a common language and identity; they were properties that monarchs acquired by inheritance, marriages of political convenience, or conquest. The Austro-Hungarian Empire ruled over peoples speaking more than a dozen different languages and territories since scattered among ten different states. The British Empire was a global empire. Its motto was that the sun never set on the British Empire, for its territories were found on every continent. Although a few parts of the empire, such as Australia and Canada, were self-governing, from the Indian subcontinent to Africa there were colonies ruled by Britain. France also had an empire, and Germany, Italy, and Czarist Russia sought to expand outside Europe too. The outbreak of World War I brought about the death of Europe as a continent of multinational empires. At the end of the war, the Austro-Hungarian, German, Ottoman, and Russian empires disappeared.

The 1919 Versailles peace conference established the idea of Europe as a set of *undemocratic nation-states.* This was welcomed in principle by many nationalities that had previously been part of multinational empires. However, national self-determination was an easier principle for President Woodrow Wilson to propose to the U.S. Congress than to apply on the ground in Europe, because several nationalities often lived in the same city or region—for example, Czechs and Germans in Prague, Austrians and Italians in Northern Italy, Germans and Poles in what had been Prussia and became western Poland, and Hungarians and Romanians in Transylvania. At Versailles new boundaries were drawn creating or changing the territory of more than a dozen states.

In the interwar period the attempt to spread democracy throughout Europe failed. Most important states of interwar Europe were undemocratic and Europe invented novel forms of totalitarian rule coercing people far more thoroughly than earlier authoritarian regimes. The Czarist empire was succeeded by the Communist Soviet Union, a state governed by Marxist-Leninist ideology without regard for bourgeois ideas of democracy. In Italy, Benito Mussolini created a Fascist regime. In 1933 Adolf Hitler took power in Germany in the name of the Nazi Party. Between the wars, no democratically elected government in Europe, except for that in Sweden, offered its depressed population the hope of a new deal similar to that of President Franklin D. Roosevelt in the United States.

The idea of Europe as a set of *democratic nation-states* came in the aftermath of World War II. The defeat of Germany and Italy meant the repudiation of Nazism and Fascism. Victory brought two new super-powers to the center of Europe, the United States and the Soviet Union, whose armies symbolically met in Berlin. Soon they became opponents, for political commissars followed Soviet troops, imposing Communist regimes across almost half the continent.

Western Europe became the defender of the idea of Europe as a set of democracies. Geographically, Western Europe was an elastic term, stretching from the Arctic boundaries of Scandinavian states to the Mediterranean. In terms of military security, Cold War Europe was a North Atlantic region. The North Atlantic Treaty Organization (NATO) was created in 1949 as a military alliance under American leadership to provide for collective defense of Western Europe against the further expansion of Soviet power. In the 1950s Franco-German initiatives in creating institutions of European cooperation began the process of submerging national antagonisms in institutions that have evolved into the European Union.

In Soviet-dominated countries from East Germany and Czechoslovakia to the Baltics and the Balkans, free elections were forbidden. Communist regimes were established with the totalitarian goal of transforming the whole society on Soviet-inspired lines. The institutions of a market economy were replaced by a command economy in which state ownership and bureaucratic controls replaced private property and markets. The Iron Curtain established by Soviet forces cut off cities such as Leipzig, Budapest, and Warsaw from their historic ties with other parts of Europe.

The latest phase in the development of twentieth-century Europe began with the opening of the Berlin Wall on November 9, 1989. The abrupt collapse of Soviet power has meant that countries traditionally considered part of Europe are no longer forcibly prevented from interacting with their neighbors. Central Europe is once again a meaningful region, embracing Germany, Austria, the Czech Republic, Slovakia, Hungary, Poland, and a few other parts of the old Austro-Hungarian Empire. East Europeans are now free to travel, trade, and study with Westerners. But their idea of a Western city may be Berlin or Vienna rather than London or Paris.

The defining characteristic of Europe today is *democracy on a continental scale*. West European countries do not want neighbors that are authoritarian regimes, whether Communist, Fascist, or nationalist. Such regimes would not only suppress their own citizens but also threaten to spill problems such as refugees across borders. This fear is especially evident in "front line" countries on the borders between Eastern and Western Europe, such as Germany and Austria. Post-Communist countries are seeking to institutionalize democracy. In 1990 free competitive elections were held in each post-Communist country of Central and Eastern Europe, and new governments formed. They have been followed by a second round of free elections and the peaceful change of control of government as the result of popular votes and votes in Parliament. The boundaries of democratic Europe are today far wider than at any time in the history of the continent. Yet the criterion of democracy also recognizes limits (see Figure Intr. 1).

Boundaries of Contemporary Europe

The member states of the European Union (EU) are the core countries of Europe today, for democracy is a requirement for membership in the Union. The EU is not a state; its old title of the European Community is a more apt description of it as a group of states bound together by treaty to cooperate for political and economic ends. The European Union has now created a single market for the free movement of goods, services, and peoples across Europe from Lisbon to Lapland and from Limerick to Lesbos. The six original members were France, Germany, Italy, and the three Benelux states of Belgium, the Netherlands, and Luxembourg. Membership has gradually expanded to include Denmark, Sweden, and Finland to the north; the Atlantic countries of Britain, Ireland and Portugal; the Mediterranean states of Spain and Greece, plus Austria.

The European Union is an open membership body. One post-Communist country, the former German Democratic Republic, immediately became part of the EU upon its integration in the Federal Republic of Germany in 1990. Six countries of Central and Eastern Europe—the Czech Republic, Slovakia, Hungary, Poland, Bulgaria, and Romania—have been identified as potential members. Three former republics of the Soviet Union—Estonia, Latvia and Lithuania—are also recognized as potential candidates for membership, as is Slovenia, the northernmost successor state of the former Yugoslavia.

FIGURE INTR.1

CONTEMPORARY EUROPE

For purposes of this book, Europe covers 23 countries from the Baltic to the Mediterranean and from Ireland to Bulgaria. The core countries are the member states of the European Union plus Norway and Switzerland, 17 countries that have been democracies for a century, a half century or, at the very least, two decades. All are advanced industrial countries belonging to the Organization for Economic Cooperation and Development (OECD); hence, the countries can also be described as OECD Europe. Six democratizing countries of Central and Eastern Europe—the Czech Republic, Slovakia, Hungary, Poland, Bulgaria, and Romania—are included here to represent post-Communist countries.

A few countries are excluded from consideration in this edition because their position is exceptional or their size marginal. The three Baltic states of Estonia, Latvia and Lithuania face distinctive problems because they lost their independence after being invaded by the Soviet Union in World War II and later incorporated into that state. With large Russian minorities and strategic proximity to Russia, their position is different from Central and East European countries that maintained their independence after 1945 (e.g., see Rose and Maley, 1994). Slovenia, the one republic of the former Yugoslavia that is clear of its war zone, is omitted because it has been part of Yugoslavia for most of this century. Small, "postage stamp" countries on the fringes of Europe, such as Iceland and Malta, are omitted to avoid distraction.

A political definition of Europe excludes countries that are not, or are not yet, democratic (see Chapter 14).Yugoslavia is geographically part of Europe, but when democracy is the criterion, Tito's independent Communist state of Yugoslavia could not be considered democratic. The war between Serbia, Croatia, and Bosnia requires a book on its own. It is misleading to treat genocidal killings in Bosnia as typical of post-Communist countries, for a striking feature of the collapse of Communism is that Bosnia is the exception. No deaths by violence occurred in the downfall of Communist regimes in the Czech Republic, Slovakia, Hungary, Poland, and Bulgaria. Only Romania experienced a violent overthrow of its national Communist dictator, Nicolae Ceauşescu. Allowing for population difference, the estimated eight thousand killed in Romania was less than a fifth the deaths in Northern Ireland from 1969 to the 1994 cease-fire. No one would project the unfinished conflict between nations and religions in Northern Ireland onto England or Europe today.

The dividing line between Eastern Europe and Asia runs through Russian territories (cf. Szporluk, 1991; Wolff, 1994). The Soviet Union was an assembly of 15 republics in Europe, the Middle East, and Asia. Russians constituted just over half the population of the USSR. The Communist Party claimed that class was more important than national identity. However, when Mikhail Gorbachev called a referendum on the maintenance of the USSR in March 1991, six republics boycotted it or held counterreferendums in which an overwhelming majority voted for independence. An attempted Communist coup in Moscow in August 1991 was an incentive to other republics of the Soviet Union to distance themselves from Moscow politics. In December 1991, Gorbachev gave up office and the USSR was formally dissolved.

Successor states of the Soviet Union have changed but have not yet established a claim to democratic status (see Chapter 14). Boris Yeltsin was elected president in 1991 when the Russian Federation was part of the Soviet Union. The conflict between the president and Parliament in the autumn of 1993 led to armed battles at the Parliament building in which hundreds died. The introduction of free elections and representative government has presented great difficulties in Russia (White et al., 1996). In December 1994, the Russian government launched a military campaign against a breakaway group in Chechnya. Russia is sufficiently different and sufficiently important politically to merit a book on its own. Other former Soviet Republics face big problems, including ethnic clashes and relations with Russia. Because new republics are not yet stabilized and many are outside historic European boundaries, the successor states of the former Soviet Union are best considered in a book on their own (cf. Laitin, 1991; Bremmer and Taras, 1993).

The end of the Cold War has reduced the priority given military security through NATO, and thus the importance of the United States in the affairs of democratic Europe. Concurrently, the growing economic importance of the European Union has increased the importance of regional ties between European states. Just as Europeans cannot influence America's negotiations with Canada, Mexico, or Japan, so important European decisions affecting international trade are made with the United States on the outside looking in.

To describe the Europe of the 1990s as a "new" Europe is half correct. It is certainly different from what went before, a continent divided between a democratic West and a Communist-dominated East. But geographically, Europe today is closer to the boundaries of Europe as it existed in 1900 or 1919 than it is to the boundaries of Cold War Europe.

WHY STUDY EUROPE?

In a world of more than 150 countries, the first question a student of comparative politics may ask is: Why study Europe? By almost any standard—democratic political institutions, economic wealth, or international security—the states of Europe collectively have much to offer anyone interested in political science. Studying Europe comparatively offers a deeper awareness of how democracies work and how they can differ; it can also increase awareness of what is distinctive about one's own country.

The Importance of Europe

There are three continents in which democracy is politically central—Europe, North America, and Australia. Because Europe is divided into dozens of countries, the majority of democracies in the world today are European. This does not mean that geography causes democracy or that a country must be European in order to be democratic: India and Japan are examples of countries that are not European yet are today established democracies (Weiner and Ozbudun, 1987). Nonetheless, any statement about democracy must fit European experience. In the world of democracies, it is the United States that is exceptional.

Europe is also important for war and peace. In the first half of this century, it was the chief battleground in world wars claiming tens of millions of lives. Since 1945, Europe has been a testing ground for institutions of collective security. World war has been avoided for half a century, for the Cold War did not develop into a shooting war. The collapse of the Soviet Union has created a new situation in which localized and civil wars appear a greater threat to peace.

The most populous single state in Europe, the reunited Federal Republic of Germany, has 80 million people, two-thirds the population of Japan and one-third that of the United States. But if we add up the total population of the 17 established democracies of OECD Europe, it is equal to the combined population of the United States and Japan (Figure Intr.2). If the population of post-Communist states of Central and Eastern Europe are added to OECD Europe, the total population becomes 200 million greater than the United States.

Economically, the European continent has the largest concentration of advanced industrial countries. The total gross domestic product (GDP) of OECD Europe is now 31 percent greater than the United States and more than double that of Japan. In sheer financial terms, Europe in aggregate is a much bigger market for production and consumption than is the United States.

From the perspective of the average individual, the total wealth of a continent is less important than individual resources. Dividing a country's gross do-

FIGURE INTR.2   EUROPE COMPARED WITH THE UNITED STATES AND JAPAN

Population (in millions)

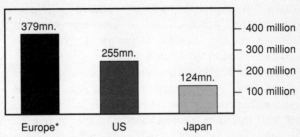

Total Gross Domestic Product (1992 US $)

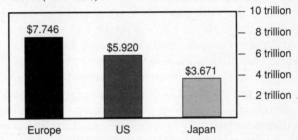

Gross Domestic Product per Capita (1992 US $)

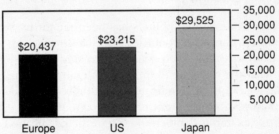

Gross Domestic Product per Capita — Adjusted for Purchasing Power Parity (1992 US $)

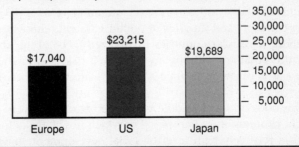

Source: OECD in Figures (Paris: Supplement to the *OECD Observer* No. 188, June/July 1994), 14-25.

mestic product by its population produces a measure of individual resources. On a per capita basis, the national product of Europe is one-eighth less than that of the United States. But comparing the whole of Europe with the United States ignores very big differences in living standards within Europe. In 1992 the gross domestic product per head in U.S. dollar terms was higher in seven European countries—Germany, Austria, Denmark, Luxembourg, Norway, Sweden and Switzerland—than in the United States.

The bottom line in comparing living standards is the goods and services that money can buy. Cross-national comparisons in terms of U.S. dollars can be misleading, for the value of the dollar in international money markets fluctuates in accord with inflation, interest rates, and speculative factors that do not reflect purchasing power. Prices of goods and services are set in national currencies, not dollars. High earnings in Scandinavia and Japan are matched by high prices and high taxes. The effect of differences in currencies can be controlled by converting current dollar values into their equivalent purchasing power parity (PPP). This deflates the Japanese national product a lot, because of very high prices in yen, and deflates European living standards a little.

When allowance is made for difference in purchasing power, the national product per European is one-quarter less than that per American, and one-eighth less than that per Japanese. After controlling for differences in purchasing power parity, Germany, Luxembourg, and Switzerland each have a higher GDP per capita than does Japan. By international standards, the average European can be described as among the relatively affluent citizens of the world.

Learning from Comparison

Traditionally, comparative politics has been taught by setting out facts about a few important European countries, such as Britain, France, Germany, and sometimes the Soviet Union. Each country is treated as a case study; little attention is given to what the cases are examples of. Memorizing large masses of information with little idea of their significance can numb the mind. Moreover, a book separating countries into different chapters cannot deal with developments across Europe—for example, democratization or the rise of the European Union.

The alternative extreme is to focus upon abstract ideas such as democracy, authoritarianism, or political development and selectively refer to different countries around the globe as examples. Britain can exemplify a stable democracy, China a stable authoritarian regime, and Nigeria a developing nation. Introducing concepts and theories of political systems shifts attention from information about particular countries to "stylized facts" about theoretical systems or illustrations that are without any context. It risks stating the obvious—for example, that it is easier to finance a welfare state in a rich country than in a poor country.

This book adopts a middle way; it compares relatively similar countries, the states of contemporary Europe, all of which now have democratic political institutions, a relatively high level of social development, and a modern economy. Such a book does not suffer from a shortage of information; instead, it risks drowning readers and author in an ocean of facts.

To compare central properties of European political systems, we need concepts. "Science depends on its concepts. These are ideas which receive names. They determine the questions one asks and the answers one gets. They are more fundamental than the theories which are constructed from them." (Thompson, 1961: 4; see also Rose, 1991). Concepts such as the state, free elections, and representation identify attributes likely to be found in every European political system; they guide the systematic collection and classification of information.

Whereas a book about a single country can describe political parties by their familiar names, a book about countries with more than a dozen different languages must translate many words into a common concept. For example, left and right are familiar concepts used to distinguish parties favoring those with lower and higher incomes. Notwithstanding differences in their names, we can group the British Conservatives and the Swedish Moderates together as parties on the right, and the British Labour Party and the Swedish Social Democratic Workers Party on the left. Once this is done, we can then address such questions as: Do parties of the right or the left more often win elections? Examining the results of hundreds of elections over the years across Europe provides a solid empirical basis and avoids misleading generalization from a single election or a single country.

Comparing European countries assumes the existence of similarities and of differences (Dogan and Pelassy, 1990). Although it is unusual for any political phenomenon to be identical in two dozen countries, it is even more unusual for political institutions to be completely different from each other. Systematically analyzing many countries makes it possible to identify patterns common in many countries. For example, a review of the electoral systems of Europe shows that in nine-tenths of the cases seats in Parliament are awarded by proportional representation. The first-past-the-post electoral system familiar in Britain and the United States is the exception, not the rule for democratic political systems.

To put flesh on the bare bones of concepts, abundant empirical evidence is presented. Empirical evidence—that is, observation based upon experience— takes many forms. It includes historical events, constitutional rules, and geographical facts as well as quantified data. Statistics are employed in the original sense of the word, data relevant to affairs of state. In some fields, such as elections, basic information is numerical. But many topics of comparative politics must be named before they can be counted (Sartori, 1984: 10 ff.). For example, we need to know what a federal constitution is before we can say whether federalism is found in Sweden or Switzerland. We can then count the frequency with which constitutions are federal or unitary and seek reasons to account for variation. The maps, figures, and tables of this book are intended to show patterns across Europe; basic information for individual countries is given in the appendix.

Every book must leave out a lot too; "*history is not a compilation of facts, but an insight into a moving process*" (Giedion, 1967: vi; italics in the original). This book is definitely not a chronicle, for a thousand-page volume would have less than a page for each year of Europe's past. Nor is it a book about current events, for the most important forms of knowledge concern durable characteristics of political systems. A book is a medium for giving depth to what can only be seen in two-dimensional sound bites on a television screen. Nor does this book give details of the minutiae of government, for doing so would obscure the forest by concentrating upon trees and individual leaves. Books and articles are frequently cited as guidance to further reading.

Intellectually, an examination of different ways in which countries govern themselves expands our idea of the possibilities of politics. This is particularly important when people are dissatisfied and regard their national institutions as unsatisfactory. To improve conditions, the alternatives are to engage in unbounded speculation about what might be done, or turn to other countries for lessons about how they have responded to similar problems, whether unemployment or drug control. In the early nineteenth century, Europeans visited the United States to study the first major example of a democratic political system. Japan's rise to world prominence was based upon the careful study of remote and powerful European countries (Westney, 1987). The division of Europe into several dozen states provides even greater scope for learning from comparison. To distinguish between applicable and inapplicable lessons, we need to know a lot about political institutions (Rose, 1993).

A STATE-CENTRIC BOOK

To view European history as if it were about the rise of democracy is to read history backward, projecting today's values upon the past. If we start at the beginning, the picture is very different. A book about the fundamentals of government in Europe must emphasize the "hard" facts of political life, such as war, revolution, dictatorship, and unsuccessful attempts to create democracies. Individuals were subjects of the state, not citizens able to choose how they should be governed. The legitimacy of the state was less certain than its claim to a monopoly of force (cf. Weber, 1972: 822). The development of a democratic state in Europe is very different from the American model of public opinion and popular wishes as the starting point of government. For most of modern European history, the state has *not* been government of, by, and for the people. The state was governed by elites that pursued their own ideas and interests, ignoring and sometimes suppressing popular views. A state-centric model is necessary to understand the politics of Europe.

Centrality of States

The starting point for the exercise of political authority is the state. The modern state is a permanent institution, consisting of organizations responsible for internal order (the police and courts); protection against foreign threats (the military); supplying money (a central bank); enacting laws of property and commerce to underpin a modern market economy; and employing officials to collect taxes and administer policies (see Rose, 1976). The state is an autonomous institution "above and distinct from both government and governed" (Dyson, 1980: 51; see also Nordlinger, 1981).

The modern state began as a "hard" state with executive, legislative, judicial, and administrative institutions sufficient to exercise authority effectively and lawfully throughout its territory. In retrospect, this seems obvious, but in the seventeenth century, enforcing the king's will was easier said than done. The modern state was not about rule by the people but about the rule of law. Law was a means of the state exercising authority over its subjects. The modern state was a *Rechtsstaat* (Rule-of-Law State). This German term emphasizes "order, certainty, predictability, equality before the judge and the tax collector," and "avoiding capriciousness, arbitrariness, and unreliability in political rule" (Freddi, 1986: 158). These are necessary but not sufficient conditions for democracy (see Table Intr.1; for detailed accounts, see Anderson and Anderson, 1967; Tilly, 1975).

Politics in a hard state arises from the clash between elite interests, ideas, and ambitions. The elites included aristocrats who owed their position to birth, leaders of the state church, officials who served the king and sometimes representatives of a country's small business class, who were not as wealthy as landed aristocrats and the state church. Although the capacity to influence the state was a privilege shared by all elites, there were always disagreements within and between elites about how the state should be governed, and who should benefit from public policies. In places such as England, Parliament became a forum in which conflicts could be expressed openly; by the seventeenth century the parliamentary elite was able to enforce its authority over the king of England.

Policy outputs of the modern state were initially few. The first concern was the maintenance of order. The term "police state" described the desire of authorities to curb disorder and protect established institutions and property, especially those of the state (see Chapman, 1970; Heidenheimer, 1986: 7 ff.). To do this required both courts and a bureaucracy, officials who followed rules laid down by their superiors and enforced laws upon subjects. To pay the state's servants required tax revenue. In the eighteenth century, Prussia and France took the lead in creating bureaucracies. Authorities could invoke the doctrine of an enlightened despot, religious authority, or both to justify telling people what they could and could not do and think. Individuals were not citizens but subjects; they were acted upon by the authorities rather than voicing demands to government.

The modern state was authoritarian, not totalitarian, for the rule of law limited what it did. Laws also licensed the formation of economic, social, and civic institutions independent of the state. This created a *civil society*, civil because it was in accord with the law, yet independent of the state. Within a framework of

TABLE INTR.1 A MODEL OF THE EUROPEAN HARD STATE

Constitutional Authority	Elite Coalitions	Policy Outputs	Civil Society
Executive	Aristocrats	Order	Economic guilds
Courts	Church	Property rights	Civic associations
Parliament	Army	Welfare	Culture
Bureaucracy	State servants		Press

Source: Prepared by the author.

law, people could pursue profit, learning, or charity. The scope for autonomy varied greatly. The continental tradition of the hard state was to control people rather than grant civil rights. By contrast, in England, freedom of association was guaranteed much earlier. Censorship could limit what was printed in newspapers and books or performed on the stage or in an opera house. Laws could grant a small fraction of males a limited right to vote, but they could also suppress political activity inconsistent with the state's wishes. France, Germany, Austria, and Italy required trade unions and political parties to register with the state, and in some cases socialist organizations and trade unions were declared illegal (Bendix and Rokkan, 1964). In places such as the Papal States of Italy, the church assumed coercive authority, controlling education and regulating public morality.

Dynamics of Change

Democratization has been a process of moving from an authoritarian rule of law state to a system of representative government accountable to a mass electorate. European countries have differed in the challenges that they have faced along the way, and in the turnings taken, including wrong turnings.

The Industrial Revolution, beginning in England in the eighteenth century, created new cities that could not be governed by methods suited to a medieval village or a Renaissance palace. Nor could order and public health be maintained by traditional means. A "revolution in government" was required, creating new institutions to deliver the goods and services necessary in an industrial society. When the modern state was founded, state and church were the only major nationwide institutions. The explosion of population, wealth, communications, and education created new institutions and new elites, based on business enterprises and associations, trade unions, the press, and universities. Such institutions have not thought of themselves as "political" in the party political sense, yet their leaders often see themselves as acting in the public interest, and many benefit from public policies, directly or indirectly.

Competition between elites is inherently unstable. Since established elites had benefited from the rules of the game, their opponents had incentives to change the rules. In France popular pressures resulted in established elites reducing their control of the state; in 1848 all adult males were given the right to vote. In the Habsburg Empire pressures from nationalities led to the creation of a dual monarchy with separate Hungarian and Austrian governments based in Budapest and Vienna. Competition between elites sometimes led to the enfranchisement of men and later of women, but sometimes it led instead to authoritarian or totalitarian regimes—or first one and then the other.

In the twentieth century world wars have demonstrated great miscalculations by national rulers, for every war produces as many losers as winners—and the price that European states have paid for victory has been great. In the economy, the great depression between the two world wars showed limits to government's capacity to give positive direction to the market. It was not until after World War II that government has been able to finance welfare states that today claim a substantial portion of a country's national product. At one point or an-

EUROPE: THE CHANGING IDEA OF A CONTINENT   15

other, all the countries examined in this book have become democracies. The introduction of free elections and mass political organization has enabled the mass of the population to influence elite coalitions. Their reactions can feed back through elections, public opinion polls, and other means, sending signals to governors about how they want their country to be governed.

Principal Themes of the Book

Today's political institutions were not chosen by today's governors; they were inherited from the past. To understand the *dynamics* of Europe, we need to *understand the past as well as the present;* that is the first theme of the book. How much history is enough? At least enough to understand current events. Joseph Schumpeter, a Viennese-born Harvard professor of economics, has described the link between past and present thus:

> No decade in the history of politics, religion, technology, painting, poetry and what not ever contains its own explanation. In order to understand the religious events from 1520 to 1530 or the political events from 1790 to 1800 or the developments in painting from 1900 to 1910, you must survey a period of much wider span. (Schumpeter, 1946:1).

We certainly cannot understand destruction of half of Europe in 1996 if we do not know what it was like before the Iron Curtain fell in 1989. Identifying connections between past and present indicates how much or how little we can expect European states to alter in the immediate future. For example, the British welfare state today is not the choice of today's governors but the inheritance of choices over nearly a century. Inherited commitments proved remarkably resistant even to Margaret Thatcher's desire to abandon them while she was Prime Minister (Rose and Davies, 1994). The economic difficulties facing Czechs today are not the choice of the freely elected Czech government but the inheritance of 40 years of Communist rule. As von Beyme (1993: 409) notes, "Ex-socialist countries suffer from the burdens of the past even when they abandon Communist ideology."

The first chapter outlines the dominant features of Europe in the first half of this century, when it was undivided and undemocratic. That period of war and revolution has left a legacy that still influences today's governors. Chapter 2 examines how Europe has been twice transformed since 1945. The first transformation turned Western Europe into a set of democratic and increasingly affluent nations, closely linked with the United States, while Central and East Europeans lived in another world, dominated by Communist institutions and Soviet troops. The second transformation, begun with the fall of the Berlin Wall, has created the Europe of the 1990s. The wall between democratic and authoritarian systems has gone, but many differences remain between East and West, and North and South too.

Democracy and democratization is the second major theme of this book. Democracy distinguishes contemporary European states from their nineteenth-century predecessors; it also distinguishes Central and East European regimes today from the regimes that governed there ten years ago. The very different routes that European countries have taken to democracy are examined in Chapter 3. It contrasts countries that have evolved representative institutions over many generations as in England or Sweden; those having democratic institutions introduced by armies of occupation, as happened in Germany; countries formulating democratic constitutions in reaction against decades of dictatorships, as in Spain; and post-Communist countries seeking to create democracy where it has not flourished before.

Creating a constitutional framework for authority is a necessary part of the process of democratization. Chapter 4 examines the different political purposes for which European states have been created, and their constitutional foundations, including institutions to maintain the rule of law. Since the foundations of post-Communist states are different, they are examined separately. Governors there are under immediate pressure to craft democratic institutions in place of a state founded on the totalitarian Soviet model. Chapter 5 describes the ways in which post-Communist states have sought to establish a new framework that grants authority to the state and freedom to civil society, and the extent to which these efforts are securing popular acceptance.

A third theme is *bringing the people into government* through the politics of representation. Elections are essential to make government democratic, and competitive elections require political parties. The choice of parties in Europe is much wider than in a two-party system, because cultural as well as economic cleavages are important, as Chapter 6 makes clear. There are often Catholic, socialist, farmers' and green ecology parties, as well as liberal and conservative parties. In Central and Eastern Europe, Communist regimes eliminated or took over institutions of civil society. Chapter 7 explains why this has created widespread popular distrust of political institutions and a "demobilized" electorate, making it difficult to establish stable parties.

The object of elections is to create a government; the British saying—"The Queen's government must be carried on"—emphasizes the need for the state to be governed, whatever the election result. Chapter 8 shows that the use of proportional representation makes coalition government the most common form of government in Europe. This offers a broader base for popular support than a single-party government; it also requires more political negotiations to secure a consensus for action. The prime minister of the day leads only one party in a coalition. The cabinet contains politicians who represent competing coalition partners and individuals with competing ambitions. When control of government is divided, there are problems of leadership and accountability. Parliament retains the power to dismiss a government that has lost its confidence, but the electorate cannot always be clear which among several coalition partners is to blame for the government's faults, as Chapter 9 explains.

In an era of big government, politics is more than a game. A fourth theme is *making and delivering public policies* of major importance to almost every household. Giving direction to government is not the exclusive preserve of the prime minister and the cabinet ministers. The delivery of public policies nationwide combines activities of public agencies administering laws, employing specialists in education or health, or promoting economic growth. Most activities of government are in the hands of civil servants. Chapter 10 emphasizes that higher civil servants have views about how the state should and should not act. Interest groups are often involved in policy making too, as lobbyists and sometimes as members of corporatist institutions in which they help make and implement policies.

From the "underall" view of ordinary people, the outputs of policies—health, education, social security, and other benefits—are as important as voting. This is particularly the case when governments claim two-fifths to one-half the national product in taxes to finance a high level of social welfare benefits. Chapter 11 systematically examines major policy concerns of European states: public order and national security, the economy, social security, health, and education. Differences between established European democracies and the post-Communist states of Eastern Europe are not due to differences in the preferences of voters; they are a legacy of decades of Communist rule. Chapter 12 documents the effects of this upon the economic behavior and welfare of people in post-Communist societies.

The basic analytic unit in this book is the state, but sovereign states can no longer be examined in isolation. European states are becoming more and more *interdependent*. The expansion of the European Union, with headquarters in Brussels, illustrates this increase in political and economic interdependence. It has grown from six states in 1957 to 15 member states today. Chapter 13 shows how the growth of the European Union has blurred the line between domestic and international politics. On many issues cabinet ministers must deal not only with competing claims in their own country but also with pressures from other states in the European Union and officials in Brussels. The authority of the European Union is limited by treaty, by politics, and by the need for agreement between member states before major steps forward can be taken.

In the contemporary world, no continent can stand alone; interdependence is global. The deutsche mark, the British pound, and the American dollar are traded in Frankfurt and London while Americans sleep; in New York when Europeans are getting ready for bed, and in Tokyo when Europeans are sleeping. The concluding chapter examines the limits of Europe's insulation from other continents. The global interests of the United States impose a different form of interdependence. In a world of flux within and between continents European governments must become adept at multilevel politics, involving national, European, and international influences.

Approaching the year 2000, Europe is a very different continent from what it was a half century ago. Increasing economic interdependence has not abolished national differences or national interests. The creation of the European Union reflects common interests and values, but the politics of the European Union emphasizes disagreements. The fall of the Iron Curtain removed an artificial barrier between countries of Europe, but it will take many years to remove the legacy of differences. A continent as full of history as Europe cannot be transformed overnight.

part **I**

A CENTURY
OF CHANGE

1

UNDEMOCRATIC AND UNDIVIDED: EUROPE UP TO 1945

The governors of European states do not inherit a blank map; they live in a continent where national boundaries have been fought over through the centuries. The Roman Empire of two thousand years ago was the first great power in Europe. It made no claims to democracy; government was in the hands of a Caesar, a word that has survived in the names of such autocrats as the German kaiser and the Russian czar. The Roman Empire was multinational, ruling over people in lands as far apart as Great Britain and Palestine; its subject populations spoke dozens of languages and had no common national identity. The Roman Empire collapsed, but its successors, whether pagan, Catholic, Orthodox, or Moslem, made no pretense of ruling a single nationality. Nor did they claim to rule with the consent of the people. Custom and coercion were sufficient justifications for authority.

The institutions of contemporary government are a matter of inheritance, not choice. The connection between past and present institutions is exceptionally long in Britain, for institutions such as Parliament trace their origins to the thirteenth century, and the prime ministership to the eighteenth century. The links between past and present are also palpable in the lives of leading politicians. Winston Churchill, Charles de Gaulle and Konrad Adenauer, each born in the nineteenth century, did much to influence the European state system in the second half of the twentieth century.

In pre-1914 Europe government was effective. States maintained large standing armies and in countries such as France and Germany, young men did compulsory military service. States could regulate trade and collect taxes on such everyday commodities as matches or tobacco. When industrialization was viewed as in the national interest, the state promoted industries through legislation that created monopolies or favored large enterprises, and financed or owned such basic services as the post office, telephones, and railways.

The state in pre-1914 Europe was also small. Education was the one social policy provided almost everyone, as basic literacy was necessary for participation in everyday life as a worker, a dutiful subject, a Christian, or a citizen. But free public education was confined to four to eight years of elementary schooling. Countries such as Britain and Germany began to introduce some social benefits for some people, but the coverage was limited and benefits few. Moreover, the

FIGURE 1.1

EUROPE : A SET OF MULTINATIONAL
EMPIRES BEFORE 1914

motive was not always democratic. Bismarck's Germany pioneered the welfare state in the 1880s in the hope that the paternalistic provision of benefits would "buy" loyalty to an authoritarian regime that denied recipients full democratic rights (Flora and Alber, 1981).

AN ERA OF UNDEMOCRATIC MULTINATIONAL EMPIRES

The map of Europe before 1914 has little relation to the map of Europe today (Figure 1.1). Most major states of Europe were multinational empires. In the Austro-Hungarian Empire, the people we now think of as Austrians were a small minority of the total population. Germany contained substantial French- and Polish-speaking minorities and had designs on territories inhabited by German-speakers outside the kaiser's empire. The empire of the Russian czar extended from Finland through Poland to part of what is now Romania; east of the Ural mountains it incorporated Moslem and Asiatic territories. The Ottoman Empire was a mixture of Turks, Greeks, and many other nationalities stretching from the Balkans through the Middle East. The United Kingdom embraced the whole of Ireland, Scotland, and Wales; it was also an imperial authority ruling colonies around the globe. France and Italy could claim to be states in which the great majority of citizens shared a common language and sense of national identity, but they were creating empires abroad. Small Scandinavian countries were distinctive in not having or seeking overseas empires.

Among the seven major states of Europe in 1914, there was little pretense of democracy in the Ottoman Empire based in Constantinople (now Istanbul) or in the Russian czar's empire. The German, Austro-Hungarian, and Italian states had representative assemblies, but they had limited influence upon government. Only in Britain and France could the outcome of a general election change control of government.

The lives of the great majority of Europeans were not much affected by what government did, for the great majority lived in rural villages or small towns remote from the national capital. In France, 61 percent of the population lived in villages of less than 5000 people, in Germany 51 percent, and in Sweden 77 percent. Britain was unusual in having most of its population living in industrial cities. Before World War I, only seven cities in Europe had more than one million people: Saint Petersburg, Moscow, Berlin, Vienna, Paris, London, and Glasgow, (Mitchell, 1975: 76–78; cf. Flora et al., 1987: ch. 3).

The isolation of the mass of the population meant that "high politics" could be conducted by elites with little need to communicate with subjects and little regard for what we now think of as public opinion. The opinions that counted most were those of government officials and those who aspired to govern. In the majority of European countries aristocrats and servants of the royal household enjoyed influence over government. Bureaucrats could claim freedom from influence by parliament on the grounds that they served the monarch. In some European countries state censors set limits to opinions that could be discussed in public; official opinion was more important than public opinion (see Anderson and Anderson, 1967: 245–271; Noelle-Neumann, 1993). Countries such as Britain, where a free press could criticize what government did and parties could hold the government of the day accountable in Parliament, were then the exception rather than the rule.

Dynastic and Absorptive Monarchies

Because the major states were dynastic monarchies, their territories could expand through wars, accidents of inheritance, and political marriages without regard to the views of subjects. For example, the Kingdom of England became a multinational state starting with the conquest of Ireland in the twelfth century. In 1485 inheritance brought to the throne a Tudor Prince of Wales. Following the death of Queen Elizabeth I in 1603, the king of Scotland inherited the Kingdom of England, and moved from Edinburgh to the more prosperous and powerful capital, London. In 1801 the United Kingdom was created when England, Scotland, Wales, and Ireland were joined in a single Parliament at Westminster. Its present boundaries were fixed in 1921, after most of Ireland won independence by force of arms.

Central Europe was full of German-speaking peoples ruled by arrangements that dated back to the origins of the Holy Roman Empire. Prussian and Habsburg monarchs competed for influence (cf. Meyer, 1955). In the Austro-Prussian War of 1866, the military strength of the Kingdom of Prussia checked the claims of the Habsburg monarchy to make Vienna the capital of German-speaking peoples. The Franco-Prussian War of 1870 brought Prussia territories to its west. In 1871 the king of Prussia was proclaimed as Kaiser (Emperor) Wilhelm I of the much enlarged German *Reich* (Empire). The Kingdom of Italy resulted from nationalist military campaigns in the Italian peninsula, leading to the gradual amalgamation of small territories and a reduction in the territory of the Papal States ruled from the Vatican. Rome became the capital of the Kingdom of Italy in 1870.

The sixteenth-century Reformation created a basic division between kingdoms on the basis of religion. Most of Northern Europe became Protestant, Southern Europe remained Catholic, and Eastern Europe was Catholic or Orthodox. Religion was a matter of state, not a matter of private conviction. The conversion of a monarch to a different religion—sometimes undertaken for political convenience—forced the mass of the population to change religion too. In many European countries, those who did not belong to the state church lacked civil rights. In Germany the population was a mixture of Protestant and Catholic, but the kaiser was Protestant and the Catholic church was part of the opposition to the government. In the United Kingdom, the great majority of the population was Protestant, except in Ireland, where it was Catholic; religious divisions became the basis of political divisions still evident in Northern Ireland today. In France and Italy all the population was nominally Catholic, but in the nineteenth century political divisions about church influence in politics resulted in anticlericals becoming dominant in the French state. The Ottoman Empire was so diverse in religion that for some purposes the population was divided and governed on the basis of religion rather than place of residence. The *millet* system created separate political jurisdictions for different religions: Moslem, Orthodox, Jewish and so forth

Dynastic empires required a common language for governance. For centuries Latin was the medium of communication between lay rulers and literate officials. As long as the majority of the population was illiterate and lived in isolated villages, the language used at court was of little consequence. Bilingualism often occurred naturally as people spoke different languages at work or in markets and at home. By the beginning of the twentieth century, the spread of mass literacy, the popular press, rapid transit by train, and the rise of big cities increased the political salience of language. Groups often began to articulate demands for national self-government, using language as a major criterion for defining nationality.

Dynastic rulers were not concerned with nationality; the right to command rested upon custom, inherited legal obligations, and force. This made it easy to accommodate territorial expansion in other continents, and global imperialism flourished. At the beginning of the twentieth century, the British crown was preeminent. India was its largest possession; it incorporated territories now divided into Pakistan, Bangladesh, and the Republic of India. The British Empire also expanded in West, East, and South Africa. A large measure of self-government was given to the dominions of Canada, Australia, New Zealand, and the Union of South Africa. Other European countries, such as France, Germany, Italy, Belgium, the Netherlands, Portugal, and Spain, developed colonial empires to a lesser extent, as did the United States. Insofar as imperialists recognized any principle of nationality, it was that European nationalities were "superior" to other peoples and should rule over them.

In 1914 Scandinavian countries were exceptional among European states in that virtually everyone living in Sweden, Norway, or Denmark was of the same religion and language and shared a common national identity. Yet this homogeneity had only been achieved relatively recently. Denmark lost Norway to Sweden in 1814 because it was on the losing side in the Napoleonic wars; it lost Schleswig-Holstein to Germany in 1864. Norway did not become independent of Sweden until 1905 and Finland did not finally become independent of Russia until after the collapse of the Czarist Empire in 1917.

Representative Institutions—Weak and Strong

Some kind of representative institutions existed in almost every European country at the beginning of the twentieth century, but they were not democratic institutions as we know them today. Although free elections were held in most states of Central and Western Europe, the majority of men were usually denied the right to vote, and everywhere except in Finland and Norway women were not allowed to vote. The franchise was limited to people with a stated amount of property or education. Second, there were usually big differences in the number of electors from constituency to constituency. In some countries there were separate electoral rolls, so that a small number of privileged voters could elect a disproportionate number of members of Parliament. Third, the absence in many countries of a secret ballot meant that individuals might be compelled to vote as their landlord or employer wanted. Fourth, nationwide political parties often did not exist to give voters a choice between alternative governments. Finally, even if a Parliament was freely elected on a mass franchise, the government did not necessarily require the confidence of Parliament to hold on to office (cf. Rokkan, 1970: ch. 3).

The typical pre-1914 European government was a *constitutional oligarchy*. Government acted according to the rule of law, but the power to make and administer the law was in the hands of relatively few. Those involved in government included representatives of the aristocracy, owners of large landed estates and manufacturing enterprises, the old professions—the civil service, law, church and state-controlled universities—and sometimes a few leaders of the new urban classes. Although participants were few, there were many divisions within government. Educated classes were more in favor of individual freedom than representatives of conservative interests such as the church. Landed aristocrats often disagreed with urban industrialists about the desirability of industrialization. Demands for language and cultural rights voiced by nationalists could conflict with established policies.

France was exceptional in having a Chamber of Deputies (the lower house of Parliament) elected by universal male suffrage from the constitution of the Third French Republic in 1875. In antimonarchical France, parliament was the legal source of national sovereignty; ministers and the president of the republic were responsible to it. However, groups of deputies tended to unite around issues that were deeply divisive—whether France should be governed as a republic with an assembly, by a monarch, or by an authoritarian leader modeled on Napoléon.

Britain had a Parliament divided into two chambers, each of which influenced government. The House of Lords consisted of aristocrats who inherited their seat. The House of Commons was elected but as of 1914 only two-thirds of adult males had the right to vote. Elections were fair, and voting was secret. A well-organized system of party competition offered voters a choice between governments, and the prime minister and cabinet were accountable to a majority in the House of Commons. However, the power of the House of Lords over legislation was substantial until a constitutional crisis between a reformist liberal government and the conservative-dominated House of Lords was resolved in favor of the House of Commons in 1911.

In Germany an authoritarian regime was sustained, notwithstanding a freely elected Parliament. The German Empire before World War I was a federal union of 26 states, dominated by Prussia, which had three-fifths of its population. In Prussia the right to vote was determined by wealth and social status. The electorate was divided into three groups of unequal size, according to the taxes paid. Each group elected one-third of the members of the Prussian Parliament. The government of Prussia was appointed by the kaiser in his role as king of Prussia. In elections to the *Reichstag,* the lower house of the federal Parliament, all adult males had the right to vote. By 1912 the Socialist Party was its largest party. However, the *Reichstag* had virtually no say in foreign policy and military matters, and its influence upon the budget was restricted (see Urwin, 1974: 115 ff).

In the Austro-Hungarian Empire the constitutional order was much more complex than in Germany. There were separate parliaments for Hungary and for territories subject to Austria, and special procedures for dealing with foreign affairs, military defense, and financial matters common to the empire as a whole. The multiplicity of nationalities within the empire meant that expanding the franchise to give everyone the right to vote was not the primary issue. The fundamental debate was whether nationalities should sit in a multinational parliament or in separate parliaments recognizing national independence.

In Eastern Europe and the Balkans the authoritarianism of the old regimes was often challenged by extra-parliamentary means. The Young Turks, a revolutionary military group, forced the sultan to grant a constitution in 1908 and deposed him the following year. Changes in the Ottoman Empire reflected a conflict between traditional and modernizing elites; they were not about introducing democracy. In Russia there was despotism tempered by intrigue. In 1905, political unrest following the country's defeat in a war with Japan led to an abortive revolution. The regime responded by creating a two-chamber *Duma* or Parliament (cf. Emmons, 1983). Duma members could challenge actions by the czar, but they could not determine the composition or direction of government.

THE GREAT WAR OF 1914–1918 AND THE GREAT COLLAPSE

When war broke out in Europe in August 1914 it was not a surprise, for major powers had been building up military forces and alliances. The assassination by a Serbian nationalist of the Austrian archduke at Sarajevo, then part of the Habsburg Empire, was the incident that brought the continent to war. It aligned the Central Powers—Germany, Austro-Hungary, and the Ottoman Empire—against the Triple Alliance of Britain, France, and Russia, later joined by Italy. The war was not an ideological conflict but a civil war between great European powers with competing interests. In April 1917 the United States abandoned the policy of avoiding conflicts in Europe, first enunciated by George Washington, and declared war on the Central Powers.

Belligerents assumed that the war would be no different from those that had gone before. However, it was different, in conduct and in outcome. The whole of the continent from France to Russia and from the Baltic to Turkey became a bloody battleground. By the time fighting ended four years later (and in the remains of the Russian and Ottoman empires, several years afterward) it had become the Great War.[1] It brought about destruction on an unprecedented scale, because it was the first major war in which all sides had modern weapons of destruction: machine guns, tanks, motorized transport, submarines, and some air power. The result was an estimated ten million deaths.

The political destruction of the Great War was on an even greater scale, for four major multinational empires were destroyed. The Czarist Empire was the first to disappear, as a consequence of the Communist-led October Revolution in 1917. The German, the Austro-Hungarian, and Ottoman empires collapsed as a result of military defeat.

The Aftermath: An Unstable Settlement

When President Woodrow Wilson asked the U.S. Congress to declare war on the Central Powers in 1917 he declared: "The world must be made safe for democracy." This goal was to be achieved by applying the principle of national self-determination, turning Europe's multinational empires into democratic nation-states that would live together peacefully without territorial grievances to

---

[1]The Great War was sometimes described as the war to end war. It did not become known as World War I until after the second world war of the century broke out in 1939.

FIGURE 1.2

Mediterranean Sea

*denotes state formed after WWI

pursue. Wilson's ideals were half-realized. Europe between the wars was converted into a set of nation-states, but many were undemocratic, and many still had nationality problems.

The 1919 Treaty of Versailles faced great difficulties in applying the principle of national determination, because many areas of Central and Eastern Europe had an amalgam of populations, German-speaking, Slav and Balkan or Baltic living in the same town or mixed together within regions such as Silesia and Bohemia. There were also millions of Jews, few of whom were then Zionists. The number of nationalities claiming independence was greater than the Versailles peacemakers were prepared to recognize as independent states. Yet some decisions about creating new states were necessary, given the vacuum created by the collapse of multinational empires.

Poland was created from territories formerly partitioned between Germany, Czarist Russia, and Austro-Hungary (Figure 1.2). Czechoslovakia was formed from parts of the Austro-Hungarian Empire; it included a large German-speaking minority in Bohemia and in Prague. Because it was on the losing side in the Great

War, Hungary lost territories inhabited by Hungarians to Czechoslovakia, Romania, and Yugoslavia. In 1918 the King of Serbia was proclaimed as the King of Serbs, Croats, and Slovenes. In 1929 the name was changed to Yugoslavia; it consisted of parts of the old Austro-Hungarian and Ottoman empires. The collapse of the Russian Empire produced substantial changes in Baltic boundaries. The former Czarist territories of Estonia, Latvia, and Lithuania became independent states, and the independence of Finland was secured too. Romania and Poland extended their territories eastward into parts of the former Czarist Empire in order to incorporate fellow nationals. Turkey became a new nation-state. To promote modernization, the state abandoned Islam and became secular, and it adopted the Roman in place of the Arabic alphabet. The capital was moved from cosmopolitan Istanbul to Ankara in the Middle Eastern land mass of Anatolia. In pursuit of the goal of a nation-state, Turkey expelled millions of Greeks who had lived there for centuries.

In Central Europe a new German state was established with smaller boundaries than before. Its population had limited national minorities, but there were German-speaking minorities in the new neighbor states of Poland and Czechoslovakia and in Alsace-Lorraine, ceded to France. To secure a Baltic port at Gdansk (in German, Danzig), Poland gained a corridor of territory separating East Prussia from the rest of Germany. Whereas before 1914 the Habsburg Empire had stretched from Prague to what is now the Western Ukraine, the new Austrian Republic was a small country with a population uncertain about whether to remain independent or seek closer ties with Germany.

Elsewhere in Europe national boundaries were scarcely affected by the settlement of the Great War. Italy gained small but significant increases in territory from the collapse of the Habsburg Empire. France, Belgium, the Netherlands, and Luxembourg sought the demilitarization of Western Germany as a guarantee of their own security. The Scandinavian countries, having remained neutral in the war, had no influence on the peace.

The Treaty of Versailles did not create a settled peace. New states created new territorial grievances, as some nationalities argued that they were on the "wrong" side of international boundaries. Poland is a textbook example of a people claiming to be a nation-state, but after 1919 one-third of its population was German, Ukrainian, Belorussian, Jewish, or Lithuanian. German, Hungarian and Austrian politicians clamored for populations and territories "lost" to new nation-states. Within multinational Yugoslavia, there were disputes between different ethnic and religious groups about who should hold most power, for the new state incorporated Moslems, Orthodox Slavs, and Habsburg Catholics. Territorial grievances arising from the settlement of World War I were significant as a prelude to World War II.

The victors were politically exhausted. Initially, the French sought substantial financial reparations from Germany and its demilitarization. In the words of a British politician during the country's 1918 post-Armistice election campaign, "The Germans are going to be squeezed, as a lemon is squeezed—until the pips squeak." The French put troops into the German Rhineland in the early 1920s in an effort to collect reparation debts. But by the mid-1920s Germany, racked by inflation and internal political problems, could not pay large sums in reparation.

The governments of France and Britain were tired of attempts to extract resources from the defeated. The United States withdrew its troops from Europe, and Congress defeated a proposal to join the new League of Nations. The American avoidance of entangling alliances was considered a return to normalcy.

NEW FORMS OF GOVERNMENT, UNDEMOCRATIC AND DEMOCRATIC

Today, the study of European government compares different kinds of democratic regimes, but to understand interwar Europe we need to understand differences between undemocratic regimes too. With the exception of Czechoslovakia, every new state created by the Versailles settlement had an undemocratic regime by the outbreak of World War II.

A distinctive feature of the interwar period was the emergence of totalitarian regimes. Initially, the modern European state was *authoritarian,* involving rule by a small group exercising power within limits specified in a constitution. Nineteenth-century authoritarian regimes such as Prussia were not democracies, but they could claim to be a *Rechtsstaat.* By contrast, the new totalitarian regimes that emerged in Europe between the wars rejected any limit to the state's power to command individuals and to take over or destroy institutions of civil society (cf. Linz, 1975: 264 ff.). *Totalitarian* regimes admitted no limits to their authority; they sought total control of society and mobilized the population to act and think as rulers commanded (cf. Arendt, 1958; Friedrich and Brzezinski, 1967; Lipset and Bence, 1994: 180 ff.).

The Rise of Totalitarian Regimes

The Russian Revolution of 1917 led to the establishment of a Communist regime in one of Europe's most backward countries. This surprised Marxists, who expected this to happen in a developed industrial country, such as Germany. The Bolshevik seizure of power was seen by Communists and anti-Communists alike as the first step in a revolution throughout Europe. However, the difficulties of the Communist Party in establishing effective authority in the Soviet Union led to its isolation with the proclaimed goal of building "Socialism in One Country"—that is, the multinational Union of Soviet Socialist Republics. The Communist decision to move the capital to Moscow from Leningrad (the new name for Saint Petersburg) symbolized the increased distance between the USSR and Europe proper.

The Soviet regime described itself as a dictatorship of the proletariat. The Communist Party had a monopoly of power and dispensed with free elections, because it was governing according to the "scientific" doctrines of Marxist-Leninism. The party was totalitarian in its goals, seeking to transform political and economic institutions to fit Communist ideology. Under Josef Stalin, who became party secretary in 1922, the Communist party used the schools, the state and secret police, and the media to propagate its views. It also used revolutionary decrees and secret police to coerce, imprison or kill its opponents; estimates of the numbers killed between the wars vary from "a few" to "many"' millions (Conquest, 1990).

In Italy, the Fascist Party of Benito Mussolini seized power from a weak and nominally democratic regime in 1922. Italian fascism rejected such democratic institutions as free elections. It held that the claims of the state were greater than the claims of individuals, thus aligning itself with traditional conservative and clerical authoritarianism. Mussolini had begun his political career as a socialist rather than as a supporter of traditional authority; he also sought to make a populist appeal. Fascism glorified a strong leader, and Mussolini proclaimed himself that leader (*il Duce*). He espoused the survival of the fittest, and glorified military activity and the use of force. Although fascism intimidated and coerced critics, it was not aggressively totalitarian. It tolerated such institutions as the Catholic Church as long as it cooperated with the party, and Italy also remained a monarchy.

The term "fascist" is often used indiscriminately to describe undemocratic regimes, but this is misleading, for it ignores the extent to which governments in interwar Europe were simply following conventional authoritarian patterns. In Poland, for example, General Joseph Pilsudski, who had organized Polish legions to fight for Polish independence and subsequently to win territory from Czarist Russia, in 1926 led a coup that made him effectively a military dictator until his death in 1935. In Hungary, after a short-lived period of communist rule under Bela Kun, subsequently murdered by Stalin, Admiral Nicholas Horthy gained power in 1920. In the absence of a monarch, he was styled the Regent, ruling in an authoritarian manner, and emphasizing nationalist grievances about the loss of Hungarian territories in the post–Great War Trianon peace settlement.

In Germany the Weimar Republic was established immediately after World War I; it was named after the city where an assembly drafted its constitution. The Weimar Republic had free and fair elections, and it allowed a multiplicity of parties to organize. However, it did not have political legitimacy. Its authority was challenged in the streets by semimilitary groups organized by disaffected war veterans. It was challenged at the ballot box by an aggressive Communist Party that won up to one-sixth of the popular vote, and conspired against the regime. Authoritarian and militarist parties sought votes too. The Nazi Party was founded by Adolf Hitler in the early 1920s; the term abbreviated the lengthy German title, the National Socialist German Workers' Party. This symbolized Hitler's desire to build a broad popular base, with a class appeal directed at workers and a nationalist appeal based on anti-Semitism and asserting the right of the German race to dominate other nations.

The Nazi Party borrowed elements from Mussolini's Fascists and Soviet Communists, and added such distinctive elements as systematic anti-Semitism and genocide. In the 1920s the Nazis organized street gangs to intimidate their political opponents; electoral support was low. The Nazis won more than one-third of the popular vote in two free elections in 1932. Hitler was made chancellor (prime minister) on January 30, 1933; he abused his powers of office to establish the Third Reich (that is, the Third German Empire). The Nazi regime was totalitarian, propagating its ideas through a monopoly of the media and education, imprisoning individuals and in the Holocaust committing mass murder of Jews.

Totalitarian regimes sought to expand their influence outside national boundaries. The Austrian Republic established after defeat in the Great War initially held free competitive elections with universal suffrage. However, the electorate divided its vote almost equally between two extremes: the Christian Social Party, whose leaders had little commitment to democracy, and the Socialist Party, which was influenced by Marxist ideas. Both parties organized semimilitary groups to protect themselves. By 1930 a third group began to organize support for a union between Austria and Germany. Christian Social leaders introduced an authoritarian regime and sought to preserve the country's independence by playing off Mussolini against Hitler. This failed. In 1938 Hitler annexed Austria as part of an expanded Third Reich.

Spain had dropped out of the mainstream of European politics in the nineteenth century, but it was European in alternating between authoritarian regimes and brief periods of republican rule. For most of the 1920s, Spain was a monarchy effectively ruled by a military dictator, General Primo de Rivera. In 1931 an uprising led to the establishment of a republic with a parliament chosen by free elections. Five years later a military uprising was launched by General Francisco Franco. Three years of bloody civil war followed, in which Nazi and Fascist regimes supported Franco's forces and the Soviet Union supported the Republic. The Civil War ended in 1939 with victory for General Franco, who established an authoritarian regime based on a coalition of the military, the Falange Party, and the Catholic Church.

A systematic comparison of major features of totalitarian and authoritarian regimes highlights what was new about the interwar Communist, Fascist, and Nazi methods of rule (see Table 1.1; for more details, see Linz, 1975; Sartori, 1993; cf. Wittfogel, 1957). Totalitarian regimes propagate an ideology that offers a comprehensive blueprint of how society ought to be governed. The ideology addresses the problems and stresses of twentieth century life—from industrialization and unemployment to conflicts of nationality—and it is used to justify extreme actions. Totalitarian ideologies are collectivist, glorifying abstractions such as nation or race or the proletariat. Individual preferences and rights are of no consequence. By contrast, authoritarian regimes usually have no pretension to an "ism." Control of the state is deemed sufficient justification for authority, supported by a few vague slogans or ideals, conservative and collectivist, or populist.

Totalitarian regimes claim to control all aspects of social life, including many normally thought of as nonpolitical, such as art, music, dress styles, the teaching of biology, and forms of addressing people—for example, Heil, Hitler or Comrade. Nothing is outside the reach of a totalitarian regime. It thus undermines civil soci-

TABLE 1.1 TOTALITARIAN AND AUTHORITARIAN REGIMES COMPARED

	Totalitarian Regimes	Authoritarian Regimes
Ideology	Comprehensive, detailed	Vague
Reach	Extensive, penetrative, undermines civil society	Limited, tolerates civil society
Party	Mass mobilization	Weak
Rule of law	Coercion and terror; enforcement is arbitrary	May or may not respect; some use of secret police
Social welfare	Positive	Variable

Source: Compiled by the author.

ety, because any independent business, trade union, or cultural or charitable group is a potential challenger of the totalitarian ideal. Authoritarian regimes, by contrast, tolerate organizations and activities that do not directly challenge their authority.

A totalitarian regime is a one-party state. Popular support is mobilized through a mass-membership political party. Communist, Fascist, and Nazi parties claimed millions of members; they were selectively recruited but not elitist. A totalitarian party offers career advancement to individuals who would have never entered government in an aristocratic regime. Hitler, Mussolini, and Stalin were each of lowly social origin and sought mass support by attacking traditionally privileged groups within society and promising benefits to the masses. By contrast, authoritarian regimes are often no-party states, for one of their first actions is to suspend parliament and elections. If an election is held, a strong party is not needed, for ministry of interior officials are expected to supervise the election and deliver the result that the regime wants.

Authoritarian regimes enact laws that empower the police to control actions of individuals, and usually keep to these laws. Antidemocratic actions are not undertaken arbitrarily but under authority conferred by law. Individuals and organizations normally have far fewer rights than in a democracy, but they usually know the limits within which they can act. By contrast, in a totalitarian regime the state acts arbitrarily. The needs of the state, as defined by officials on the spur of the moment, are regarded as sufficient to justify any action, however arbitrary. The Soviet KGB and the Nazi gestapo went one step further: They used terror to intimidate and coerce their political opponents and the population at large.

Both Nazi and Communist regimes proclaimed a desire to promote the material welfare of the people. Nazi Germany and the Soviet Union each boasted that they avoided the worst problems of unemployment during the world depression of the 1930s. To encourage mass support, expenditure on social security policies was increased. The Nazi regime spent a larger share of its national product on social programs than democratically elected governments in France and Sweden. Until war materials became of overriding importance, the Nazi regime also spent more on social policy than defense (see Flora, 1983: ch. 8). By contrast, most authoritarian regimes have been right wing in economic policies, and spent little on social policies.

There were major differences between Nazi and Soviet totalitarianism. The Nazi regime was virulently nationalist, proclaiming the German race as the master race. By contrast, the Soviet regime granted parity of esteem to nationalities; class, not nation, was deemed of first importance. Communists governed a Union of Soviets, that is, people's councils controlled by the party, ruling in the name of the international working class rather than in the name of the Russian people.

An Expansion of Democracy

Simultaneously with the eruption in Europe of new forms of undemocratic government, states in northwestern Europe were peacefully evolving into democratic regimes by greatly increasing the number of citizens with the right to vote. It was administratively simple to do this, for traditional qualifications for voting were complex; individuals had to demonstrate that they had at least a certain amount of property or education or met other restrictive requirements. The logic of franchise reform was that everyone, or at least every male above a given age should have the right to vote. By 1939, in nine European democracies—the four Scandinavian countries of Denmark, Finland, Norway, and Sweden, plus Czechoslovakia, Ireland, Luxembourg, the Netherlands, and United Kingdom—all men and women had the right to vote.

It was politically difficult to get reform acts approved, for it meant that those long accustomed to office had to put at risk their hold on power. Giving the vote to manual workers, the majority of the population, raised the novel prospect of socialist or communist parties winning office, a prospect that made many conservatives anxious. Hence, the great majority of European democracies adopted a new electoral system, proportional representation, at about the same time that they enacted universal manhood suffrage. Proportional representation gives parties seats in parliament in proportion to their share of the popular vote (see Chapter 8). Antisocialist politicians were prepared to accept proportional representation because it assured them some members of parliament in an electorate in which the majority of voters were manual workers. It also raised to 50 percent the threshold that socialists required to cross in order to be sure of controlling government. In culturally heterogeneous societies such as Switzerland and Belgium, proportional representation was also popular because it guaranteed representation to minorities that risked being greatly underrepresented in a parliament elected by the first-past-the-post electoral system (Rokkan, 1970: 157 ff.).

Coalition governments are the normal outcome of the introduction of proportional representation, because no one party gains a majority of seats in parliament. This meant that socialists normally entered office in a government that also included nonsocialists. In Britain, the Labour Party twice formed a government, but each time it depended on the support of other parties because it lacked an absolute majority of seats in the House of Commons. By 1939, Socialists had experienced a term of office in most European democracies. Sweden was exceptional in having a Socialist-led government from 1932. Elections on a democratic franchise did not guarantee political stability. This was most evident in Weimar Germany, where by 1932 extreme parties of the right and left together won more than half the total vote.

The expansion of democracy divided Europe. By the end of the 1930s, the big division was not within countries but between democratic and undemocratic countries. Democratic countries ranged from Scandinavia to the Alps, while authoritarian or totalitarian regimes ranged from the Baltic to the Mediterranean. Many democracies were small in population. The five democracies of Denmark, Finland, Ireland, Luxembourg, and Switzerland had fewer people than a traditional authoritarian state such as Romania. Excluding the Soviet Union, by the late 1930s three-fifths of the peoples of Europe lived under an authoritarian or totalitarian regime; if the USSR is included, more than three-quarters of Europe's population was ruled by undemocratic regimes.

War

The first move toward another war in Europe occurred in 1936, when Hitler sent German troops into the Rhineland, a previously demilitarized German province on the border with France. In March 1938, Hitler annexed Austria after intimidat-

TABLE 1.2   HOW EUROPEAN STATES LINED UP IN WORLD WAR II

Allies	Invaded by both Germany and USSR	Axis	Neutral
BELGIUM*	Estonia	Austria	IRELAND
CZECHOSLOVAKIA*	Finland	Bulgaria	Portugal
DENMARK*	Latvia	Germany	Spain
FRANCE*	Lithuania	Hungary	SWEDEN
Greece*	Poland	Italy	SWITZERLAND
LUXEMBOURG*		Romania	
NETHERLANDS*			
NORWAY*			
Soviet Union*			
UNITED KINGDOM			
Yugoslavia*			

Note: The asterisk indicates occupation by Axis powers; democracies are indicated in capital letters.

Source: Compiled by the author. As the tides of war flowed to the allies, some countries, such as Italy, changed sides.

ing an authoritarian Austrian government by a show of force. In September 1938, Hitler claimed the Sudetenland, a German-speaking part of Czechoslovakia. France and Britain were alarmed, but reached agreement with Hitler at Munich that Germany could take this territory, provided that it would be Hitler's last territorial claim. In the spring of 1939, Hitler seized the remainder of Czechoslovakia. Ten days before the invasion of Poland, Nazi Germany negotiated a nonaggression pact with the Soviet Union. This gave Russia a free hand to invade the Baltic states of Finland, Estonia, Latvia, and Lithuania, and Poland from the east.

World War II broke out on September 1, 1939, with the German invasion of Poland. Britain, France, and their allies declared war on Germany. After months of inaction on the Western front, in the spring of 1940, the German army made a *blitzkrieg* (literally, lightning war) attack that overran Belgium, the Netherlands and Luxembourg, France, Denmark, and Norway in a matter of weeks. Mussolini's Italy then joined the war as a belligerent on the Nazi side. By June 1940, Britain, under a new government led by Winston Churchill, stood alone against the German-led Axis. Britain was subject to a blitz of bombs from the air but not invaded.

Hitler's forces occupied almost all of the continent of Europe. Only four small countries, plus Spain, exhausted by civil war and sufficiently pro-German to be no risk to Hitler, remained neutral (Table 1.2). Nazi Germany secured allies in the Balkans as Hungary, Bulgaria, and Romania advanced territorial claims by joining the Axis side. The German attack on the Soviet Union in June 1941 made Eastern Europe the main military field of operation, as German troops advanced to the gates of Moscow and, further south and east, to Stalingrad. The fall of French North Africa and Italy's control of Libya brought the Axis to Egypt, then a British protectorate. The Japanese attack on Pearl Harbor in December 1941 was followed by Germany and Italy declaring war on the United States. The second great war of the century became global.

In World War II the Axis powers unambiguously rejected democracy. Most but not all of the allies were committed to democracy; Greece, Yugoslavia, and the Soviet Union fought as allies because they had been invaded by armies of the Axis. Three democracies, Ireland, Sweden, and Switzerland, remained neutral, as did two dictatorships, Spain and Portugal. The allies fought to prevent invasion; only Britain succeeded completely. In occupied countries, resistance groups fought German and Soviet invaders; they sometimes fought each other too. They could not secure their own liberation. This came with the advance of American and British troops from the south and west, and Soviet troops from the east.

2

EUROPE TWICE TRANSFORMED SINCE 1945

World War II transformed Europe physically and politically. Military occupation brought home to the civilian population of Europe the full impact of war. Racist Nazi beliefs led occupied peoples to be treated as inferior races subject to arbitrary arrest, deportation or death. The Jews of Europe suffered most; an estimated six million perished in Nazi extermination camps during the Holocaust. Millions of Russians in the path of the invading German army also suffered. In many countries of Central and Eastern Europe there were divisions between groups supporting the Axis and those favoring the allies. In Europe, World War II took more than 20 million lives.

The tide of war began to turn in 1942, when the advance of the German army was stopped in Russia at Stalingrad (since renamed Volgograd) and in Egypt by British forces at El Alamein. In the autumn of 1942, American and British troops under the command of General Dwight Eisenhower landed in North Africa, and the following year invaded Southern Italy. By 1944 Soviet troops were advancing into Eastern Europe. Allied troops landed in France on D-Day, June 6, 1944, and began to march toward Germany. The war in Europe ended on May 7, 1945, and in the Pacific in August of that year. Both the victors and the vanquished were exhausted by six years of fighting.

Reconstruction was necessary because the destruction by ground fighting, bombs, and scorched earth policies of retreating armies destroyed millions of homes and places of work. Money had lost its value; cigarettes or chocolate bars were sometimes used instead as currencies. People whose house had lost a roof needed shelter, farmers whose livestock had been slaughtered needed new breeding animals, people returned from prisoner-of-war or forced-labor camps needed to regain their health. There was a need to rebuild city centers destroyed by bombing. But it was not possible to restore what had been before. For example, the blitz of the city of London destroyed churches and other buildings that dated back to the Great Fire of 1666. Factories did not need restoration, but they did need new equipment to replace obsolete facilities. Rebuilding and modernization thus occurred simultaneously.

Rebuilding political regimes was necessary too. Most countries on the allied side had been occupied for four or five years. In France, a regime that had collaborated with the Nazis was replaced by the Fourth Republic. In other parts of Western Europe restoration of the old constitution was the norm, often under new leadership. In the Axis countries the allied occupying armies supervised the introduction of new regimes, democratic in Western Europe and Communist in Eastern Europe.

By the mid-1950s the momentum of reconstruction had created a new dynamic. Democratic regimes were consolidated. Investment in the economy was producing a steady and high rate of growth. By the 1960s, the fruits of economic growth were showing up in rising standards of living in the households of ordinary families. A new generation was coming forward whose political outlook had been formed in a period of peace and rising prosperity. Small groups of students challenged these foundations in highly publicized student demonstrations in Paris in 1968. The great majority of Europeans were satisfied. Rising inflation in the 1970s, followed by increased unemployment, disturbed governors and governed, but it did not shake the foundations of democratic regimes.

Political divisions between Western Europe and the Communist bloc lasted for more than a generation. The abrupt collapse of Communist authority between 1989 and 1990 brought about the second transformation of Europe since 1945. The removal of the Iron Curtain marked a return to a pre-1914 era, characterized by a British foreign secretary as a period when you could go down to the railway station and buy a ticket to wherever you pleased. Today Central Europe is once again central to the continent. The consequences of this second transformation are still being worked out.

DIVISION AND DEMOCRACY

Whereas World War I broke up empires, World War II broke up Europe. Social changes underway in the interwar period were accelerated by war, occupation, and liberation. Distinctions of class and status became unimportant when millions lost their lives. Those who backed the Axis lost honor and property too. At the end of the war, there were three major powers. Two—the United States and the Soviet Union—were new to their role. The third, Britain, was economically weakened by war and had a less big population; it could not compete with a claim superpower status.

Need for Reconstruction

Germany was a ruin, physically and politically, and it was occupied by the victorious allied armies. In many occupied countries the Germans had found collaborators who served the German occupation powers. France was exhausted politically as well as economically, and Hitler had created a puppet pro-Axis regime at Vichy under the aging Marshall Petain, and some French had supported it.

Politically, West European countries divided into three groups. Those that had not been invaded retained the same regime as before 1939, whether it was democratic or, as in the case of Spain and Portugal, authoritarian. A second group consisted of occupied countries such as Belgium, the Netherlands, Luxembourg, Denmark, and Norway, which restored their pre-war constitution, often with a government formed by those who had been leaders in exile. New institutions were needed to replace discredited regimes in Germany, Austria, Italy, Greece, and Finland.

In occupied Europe, resistance groups had been formed, but there was no agreement among Catholic, Liberal, Socialist, and Communist groups about how to govern in peacetime (see Urwin, 1989: ch. 2). The interwar depression left Western European governments with little faith that the market could solve their massive economic problems. On the right, extremists were discredited and traditional conservatives few. Social democratic parties declared that the postwar reconstruction should use the powers of the state to promote social welfare for the majority, and so too did Communist parties. Catholic parties were an important third force between market-oriented and Socialist parties. They favored a positive role for government in developing the economy, while applying traditional religious values to social policy.

The reconstruction of Europe required a mass commitment of effort by individuals and families to renew the fabric of everyday life. It also required large amounts of money to rebuild infrastructure and industry. The shortage of equipment required imports from the United States, which had expanded its economy during the war because it was neither invaded nor bombed. However, there was a shortage of dollars to pay for such imports. There was fear on both sides of the Atlantic that, in default of reconstruction, there would be another global depression, and that this could lead to a return to authoritarianism and then to World War III.

A Look Across the Atlantic

At the 1945 Yalta and Potsdam conferences the victors accepted the situation created by force of arms during the final months of the war. Soviet troops had fought their way across Eastern and Central Europe from the Baltic to the Black Sea and had reached as far west as Germany, the Czech Republic, and Austria. Most of these territories fell within the Soviet sphere of influence. Parts of Romania, Poland, and East Prussia were annexed by the USSR, adding to Stalin's earlier annexation of Estonia, Latvia, and Lithuania. Soviet troops were spread throughout Central and Eastern Europe; the greatest concentration was in East Germany, and remained there until 1991.

Across the territories it invaded, the Soviet Union sponsored new Communist regimes. In the spring of 1946, Winston Churchill warned of an "Iron Curtain" falling across Europe from the Baltic to the Adriatic, separating countries in the Soviet sphere of influence from European countries to the West. This dividing line meant the disappearance of Central Europe, for countries were placed either east or west of the Iron Curtain, according to whether they were subject to Soviet dominance. Germany was unique in being divided into two separate states, the western-oriented Federal Republic of Germany with its capital in Bonn and, as part of the Communist bloc, the German Democratic Republic, with its capital in East Berlin.

Whereas after World War I Europe was able to arrive at a postwar settlement on its own this was not possible in 1945. Instead of being the home of great powers securing peace, Europe was a political vacuum. The nearest country powerful enough to impose a settlement was the Soviet Union. The United States was the only alternative.

There were fears in Washington that Western Europe might suffer a Communist takeover. In a speech at Harvard in June 1947, the U.S. Secretary of State, George Marshall, offered American economic aid if European countries could agree among themselves about the use of the aid. The Marshall Plan objectives were political cooperation within Europe and with the United States; the peaceful reconstruction of Germany; and the promotion of international economic expansion, in which the United States had a material interest. Although Central and Eastern European countries showed interest in the Marshall Plan, Soviet pressure forced their abstention, thus reenforcing the Iron Curtain. The U.S. Congress over four years authorized $12 billion to promote economic recovery, a huge sum in those days. Combining domestic resources and aid from abroad, European nations began to recover economically. Recovery took time. For example, France did not regain its 1929 level of production until 1950, and Germany did not attain prewar levels until 1952 (Mitchell, 1975: table K1).

Old enemies in battle took steps toward institutionalizing cooperation among themselves by founding the European Coal and Steel Community (ECSC) in 1951. Symbolically, it was proposed by Robert Schuman, a leading French politician born in Lorraine when it was part of Germany. The six countries joining in this partnership—France, Germany, Belgium, the Netherlands, Luxembourg, and Italy—had been enemies in World War II. The Schuman plan was based on an assumption common to many European economic philosophies— conservative, Catholic and social democratic—namely, that the state should play an active role in promoting economic development. The ECSC had two primary objectives: to coordinate investment in basic industries in order to prevent the recurrence of earlier boom and bust cycles in the economy, and to reduce the risk of war between historic enemies by integrating industries essential for war production.

Western Europeans watched with alarm the purging of social democrats, liberals and other democratic groups in Soviet-occupied Central and Eastern Europe. Civil war in Greece showed that even in the absence of Soviet troops Communist groups were capable of moving the struggle for power from the ballot box to the battlefield. In 1946 Britain was forced by economic difficulties to withdraw military support from Greece and Turkey, countries bordered by Soviet forces.

The United States stepped in to fill the vacuum in military security. The Truman Doctrine committed the United States to provide military aid to European countries threatened by Soviet attack or subversion from within. In 1948 the Soviet Union shut off land access to West Berlin by Western Europeans. The result was the Berlin airlift, in which all manner of goods, from coal to medical supplies, were flown there by American, British, and French planes. The Cold War had begun. The reference to "war" emphasized the intensity of the conflict between the protagonists. But the conflict was not a "hot" war.

The convergence of Western European and American security concerns led to the establishment in 1949 of the North Atlantic Treaty Organization (NATO) to promote collective military security. In addition to the United States and Canada, ten European countries were founding members. The United States was the only country with sufficient population and economic resources to build a military force equal to that of the Soviet Union. The United States pledged to regard an attack upon any one of the signers as an attack upon itself. The presence of American troops in front line positions in Europe meant that if war broke out European countries would not have to endure years of uncertainty before the United States joined in. Keeping the finger on the trigger of nuclear weapons in American hands was a necessary condition of NATO's acceptance in Washington. There were wars in many parts of the globe after 1949, but Europe did not become a battleground. The subsequent expansion of NATO created a military alliance reaching from Norway and West Germany to Portugal and Spain, and eastward to Greece and Turkey.

By 1949 the division of Europe was complete. Integration across the North Atlantic was paralleled by Soviet efforts binding East European countries closer to Moscow. Instead of being a barrier, the North Atlantic had become a sea and air link between the United States and European countries outside the Soviet orbit of influence.

The creation of NATO was a fundamental change in transatlantic relations. It marked the abandonment of the traditional belief that the United States was outside the European balance of power, a belief held in Washington as well as in Paris, London, and Berlin. In the words of Owen Harries (1993: 42), "The political 'West' is not a natural construct but a highly artificial one. It took the presence of a life-threatening overtly hostile 'East' to bring it into existence." The Western alliance was not a European alliance; America was the premier country in the alliance because of the preponderance of American arms and American dollars.

In economics, the foundation of the Organization for Economic Cooperation and Development (OECD) in 1961 reflected Western Europe's divisions and links with other advanced nations around the globe. It has sought to promote economic growth, full employment, rising living standards, stable prices and free trade among advanced industrial societies. Its membership is not confined to one continent. The 24 member countries of OECD span four continents, including the United States and Canada in North America; Australia and New Zealand in the South Pacific; and Japan as the major Asian economic power. If number of countries is the criterion, then OECD is primarily an association of European states, but if economic wealth is the measure, then no continent can claim dominance (cf. Figure Intr.2).

The designation *North Atlantic Europe* registered the Cold War division of Europe along lines of opposing military alliances (Figure 2.1). The term is politically more accurate than the distinction between Western and Eastern Europe, for the guarantor of Western European security has been the United States, a North Atlantic but not a European country, and the chief military power in Eastern Europe, the Soviet Union, straddled three continents.

North Atlantic Europe excluded lands that had been part of Europe for centuries but were now on the other side of the Iron Curtain. Thus, even though Prague is well west of Vienna, it was defined as in the other Europe, and even though Athens is east of Warsaw and Sofia, Greece was included in North Atlantic Europe. The disappearance of Central Europe destroyed the traditional position

FIGURE 2.1

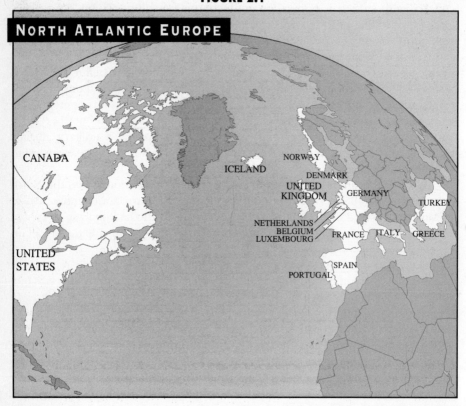

NORTH ATLANTIC EUROPE

of many countries between East and West. Countries that did not join NATO because of neutrality, such as Sweden and Switzerland, or to avoid Russian counterpressures, such as Austria and Finland, oriented themselves to North Atlantic Europe rather than to Moscow.

Politically, North Atlantic Europe sought to promote democracy. In the early days, the majority of NATO members were established democracies; others were new democracies seeking to avoid a Communist takeover (cf. Chapter 3). By the end of the Cold War the only member state that did not have a consolidated democracy was Turkey, which has alternated popularly elected governments and periods of military rule. Turkey was included in NATO, even though it was just outside the border of Europe, because of its strategic borders with the Soviet Union.

THE CHALLENGE OF CHANGE WITHIN A DEMOCRATIC FRAMEWORK

Even when a democracy remains the same in constitutional form, significant changes occur, as democratic institutions offer means of responding to fresh demands. Because politics is about voicing competing demands about how a country ought to be governed, democratization is not the end of politics. Every free election reveals that the population is divided about who ought to govern, and what government ought to do. Governments frequently are challenged by changes in the national and international environment, too.

Gradual Changes

The momentum of postwar economic reconstruction was sustained for decades after recovering from World War II. In every country average real income more than doubled in a matter of decades—and it has kept on increasing since. Consumer goods such as automobiles, once thought the privilege of a few, are now mass consumption goods. Increased national income funded increased public expenditure. European states expanded social security to guarantee incomes to everyone in retirement and to the unemployed; national health systems were also introduced and educational opportunities expanded. The collectivist ideal of the nation-state was replaced by the collectivist ideal of the welfare state.

Economic change has transformed the way in which people live. Rural villages that were traditional societies have lost population. In cities people have moved from traditional working-class quarters to new houses and flats in suburbs, where they meet new faces and new ideas. The population of cities has fallen as employers have moved into areas that were formerly rural. The majority of Europeans now live in modern houses and often in new communities.

The turnover of generations has brought forward new political leaders across Europe. Britain provides a dramatic illustration. The prime minister at the end of World War II, Winston Churchill, had been born in 1874, served as a soldier under Queen Victoria, and entered Parliament in 1900. Today's British Prime Minister, John Major, was just two years old at the end of World War II; Tony Blair, the leader of the opposition Labour Party, was born eight years after the war ended. When leaders of countries that fought each other in World War II meet, much of what they know about war consists of what they have heard from parents or grandparents or seen on old television films.

Democracy implies frequent changes of rulers, and this has been common across Europe. Since 1945, the average prime minister has held office for less than two and one-half years. Even in Sweden, where the Social Democratic Party enjoyed uninterrupted control of government for three decades after World War II, the pendulum has since swung back and forth between left and right. In Italy, the Christian Democratic Party dominated government for nearly half a century, only to collapse in 1994 in the wake of corruption charges against many national officeholders. Everywhere in Europe the In party sooner or later becomes the Out party, and some of the Outs go into government.

The electorate is changing too. The median voter today was born in the 1950s, the beginning of a long era of affluence. She or he has been socialized into politics by television as well as by learning from older generations. An explosion of education has widened the horizons of tens of millions of Europeans. Before World War II, the majority had only an elementary education, and very few Europeans went to college. After World War II, secondary education was made compulsory and free. By the 1960s, youths of the postwar baby boom were pressing for a state-subsidized university education; new institutions were opened and old universities expanded. An increasing majority of Europeans have a general education suitable for earning a good wage in a modern economy. In particular, Europeans are well educated in languages, important for following events in other countries and realizing that one's own country is not the only country that counts in contemporary politics and economics.

Leaders of democratic parties must respond to changes in society or lose votes (see Chapter 6). Among social democratic parties, the Germans took the lead in 1959 in adopting a "reform" (that is, post-Marxist) program. The British Labour Party hesitated to abandon traditional socialist principles and suffered a series of electoral defeats. In 1995 it finally abandoned a commitment to wholesale nationalization introduced in the 1918 Labour Party constitution. In the Netherlands, changes in churches and a decline in church attendance have led the Catholic Party and two Protestant parties that previously contested elections separately to merge under the banner of the Christian Democratic Appeal.

The prospect of a new party entering the political system poses a challenge to all parties, for even if it wins only 5 or 10 percent of the vote, this can be the margin between victory and defeat for a larger party. Many new parties have been formed in the postwar era, but few have lasted. The most conspicuous examples of "new" new parties are the Greens or Ecologists, who now hold seats in most parliaments. Racist anti-immigrant parties with appeals echoing Fascism occasionally contest elections but almost invariably do badly. Competition for votes has become competition for votes between democratic parties.

While European countries depended upon the United States for military security, they were simultaneously becoming more dependent upon each other economically. Interdependence was given institutional form by the creation of the European Community. The 1957 Treaty of Rome established the European Economic Community (EEC) and the European Atomic Energy Community (EURATOM). The EEC was founded to promote economic development by establishing a common market for France, Germany, Italy, Belgium, the Netherlands, and Luxembourg. Economic growth resulted in each EEC country increasing trade with other countries in absolute and in relative terms. Although progress has been irregular, membership has gradually expanded to 15 states and the EEC has become the European Union, which has substantial influence upon economic activity across Europe.

Unexpected Challenges

Two major postwar developments were interpreted at the time as threatening political destabilization. The first was a series of student protests in 1968, which started in Paris and Frankfurt and spread to many university communities across Europe. In Germany student protests brought back memories of the Weimar Republic, when protests turned to violence and worse. Sometimes the protests were described as student "risings," as if they were an attempt to seize government. Whereas in the United States student protests were often directed against American involvement in the Vietnam War, in Europe they were primarily aimed at university authorities. Studies of mass attitudes showed that every country had a protest potential. However, events since have shown that this potential has failed to materialize in mass movements in the streets undermining democratic regimes (cf. Barnes and Kaase, 1979).

A bigger and broader challenge was world recession. After the first big increase in world oil prices, the economies of the majority of European states contracted in 1975. Inflation and unemployment rates rose higher than at any time in the previous quarter-century. Doomsayers forecast that if popularly elected politicians could not maintain continuously rising standards of living, prevent unemployment, and stop inflation, not only would governing parties lose elections but also democracy itself might be threatened (e.g., see Brittan, 1975). Mistaken analogies were drawn with conditions in Weimar Germany, where inflation had destroyed the currency in 1923. But postwar Europe was not Weimar Germany. Notwithstanding economic difficulties, since 1975, European countries, have produced neither a Hitler nor a Marlene Dietrich (see Rose and Peters, 1978).

Undemocratic regimes faced the biggest challenges to political authority, and they failed to maintain themselves. At the start of the postwar era, Spain and Portugal were governed by stable authoritarian regimes. Since the mid-1970s, both have become stable democracies. Greece has defeated two challenges to democracy, a civil war at the end of World War II between Communists and defenders of the regime, and a short-lived military dictatorship that seized power in 1967.

BEHIND THE IRON CURTAIN

From 1949 to 1989 the Iron Curtain was a heavily militarized dividing line between lands that had normally been regarded as European. The justification was simple: In political and economic terms Communist-dominated states were fundamentally different from the political systems of North Atlantic Europe. While West European states constructed democratic political systems and market economies, Communist regimes constructed one-party states and nonmarket command economies modeled on that of the Soviet Union.

Politics transformed geography (Figure 2.2). Warsaw is as close to Zurich as it is to Moscow, Budapest closer to Paris than to Moscow, and Prague is actually closer to Dublin than to Moscow. But the important political point was the direction in which countries were forced to be oriented politically. Soviet troops on the boundaries of Communist bloc countries forced people to turn their attention east.

In Communist Europe independent institutions were broken up or brought under the control of the party-state. There was no freedom of speech and no choice about which party should govern. The party's control of the police and army enabled it to coerce the populace. The Communist Party proclaimed that the "correct" way to advance toward Communism was to base actions on Marxist-Leninist principles, which held that the state could not be neutral: Either it was used to build socialism or else to support capitalism. There was thus little scope for institutions of civil society to operate freely. The postwar settlement in Communist Europe was a story of the systematic elimination of other political parties and free elections (cf. Alex Pravda, 1978).

FIGURE 2.2

COMMUNIST BLOC IN EASTERN EUROPE

*Albania withdrew from Warsaw Pact in 1968

Throughout the bloc, an aggressive effort was made to propagate Communist values through the schools, the media, and political education at the workplace. Marxist-Leninist ideology emphasized that Central and East Europeans were living in a different world than people in North Atlantic Europe. Communist regimes insulated their citizens from contact with other Europeans by censoring the media, prohibiting travel outside the Communist bloc and controlling visitors from abroad. Schools gave priority to teaching Russian and limited the teaching of "subversive" languages such as English.

The economy was a command economy; private property and capitalist transactions were made illegal. Decisions about the production and consumption of goods were made not in the marketplace but in government ministries. Instead of consumer demand stimulating the supply of goods and services, the government made an annual plan directing the production of enterprises. Politics not the market was the basis of the command economy. To make it operate required the creation of a command structure; this was the party-state (see Kornai, 1992). The Council of Mutual Economic Assistance (CMEA, also known as COME-

CON) extended the practices of the planned economy to trade between command economies. Whereas before World War II most Central and Eastern European countries had traded principally with developed capitalist nations such as Germany, after the creation of the Soviet bloc trade was concentrated behind the Iron Curtain.

In the course of four decades, command economies raised living standards. Given the amount of investment, it would have been extraordinary had this not been the case. Such basics as food, housing, and fuel were provided at heavily subsidized prices. Everyone was guaranteed a job, even though wages were often low and workers did not have the right to strike. Public spending on cultural facilities was lavish; so too was spending on military defense and party activities. Shortages controlled consumption; for example, people might have to wait five years to buy a car. Inequalities of the market were abolished and replaced by the inequalities of rank; those who were high in the ranks (*nomenklatura*) of the Communist Party or favored by it were given material privileges denied the majority (cf. Grossman, 1977; Castles, 1986; Winiecki, 1988).

The Warsaw Pact bound Communist countries to Moscow in a military alliance under the control of the Soviet Union, by far the most populous state in the region and the only country with nuclear weapons. In addition to the USSR, the founding members were Albania, Bulgaria, Czechoslovakia, the German Democratic Republic, Hungary, Poland, and Romania. Albania left the alliance after ideological clashes with Moscow and turned to China. The alliance enabled the Soviet Union to station troops as far west as Berlin and Prague. For the Soviet Union, which had twice been invaded by Germany in the twentieth century, moving military borders west was self-defense. In the name of "mutual assistance," Warsaw Pact troops were also used to suppress political changes in member countries, most notably the invasion of Hungary in 1956 and Czechoslovakia in 1968.

Differences Between Communist Regimes

The institutions of totalitarianism were most fully developed in the Soviet Union under Josef Stalin. After his death in 1953, Nikita Khrushchev's regime (1953–1964) purged some of Stalin's associates and denounced his dictatorship. He and his conservative successor, Leonid Brezhnev (1964–1982) remained firmly committed to Communist Party rule throughout the Warsaw Pact region. There was no talk of reform until after Mikhail Gorbachev took office in 1985. Throughout most of the postwar era, the leaders of the Soviet Union were ready and willing to maintain the division between Communist Europe and North Atlantic Europe. How this was done varied in significant detail from one country to another.

East Germany was created as the Soviet zone of occupation at the end of World War II. In 1949 it was proclaimed as a separate state, the German Democratic Republic, under the control of German Communist leaders Otto Grotewohl and Walter Ulbricht. In 1953 workers in East Berlin publicly demonstrated against the regime, but were suppressed by Soviet forces. During the 1950s, East Germans dissatisfied with the regime could leave by taking a subway or bus from

East to West Berlin, where they were accepted as citizens of the Federal Republic. The construction of the Berlin Wall in August 1961 closed this exit route. East Germans were trapped in a Communist system which repressed dissent and shot persons trying to flee across the Berlin Wall.

Czechoslovakia, unique in having an interwar democratic regime, was subject to particularly harsh repression. Initially, it had a coalition government of democratic and Communist parties. In 1948 a new constitution was adopted, making it a Communist party-state. A series of Stalinist trials purged Czechs accused of being "home Communists," that is, their loyalty to Moscow was suspect. In 1968 there was a brief Prague spring, as a new party leader, Alexander Dubcek, introduced measures promoting individual freedom. Warsaw Pact troops invaded Czechoslovakia, and Dubcek was arrested and taken to Moscow. The new regime under Gustav Husak re-imposed authoritarian controls and aggressively suppressed dissent until the collapse of Communism.

Poland has been violently anti-Russian and anti-German due to being partitioned between German, Russian, and Habsburg empires. During World War II, there was tension between the London-based Polish government in exile and Soviet-backed Poles, arising from the Soviet Union's collaboration with Nazi Germany in dismembering the country in 1939. The political fate of postwar Poland was decided in the closing months of World War II. At the Yalta Conference in 1945, the Western allies accepted Soviet proposals to redraw Poland's boundaries, since Soviet troops were already in control there. Within a few years, a Soviet-backed regime had taken complete control. The fiercely nationalist Catholic Church was a focal point of resistance to Soviet domination. The first of a series of popular demonstrations against the regime occurred in Poznan in 1956. In 1980, following demonstrations in Gdansk led by Lech Walesa, the Polish government recognized the right of protesters to organize in trade unions such as Solidarity. In 1981 this was revoked and martial law proclaimed under General Jaruzelski (for accounts of everyday life in Communist Poland, see Wedel, 1992).

After being on the losing side in World War II, Hungarians established a republic with a government based on competitive elections; Communists won less than one-fifth of the vote. However, the Communists used control of the Ministry of Interior and police to arrest their opponents and seize control in 1948. Following a period of intense repression, there was a popular uprising against Communist rule in Budapest in 1956, a new coalition government was formed under Imre Nagy, and Hungary announced its intention to withdraw from the Warsaw Pact. Soviet troops crushed the new government and installed Janos Kadar in power; Nagy was executed. Subsequently, an understanding was reached. Hungarians would not overtly challenge Soviet dominance or one-party rule, and repression would be relaxed. The Hungarian state could thus cynically claim: "Those who are not against us are with us." The economy was modified to benefit consumers; the policy was described as "Goulash Socialism." Hungary became the least repressive of Communist regimes (Andorka, 1993).

Bulgaria, caught between the Ottoman Empire and Czarist Russia, had traditionally sought alliances with Russia. However, in World War II the monarchist regime sided with Hitler to advance territorial claims against its Balkan neighbors. Bulgaria signed an armistice agreement in 1944. Within five years, it had become a Communist party-state under the leadership of Georgi Dimitrov and closely linked with Moscow. In 1954 Todor Zhivkov became general secretary; he held this post until the upheavals of 1989.

During World War II, Romania had attacked the Soviet Union but later changed sides following domestic political initiatives led by King Michael. In 1947 he was forced to abdicate and a Communist party-state was established. Although poor by European standards, because of its oil fields Romania had a major economic resource lacking in most Communist states. In 1965 Nicolae Ceauşescu became Communist leader and initiated an increasingly independent foreign policy, which won some favor with Western leaders. Domestically, the Ceauşescu regime was exceptionally repressive, ruling by terror through police institutions loyal to the ruler.

Unlike other East European countries, Yugoslavia did not rely upon Russian troops to gain liberation from German occupation; a multiplicity of partisan armies fought the occupiers. Partisan armies were divided along ethnic lines and between royalists and Communists. The Communist forces of Marshal Tito triumphed in the civil war between partisan armies, and Yugoslavia was established as a Communist state with six republics. Initially, Tito aligned the country with Moscow. However, in 1948 Moscow and Tito broke ties. Because it was anti-Soviet, Yugoslavia received military and economic assistance from the West, but it did not join NATO. Nor did the country abandon pursuit of a distinctive economy, promoting what it called Socialist self-management at the enterprise level. Following the death of Tito in 1980, ethnic differences between its republics became increasingly difficult to contain.

The regimes of Communist Europe systematically repressed opportunities for individuals to express their views or to organize politically. Individuals could only cultivate what a Hungarian sociologist, Elemer Hankiss (1990: 7; italics in the original), called "ironic freedom," that is, "the freedom of *living outside the system in which they lived;* the freedom of not identifying themselves with the system." The choice of government was not between democratic alternatives, but between endorsing or refusing to endorse an authoritarian regime that proclaimed totalitarian goals.

THE FALL OF THE BERLIN WALL—AND MUCH ELSE

In Marxist-Leninist theory, the peoples of the Communist bloc should have supported regimes that placed power in the hands of a party that claimed to know their interests. But in practice they did not. Governments were not chosen by free elections, and by contrast with prewar authoritarian regimes, the regime was not nationalist but a dictatorship subordinate to Moscow.

Unintended Consequences of the Gorbachev Reforms

In 1985 Mikhail Gorbachev began initiating change within the Soviet Union, with the intention of strengthening the USSR and preserving the Communist bloc. He invoked the prospect of a return to an undivided continent, "our common house of Europe." In this vision Russia was to be an active force up to the English Channel, and U.S. troops would no longer be in Europe.

In actuality, Gorbachev's pursuit of *glasnost* (openness) and *perestroika* (reform or restructuring) resulted in the collapse of the Communist bloc and the dissolution of the USSR (for interpretations, see e.g. Fleron and Hoffmann, 1993; Roeder, 1993). The Soviet leader had not anticipated that Central and Eastern Europeans would interpret reform as meaning the *removal* of Soviet political, economic, and military influence. Nor had he allowed for the fact that suppressing dissent with tanks, as his predecessors had done, was inconsistent with his claim to be tolerant of political differences. The proclamation of the "Sinatra" doctrine granted Central and Eastern European governments the right to introduce reforms on a "do it your way" basis. The result was the peaceful abandonment of Communist regimes.

Opposition to Communist rule existed prior to Gorbachev. Patriotism was one source. Sovietization was widely resisted as the imposition of an *alien* authoritarian rule. Some people listened to Western radio stations, exchanged antiregime thoughts with trusted friends, and a few circulated antiregime demands in *Samizdat* publications. Groups of dissidents demanded civil rights taken for granted in civil societies, such as freedom of speech, freedom of association, and freedom of movement. In Czechoslovakia dissidents organized a group called Charter 77, but Communist authorities greatly restricted their activities. In Poland, Solidarity organized mass demonstrations; these were met by martial law. The relaxation of suppression under Gorbachev encouraged dissidents to express opposition to Communist authority in public.

In October 1989, hundreds of thousands of East Germans began weekly candlelight street protests in Leipzig and Dresden. These demonstrations were the more impressive because East Germans had previously been the most submissive of Communist subjects. Communist authorities faced a simple question: whether to accept reform or use massive force to break up demonstrations. A regime that had previously had the confidence to kill individuals trying to leave the country no longer had the political will to shoot. The opening of the gates in the Berlin Wall in November 1989 is a symbolic turning point of the end of Cold War division of Europe. Once Soviet backing was withdrawn, the East German state disappeared. The reunification of Germany occurred in October 1990 by the five East German *Laender* becoming additional regions of the Federal Republic of Germany. East Germans thus instantly gained citizenship and major claims on the established welfare state services of the Federal Republic.

The tempo and form of change differed from country to country. Before Gorbachev, Hungarians were in the best position to debate ideas and travel, and opposition groups were allowed to organize in 1987. When Hungary opened its border with Austria in May 1989, this not only eased Hungarian travel to the west but also enabled other nationalities, such as East Germans, to flee to West Germany by traveling via Hungary and Austria. Big changes in Poland commenced in April 1989, when the Communist regime granted legal recognition to the anti-Communist trade union Solidarity. In June, elections were held to a National Assembly; Solidarity swept the popular vote. By January 1990, Lech Walesa, the Solidarity leader, had become president.

In Czechoslovakia the transition between regimes was described as the Velvet Revolution, because of its smoothness. In Bulgaria change began with a coup of reform Communists, backed by the army, deposing Zhivkov in November 1989. Under pressure from demonstrators in Sofia, the Communist regime agreed to a new constitution, and free elections were held in June 1990. In Romania the change was violent, starting in 1989, in Transylvania, a Hungarian-speaking area of western Romania. Military dissidents and reform Communist revolted against the Ceauşescu regime; an estimated eight thousand died in the fighting that followed. Ceauşescu and his wife were tried by a military court on charges of genocide, embezzlement, and perverting the authority of the state, and summarily executed.

The dissolution of the Warsaw Pact in 1991 freed Central and Eastern European states from being military allies of the Soviet Union and removed the justification for stationing Soviet troops there. COMECON, which had organized trade and distributed covert subsidies among command economies of Eastern Europe, was dissolved in September 1991. The trade was often to mutual advantage—for example, the export of Russian raw materials to Bulgaria and Slovakia in exchange for manufactured products. But COMECON no longer had any purpose when Russia wanted hard currency for its exports, especially oil. In most post-Communist countries, the abrupt cessation of trade was a disruptive influence in the transition from a command to a market economy.

Although Yugoslavia was not directly affected by changes in the Soviet bloc, its leaders were challenged by internal demands for independence. Tito established the post–World War II country as a federal state with six republics: Serbia, Croatia, Slovenia, Bosnia and Herzogovina, Macedonia, and Montenegro. In 1963 two autonomous provinces were recognized within Serbia, Kosovo (largely Albanian) and Vojvodina, with a large Hungarian minority. There were big differences between republics in their level of economic development; the richest, Slovenia, had about eight times more income per head than Bosnia or Macedonia (Sicherl, 1992). In January, 1990 the federal government promised to abolish the Communist Party's monopoly of power and hold free elections. Separately elected governments soon became opponents. In June 1991, Slovenia and Croatia declared independence. Concurrently, there were conflicts within republics containing more than one ethnic group. In Bosnia neither Moslems, Croats, or Serbs are a majority. Armed conflicts broke out between Serbia and Croatia in 1991 and spread to Bosnia; most of the federal Yugoslav army sided with Serbia. Notwithstanding a United Nations arms embargo in September 1991 and the dispatch of UN peacekeeping forces, fighting in Bosnia resulted in ethnic-cleansing atrocities.

Since 1989, Communist regimes have been assigned to what Marxists once described as the "ash can of history." The depth of rejection of the Soviet Union is illustrated by answers given to the question: Which country would you most like this country to be like? Even though everyone in post-Communist countries had been exposed to 40 years of Soviet culture, history, and practice, Central and Eastern Europeans rank Russia at the bottom in a list of countries considered worth emulating (Table 2.1). The countries that people most admire are democratic countries of North Atlantic Europe. The two most frequently named are social market or social democratic, Germany and Sweden. The United States is mentioned far more often than the Soviet Union.

TABLE 2.1   COUNTRY THAT WE SHOULD MOST TRY TO EMULATE

	Czechoslovakia %	Hungary %	Poland %	Average
Germany	31	38	37	35
Sweden	32	34	21	29
United States	14	10	30	18
Italy	9	9	0	6
France	5	2	7	5
Britain	3	3	3	3
Other	6	2	2	3
Soviet Union	0	1	0	0.3

Source: Freedom House, *Democracy, Economic Reform and Western Assistance; Data Tables* (New York: 1991), 154.

Differences Remain Within a Democratic Continent

Europe is once again an undivided continent. But it is not the same Europe as in 1939 or in 1914. The states of Europe today are nation-states rather than multinational empires. And the governments of Europe today are democratic or striving to become democratic rather than authoritarian. Even in countries with little or no tradition of democracy, free elections are being held and governments turned out of office when they lose the confidence of voters.

The old map of Europe is back, and Central Europe is once again central to the continent. Germany not only borders West European countries such as Denmark, the Netherlands and France, but also Poland and the Czech Republic. Austria too is once again at the center of Europe; it borders the Czech Republic, Slovakia, Hungary and Slovenia as well as Switzerland, Italy, and the Federal Republic of Germany. Vienna is closer to the capital of five former Communist states than it is to some major cities in Austria. The European Union is turning eastward, for three of its new member states in 1995—Finland, Sweden, and Austria—are Central European states.

The return to a continental system implies a relative decline in the significance of North Atlantic ties. This is specially evident in military defense, the most important North Atlantic link. NATO was founded to defend its members against the threat of Soviet aggression. The collapse of the Soviet Union has removed that threat. There remain threats to the security of European states, but there is no agreement about how big or small these are, or what should be done about them.

Big differences in standards of living exist, and they are found not only between the North and the South of Europe, that is, Scandinavia and poor Mediterranean countries such as Greece, but also between East and West. In economic terms we can think of Europe as divided into four different quadrants, with the richest part being the Northwest and the poorest the Southeast (Table 2.2)

In the Northwest of Europe, per capita national income is high, averaging $18,192 per person after controlling for purchasing power parity. Prosperity is not confined to a few Scandinavian countries; it now extends across 13 countries from Britain and Italy to Finland. Nor is prosperity limited to a few people; prosperous countries have a combined population of 316 million people, larger than the United States or the whole of the former Soviet Union.

The states of less well off Southwest Europe—Greece, Portugal, Spain, and Ireland—are few. By their own standards they are much better off economically than in the past, each country is dynamic, having experienced sustained economic growth for decades. This has reduced differences in income between north and south. The model for these countries is not Sweden but Italy, which has moved from being a relatively poor Mediterranean country to a prosperous Northwestern country in little more than a generation.

Evaluating the economic wellbeing of post-Communist countries is difficult, because standard measures of market economies do not apply there. Official statistics of gross domestic product are inadequate because they leave out second or shadow economies that deal in cash in hand. They also leave out household production of goods that are not sold, such as food grown for domestic consumption, an important resource for avoiding destitution. Furthermore, there is no satisfactory method for converting currencies that have not yet stabilized into current or PPP dollars (cf. Holzmann et al., 1995). Moreover, there are substantial differences in living conditions between post-Communist countries.

Car ownership offers a rough guide to differences in living standards, for buying a car requires more money than a poor person will have, and money is also needed to buy gasoline to keep a car running. On this basis, the Czech Republic, Hungary, Slovakia, and Poland can be grouped in Northeast Europe, as 48 percent of households own cars. This is more than a third higher than car ownership in the Southeastern European countries of Bulgaria and Romania.

TABLE 2.2   ECONOMIC DIFFERENCES WITHIN EUROPE

Northwest	Northeast
(High GDP per capita: $18,235 market economy)	(Post-Communist economy; 48% households with cars)
Population: 316 million Austria, Belgium, Britain, Denmark, Finland, France, Germany, Italy, Luxembourg, Netherlands, Norway, Sweden, Switzerland.	Population: 63 million Czech Republic, Slovakia, Hungary, Poland
Southwest	**Southeast**
(Not so high GDP per capita: $10,833; market economy)	(Post-Communist economy; 35% households with cars)
Population: 63 million Greece, Ireland, Portugal, Spain	Population: 32 million Bulgaria, Romania

Source: GDP per capita data (purchasing power parity) and population data for OECD nations: *OECD in Figures* (1994), 6-7, 24-25. Population, post-Communist countries: *Historically Planned Economies: A Guide to the Data,* 2nd ed. (Washington: World Bank, 1993), 37. Car ownership: Paul Lazarsfeld Society, Vienna, *New Democracies Barometer III* (1994).

Whether one counts countries or peoples, economic well-being is now widespread throughout Europe. The 13 prosperous countries of the Northwest of the continent collectively have two-thirds of its population. Similarly, the relatively better off post-Communist countries of Northeastern Europe have almost double the population of the least prosperous Southeast. Bulgaria and Romania account for only 7 percent of the total population of Europe. By any measure, the great majority of Europeans today live in countries that are relatively well off by the standards of market or post-Communist economies.

In politics, big differences are about timing. Throughout Western Europe, democratic institutions have had a quarter-century to a century to become established. In post-Communist societies governors have inherited discredited political and economic institutions. Politicians who have never held elective offices must learn how to compete in elections and wield power without crushing opponents or being crushed. The problems are not unprecedented: They were faced and overcome in postauthoritarian regimes of Western Europe not so long ago.

part **II**

DEMOCRATIZATION

3

THE DYNAMICS OF DEMOCRATIZATION IN EUROPE

Democracy is a set of institutions and a valued political symbol. It can therefore refer to anything from an impossible ideal to a realistic system in which democracy is seen as the lesser evil (see Sartori, 1987: 7 ff., 271 ff.). The word can also be qualified by adding an adjective—for example, "social democracy," "economic democracy," or "participatory democracy"—or it may even be used to describe how authority may be exercised within a family, a trade union, or a university. Because of its symbolic value, the word is also appropriated by dictators, as it was in the German Democratic Republic.

Literally, democracy means rule by the people, but in a populous modern state representative institutions are needed to give effect to popular preferences. The classic realist definition is that of Joseph Schumpeter (1952: 271), who defined democracy as the choice of government through "free competition for a free vote." Competition between parties distinguishes democracy from government by a nonelected monarch, authoritarian dictator, or totalitarian party endorsed in elections without choice (cf. Hermet et al., 1978). Making government accountable to elected representatives distinguishes democracies from regimes in which free elections may be held but rulers govern without being accountable to elected representatives (e.g., see Inkeles, 1991; Schmitter and Karl, 1991; Beetham, 1994; Shin, 1994).

Democracy requires a regime to recognize a few basic conditions. First, there must be a civil society; that is, the law must grant freedom of association, so that businesses, trade unions, churches, farmers, environmentalists, and other bodies can form political parties and pressure groups. The absence of organized parties reduces the opportunity for voters to influence who governs. A multiplicity of parties ensures that government faces opposition in Parliament, and opposition parties criticize what the government does in an effort to win political control at the next election.

Second, all adults should have the right to vote. Free competitive elections were held long before the franchise was granted to everyone. For most of the nineteenth century, the right to vote was limited to a small minority of males, usually people who met traditional criteria unrelated to an industrial society, such as having property, education, or inherited claims to vote. France was the first major European country to give all adult males the right to vote. This was done initially after the French Revolution, but political upheavals led to regime changes in which this right was suspended. France did not grant women the right to vote until 1944.

Third, the government of the day must be accountable to the electorate. In a parliamentary system of government this is done by requiring the prime minister and cabinet to maintain the confidence of a popularly elected Parliament. In the nineteenth century the heads of executive departments of government, including the prime minister, were often appointed by the monarch and responsible to the Crown rather than Parliament. This was the case, for example, in Germany up to World War I.

Finally, a democratic government should not be controlled by extra-governmental institutions or under foreign domination (cf. Dahl, 1971: ch. 9). In a civil society, a government may be influenced by pressure groups, but if such groups consistently dictate what it does, it loses a claim to represent the electorate. In a world of interdependence, every country is influenced at least a little by other countries and by movements in international markets. However, vulnerability is not the same as subservience. Subservience was the unique and unpleasant fate of Central and Eastern European Communist governments compelled to follow the dictates of Moscow by the threat or use of force.

Democracies can differ greatly in their institutions. The usual European method of holding government accountable is through a popularly elected Parliament. In the United States, the president is not accountable to Congress but to the national electorate. Representatives can be elected by proportional representation, as happens almost everywhere in continental Europe, or by a first-past-the-post ballot, which is normal in Anglo-American democracies. Some democracies centralize authority at the national level; others are federal systems.

A democracy does not require every citizen to hold democratic values. This would be an impossible requirement to fulfill, for democracy is about the articulation of conflicting political views. Thus, one person's idea of basic democratic values may be considered a partisan political claim by opponents. Surveys in Europe and the United States show that a significant minority of the population consistently endorses some views that researchers consider antidemocratic. The conduct of free elections presupposes the right of people to vote for any party of their choice, including antidemocratic parties. A regime is consolidated if antidemocratic parties receive only a small share of the popular vote if they contest elections.

Even though democracies are usually economically advanced, this is not a necessary condition for the creation of a democratic regime (see Weiner and Ozbudun, 1987). India, one of the poorest countries of Asia, has held free elections longer than Portugal and Spain. When Japan established a democratic political system under occupation tutelage, this was well before it became a wealthy country. Nor is it necessary for a democracy to guarantee welfare through the state to secure legitimacy. The dominant political values in Switzerland, as in the United States and Japan, are against high-tax, high-spending welfare state policies (see Rose, 1989).

ALTERNATIVE PATHS TO DEMOCRACY

Modern European states have reached democracy by very different routes. The normal starting point was a regime governing by the rule of law but not accountable to the populace through free elections. Elites confronted with pressures to become democratic had the option of seeking to repress demands and risk a popular back-lash, or of broadening the franchise and risking the loss of power. Some regimes chose democratization, others tried repression, and some chose each option in turn.

Progress toward democracy can be evolutionary or it can occur after the abrupt collapse of an authoritarian regime. Evolution avoids any abrupt break with the past; however, the creation of stable democracies takes time, and politi-cians confronted with the collapse of an authoritarian regime have no time to lose. A second consideration is whether pressures to change are internal or exter-nal. In a country such as Greece and Spain in which democracy has been aban-doned more than once, each new attempt at democratization is threatened by domestic challenges. A country defeated in war must heed occupation forces. In Central and Eastern Europe after 1945, Soviet armies supported the imposition of Communist rule while in Western Europe occupation armies supported the cre-ation of democratic regimes.

There are four different paths to democracy in Europe, varying with the tempo and pressures to change (Table 3.1; see also Huntington, 1991; Dix, 1994).

TABLE 3.1   ALTERNATIVE PATHS TO DEMOCRACY

| | *Primary pressure* | |
	Internal	External
Gradual	EVOLUTION (9)	TUTELAGE (1)
	Belgium	Ireland
	Britain	
	Denmark	
	Finland	
	Luxembourg	
	Netherlands	
	Norway	
	Sweden	
	Switzerland	
Abrupt	DOMESTIC TRIAL AND ERROR (4)	DEFEAT and OCCUPATION (3)
	France	Austria
	Greece	Germany
	Portugal	Italy
	Spain	
		LIBERATION (6)
		Bulgaria
		Czech Republic
		Hungary
		Poland
		Romania
		Slovakia

Tempo is indicated on the left axis (Gradual / Abrupt).

Source: Prepared by the author.

The textbook path to democracy is through evolution. However, uninterrupted progress toward democracy, as in Britain, the Benelux countries, and Scandinavia, has occurred in only a third of contemporary European states. A deviant path is the gradual development of democratic institutions under the tutelage of a foreign country. The Republic of Ireland is unusual in Europe in following this path, for as a part of the old United Kingdom it had participated in democratic elections for generations prior to winning independence.

The majority of European states have been unable to evolve democratic institutions because of the abrupt collapse of authoritarian regimes under internal or external pressures. Democratic institutions have been introduced in a vacuum. In 1945 the defeat and occupation of Germany, Austria, and Italy led these countries to adopt democratic constitutions. In Communist Europe, the withdrawal of foreign influence was critical, for when Moscow showed it would no longer use Soviet power to support Communist regimes, countries were free to create a new regime of their choice. The domestic collapse of an authoritarian regime can offer conditions for the abrupt introduction of democracy. In Spain the death of a dictator, General Franco, was the trigger; in Portugal it was a colonels' coup, and in Greece the surrender of power by colonels. France has been exceptional in replacing one democratic regime, the Fourth Republic, with another, the presidentialist Fifth Republic under General de Gaulle, as a consequence of a military coup in 1958. In each of these four countries democracy has been established by domestic trial and error.

Crafting the Transition

Democratization is the process of moving away from authoritarianism and establishing new institutions of governance. Establishing a democracy is far more difficult than governing an established democracy. In an established democracy there is a reservoir of popular support as each generation is socialized to take democracy for granted. In such circumstances politicians need only worry about what the government of the day should do. However, when a regime is visibly collapsing and the direction of transition is uncertain, a key question remains: What kind of regime will this country have?

At the start of any democratization, there are two groups of politicians: a group benefiting from power under the authoritarian regime and a group hoping to benefit by introducing democracy. The interests of both must be taken into account. Representatives of the authoritarian regime cannot be ignored because they usually control such important institutions as the military, police, central bank, and higher civil service. To dismiss all these high officials would disrupt everyday activities on which the state relies for revenue and public order. It would also make enemies of people whose expertise and experience may be needed to establish a new regime. The bargaining power of the old regime will depend upon whether it has collapsed or is subject to a gradual erosion of its authority.

The entrenched position of leaders of the old order is, however, an ambiguous asset, for their shortcomings have created the situation in which opponents demand fundamental change. Representatives of the old order must extricate themselves from their ties with a regime that is less and less viable. Cooperation with emerging democratic groups is a necessary condition of maintaining their place in the new regime (cf. di Palma, 1990: 37 ff.). Once a new democracy is established, former opponents can become converted to democracy on grounds of political self-interest.

In a relatively tolerant rule-of-law regime, proponents of democratization can campaign for change from within the system—for example, seeking election to Parliament, even if the government is not accountable to it. Challengers can press for reforms that expand the sphere of popular influence upon government. When the great majority of adults do not have the right to vote, democrats may lobby through demonstrations outside Parliament. In extreme form, democrats may be driven into exile by a totalitarian regime and carry on their campaign from abroad. This was the case with Willy Brandt, a social democrat who fled Nazi Germany and subsequently became a German chancellor.

Elite bargains between radicals seeking to introduce democracy and those wanting to salvage as much as possible from the old system facilitate the peaceful change from an oligarchic regime to a democracy (see Almond et al., 1973). Bargaining has also been important in the swift conversion of some authoritarian regimes into democracies; for example, in Spain there was bargaining between politicians who served Franco and opponents of that regime. The compromises and deals that lead to a democratic bargain involve a mixture of motives among participants, including personal ambitions (Bogdanor, 1988; Banting and Simeon, 1985). After military defeat or the collapse of a police state, fear of returning to the past is a negative incentive to agree. This motivation was palpably evident in Central Europe after 1945. It is also evident in the post-Communist states of Europe today.

Bargaining between pro-democratic and pre- or anti-democratic groups often makes it difficult to draw a line between reform and revolution, for agreement normally includes some continuities with institutions and personnel of the old regime (cf. O'Donnell and Schmitter, 1986; Linz, 1990: 150 ff.). Rustow (1970: 357) describes the "democratic deal" as being a second-best solution; it is not so much a consensus about fundamentals as it is an agreement about rules for reconciling conflicting interests. It offers guarantees to all sides, losers as well as winners of the first free election, in circumstances in which elites may be uncertain about whether they will win or lose that ballot.

Because the problems of governing are endless, the adoption of democratic institutions is not the "end" of history. Democracy does not ensure economic growth, full employment, or the absence of crime. It is about procedures. Democracy presupposes that the government of the day will generate disagreements about what ought to be done and will sometimes fail to satisfy voters. Democracy is tested by "the way in which political leaders respond to their inability to solve the problems confronting their country" (Huntington, 1991: 258). It gives voters the right to show their dissatisfaction by turning the government of the day out of office and allowing the Opposition to try its hand. The "crisis of confidence" that faces many elected governments is definitely not the same as a crisis of confidence in the regime itself.

The argument for democracy is not that it is perfect but that it is preferable to alternatives. The history of Europe shows that alternatives to democracy are numerous and have imposed great costs in human life and dignity. As Winston

Churchill told the British Parliament shortly after the end of the Second World War:

> Many forms of government have been tried, and will be tried in this world of sin and woe. No one pretends that democracy is perfect or all wise. Indeed, it has been said that democracy is the worst form of government, except all those other forms that have been tried from time to time (House of Commons, *Hansard,* November 11, 1947, col. 206).

ESTABLISHED DEMOCRACIES

A democracy is established when all politically significant groups regard its key political institutions as the only legitimate framework for political contestation (cf. Higley and Gunther, 1992). Political debate continues, but it is about who governs rather than about whether a democratic or authoritarian regime should wield power. Acceptance of a new regime is a process of consolidation; it is the opposite of the political disintegration that occurred in interwar Europe, when defenders of democracy quarrelled and substantial groups emerged to challenge democratic regimes.

Democracy by Evolution

The gradual introduction of democratic institutions depends not only upon pressures from the masses "below," but also upon how those on top respond. If established elites are prepared to share power with new claimants, progress can be made step by step. Adaptation is facilitated if there is already in place an assembly representing some major interests in society, including aristocrats, ecclesiastical authorities, landowners, and urban merchants. In such circumstances:

> Bargaining could proceed by a process of careful adjustment, of shared responsibility, of due respect for ancient privileges. Attempts at absolute kingship eventually broke on the concerted strength of particularist interests, whether corporative, regional or social. As the political order was in a very real sense built upon parts, the idea that men could reasonably be partisans found ready recognition. . . . Intra-elite competition made it easier to weather the crisis of participation (Daalder, 1966: 47 f.).

To describe such institutions as undemocratic is anachronistic, projecting contemporary values backward in time; they are best described as *pre*-democratic. They constituted a check on absolutist rule and allowed political leaders to mobilize support outside the ruling elite in support of demands for democratizing the regime (see Lipset and Rokkan, 1967).

Evolution to democracy was also facilitated by the existence of a *Rechtsstaat.* Where the state was limited by the rule of law, liberalization could advance through the enactment of new laws (Marshall, 1950). The move from civil society to democracy required three additional steps. First, the right to vote had to be extended until universal suffrage was achieved. In evolutionary democracies the right to vote was granted all men around the time of World War I; women did not gain the right to vote until as late as 1971 in Switzerland. Second, the state had to recognize freedom of speech and association, including the right of political parties, trade unions, and other groups to organize (Bendix and Rokkan, 1964). Third, an elected Parliament had to gain the power to hold the government of the day accountable.

Britain was early in developing representative institutions from which democracy evolved. Parliament dates from the thirteenth century. The supremacy of Parliament over the king was established in the seventeenth century by the beheading of King Charles I. The first reform of the franchise laws occurred in 1832. The supremacy of the elected lower chamber of Parliament, the House of Commons, was established before World War I. The slow tempo of evolutionary change is illustrated by the fact that all men and women did not enjoy an equal right to vote until 1928, and it was not until 1950 that the rights of a favored few to more than one vote were abolished.

In Sweden an assembly representing four estates—nobles, clergy, burghers from the cities, and freehold farmers—first met in 1435. The Constitution of 1809 ended royal absolutism and gave a significant role to the assembly, which had evolved into a Parliament. A century-long struggle followed between adherents of royal and parliamentary authority. Industrialization brought demands for the right to vote from workers, who had no representatives in Parliament. Conflicting interests in the old regime bargained about bringing in new interests that coincided with their own. Motives were mixed: traditionalists reckoned that gradual reform was better than risking revolution, and reformers took what they could get when they could get it. By 1907 the right to vote was granted all adult males and by 1921 to women too. Sweden had become a democracy in the modern sense (cf. Rustow, 1955).

When democracy developed early, subsequent challenges to effectiveness did not become entangled with disputes about the regime. Sweden responded to the interwar world depression with an innovative economic program hailed as a middle way between a laissez-faire economy and state socialism. In Britain the same problem was met by the formation of a coalition government under Ramsay MacDonald, an ex-Labour leader; it secured the biggest electoral majority in British history in 1931 (Kavanagh, 1973). Regimes that evolved into democracy were able to survive military defeat and occupation in World War II. Following liberation at the end of the war, their prewar constitutions were restored.

Tutelage and Independence

Ireland participated in the extension of British democracy in the nineteenth century, because it was then part of the United Kingdom. The extension of the right to vote to all religions and to the majority of adult males resulted in Irish Nationalists winning sufficient seats in the British Parliament to hold the balance of power off and on from 1885. This gave Irish political leaders substantial experience of parliamentary democracy. Opposition to Irish home rule in the British Parliament eventually led to the creation of an extraparliamentary Irish republican movement, that rose in arms against Britain in 1916 and to a bloody war of independence concluded in 1921. The new Irish state was founded on the rejection of British rule and English culture. But it did not reject democracy. The Republic of Ireland is a democracy combining familiar British and distinctive national elements (cf. Chubb, 1982: 5 ff.; Rose and Garvin, 1983).

Defeat and Occupation: Getting Rid of Tangible Evils

The majority of countries in Europe have not enjoyed sufficient domestic harmony or freedom from war to maintain a regime without interruption. The most characteristic route to democracy has been an abrupt transformation from one regime to another after a trial-and-error process of trying undemocratic and democratic alternatives. In some countries the trigger for change has been external and in others internal.

Writing after the First World War, James Bryce (1921: II, 602) described the road to democracy as expressing "the wish to be rid of tangible evils." European states were capable of producing great evils. Military defeat and occupation brought home to Germans, Austrians, and Italians the evils of totalitarian regimes. Yet there could be no confidence about establishing democracy, for in each country it had been tried and failed before World War II. Each succeeded in establishing a democratic regime. But given the costs, no one would choose to arrive at democracy by a path that led through defeat and occupation.

Germany is an extreme example of a country that proceeded to democracy through great trials and errors. The pre-1914 German Empire recognized the rule of law and allowed elections, but the regime was not democratic. The Weimar constitution sustained a democratic regime from 1919 to 1933; it was supplanted by Hitler. In 1945 occupying powers—Britain, France and the United States—initially promoted the de-nazification of administration. The idea of removing from public office all former members of the Nazi Party was soon abandoned, because, as a mass membership party, it had enrolled millions. Many nominal Nazis were not ideologically committed, especially in the wake of defeat. For the allies, coming to terms with the past meant recognizing that people who were once members of the National Socialist Party would not necessarily remain Nazis for the rest of their lives. The occupying forces began to give Germans responsibility for administration at local level (see Loewenberg, 1968).

In 1945, German parties began competing in local elections to give both politicians and voters the experience of democracy. The occupation forces licensed political parties if they could demonstrate that they were free of Nazi sympathies. Any German above the age of 42 when the war ended had been an adult longer in a democratic Germany than in Hitler's Third Reich. The first Christian Democratic chancellor, Konrad Adenauer, had gone into local government under the Kaiser, and the first Social Democratic chancellor, Willy Brandt, had entered politics in the days of the democratic but failed Weimar Republic. These initial steps toward democratization were taken while food was rationed and malnutrition widespread.

The drafting of the constitution of the Federal Republic of Germany began in "a vacuum as complete as any that Western civilization has ever known" (Merkl, 1963: ix; see also Golay, 1958). The 1949 Basic Law (*Grundgesetz*) was prepared quickly under supervision of the Allies by representatives of the regional *Länder* and of all the major West German parties. Competing Catholic, socialist, and liberal elites disagreed about many things, but they agreed in rejecting a return to the past. So too did the populace. At the first national election in 1949, 92 percent of the German vote was cast for democratic parties. Popular support for democratic institutions and moderation in partisan conflict followed (e.g., see Baker et al., 1981; Klingemann and Wattenberg, 1992).

Austria became a nation-state as a consequence of defeat in World War I, but the collapse of the Habsburg Empire left Vienna the capital of a small fraction of its former territory. The First Austrian Republic had parties that were too competitive; conflict sometimes erupted into street battles between armed groups. In 1934 Parliament was suspended and an authoritarian regime introduced. In 1938 Hitler annexed Austria to Nazi Germany. In 1945 Austria was subject to military occupation by the four Allied powers; Russian troops controlled Vienna and its hinterland. The first goal of Austrian politicians was to secure the removal of foreign troops. Experience of annexation to Nazi Germany made traditionally antagonistic Austrian parties willing to cooperate with each other, if only as a "lesser evil." Socialists and clericals formed a coalition government. Undemocratic parties secured few votes. In 1955 a peace treaty was negotiated and military forces, including Russia, withdrew (Engelmann, 1966).

Italy had weak democratic institutions before going fascist in 1922 when Mussolini seized power by a march on Rome. It was an original partner in the Axis. The Allied invasion of southern Italy in 1943 was followed by the king dismissing Mussolini and the new Italian government surrendering to the Anglo-American armies; the Soviet Union had no troops on the Italian front. Italian politicians were thus much freer to adopt a new constitution than were Germans or Austrians, but they had a large Communist and a small neo-Fascist party in Parliament (see Pasquino, 1986). The left feared an authoritarian takeover from the right, and the right feared a Communist takeover. Hence, the negotiation of a new constitution was driven by demands from both sides for protection against its worst fears through *garantismo,* the pursuit of guarantees protecting any party in opposition from repression as a consequence of losing a democratic election (di Palma, 1990: 46 ff.). A new democratic constitution for the Republic of Italy was adopted in 1948.

For 40 years the Christian Democratic Party won the most votes at each Italian election. Because the party did not win a majority of seats in Parliament, it formed coalitions with small parties to stay in office. The Socialists distanced themselves from Communists and entered an enlarged coalition with the Christian Democrats in 1962. In the 1970s armed underground groups from the left and right attacked the regime; the regime successfully defended itself. Italian Communists broadened their popular appeal by adopting a Euro-Communist position independent of Moscow; this failed to gain office. In the 1990s widespread corruption within the regime was exposed by judicial action. Governing parties broke up and new parties were formed. After the collapse of the Soviet Union, the Communist Party broke up too. At the 1994 election, old parties were replaced by new. The rejection of four decades of Christian Democratic rule occurred through the democratic process.

Domestic Trial and Error

A third group of European states—France, Spain, Portugal and Greece—demonstrate that the absence of war does not guarantee an uninterrupted evolution to democracy. Each country has had a political history of trial and error alternations between democratic and authoritarian regimes as a result of domestic upheavals, a pattern familiar in Latin America too (see O'Donnell and Schmitter, 1986).

Following the Revolution of 1789, France alternated for a century between rule by popularly based assemblies and rule by descendants of the royal family or Napoléon Bonaparte. Between 1871 and World War II, France had democratic institutions, but there was a substantial minority on both the right and left against democracy. The creation of the Vichy Regime under Nazi protection in 1940 appealed to the authoritarian right. Immediately after the war, elections in the Fourth Republic showed antiregime Communists and Gaullists each securing up to a fifth of the popular vote. The leaders of the Fourth Republic were further challenged by an anticolonial uprising in Algeria, then regarded as an integral part of France. In 1958 a military uprising in Algeria against the Fourth Republic led to General de Gaulle being invited to take office. He sponsored a new constitution for the Fifth Republic, democratic in form and in practice, and a referendum endorsed it with almost four-fifths of the vote. Since 1958, France has become a stable democracy, but it took a century and a half of disagreements among French people before this could be achieved.

In the history of Spain, Portugal, and Greece, democracy appears as the exception rather than the rule. Spain alternated between authoritarian or oligarchic rule and brief periods of democracy. The 1936–1939 Spanish Civil War ended with the establishment of a dictatorship under General Francisco Franco. While not accountable to the electorate, Franco had to balance competing influences of the church, the army, and the fascist Falange Party that he created. To ease the transition to the post-Franco era, in 1969 Prince Juan Carlos, grandson of a former king, was named as Franco's heir apparent to the position of Head of State. Franco's death in 1975 meant the end of his personalistic regime (Alba, 1980).

The problem facing Franco's heirs was how to extricate themselves from a situation in which the authoritarian source of legitimacy was no longer there. The right wanted to keep as much power as possible; the left wanted a democracy in which it might someday win power. The bloodshed of the 1936–1939 civil war made Spanish politicians think twice about pushing their differences to the extreme. Democracy appeared preferable to the alternatives of uncivil repression or civil war (see Share, 1985; Gunther, 1992). Compromise thus appealed to all sides. Juan Carlos was proclaimed king, free elections were held, and a democratic constitution was drafted and ratified by referendum in 1978 (see Bonime-Blanc, 1987: 66 ff.; Hermet, 1988). Spain has since shown commitment to democracy through the alternation in office of conservative and social democratic administrations, and by the failure of an attempted military coup in 1981. The turnaround was as abrupt as in Germany and Austria, and without external pressure.

Although the word democracy is derived from the Greek, since gaining independence from the Ottoman Empire in 1832 Greece was usually ruled by a regime in which a small number of oligarchs manipulated elections. At the end of

World War II, the country plunged into civil war between resistance forces allied to the monarchy and Communists. Allied liberation armies were caught in the middle. Fighting between rival Greek forces did not cease until 1949. After almost two decades of free elections, a military junta seized power in 1967, driving the king into exile and suppressing all opponents. The military did not like having responsibility for civil authority in a country historically difficult to govern (Featherstone and Katsoudas, 1987; Doukas, 1993). Divisions within the military were followed by a return to civilian rule in 1974 and free elections, and the adoption of a new constitution. In 1981 the Socialist Party won a majority of seats in Parliament and took office for the first time, thus showing that the new regime had sufficient legitimacy to accept the alternation of power between the right and the non-Communist left.

Portugal too has lacked a democratic tradition. The abolition of the monarchy in 1910 was followed by authoritarian rule under a succession of civil and military authorities. A very long period of stable authoritarian rule ran from 1932 to 1968 under the dictatorship of a civilian, Antonio Salazar. Elections were intermittently held, but they were "managed" by government rather than free. Following unrest in Portuguese colonies and in Portugal itself, a military coup seized power in 1974. Divisions developed within the military about whether to institutionalize a radical left-wing economic program through control of the state apparatus or give priority to a democratic constitution. The outcome was a constituent assembly being called and a new constitution adopted in 1976, authorizing a popularly elected president and a government under a prime minister appointed by the president and accountable to Parliament. This constitution has demonstrated its effectiveness by surviving the alternation of office between parties of the democratic left and the democratic right (Gallagher, 1983; Graham, 1992).

Today all 17 countries of North Atlantic Europe can be considered established democracies. In countries that achieved this by evolution, disputes were about the specifics of gradual change. In countries where democracy has been established by trial and error, consolidation occurred relatively quickly in Germany and Austria, where occupation forces and national leaders were on guard against a return to totalitarianism. Consolidation was slowest in France and Italy, where for decades after the war Communist parties presented themselves as "parties of combat," and extreme right-wing parties proclaimed themselves ready to defend the nation by undemocratic means.

The consolidation of democratic regimes did not require the creation of a new political culture. New institutions have become effective *before* mass values could be transformed. Changes in political culture have followed rather than preceded the introduction of democratic regimes. A lengthy analysis of German public opinion data indicates that only one-third of Germans supported democracy in 1950, a year after the Federal Republic's constitution was introduced; by 1964 two-thirds did so and since the mid-1970s, five-sixths or more of Germans endorse democracy (Figure 3.1). In Spain, where democracy was introduced much later, the evidence shows an even quicker rise in public support for democracy in order to avoid the recurrence of tangible evils (Weil, 1989).

FIGURE 3.1   CONSOLIDATION OF POPULAR SUPPORT FOR DEMOCRACY
(% showing support)

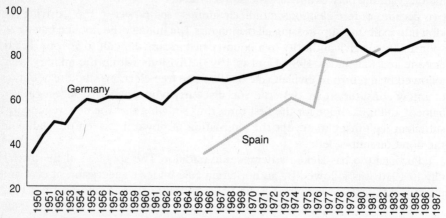

Source: Abstracted from Frederick D. Weil, "The Sources and Structure of Legitimation in Western Democracies," *American Sociological Review,* 54 (1989), table 1.

POST-COMMUNIST EUROPE: FREE TO CHOOSE

Central and Eastern European societies did not choose to become Communist: Communist regimes were imposed under the supervision of Soviet occupying forces. The moment for replacing these regimes was also unplanned. A consequence of the Gorbachev reforms was the withdrawal of Soviet support for national Communist regimes. The unexpected liberation from an established authoritarian regime created a political vacuum. It challenged national politicians with a crucial question: How to fill the vacuum? National histories offered many examples, but few that were democratic. The experience of countries evolving democratic regimes over a century was irrelevant. Since the crisis of democratization was due to the withdrawal of Soviet authority, the experience of countries subject to occupation in the aftermath of World War II was also irrelevant. By default, the only way to proceed was by trial and error. But such a course might lead in more than one direction. As Poland's first president, Lech Walesa, cautioned the Council of Europe, "Democracy might just be a passage between Communism and another form of authoritarian rule" (quoted in Lomax, 1995: 188).

Extrication from Communist Rule

The abrupt collapse of Soviet power forced opponents and defenders of Communist regimes to act quickly to remove coercive control from Communist hands and introduce institutions for a new regime. The uncertainty of events— would the Soviets abandon *glasnost* and return to repression? Who would the masses favor as their new governors? What would happen to the economy in transformation?—made calculation difficult (see Welsh, 1994, for a review).

Regime transformation immediately affected members of the Communist elite. By the end of 1989, most national Communist parties were divided between hard-line factions that did not wish to adapt their behavior to new circumstances, and reformers who, for reasons of self-interest or conviction, were ready to introduce a multiparty regime. There was also a significant group that was prepared to leave politics to make money in the emerging market place—taking with them assets that they had accumulated in the *nomenklatura*. In a few countries there were recognized representative institutions independent of the Communist regime. Poland had two groups, the Catholic Church and the independent trade union, Solidarity. In most countries there were small dissident groups that had articulated a clear moral critique of the regime, often at some risk to their personal well-being. Yet however acute their analysis, such elites were inexperienced in designing or governing an alternative regime. Veteran Communists had lots of experience in administering an undemocratic regime, but none of democracy. At the moment of transition, the proposals and calculations of each group often veered between unwarranted optimism and unwarranted pessimism (see Lijphart, 1994: 208 ff.).

The transition from Communist to post-Communist regime occurred in a matter of months. Where negotiations started before the fall of the Berlin Wall, the goal of opponents of the regime was to make it pluralistic or to share in power. As the old regime visibly weakened, its opponents began to insist on the announcement of a date for a free election, even before the new form of government or the electoral system had been decided. The position of the Communists was the reverse. Initially, they approached roundtable negotiations from a position of apparent strength. But as it became apparent that Soviet influence would not be exercised on their behalf, a new goal was adopted: How could Communists extricate themselves from their commitment to a collapsing regime and secure the best possible position in the regime that followed?

The first roundtable negotiation began in Poland in February 1989, when participants were still reflecting the lessons of martial law. Communists had no wish to provoke massive demonstrations by Solidarity, and Solidarity leaders reckoned that their demands had to be "self-limiting"; they could not threaten the Communist hold on power and dominance of the Soviet Union without inviting a return to martial law (cf. Staniszkis, 1984). The roundtable agreed to an election law in which the Communists were assured a majority of the seats in the lower house of Parliament. In the June 1989 elections, Solidarity won virtually all the freely contested seats in Parliament. Lech Walesa, leader of Solidarity, was unprepared for this outcome, hoping that Solidarity would be able to remain in opposition, criticizing Communists responsible for difficult reforms. However, as Walesa wryly noted, "By a stroke of bad luck, we won the election" (quoted in Przeworski, 1991: 79). Communist rule ended when a Solidarity leader became prime minister in August 1989.

Hungary began roundtable negotiations in June 1989 and was able to agree to a constitution in October 1989. The preamble shows the marks of a compromise document satisfying all groups, including Communists. It balanced references to democratic socialism with a commitment to bourgeois democracy:

> The Hungarian Republic is an independent democratic, law-based state in which the values of bourgeois democracy and democratic socialism hold good in equal measure. All power belongs to the people which they exercise directly and through the

elected representatives of popular sovereignty. . . . No party may direct any organs of state.

In an effort to maintain power, the Hungarian Communist party dissolved in October 1989 and reconstituted itself as the Socialist Party, with many of the same leaders. It declared itself the legal heir of the Communist Party but rejected its "crimes and mistakes." Hungarian Communists believed that the popularity of the leader of the reform wing of the Communist Party would help it win the presidency, if the office was filled by popular election. Opposition parties were sufficiently impressed with this argument to oppose direct election of the president. A proposal for direct election was put to a referendum and failed. By May 1990, a free election had led to the rejection of ex-Communists and a conservative government. The 1989 constitution has now been amended so much that it is virtually a new document.

In Romania the violence accompanying the death of the old regime and its totalitarian character meant that the resulting power vacuum was filled by anti-Ceauşescu Communists. A provisional government took office. Without a round-table, it promulgated an election law and a ballot was held five months after Ceauşescu's execution. The result was an overwhelming victory for the party of government, the National Salvation Front (NSF). It won 66 percent of the votes and seats in Parliament. The remainder of the vote was fragmented; the second largest parties won only 7 percent of the vote each. The NSF presidential candidate, Ion Iliescu, won 85 percent of the vote. Subsequent splits in the National Salvation Front created competitive party politics.

The need to make a double transformation—from a Communist to a democratic regime and from a nonmarket to a market economy—differentiates changes in Central and Eastern Europe from other European countries abruptly forced to introduce a new regime. Greece, Portugal, and Spain each had market institutions operating *before* the establishment of democratic regimes. External intergovernmental institutions such as the European Union or world summit meetings offer moral support, and there is no external threat equivalent to Communist power prior to 1989 or Nazi power in the 1930s. But the help offered by financial institutions such as the International Monetary Fund and the World Bank is limited. They are not an army of occupation but a small body of "fly in, fly out" advisors, who cannot substitute for the missing persons of a market economy, accountants, bankers, lawyers, and marketing managers.

Leaders of post-Communist regimes have been successful in tasks of "deconstruction"—that is, the dismantling of the repressive apparatus of the Communist party-state. Soviet agents have gone, the secret police has been dismantled, censorship is no more, and border guards are more likely to be looking for bribes from illegal immigrants or traders than to shoot to kill. However, in post-Communist societies democratic institutions remain novel.

Testing the Churchill Hypothesis

New regimes do not have to be or do not have to remain democratic. A trial-and-error search can lead politicians in many directions, including authoritarian rule. In established democracies it is often assumed that voters are impatient and will withdraw support from the government of the day if it does not deliver what they want, particularly economic benefits. The problems inherited from Communist days, such as the transformation of a command economy into a market economy, cannot be resolved overnight. But do people have patience?

When the third *New Democracies Barometer* asked people in 1994 whether they thought it would take years for government to deal with the problems inherited from the Communists or whether it would be better to try another system of government soon, an average of 65 percent in Bulgaria, the Czech Republic, Slovakia, Hungary, and Romania said they thought it would take years to deal with the legacy of the past, as against 35 percent indicating impatience (Rose and Haerpfer, 1994: question 28).

Impatience does not necessarily imply the rejection of democracy. The Churchill hypothesis recognizes that ordinary people have reasons to be dissatisfied with a democratic government. It simply states that democracy is preferable to any alternative. To probe what people in post-Communist countries think about the alternatives, the *New Democracies Barometer* also asked whether people thought they would be better off if their country was governed differently, and offered five alternatives (Table 3.2; Rose and Mishler, 1995).

A *Communist regime* cannot be dismissed on the grounds that "It can't happen here," since it has. But insofar as the previous Communist regime rested upon Soviet domination, its collapse makes it impossible to return to the pre-1989 regime. Nonetheless, the familiarity of the old regime, and the stability it offered, could give it some appeal amidst the turbulence of transformation. This hypothesis is reinforced by the capacity of ex-Communists to retain some

TABLE 3.2   WHAT ARE THE ALTERNATIVES TO DEMOCRACY?

Q. *Our present system of government is not the only one that this country has had. Some people say that we would be better off if the country were governed differently. What do you think?*

	BUL	CZ	SVK	HUN	POL	ROM	NDB mean*
				(% endorsing)			
Return to Communist rule	25	6	16	17	18	12	16
Army should govern	14	2	4	2	11	19	9
Monarchy	19	3	2	5	6	18	9
Strong leader to decide	45	16	24	18	35	30	28
Experts should run economy	66	79	89	82	60	57	72

*Average of responses across all six countries.

Source: Paul Lazarsfeld Society, Vienna, *New Democracies Barometer III.* A multi-national survey conducted between late November, 1993, and early March, 1994, sponsored by the Austrian Federal Ministry for Science and Research and the Austrian National Bank. Total number of respondents: 7,020. For full details, see Rose and Haerpfer, 1994.

vote-getting capability in a competitive party system. Yet five-sixths of people in Central and Eastern Europe reject the idea of a return to the old Communist system. Even in Bulgaria, where support for the old regime is highest, three-quarters are against going back to that past.

Military rule is a familiar form of authoritarianism throughout the world. However, it requires military personnel who see their role as guaranteeing order within their society, and who are organized to run the state. These conditions are met in many Latin American, African, and Middle Eastern states. In Communist political systems, however, the military was subject to a high degree of political control by the Communist Party. It led the military to define its role as that of professional soldiers supporting the rulers of the day rather than seeking to supplant them. The problems facing post-Communist countries underscore the limitations of the military's effectiveness. Even if bayonets can suppress dissent, they cannot make factories efficient or promote exports. The aversion of the military to seizing power is matched by public opinion. An average of only 9 percent endorse military rule, and in Hungary and the Czech Republic, only 2 percent do so.

The *monarchy* has a minimum of support too. National revolts against multinational empires led to a rejection of imperial monarchies and turned most successor states into republics after 1918. Of the six countries covered in Table 3.2, only Bulgaria and Romania were monarchies between the wars, and even there four-fifths reject a return to the monarchy.

A regime founded on *strong leadership* is consistent with twentieth-century Central and Eastern European history, including Communist rule. However, the demand for effective leadership is not necessarily undemocratic: It can be heard in every American presidential election and in Western Europe, too. When respondents to the New Democracies Barometer were asked whether they would welcome a strong leader, 72 percent adopted the cautious democratic stance of saying no. After generations of rule by leaders who repressed debate, they prefer government through a Parliament in which different parties can voice views, even if they contradict one another. Of the 28 percent who endorse a strong leader, half this group wish to see Parliament remain in operation (cf. Rose and Mishler, 1996). Only one in seven Central and Eastern Europeans support government by a strong leader without regard to Parliament and elections.

The idea that post-Communist regimes will be judged by their performance in transforming their economic system is widespread (e.g., see Przeworski, 1991). Communist regimes claimed to be technocratic, albeit relying upon Marxist-Leninist rather than Anglo-American neoclassical economics for their economic policies. When the *New Democracies Barometer* asked people to respond to the statement—*The most important decisions about the economy should be made by experts and not the government and Parliament*—agreement shot up to 72 percent. However, those wanting experts to make decisions are not endorsing any old Ph.D. The definition of an expert is a person who is effective in delivering economic reform. People holding this view are not against democracy; they simply believe that technical decisions should be made by qualified and effective technicians. There is no contradiction between democracy and expertise (Dahl, 1970). Elected politicians need not fear being supplanted by economists; their problem is to decide which economic policies and which economic advisors offer the best prospect of producing what the people want.

Given the lengthy duration of Communist regimes and the recency of their overthrow, it is not possible to describe the new regimes of Central and Eastern Europe as established democracies. But given experience to date, it is possible to say that post-Communist regimes are following the path of democratization.

4

THE CONSTITUTION OF ESTABLISHED DEMOCRACIES

The goal of democracy is to complete the state, not to replace it. Without the institutions of a modern state, a newly elected government could not fulfill its mandate from the electorate. Even if Parliament were to decide what the government ought to do, there would be no civil servants to deliver public policies. In Europe the state is much more than a philosophical abstraction; it is a fact of life. A state orders subjects to obey its laws, pay taxes, and risk their lives in military service. Within its territory, the state claims a monopoly of coercive power.

The institutions for governing a state constitute a *regime;* they are normally set out in a constitution. A regime does not change when a general election changes the parties and people giving direction to government. As the British saying puts it, the Queen's government must be carried on. France illustrates the importance of the distinction between the state and the regime. Since the French Revolution of 1789, the state has been in continuous existence, but France has had many different regimes, including five republics, two constitutional monarchies, and empires under two different Napoléons.

The *government of the day* (or the administration, to use a Washington term) should not be confused with the regime. A particular administration is a transitory tenant in the house of power. A newly elected government does not choose the institutions by which it governs; it must take the institutions of governance as given by the constitution. The government of the day uses the institutions of the regime to give direction to the ship of state. Unfortunately, the English language often uses the word government to refer indiscriminately to the current administration, the regime, and the state.

The Anglo-American tradition is stateless or assumes a "soft" state, in which the state's powers are limited in relation to the people or their representatives (cf. Nettl, 1968; Tilly, 1975: 32 ff.). In Britain the concept of the Crown replaces the continental European concept of the state; power is in the hands of a party government accountable to a popularly elected Parliament (Rose, 1982). The American political tradition owes much to the English heritage of "statelessness" (cf. Hartz, 1955). In America the individual rather than the state is the foundation of political authority. The study of American government emphasizes the political behavior of individuals, whether voters, members of Congress, or the president.

The "statelessness" of Anglo-American politics explains the tendency of many social scientists to define democracy as existing in the political culture or minds of individuals rather than as a set of permanent institutions. But public opinion cannot carry out the activities of the modern democratic state, such as administering laws, delivering social benefits, and making decisions about war and peace. These actions require institutions with the capacity to make sure that its laws are obeyed. In Europe this is taken for granted; the institutions acting on behalf of society are part of the state.

In Europe today the state is no longer glorified as an end in itself; it is a means of democratic governance. However, the purposes of a regime differ between democratic states. The first section of this chapter draws on constitutions to show this. The second section shows how a constitution can give rights to individuals as well as governors, and require courts to decide disputes about what government can and cannot do. Although every country has a national capital, a modern democracy must deliver public policies nationwide, and this requires the territorial division of power, the topic of the concluding section.

THE VARIABLE PURPOSES OF STATES

In writing a constitution, choices must be made about political values, for a constitution has political purposes. Many different values may be considered—for example, national unity, social justice, peace, democracy and economic growth. But all the goals of politicians cannot have priority; one or two must come first.

The preamble of a constitution sets out the purposes of the regime. Its rhetorical flourishes contrast with the dry legal language of subsequent clauses. The preamble invokes values with a deep symbolic meaning. The preamble of one constitution, read on its own, may appear platitudinous. But comparing preambles of different countries identifies the significance of selected values. When a country changes its constitution, the new preamble invariably emphasizes different values than the old.

Sources of Authority and Unity

A preamble often identifies the source of authority of the regime. The U.S. Constitution, for example, derives its authority from "We, the People," who "do ordain and establish this Constitution." When this document was adopted in 1787, proclaiming the people as the source of authority was subversive of the claims of kings to inherited and divine authority. The adoption of the Bill of Rights made explicit the rights of the people, prior to and independent of the government authorized by the constitution.

The French Declaration of the Rights of Man of 1789 similarly derived authority from the French people and listed many political freedoms and rights. However, such republican ideals were continuously interrupted by the proclamation of undemocratic regimes (for texts of a sequence of French constitutions, see Finer et al., 1995: 208–244). The preamble to the Fifth Republic's constitution reaffirms the old republican ideal: "The French people solemnly proclaim their attachment to the rights of man and to the principles of national sovereignty as defined by the declaration of 1789."

National unity is a particular concern in states created to build a nation. Germany is an example of a state created much later than the German people. The 1919 Weimar Constitution opened by referring to "the German people united in all its tribes." Such a phrase was potentially explosive because of the dispersion of ethnic Germans throughout Central and Eastern Europe. The 1949 Basic Law drew its authority from the people of the *Länder* of West Germany. It was also enacted "on behalf of those Germans to whom participation was denied," that is, Germans living in Soviet-occupied East Germany. It stated the aspiration for the unity of "the entire German people"; this was achieved in 1990. In view of its military past, the post–World War II German constitution emphasized peace too. The preamble declared that the German nation was "conscious of its responsibility before God and Man, animated by the resolve to serve the peace of the world as an equal partner in a united Europe."

National unity is a major concern in the constitutions of multinational states too. The Swiss constitution is written in three languages, German, French, and Italian. The preamble states that it has "the intent of strengthening the alliance of the Confederation and of maintaining and furthering the unity, strength, and honor of the Swiss nation." The text of the Belgian constitution is published in parallel French and Flemish-language columns. In an attempt to stabilize intergroup relations, the abnormally long first article sets out in detail the respective position of the Walloons, the Flemings, and residents of the bi-lingual region of Brussels.

Close ties between church and state characterize the history of many European countries and are sometimes embedded in the constitution. The preamble of the 1937 Irish Constitution affirms:

> In the Name of the Most Holy Trinity, from Whom is all authority and to Whom, as our final end, all actions both of men and States must be referred, We, the people of Eire, humbly acknowledging all our obligations to our Divine Lord, Jesus Christ, Who sustained our fathers through centuries of trial, gratefully remembering their heroic and unremitting struggle to regain the right of independence of our Nation and seeking to promote the common good, with due observance of Prudence, Justice and Charity, so that the dignity and freedom of the individual may be assured, true social order attained, the unity of our country restored, and concord established with other nations, do hereby adopt, enact and give to ourselves this Constitution.

The reference to "We, the People of Eire" (Eire is the Gaelic name for Ireland) is a reminder of the support that Irish revolutionaries have drawn from the United States.

A comparison of the 1809 and the 1975 Swedish constitutions shows how values have changed from predemocratic days. The first article of the 1809 Swedish Instrument of Government declared: "The realm of Sweden shall be governed by a King and shall be a hereditary monarchy with the order of succession which is established by the Act of Succession." It described the King's person as "sacred and reverenced." By contrast, the 1975 Swedish constitution starts: "All public power in Sweden proceeds from the people. Swedish democracy is founded on freedom of opinion and on universal and equal suffrage. It shall be realized through a representative and parliamentary polity and through local self-government."

Changes in the Greek constitution also highlight shifts in values. The 1952 Greek Constitution was a traditional document. The opening invoked the "Holy Consubstantial and Indivisible Trinity" and proclaimed the Eastern Orthodox Church as the state church of Greece. After the end of a military dictatorship, the 1975 constitution opened with the following statement: "Greece shall be a parliamentary democracy with a President as head of state. Popular sovereignty is the foundation upon which the form of government rests." To reassure religious interests, article three confirmed the position of the Eastern Orthodox Church.

The values addressed in the preamble of a constitution are priceless values. Even though European states today spend most money on social programs (see Chapter 11), constitutions do not give citizens the right to social benefits. To do so without specifying their cash value and the taxes necessary to finance such benefits would be an empty gesture. A British think tank's attempt to write a social democratic constitution shows the limits of promoting social welfare through a constitution. It enumerates concerns common to social democratic parties of Europe. But since social security, health care, and education make big claims upon tax revenues, it concludes: "The provisions of this Article are not enforceable in any court." An interpretive note adds, "Unlike the rights secured in the Bill of Rights, such matters are essentially political and best determined by political means" (Institute for Public Policy Research, 1991: sect. 27.3). Democratic constitutions leave to popularly elected governments decisions about which social programs to enact and how much to spend on them.

THE RIGHTS OF THE STATE AND OF INDIVIDUALS

A constitution is a political document, for it sets out the rules under which groups compete for power, and it states rules for reconciling conflicts that are the lifeblood of the political process. It allocates functions and powers among various institutions of government and regulates their relationship. The constitution also defines the status of citizens' rights in relation to government (see Finer et al., 1995). A constitution is not negotiated above politics. When new institutions are introduced, "problems of the country tend to take a back seat to the problems of the people at the negotiating table" (Weaver and Rockman, 1993: 465). Making a new constitution effective is a political problem, for neither the governors nor the governed have experience of novel rules and institutions.

Limited Checks and Balances

The extent to which a constitution ought to restrain the state is a political judgment. The founders of the modern state were not interested in creating checks on their authority; they were concerned with increasing the capacity of the state to act. Aware of the dangers of tyranny arising from absolutely unchecked power, Montesquieu propounded the doctrine of the separation of powers, assigning different responsibilities to the executive, the legislature, and the judiciary; they were intended to act mechanically as a system of checks and balances. The idea of checks and balances influenced the authors of the U.S. Constitution, which guards against the abuse—or even the use—of power. However, in Europe the idea did not take so strong a hold. Unchecked authority has been justified by arguments drawn from such very different principles as absolute monarchy, parliamentary democracy, or social democracy.

The constitution of the Fifth French Republic, for example, was designed to strengthen central authority, and it reflected a distrust of elected representatives. General de Gaulle sponsored it in reaction to what he regarded as the weaknesses of the Fourth French Republic, in which the fragmentation of parties in the French Assembly made it difficult for the government of the day to have a stable majority (cf. Hoffmann, 1959; Keeler, 1993). The office of president was made a political rather than a ceremonial office. The constitution contains emergency clauses allowing the temporary suspension of constitutional rules when the president deems there is a risk to the republic, to public order, or to the territorial integrity of the state. Constitutional suspension of elected government is justified by *raison d'état* (reason of state), a European doctrine dating back to Machiavelli. The doctrine justifies doing whatever is necessary to defend the state (cf. Meinecke, 1957).

The goal of the modern democratic state is to govern by the rule of law; the law confers rights and obligations upon citizens and upon governors. But what happens when disputes arise about who is a citizen or what rights an individual has? And what happens when disputes arise about whether the government of the day is acting constitutionally?

The Rights and Obligations of Citizens

In every European country the population can be divided into two groups: citizens who are full members of the political community and those who are residents but not citizens. The simplest way of defining citizenship is by the place of birth (in Latin, *jus soli,* the law of the soil). Being born in a country is sufficient to establish citizenship in most European countries. But the boundaries of European states have been changing throughout this century, and there have been big migrations of people across Europe, sometimes voluntary and sometimes due to war. Today, there is also a migration to Europe from other continents. In Switzerland, 18 percent of the population are foreigners, a combination of people who have moved there as a safe haven for themselves and their money, and immigrants from poorer countries who are there as temporary workers.

Each European state has standards for determining whether or not immigrants can become citizens. France is an example of an open, assimilationist European country. Anyone born in France can claim French citizenship. Waves of politically and economically induced immigration have created millions of French citizens with parents born in other parts of Europe or former French colonies in other parts of the globe. The French faith in the "civilizing" mission of the Empire and the superiority of French culture has made the country ready to grant citizenship to immigrants who want to assimilate French culture. Today, the substantial number of immigrants, including more than half a million each of Portuguese, Moroccans, and Algerians, has been seized upon by the French National Front to launch an antiimmigrant party.

Germany, by contrast, defines citizenship by blood (*jus sanguinis*); wherever a person is born, he or she can claim German citizenship if parents or more distant ancestors were German citizens. This definition grants citizenship to several million *Volksdeutsche,* descendants of Germans who in past centuries migrated to Eastern Europe and lands of the former Soviet Union. Over a million ethnic Germans, some knowing no German and never having lived there, have been resettled in the Federal Republic in the past decade, the great majority coming from formerly Communist countries. Concurrently, Germany has had laws making it very difficult to obtain citizenship for upward of six million *Gastarbeiter* (guest workers) and their families who came from Turkey, Italy, and other Mediterranean countries in search of work. Since 1990, long-term residents and their children have had opportunities to become German citizens, but the process is more difficult than in France (cf. Brubaker, 1994).

The European Union endorses the principle of the free movement of people between its member states. Some European Union countries such as Sweden and Denmark have given foreign residents the right to vote in local elections. In Britain, people from any territory of the former British Empire had traditionally had a right to come to Britain and participate in politics. But immigration from nonwhite parts of the British Commonwealth provoked a political backlash from whites in the 1960s, leading to the introduction of restrictions on immigration. This is complicated because Britain lacks a clear definition of who is and who is not a citizen. Under certain circumstances people born in far-flung parts of the old empire can claim citizenship (Rose, 1982a: 35 ff.).

Residents of a country are obligated to obey laws and pay taxes, whether or not they are citizens. Noncitizens normally have a right to such social benefits as education for their children, health care, and, if they have paid the appropriate taxes, to unemployment benefit or an old age pension. All residents can claim equal treatment by the courts, although a noncitizen may be deported if convicted of certain crimes. The chief difference between citizens and resident noncitizens is that the former have the right to vote.

Treating everyone alike need not confer rights on individuals. Most European countries do not have an American-style Bill of Rights or a constitutional court active in defense of individual rights. In the Roman or civil law countries of Europe, there is much less emphasis upon rules of due process intended to protect individuals accused of crimes. Judges see their first responsibility as uncovering all the facts relevant to a case in order to arrive at substantively accurate judgments. Judges usually play an active role in fact-finding and probing the arguments of both prosecution and defense, whereas in the common law tradition of England and the United States a judge is expected to be an impartial umpire (Ehrmann, 1976: 86 ff.).

Cultural norms about what governors should and should not do are often claimed to be the best protection of individual rights. In England, the self-restraint of public officials has been considered a better guarantee of individual rights than statutes that could be subverted, as in Germany in the 1930s, or abused, as in the heyday of J. Edgar Hoover's FBI and McCarthyism in the United

States (Shils, 1956: chap. 2). However, the protection of individual rights by custom requires a very high degree of civility and trust not present in many societies. Northern Ireland demonstrates that the traditional English respect for individual rights does not extend to all parts of the United Kingdom. In the absence of rights confirmed by a written constitution or statute laws, Catholics who considered that they had been discriminated against could not appeal to courts. In a society in which religious identification determined voting behavior and Protestants were in a majority, Catholics could not hope to win an appeal at the ballot box. Since the courts and ballot box could not offer relief, in 1968 the Northern Ireland Civil Rights Association took to the streets. When their protests were met by police and Protestant mob violence, the Irish Republican Army (IRA) stepped forward with guns in hand. The result was a quarter-century of violence in which Protestants, Catholics, and British security forces killed each other. Judicial inactivism in Northern Ireland is in extreme contrast with the United States, where black minorities nonviolently and successfully used the courts to overturn discrimination in the Deep South (Rose, 1976a; Hadfield, 1992).

To protect individual rights, the multinational Council of Europe has sponsored the European Convention on Human Rights, and 23 European countries have agreed to it. A European Court on Human Rights was established in 1959, and there is a commission to investigate complaints about violations of rights. To date the convention has had limited practical effect, for it is difficult to bring a case to the European Court and takes years before a decision is reached. If a case does come before the Court, a binding verdict requires a two-thirds majority vote by the judges. The convention does not have the sanctions of a national court or the European Union's Court of Justice. Nonetheless, a state's signature of the convention creates an opening for judges in national courts to cite it as a reason for upholding individual claims against infringements of rights, and critics of a national government's actions can cite findings under the convention to support demands for change (Shapiro and Stone, 1994: 409 ff.; Moravcsik, 1994; Robertson and Merrill, 1993).

Global measures of human rights and freedom consistently show that European democracies rank very high in respect for individual rights. Freedom House, a New York research institute, groups countries into three categories: free, partly free and unfree. On the basis of a detailed assessment, 21 of 23 European countries are rated as free, and two, Romania and Slovakia, as partly free (Table 4.1). By contrast, in the Middle East no country is completely free, and the majority of countries there are classified as not at all free. In Asia, Africa, and South and Central America the partly free and unfree countries also predominate. The only other continent where individuals are as free is North America, but if Mexico is included, the picture is less favorable.

INTERPRETING THE CONSTITUTION

Most European countries are governed under the Roman or civil law, in which legal principles are regarded as comprehensive and fixed. When a dispute arises, a judge may place the yardstick (or the metric stick) of the constitution against a

TABLE 4.1   EUROPE—THE FREEST CONTINENT

	States that are:		
	Free	**Partly free**	**Not free**
Europe	21	2	0
North America	2	0	0
South and Central America	11	13	2
Asia	5	12	11
Africa	4	19	26
Middle East	0	4	11

Source: Calculated from 1994 Freedom House assessment, as reported in *Freedom Review* 25,1 (1994). Minicountries, Yugoslavia, and all former republics of the Soviet Union are omitted.

given action of government to determine whether it is constitutional. Max Weber (1972: 826) characterized the German version of this theory as making the courts a legal vending machine (*Paragraphenautomat*): "legal submissions are put in at the top along with the fees and costs and a judgment comes out at the bottom along with a standard printed justification." Even though laws and constitutions are printed in black and white, their interpretation involves many shades of gray. Constitutional cases focus on politically controversial actions, in which competing definitions of the constitution are advanced.

There are two very different arenas for resolving constitutional conflicts. The courts can decide the constitutionality of an action or a dispute can be resolved in the political arena, for example, by a parliamentary vote of confidence or a general election. Faced with this choice, most European constitutions favor the resolution of constitutional disputes in political arenas. The Dutch constitution explicitly forbids the courts considering the constitutionality of a law (cf. Waltman and Holland, 1988; Volcansek, 1992).

In European countries judges usually do not see their role as making law through the creative interpretation of statutes. Courts predate democracy; they rest upon doctrines of royal prerogatives that granted wide latitude to the king's servants. Judges are civil servants, spending their career as state officials and having the typical bureaucrat's desire to avoid controversy. Even in social democratic Sweden, judicial officials "generally continue to see themselves as enforcers of governmental administrative, statutory, and constitutional authority" (Schmidhauser, 1992: 297). Judges with a "timid" approach to constitutional issues see the primary role of the courts as clarifying legislation in advance of a law being enacted or applying it in circumstances in which interpretation is unclear (see Meny, 1990: chap. 8). Lawmaking is the prerogative of Parliament and the executive.

In the extreme case of Britain, Parliament is the High Court of the land; this means that an act of Parliament cannot be declared unconstitutional by a court. British judges normally do not evaluate the wisdom of a law or its consequences; the chief test is whether actions are taken within powers conferred by statute.

Since an act can be passed by a simple majority of MPs, the government of the day effectively decides what is and is not constitutional, and it can even pass an act that reverses a judicial decision. Acts of Parliament can give government departments very broad discretion in setting pollution standards, and health and safety regulations. An act may simply authorize a minister to do whatever he or she regards as "reasonable," a condition that the courts have interpreted as satisfied if the minister gives a reason for an action (cf. Jowell and Oliver, 1994).

The British left has historically regarded keeping the courts out of politics as a protection of democracy. By contrast with the United States, where liberal Democrats have relied upon the courts to advance their causes, the British Labour Party has distrusted courts because early in the century they tended to rule against trade unions. Subsequently, the distrust has been sociological: judges as a class are well educated, well paid, and remote from the everyday life of manual workers. Labour leaders have believed that the best way to pursue their goals has been to win an absolute majority in Parliament, and enact laws that no court can void. Conservative governments also prefer to have their decisions subject to political not judicial restraints.

Germany is at the other extreme from Britain. In reaction against the unbridled power of Hitler's Third Reich, the Federal Republic has a Constitutional Court ruling on the constitutionality of acts of Parliament and actions of the government of the day. To make the Court a bipartisan institution, appointment of judges is shared between the two houses of Parliament. Half the judges are appointed by the lower house, which is popularly elected; the other half by the upper house, which represents the *Länder* (regional governments the equivalent of American states) and has a major stake in the enforcement of the Constitution of a federal system (Landfried, 1994). Cases coming before the German Constitutional Court can involve controversial political issues, such as abortion or election laws, or an individual alleging a violation of constitutional rights. The federal government or *land* governments can ask the Court to decide whether an action by one tier is consistent with its constitutional authority. The Court has declared more than 270 federal laws invalid and ruled against the constitutionality of more than 121 *land* laws (Kommers, 1994).

In France, popular sovereignty took precedence over the views of judges until the Fifth Republic. A Constitutional Court was established in 1958. Its independence was secured by giving the right to nominate a third of the judges to the presidents of each house of Parliament and the president of France. The scope for action was initially extremely limited, for cases could only be brought before the Constitutional Court by the president of the Republic, the prime minister, or the head of either of the two branches of Parliament. Since they are much involved in lawmaking, there were few occasions in which they wished to invite a judicial challenge to what they had done. In 1974 a major change was introduced; any 60 members of Parliament can appeal to the Court. This allows a minority of MPs who have voted against a bill to pursue their opposition in the Constitutional Court. Appeals now run at the rate of 10 to 20 cases a year. The Court rules on such controversial political matters as the nationalization or privatization of enterprises, and regulation of the media (Stone, 1992).

Italy shows how the judiciary can transform a political system. For most of Italian postwar history, corruption was a fact of life in politics. No party complained about the way in which money was distributed in return for favors, for all parties were involved in what one sympathetic analyst described as "the spectacle" (LaPalombara, 1987). In 1992, a few judges began to probe deeply into bribery in Milan, also known as "*Tangentopoli*" (Kickback City). As investigations extended throughout Italy, a large number of leaders in government and industry were indicted for bribery and associated crimes; the established governing party, the Christian Democrats, was discredited and dissolved, and in 1994 a new reformist alliance was voted into office.

In recent years judges have shown signs of increasing their involvement in disputes about public policy (see Shapiro and Stone, 1994; Vallinder, 1994). The European Union introduces a new source of law that in certain circumstances is binding upon member states. On European Union matters, the ultimate court of appeal is the European Court of Justice (see Chapter 13). Nonetheless, in the majority of countries, the courts continue to exercise limited powers and hesitate to overrule a popularly elected government acting with the authority of an act of Parliament. This is not because judges are indifferent to law enforcement but because they believe in more self-restraint than American judges.

> At least in the European democracies the democratic principle of national or popular sovereignty and the representative principle that Parliament rules supreme have long been regarded as more important than the third liberal principle underlying Western political systems, that of the separation of powers (Meny, 1990: 296).

Survival Through Adaptation

If a constitution is to remain relevant long after its authors are dead, it must be adaptable, for a rigid set of rules can become an obstacle to effective government. One way to avoid rigidity is to have a short constitution, establishing basic institutions and regulating relationships between them but leaving out contentious political concerns, such as the amount of taxation. When this happens, politicians can debate policies within an agreed set of rules of the game.

Evolution is the simplest method of altering a constitution. The British Constitution is unique because it has evolved from medieval times by a process that Walter Bagehot (1867) described as "keeping the ancient show while we secretly interpolate the new reality." It is not a single document but a collection of laws, official statements, and conventions. There are also unwritten assumptions about what the government should and should not do. The government of the day can alter constitutional statutes by a simple majority vote in Parliament. Unwritten and nonstatutory elements of the constitution can be altered by ministers introducing new customs or conventions or by ministers ignoring old customs and conventions (cf. Marshall, 1984; Turpin, 1985).

Norway is an extreme example of flexibility, for its 1814 constitution was written almost a century before it gained independence from Sweden. The document recognized a constitutional monarchy but did not specify who the monarch should be. From 1814 to 1905 the king of Sweden was also the king of Norway. When Norway gained independence in 1905, the vacant position of head of state was filled by a Danish prince without any need to write a new constitution.

A constitution can change by amendment. Constitutional amendment usually takes place by complex procedures that require a "more than majority" vote. The Basic Law of the Federal Republic of Germany requires a two-thirds majority vote in each house of Parliament. Since the lower house is elected by proportional representation, this effectively requires the support of the two largest parties. Since the upper house is composed by a federal formula rather than directly elected, it has a different partisan composition. Securing a consensus in both houses of the German Parliament is as difficult as winning a two-thirds majority in the U.S. Congress.

A popular referendum can be required to approve constitutional changes. The 1937 constitution of Ireland, written in the aftermath of a nationalist revolution and civil war, made amendment difficult. Changes require approval by both houses of the Irish Parliament, and then by a popular referendum (Chubb, 1991: 118 ff.). In Switzerland constitutional amendments can be proposed by Parliament and then put to a referendum, or proposals for constitutional amendments can be initiated by a petition signed by a limited number of electors (see Butler and Ranney, 1994). Because of the federal structure of Switzerland, a proposed constitutional amendment must be approved not only by a majority of voters but also by majorities in more than half of Swiss cantons.

From the perspective of the 1990s, the greatest problems of constitution-making appear to have been resolved. Yet the postwar history of Belgium is a reminder that even an agreed constitution can become the subject of rancorous conflict. Belgium has always been bilingual—Flemish is spoken in Flanders, French in Wallonia, and the capital, Brussels, is linguistically mixed. However, these differences were not politicized. The major political cleavages within Belgium were between liberals in favor of democracy and conservatives against it; between Catholics and anticlericals; and between Socialists and business enterprises (Lorwin, 1966). The Belgian constitution adopted in 1831 lasted with minor amendments for a century and a quarter. Since the 1960s, however, Belgium has been racked by divisions between the two linguistic communities resulting in constitutional changes turning a unitary state into a federal state, because of a fear that the alternative is a breakup along linguistic lines.

EXERCISING POWER NATIONWIDE

For most of European history, states have not been nation-states; they have been amalgams of peoples, territories, principalities, and postfeudal fiefdoms. Much of the politics of Europe from 1815 to 1918 was about the creation of new states with boundaries more or less coterminous with a particular nationality (Linz, 1993). In writing a constitution for a national (that is, central) government and government nationwide, the question inevitably arises: How should the powers of the state be divided territorially?

The territorial division of government is an issue of power as well as administration. The alternatives are a unitary or a federal state. The theory of the unitary state is that the central government is all-powerful; it has the primary responsibility for taxing and spending, enacts laws that determine the institutions and functions of local and regional authorities, and can even abolish them. Federalism gives constitutional rights to regions or *lands*. The constitution distributes powers between two tiers of government, each of which must approve the constitutional compact. The national government cannot abolish the constituent units of a federal system, and the constituent units cannot secede from the state.

To administer and deliver public policies, every European state is divided into several tiers of government (Table 4.2). Even the ministate of Luxembourg has 118 communes. The names of tiers differ but the logic is clear. Federal systems have a regional level of government, embracing a geographical area combining cities and countryside and covering thousands of square miles. In law such units are analogous to American states, but in population they are much

TABLE 4.2   THE TERRITORIAL DIVISION OF GOVERNMENT

Unitary States	Region	District (number of units)	Local, commune	Population per local unit
Denmark	—	14	275	19,000
Finland	—	12	455	11,000
France	22	96	36,551	1,600
Greece	13	51	6,023	17,000
Ireland	—	38	75	47,000
Italy	25	94	8,075	7,000
Luxembourg	—	—	118	3,000
Netherlands	—	12	646	23,000
Norway	—	19	448	9,000
Portugal	20	305	4,209	2,000
Spain	17	50	8,077	5,000
Sweden	—	24	286	30,000
United Kingdom	4	65	422	134,000
Federal States				
Austria	9	—	2,300	3,000
Belgium	3	9	589	17,000
Germany	16	543	16,043	5,000
Switzerland	26	—	3,003	2,000

Source: Statesman's Year-Book, 1994–1995 (London: Macmillan, 1994). United Kingdom figures exclude Northern Ireland, under direct rule from London since 1971.

smaller. Unitary states often have a regional tier of government too. The next tier is the district, normally populous enough to deliver such major services as education and police, yet geographically small enough to be as close to its residents as an American county or city. The bottom tier is the commune. Many European countries have thousands or tens of thousands of communes. Communes appear to bring government close to the people. But in practice their small size—in France the average commune has about 1600 inhabitants—means that communes lack the money and staff to finance local services.

The current structure of local government is the result of a wave of reorganizations a generation ago, which greatly reduced the number of local authorities in order to make each larger and give them greater resources (Gunlicks, 1981; Dente and Kjellberg, 1988). The underlying assumption was that larger authorities are likely to be more expert and efficient. But there is a political cost in the creation of larger areas: in many places local government is no longer local.

Strength at the Center

In a unitary state, the constitution grants the central government supreme power to determine policies, whether these are delivered by themselves or delegated to regional or local government or other public agencies. Three-quarters of European countries are unitary states. Scandinavian countries, with relatively small populations and ethnically homogeneous, are unitary states. But large states such as France are also unitary. In the 1980s new regional structures of government were introduced, but Paris remains on top. In the words of the first article of its 1793 constitution, France is "one and indivisible" (cf. Schmidt, 1990). Even though there is a measure of administrative devolution to Scotland, Wales, and Northern Ireland, Britain too is a unitary state. All parts of the United Kingdom are governed by Acts of Parliament enacted at Westminster and by Cabinet ministers answerable to the United Kingdom Parliament (Rose, 1982a).

Among unitary states exceptional arrangements are sometimes made to accommodate particular regions without detracting from the overall authority of the central government. Spain has been a unitary state for centuries, but the post-Franco regime faced demands for greater local power from Catalonia and the Basque region in the north and Andalusia in the south. In the Basque region there are also armed groups seeking independence. To avoid exceptional treatment for these three major areas, the 1978 constitution created elected regional councils covering the whole of Spain (Cuchillo, 1993). Italy has five special autonomous regions and 20 regions with elected councils. Popularly elected regional bodies offer a political forum for articulating demands, but the central state keeps a tight hold on resources. Regional personnel make up only 2 percent of civil servants, and account for 21 percent of total public expenditure (cf. Cassese and Torchia, 1993: 108 ff.; Putnam, 1993).

Politically, the unitary state can be advocated as the best way to secure "territorial justice" (Davies, 1968)—that is, equality in public services for everyone regardless of where a person lives. The value of a pension does not depend upon whether a person lives in a prosperous or depressed area, and hospitals can offer people in poor or remote areas the facilities available in hospitals in large cities. Centralization is a necessary condition of equalizing benefits nationwide, for national laws are needed to create common standards of entitlement and administration, and to redistribute tax revenue between richer and poorer areas.

The leaders of central government are primarily concerned with "high" politics, such as the management of the national economy, the politics of the European Union, and foreign policy (cf. Bulpitt, 1983). High politics is the concern of *ministries* that collectively constitute the cabinet. Each ministry concentrates upon a single function of concern to the whole country. Foreign affairs is a classic example of "high" politics at the center of central government. So too is defense; it has a chain of command that leads from soldiers, sailors, and air force personnel to the minister of defense and the government collectively. The administration of justice is organized through a hierarchy of courts and central government officials.

National leaders seek to conserve scarce political resources and time by distancing themselves from "low" politics, such activities as delivering education or collecting garbage. Yet in an era of big government, such everyday tasks are the bulk of the activities of government (Rose, 1985). Giving local authorities responsibility to deliver such services, subject to central direction and finance, insulates national leaders from criticisms about what happens in hundreds of localities distant from the national capital. In an era of financial retrenchment, central government is likely to give more responsibility for services than money to pay for them, thus making subordinate agencies responsible for cuts in services. This is known as passing the poisoned chalice, a drinking cup that can be politically fatal to the recipient.

Collectively, the institutions delivering public services can be described as public agencies. Every unitary state has three types of agencies to deliver public policies: (1) regional and local government, (2) functional agencies, and (3) public enterprises. They differ in their territorial breadth and the variety of services for which they are responsible. In a unitary state they are agents of central government. Central government enacts laws establishing agencies, controlling their revenue and expenditure, and supervising and inspecting what its agencies do. This is usually true of popularly elected local government as well as of agencies under nonelected heads.

Regional and local governments have a multiplicity of functions but are limited in territorial scope. Many services of concern to citizens and communities, such as police, fire, housing and land use, social services, and sewers are deemed beneath the notice of ministers dealing with high politics (see Page, 1992; Sharpe, 1993). Local authorities have some discretion in how they deliver services; the limits are set by central government. Local authorities also have some discretionary powers that can be supported from local funds—for example, promoting local tourist attractions. Local authorities have major patronage powers, for they are significant employers and purchasers of services. Symbolic actions can be taken, such as naming streets after local people or political heroes.

Local councils responsible for delivering services are popularly elected but often lack the money or legal authority to do all that their voters want. When a local council faces this limitation, and especially if it is controlled by different parties than the government of the day, it can blame central government for not providing enough money from central funds. It can also claim to be the legitimate voice of the community because it is elected locally. Central government claims that victory in national elections gives it superior legitimacy. However, the controversy is not carried out between equals. In a unitary state, local councils can be compelled by law or by financial sanctions to carry out measures with which they are out of sympathy.

Functional agencies that depend on central government for their legal authority, finance, and policy direction can deliver major services. Functional agencies vary enormously in size and purpose. Most are nationwide in territorial responsibilities but limited in what they do. They are often created to distance central government from day-to-day responsibility for operations—for example, a parole board decides whether to release a prisoner—or because government lacks specialized knowledge—for example, in aviation (cf. Hood and Schuppert, 1988). The health sector is the biggest functional category; it actually combines different agencies, including hospitals operated by health authorities, religious or charitable bodies, or local government; medical clinics run by doctors or by local authorities; private medical practices where patient fees are paid by the state; and insurance funds receiving compulsory payments from members as part of a government policy of mandatory health insurance.

Public enterprises derive most of their revenue from sales but are owned by the state. Enterprises cover such diverse fields as gas, electricity, coal, transport, and postal services, and some states own enterprises making or selling steel, cigarettes, gasoline, or liquor. Enterprises deemed central to the management of the national economy—for example, the railways or telephones—are sometimes state-owned. Others have been taken over by government because of political problems raised by the threat of bankruptcy; shipyards would be an example. Public enterprises are distinctive in being accountable to the market as well as to the state.

In the 1980s governments, led by the Thatcher administration in Britain, began to privatize state enterprises, selling ownership of gas, electricity, telephones, and other services to the private sector so that they could operate according to market principles. The sale of profitable enterprises raised money to reduce soaring deficits; the disposal of unprofitable enterprises reduced claims on the public purse for subsidies. Privatization has also reduced the influence of public sector unions, which lobby ministries to support their wage claims. However, the privatization of public utilities has not altered the fact that many are still regarded as affecting the public interest, and often have monopoly or near-monopoly powers. Even the Thatcher government was forced to recognize this, for the Acts of Parliament that authorized privatization also established agencies to regulate the prices and activities of newly privatized firms (see Rose, 1989; Majone, 1994; Moran and Prosser, 1994).

The existence of a multiplicity of public agencies—ministries, regional and local government, functional authorities, and public enterprises—creates major problems of *intra*-governmental relations. In a unitary state ministries are dominant in terms of constitutional authority and fiscal power. But because other agencies have their hands on the delivery of services, there is an interdependence between central government and agencies delivering services. In this relationship, the partners are not equal, for central government has the power to amend or abolish agencies that it creates. The Thatcher administration provides an extreme example. It sold off many public enterprises; abolished the Greater London Council and metropolitan authorities covering other major cities; placed ceilings on local expenditure; and against the protests of local authorities replaced property taxes with a novel (and politically disastrous) poll tax (see Butler et al., 1994).

Unity and Diversity: Federalism

Federalism is a word that has many definitions; one scholar has counted 44 and another 326 uses (cf. Davis, 1978; Stewart, 1982; Burgess and Gagnon, 1993). In Europe federal governments are the exception rather than the rule. Germany and Switzerland are the pre-eminent federal countries. Austria was created as a federal state after World War II, in part to guard against the risk of a centralized state being taken over by an authoritarian regime and in part because of regional differences. However, economic and religious divisions cut across regional boundaries. Linguistic frictions have turned Belgium into a federal state with three parts, each with substantial tax revenues and policy responsibilities—Flemish-speaking Flanders; French-speaking Wallonia; and the capital city, Brussels, with special institutions and problems because it contains both language groups.

A federal system is created by a constitution agreed to by the regions that are constituent parts of the new federal system. Each is given exclusive responsibility for some policies, and some responsibilities are shared between both partners to the federal compact. A federal constitution establishes rules for jointly agreeing policies, and the terms under which each partner can act on its own. Because levels of government are likely to differ in political priorities, disputes are inevitable. A federal constitution normally establishes a court to resolve disputes between the federal government and regions about the exercise of their powers.

The federal government claims exclusive responsibility for such sovereign concerns as defense and diplomatic representation abroad. Lower-level partners usually have primary or exclusive responsibility for such matters as education, police, and fire. Many policies involve concurrent jurisdiction by both federal and regional governments. Taxation is one example. Roads are another, for cities and regions maintain local roads and the federal government takes responsibility for nationwide highways. In Germany the constitution gives the federal government the right to enact laws setting out the broad guidelines of policy in fields where a degree of consistency may be desirable—for example, university education or regional planning. Within this framework regional governments are authorized to enact detailed legislation and administer programs. Local government is usually a regional responsibility.

Politics in a federal system involves incessant *inter*-governmental negotiation. Insofar as the assent of the upper house of Parliament is needed to enact government proposals and the regions are strong there, national institutions reinforce regional influences. In Germany each *Land*'s representatives vote in the upper chamber of Parliament as a block in accord with the wishes of the regional government. The minister president of the *Land* is thus a significant figure in the national capital. Differences in the dates and outcomes of *Land* and federal elections can deprive the majority party in the federal government of a majority in the upper house of Parliament.

Switzerland is an extreme example of federalism, arising from the fact that the Swiss Confederation was created in the nineteenth century as a league of previously independent cantons divided by language and religion, as well as by mountain ranges. Under the 1874 Swiss constitution, all powers not explicitly granted to the federal government remain in the hands of the cantons, which today number 26. The federal government is subject to multiple checks by the Council of States, the upper house of Parliament where members sit as representatives of cantons; by the coalition structure of the federal cabinet; and by popular referendum (Linder, 1994).

If the political goal is to maximize consensus, a federal constitution promotes this goal. The Belgian and Swiss concern with consensus arises from the need to accommodate differences in language and religion. In Germany and Austria the federal constitution is an explicit attempt to divide power in countries where the previous regime had been the centralizing Third Reich of Adolf Hitler. One way in which federalism promotes consensus is by reducing the need for centralized bargaining and agreement. Regional governments have some powers to take decisions in accord with their assessment of regional circumstances. Pluralists regard the resulting variety as desirable, but in social policy it can be criticized as a departure from the principle of territorial justice.

Federalism also promotes consensus insofar as national decisions require a concurring majority—that is, positive endorsement by a majority at different levels of government within a state and by both chambers of the national Parliament. This requires continuing negotiation between institutions that each have entrenched constitutional powers and claims to electoral legitimacy.

5

POST-COMMUNIST EUROPE: THE NEED TO TAME THE STATE

To the old European tradition of the hard state, Communist regimes added the idea of an alien state, supported by the forces of a foreign power. In reaction, the first priority of post-Communist regimes has been the "deconstruction" of the old regime. The second goal has been to tame the state through the construction of new constitutional regimes that respect individual freedoms and are prepared to govern by the rule of law.

The first step—the deconstruction of the old regime—could occur quickly. Every post-Communist capital now boasts as a monument to freedom an empty plinth where formerly stood a statute of Marx, Lenin, Stalin, or some local commissar. Censorship no longer restricts what can be said in public, and the state security police no longer instills fear. The bookstalls that have sprouted everywhere are testimony to a boom in the marketplace for ideas. Even if many ideas expressed are banal or sensationalist, their expression is evidence that people can now voice private opinions publicly.

The elaborate system of visas and armed border guards that prevented the movement of individuals and ideas across the Iron Curtain has been dismantled. This is especially visible in Berlin, where all that remains of the Berlin Wall is the monument to those killed on the wall trying to flee to freedom. Czechs who want to go shopping in Bavaria or Vienna are no longer confronted with high barbed wire fences strung across Bohemia's woods and fields. Westerners can visit Central and Eastern European countries to discuss how to build new institutions in place of a Communist regime. The chief barriers to travel are now money and time.

The construction of a democratic regime is a complex process. The rule of law requires a source of law—namely, a constitution to replace the instrument of government used in Communist days. Some countries, including Poland, held elections to determine who governs before agreement was reached on a constitution setting out rules by which a country should be governed. Even when agreement on a constitution is reached, it takes time for new leaders to make new procedures and institutions work as in an established democracy.

In the days of an alien regime, Central and Eastern Europeans could express their feelings by being politically irresponsible. An alien regime made circumventing or scoffing at commands of the party-state a moral virtue, a small gesture of protest. Today, people have a harder task.

The new political class, and society as a whole, have to learn how to build up and run a democratic system. This will be a new experience and a long learning process. People will have to realize that the fight for a free and prosperous society is a much more difficult and complex task than they had imagined in the years and decades of despair and servitude. The golden age of innocence and simplicity has passed (Hankiss, 1990: 265).

Three central problems in the taming of the state are reviewed in this chapter: (1) the problem of constitutional transformation; (2) the establishment of rights in a civil society; and (3) the commitment to democracy.

PROBLEMS OF CONSTITUTIONAL TRANSFORMATION

Dissatisfaction is the starting point for constitutional change. The great majority of Central and Eastern Europeans reject regimes from the past, associated with repression and failure (see again, Table 3.1, p. 59). Dissatisfaction provides an impetus to action—but it is not a blueprint for constructing a new state. The institutions of Western democracies are attractive but distant goals. Immediately, politicians must cope with the problems of producing a constitution for a new regime.

Communist Constitutions

In the old Communist regimes authority was not vested in the people as a whole but in politically correct people, as that term was defined by Marxist-Leninist doctrine. The rule of law was interpreted as socialist legality, which allowed the party-state to do whatever it deemed necessary in pursuit of its goals. For example, the 1936 Soviet Constitution authorized the Communist Party to give direction to all social institutions, including churches, trade unions, newspapers, publishing houses, and political associations, and to expropriate property. The Soviet Constitution has been described as "the first fully fledged totalitarian constitution. In Weberian terms, it routinizes totalitarian procedures" (O'Brien, 1978: 70).

The character of Communist constitutions is given by the preamble to the 1952 Polish constitution:

> The Polish working people under the leadership of the heroic working class and on the basis of the alliance between workers and peasants fought for many decades for the liberation from national enslavement imposed upon the nation by the Prussian, Austrian, and Russian conquerors and colonizers, just as they fought for the abolition of exploitation by the Polish capitalists and landlords.
>
> During the occupation, the Polish nation waged an unflinching heroic fight against the murderous Nazi invasion. The historic victory of the Union of Soviet Socialist Republics over fascism liberated Polish soil, enabled the Polish working people to take power into their own hands, and established conditions for the national rebirth of Poland within new and just frontiers.

This Soviet-inspired constitution denied such things as the 1939 partition of Poland by Nazi Germany and the Soviet Union and the incorporation of territory formerly part of Eastern Poland into the Soviet Union. The response to aggressive

Communist propaganda was alienation. In the words of a Polish lawyer, "Everything is so impossible that we have to avoid the law" (quoted in Wedel, 1986: 17)

The totalitarian aspiration of Communist leaders made little allowance for individual rights. This can be seen by examining the ranking of countries around the world on Gastil's (1987: 10 ff.) human rights index, a composite measure of 14 indicators, such as freedom from unlawful arrest or torture; the absence of censorship; the right to organize trade unions, businesses or professional associations, freedom of religion and so forth, rights taken for granted in North Atlantic Europe,

In Communist regimes the majority of civil rights were not respected by the state (Table 5.1). The only difference between countries was in the intensity with which rights were denied. Given rejection of so-called bourgeois freedoms, the Soviet Union was positioned worst, along with Bulgaria and Romania and such non-Communist countries as Saudi Arabia and Iraq. Czechoslovakia, between the wars an outpost of democracy in Central Europe, was only one step above the bottom on civil rights, at the same level as Iran and Togo. Hungary, Poland, and Yugoslavia were also below the midpoint.

Even though people living in Communist regimes were highly educated and prosperous relative to developing countries, their civil rights were lower. No Communist regime granted its citizens the civil rights of India, Turkey, Mexico, or Egypt. Nor could a lack of economic resources be used to justify the absence of rights, for a poor African country such as Togo was no more repressive than Czechoslovakia, which had a European living standard but not the standards of a *Rechtsstaat*.

Agreeing on a New Constitution

A new constitution must do much more than set out broad purposes in a symbolic preamble. It must also identify the basic institutions for the organization of power, such as whether the state will be unitary or federal, or governed by a pop-

TABLE 5.1   GLOBAL RANKING OF COMMUNIST REGIMES ON CIVIL RIGHTS

Non-Communist examples	Ranking	Communist
United Kingdom, United States, + 11 European states	1	
Greece, Spain + 6 European states	2	
Colombia, India	3	
Egypt, Mexico, Turkey	4	
Jordan, Tunisia, Pakistan	5	Hungary, Poland, Yugoslavia
Algeria, Iran, Togo	6	Czechoslovakia
Iraq, Saudi Arabia	7	Bulgaria, Romania, USSR

Source: R. D. Gastil, *Freedom in the World: Political Rights and Civil Liberties* (New York: Greenwood Press, 1987), 41.

ularly elected president or a prime minister accountable to Parliament. It must also identify who is and is not eligible to be a citizen. If a civil society is to be established, the rights of individuals and institutions must be clearly stated and procedures set out for their enforcement.

Because of the simultaneity of problems, constitutional issues get caught up with other political issues. From the perspective of a harried minister of finance, the prevention of runaway inflation is more immediately important than writing a constitution, and ministers for industry, employment, and social security are likely to give priority to economic and social issues too.

If a new constitution is to be institutionalized, the "rules of the game" must be accepted by major political groups when they lose as well as when they win. Since the new constitution will determine the pattern of power for a generation ahead (assuming the constitution lasts), ambitious politicians fight hard for terms that will best serve their group and personal interests. Political realism replaces the idealism of opposition to a repressive regime. A Western expert notes, "Legislators should not renegotiate the rules of the game while they are playing the game, but since ordinary parliaments are everywhere doubling as constituent assemblies, this is exactly what East European politicians are doing" (Holmes, 1993: 22; see also Howard, 1993).

Czechoslovakia is an extreme example of the problems of constitution making, for the outcome of constitutional efforts to define the powers and rights of Czechs and Slovaks in a federal constitution was the breakup of the country into two independent states, the Czech Republic and Slovakia. The two groups had always had differences. The Czech region, in the western part of the country, was more secular, social democratic, prosperous, and larger. The Slovak region was more Catholic and conservative, and it had depended on Soviet support for its heavy armaments industry. In the June 1992 election the pro-autonomy Slovak National Party won the largest share of the vote in Slovakia but was a minority in the Federal Parliament in Prague, because Slovakia accounted for only one-third of the federation's population. The Czech parties initially affirmed the unity of the federation, but when Slovak politicians persisted in making claims for more and more autonomy, they did not press to continue the federation. Instead they negotiated what has been called a "Velvet Divorce," a prompt and peaceful separation giving Czechs as well as Slovaks the right to determine their own political future. The independent states came into being on January 1, 1993.

While disagreeing about how to share power, Czechs and Slovaks still agree about many basic values, including representative democratic institutions. Constitutional preambles invoke "all good traditions of ancient statehood" (Czech) and "the political and cultural heritage of our forefathers and of hundreds of years experience in the struggle for our national existence" (Slovak). They differ, however, in how the traditions are identified. The Czech constitution sees its land "as part of the family of European and world democracies" and the Slovak as "in the spirit of St. Cyril and St. Method and the legacy of the Great Moravian Empire."

East Germany was unique in having no need to adopt a new constitution, for so discredited was the East German regime, even in the eyes of its own people, that once Soviet backing was withdrawn its leaders no longer claimed to be heading a sovereign state. The collapse of the Communist-controlled German Democratic Republic was followed by reunification with West Germany. The 1949 constitution of the Federal Republic was written in such a way that the five *Länder* of East Germany could be incorporated in the Federal Republic by a process analogous to the nineteenth-century addition of states to the United States of America. As citizens of the Federal Republic, East Germans immediately became subject to all laws enacted in Bonn, including those conferring the benefits of the German welfare state (Goetz and Cullen, 1995).

Poland is a leading example of the difficulties of agreeing on a new constitution, for the Soviet-style constitution of 1952 has been much amended but not yet replaced. The first changes were agreed to in 1989, when Solidarity leaders were willing to accept compromises to avoid the risk of a Soviet backlash. Since then the fragmentation of parties, urgent economic problems, and the unclear division of authority between an elected president and a prime minister accountable to a separately elected Parliament has made agreement difficult.

> The broad consensus among the members of the erstwhile opposition to the Communist dictatorship tended to disintegrate rather quickly, once the enemy had been defeated. Their consensus was not shallow, insofar as it expressed a shared commitment to the most fundamental values of personal liberty and political democracy. But precisely because the consensus was extremely broad and opposition to the Communists did not require the elaboration of a more concrete conception of democracy and its institutions, those opposed to the Communists never developed a unified vision of the institutional arrangements that must now replace the old dictatorship (Rapaczynski, 1993: 125).

There are also fundamental differences about what rights should and should not be included in a new Polish Constitution, such as a clause permitting or forbidding abortion.

ESTABLISHING CIVIL RIGHTS

A constitution is supposed to establish rights, but this leaves open the question: What rights? Communist regimes told their subjects that the rights that count are social rights, such as an entitlement to social security, health care, and employment, and Communist regimes proclaimed the delivery of these benefits as a major achievement. It was also regarded as *substituting* for civil and political rights; Breslauer (1978; see also Cook, 1993) has described this as a form of "welfare state authoritarianism." By contrast, in North Atlantic Europe social security benefits have been regarded as additional to political and civil rights.

In "*Two Concepts of Liberty*" Isaiah Berlin (1969: 122) has given classic expression to the idea of freedom as a negative condition, *freedom from,* defined as "the degree to which no man or body of men interferes with my activity . . . the area within which a man can act unobstructed by others." The brevity of the definition is a strength; it avoids overloading the idea of freedom with many other desirable political goals. It concentrates on the presence or absence of coercion by the state, a point especially relevant in the aftermath of an authoritarian or to-talitarian regime.

Denying Freedom—Creating a Demand

The intrusiveness of a state that did not recognize rights has heightened individual awareness of civil rights that citizens of established democracies take for granted. Even before post-Communist regimes become established democracies, they can promote freedom through weakness; a weak state cannot prevent individuals from saying and doing what they like.

Berlin's idea of negative freedom is readily quantifiable. Freedom is the *degree* to which individuals can act without interference. It is also possible to identify a number of different areas in which individuals can act without obstruction. Freedom is thus a variable that can be more or less present within a society. Asking people to compare what they can do today with what they could do in a Communist regime produces a consumer assessment of freedom. The *New Democracies Barometer* found on each of six measures of freedom a majority of people in post-Communist societies report that they feel freer than under the old regime; the only difference is the size of the majority who feel freer today (Table 5.2; for more details, see Rose, 1995).

- *Religion: 89 percent freer.* Communist regimes were not secular, they were militantly atheist. Today people feel free to make up their own minds about religion. Turning off propaganda for Marxist-Leninist materialism does not mean people are flocking back to churches. In every country except Poland, a big majority are infrequent churchgoers, agnostics, or atheists by their own choice.
- *Joining any organization: 88 percent.* The suppression of organizations independent of the state was a defining mark of the totalitarian aspira-

TABLE 5.2 INCREASED FREEDOMS IN POST-COMMUNIST SOCIETIES

	Speech	Join any organization	Travel	No fear of arrest	Interest in politics	Religion
	(% feeling freer now than under a Communist regime)					
Bulgaria	90	95	95	88	97	98
Czech Republic	84	90	96	73	84	94
Slovakia	82	88	88	62	80	96
Hungary	73	81	76	59	na	83
Poland	83	78	75	71	69	70
Romania	94	94	90	81	92	95
	-	-	-	-	-	-
Mean	84	88	87	74	84	89

Source: Paul Lazarsfeld Society, Vienna, *New Democracies Barometer III* (1994). For full details, see Richard Rose, "Freedom as a Fundamental Value," *International Social Science Journal* no. 145 (1995).

tions of Communism. Yet if a civil society is to come into being, individuals must have the right to start their own business or join a union or voluntary association of their own choice. Everywhere this freedom is now much greater than before.

- *Travelling and living where you want: 87 percent.* In Communist societies the right to travel abroad was severely restricted by the need for exit visas, and controls were also imposed upon moving from one city to another. This system has disappeared. A shortage of cash is now the commonest restriction on travel.

- *The right to say what you think: 84 percent.* If people cannot say what they think, then public opinion must be kept private. This is no longer necessary in post-Communist societies. Nor can official opinion be presented by state officials as if it represented what people really do think.

- *Whether or not to take an interest in politics: 84 percent.* Voluntary political participation is a civic virtue in democracies, but in a one-party state it was a necessity. People were compelled to vote and participate in party-controlled activities. Given this experience, the important civil right today is freedom from compulsory mobilization in support of a party. The collapse of Communism has given people freedom to decide for themselves how much or how little attention to give politics in their everyday life.

- *No fear of unlawful arrest: 74 percent.* Terror was important for securing compliance in Stalinist regimes. Destalinization prior to the collapse of Communism reduced the significance of terror, but it did not remove it. The collapse of Communism has reduced fear of unlawful arrest much further.

The past half dozen years has made a big difference to the everyday lives of people across Central and Eastern Europe. Whereas the right to vote can only be exercised occasionally, the freedoms examined here affect what a person can do each day. The gains in freedom are greatest where regimes were previously very repressive, such as in Ceauşescu's Romania, and in Bulgaria. They are also very high in the Czech and Slovak republics, where Soviet troops remained in place until the end to prevent the recurrence of another outburst like the 1968 Prague spring.

East Germany presents an equally revealing test of popular recognition of freedom. During Hitler's Third Reich, it was sometimes argued that the political culture of Germany was inimical to freedom; the concept of the authoritarian personality was developed by exiled German social scientists in the United States. The German Democratic Republic demonstrated that 16 million Germans could shift from Nazi to Communist rule. Its inhabitants were families who did not move West before the Berlin Wall was built in 1961. Instead, they bowed to a repressive regime based on coercion and informers, in which the state security police (the *Stasi*) maintained elaborate files on what individuals said and did at home. Even though East Berlin was not as prosperous as West Berlin, it was far more prosperous than Warsaw or Moscow. The concept of "welfare state authoritarianism" aptly describes the old GDR, for it shot citizens fleeing a country with the highest material living standard of any Communist country.

FIGURE 5.1   EAST GERMAN EVALUATION OF REGIME CHANGE
(% endorsing government measures)

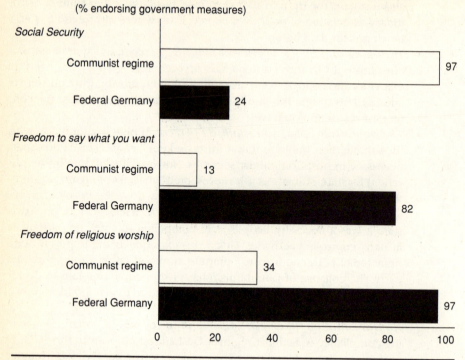

Source: Richard Rose, Wolfgang Zapf et al., *Germans in Comparative Perspective* (Glasgow: University of Strathclyde Studies in Public Policy No. 218, 1993); 1,117 interviews in East Germany, March/April 1993.

When East Germans are today asked to rate their old and new regimes in terms of social security, the Communist regime comes off best by a margin of four to one (Figure 5.1). However, notwithstanding the recognition of greater social welfare benefits under the Communist regime, East Germans do not ignore the big gains in freedom achieved by becoming part of a *Rechtsstaat*, the Federal Republic of Germany. More than four-fifths now feel free to say what they think compared to one in eight in the Communist era. Similarly big gains have been made in religious freedom. In a perfect world, East Germans might like to have both the social security of the past and the freedoms of the new regime. But life does not offer such choices. When asked to evaluate the old and the new regimes, East Germans give a much higher rating to the regime that has increased their freedom than to the regime better for social security. Only 32 percent approve the old Communist regime, compared to 60 percent endorsing the Federal Republic of which they are now a part (Rose and Page, 1996).

Popular appreciation of freedom may seem "obvious." But the point was not so obvious to analysts of the Soviet bloc prior to the collapse of that system. Whatever credit Communist regimes gained for their material achievements, this did *not* blind subjects to the regime's interference with activities that in a civil society are outside state control. Today citizens of post-Communist countries complain about the ineffectiveness of the new regime in dealing with problems arising from the transformation of a command economy into a market economy. There is a need "to liberalize and strengthen the state simultaneously (Holmes, 1995: 78). Yet in terms of freedom from the state, the *weakness* of political authority can be an advantage when it replaces an authoritarian regime that sought social control through coercion.

New regimes in post-Communist lands are far from ideal. Yet Freedom House ratings of Central and Eastern European countries confirm that all countries in the region are freer today than under the Communists (Figure 5.2). In the case of the Czech Republic and Hungary, ratings have risen as high as in Britain, France, and Germany. In Bulgaria and Poland, each country has risen as high as Greece or Italy. Slovakia and Romania are rated as "partly free" today. This is a significant improvement from the past, if only because the starting point was so low.

FIGURE 5.2   CHANGES IN FREEDOM FROM COMMUNIST TO POST-COMMUNIST REGIMES

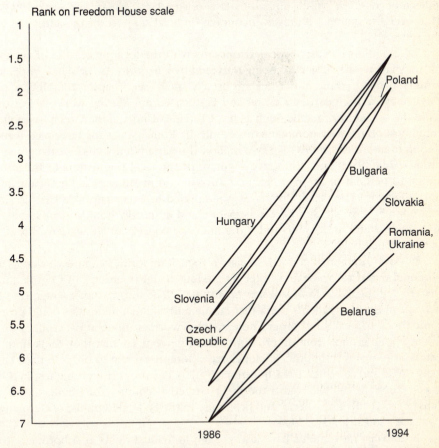

Sources: R. D. Gastil, *Freedom in the World* (New York: Greenwood Press, 1987), 41; Freedom House, "1994 Freedom Around the World," *Freedom Review* 25, 1 (1994), 20.

Protecting Majorities and Minorities

In a country governed by the rule of law, the guarantees of majority and minority rights are multiple. Individuals, including public officials, are accustomed to respect the rights of others; laws exist to safeguard rights; and courts exist to enforce laws protecting rights.

In post-Communist states the role of the courts in protecting rights is limited, as is the case in many Western European countries. Post-Communist constitutions often make provision for courts to review the constitutionality of legislation and executive action. Hungary has gone furthest in allowing any aggrieved individual or organization to challenge the constitutionality of government action in the courts. Hungarian courts have dealt with such politically controversial topics as the powers of the president, the restoration of property to people from whom it was seized in authoritarian times, and capital punishment. However, in most post-Communist countries access to constitutional courts is restricted and the exercise of constitutional rights may only be recognized "unless the law provides otherwise" or "unless limited by law" (Elster, 1991: 465 ff.; Schwartz, 1993). Moreover, the training of judges encourages judicial support for the authority of the state.

Ethnic minorities have special concerns with the legal protection of rights, for they are always subject to being outvoted by a majority. As the name implies, groups forming ethnic minorities are usually small (see Chapter 7, Table 7.4, p. 143). Many minorities fled Central and Eastern Europe during World War II or were the object of genocide, such as Jews. Today, Poland and the Czech Republic are almost completely homogeneous ethnically. Romania has the largest concentration of minorities, more than two million Hungarians and gypsies, each constituting a significant and distinctive segment of the total population. In Bulgaria about 10 percent of the population is Turkish and in Hungary a significant minority is gypsy. The velvet divorce was simplified in Czechoslovakia because in that country it was easy to create separate and ethnically homogeneous Czech and Slovak states. In Slovakia today the minority consists of Hungarians, a tenth of the population.

In post-Communist countries, relatively small minorities can be viewed as a potential threat to peace and order by anxious majority groups. In Central and Eastern Europe, *New Democracies Barometer III* found that an average of 32 percent of the respondents think that ethnic and national minorities could pose some threat to peace and order. There are also worries about an overspill of different ethnic groups from other countries; 24 percent say that they think immigrants or refugees from other societies are a potential threat to order in their society (Rose and Haerpfer, 1994: questions 69, 70). The proportion is highest in the Czech Republic, which is also the most attractive country for immigrants because of its relative prosperity and proximity to the Federal Republic of Germany (Wallace and Palyanitsya, 1995).

Nationalist movements have always seen individual rights as subordinate to collective rights of a nation with a common identity, language, and religion. But one community's nation-state can exclude other nationalities. Estonia and Latvia were independent Baltic states occupied by Nazi and Soviet troops as a consequence of the 1939 pact between Hitler and Stalin. They were incorporated into the Soviet Union during World War II. After 1945, many Russian-speaking Soviet citizens moved there as part of a Soviet military and industrial buildup. Russian-speaking former Soviet citizens now constitute more than one-third of the population of Estonia and Latvia, whereas before World War II they were small minorities. Since Russian was the official language of the Soviet Union, emigrants normally did not learn Estonian or Latvian, and the majority was compelled to learn Russian. The third Baltic state, Lithuania, is different, for 85 percent of its population is Lithuanian, and the rest is divided between Russian-speaking and Polish-speaking minorities.

Estonia and Latvia are each small countries with distinctive national languages and non-Russian cultures. Estonia has close ties with Finland; the capital of Latvia, Riga, is an old Baltic trading city with a Western orientation. To grant citizenship to Russian-speakers would transform these nation-states into multinational states. If Russian-speakers voted as a bloc, then so too could Estonians and Latvians, thus creating permanent polarization between an ethnic majority and an ethnic minority. Yet not to grant citizenship is to deny Russian-speakers political rights and risk their alienation from the new state. Estonians and Latvians are divided about policies on citizenship. Both are prepared to recognize rights based upon the rule of law, such as freedom of speech and freedom from unlawful arrest. Russian-speakers also have rights to employment and social benefits. The states are prepared to offer citizenship on terms that combine a test of residence and knowledge of a Baltic language, but neither is prepared to give citizenship and the right to vote immediately to every Russian resident (see Rose and Maley, 1994).

The importance of civil rights as distinct from such political rights as voting is demonstrated by the way in which the Russian minorities in the Baltic states rate their freedoms today by comparison with life in the Soviet Union (Rose, 1995: table 1). More than three-quarters of Russians feel freer in the independent Baltic states than they did when they were part of the Russian-dominated Soviet Union. This is the case even though many cannot vote. Moreover, Russians in the Baltic states feel freer today than do Russians living in the Russian Federation.

HOW MUCH COMMITMENT TO DEMOCRACY

The evaluation of democracy depends upon the standards chosen. If democracy is defined in an idealized form, comparing the ideal with the reality will make reality appear deficient, whether in Britain, Germany, or America, for democracies encourage criticism. New regimes in post-Communist countries show even more deficiencies, for institutions there are untried, and governors are inexperienced. However, if comparison is made between the experience of actual regimes, the evaluation changes. Even if both past and present regimes appear unsatisfactory, people are likely to prefer the regime that they regard as the lesser evil. An ineffectual democracy can appear preferable to a Communist regime effective in suppressing individual rights.

FIGURE 5.3   EVALUATION OF REGIMES—PAST, PRESENT, FUTURE

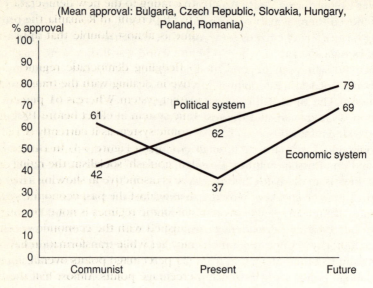

(Mean approval: Bulgaria, Czech Republic, Slovakia, Hungary, Poland, Romania)

Q. Here is a scale for ranking how the government works. The top, plus 100
    is best; the bottom, minus 100, is the worst. Where would you place:
    a. The former Communist regime? The socialist economy?
    b. Our current system of governing with free elections and many
        parties? Our current economic system?
    c. Our system of governing in five years time? Our economic system in
        five years?

Source: New Democracies Barometer III (1994): Paul Lazarsfeld Society, Vienna.

Comparing Past, Present, and Future Regimes

The starting point for assessing post-Communist commitment to democratic regimes
is the past, not the present. How strong is the rejection of the old Communist
regime? The greater the dissatisfaction generated, the more likely any regime, including a fledgling democratic regime, will appear preferable. To make this comparison,
we need to think of popular evaluations of regimes on a "heaven/hell" scale ranging
from total satisfaction (plus 100) to total dissatisfaction (minus 100) (see Rose, 1992).

In Central and Eastern Europe today, the majority of people have a negative
view of the former Communist regime (Figure 5.3). Across six countries, only 42
percent overall give it a positive rating. In the Czech Republic, where Soviet dictates made the old regime particularly repressive, only 23 percent give a positive
rating to the old system. The highest rating, 58 percent positive, is given in Hungary, where the old regime was cynically rather than oppressively Communist.

Although a new regime is limited in what it can immediately achieve, by definition it has one distinguishing feature: It is *not* the old regime. Simply by allowing scope for a civil society to develop and giving individuals much more free-

dom to do and say what they wish, the new regime shows itself different from the old. Overall, 62 percent give a positive rating to the new democratic regimes. In the Czech Republic, the rating rises to 78 percent. In Romania, the proportion approving the current Romanian regime is almost double that approving the Ceauşescu regime.

The substantial approval given to fledgling democratic regimes does not mean that people regard them as effective in dealing with the transformation of the economy from a command to a market system. Whereas 61 percent have a positive view of the nonmarket economic system in effect before 1989, a majority disapprove the operation of the economic system as it currently is. The overall rating drops by 24 percentage points (see again Figure 5.3) In Hungary, which was relatively prosperous under so-called "goulash" socialism, the rating drops by 48 percentage points. The Czech Republic is distinctive in showing a higher level of positive endorsement for the present as against the past economic system.

The positive attachment to new democratic regimes is not economically determined. If that were so, everyone dissatisfied with the economic system today would also be dissatisfied with democracy. Yet while transformation has seen approval of the economic system fall by 24 percentage points overall, approval of the political system has risen by 19 percentage points. Almost half those disapproving of the current economic system nonetheless give a positive rating to the political system. The median post-Communist citizen approves of the new political regime but disapproves of the new economic system.

Polarization or Leaders and Laggards?

Majority support for the new regime is a necessary condition of maintaining a democracy. However, a positive judgment in aggregate masks differences of opinion between individuals. In the fluid circumstances of post-Communist countries, some people can become more favorable while others are becoming less favorable to the new regime (Rose and Mishler, 1994). Classifying *New Democracies Barometer III* respondents by their approval or disapproval of the old Communist regime and the fledgling democratic system produces four groups of unequal size:

- *Democrats (disapprove of Communist regime, approve of new regime: 38 percent).* This group is the largest and most positive about political change. Their average rating of the old regime on the heaven/hell scale is minus 57; their average rating of the new regime is plus 44.
- *Skeptics (disapprove of both regimes: 20 percent).* Churchill was a skeptic, endorsing democracy as a lesser evil. A fifth of Central and Eastern Europeans share his view. They are negative about both past and present political regimes. On average, they view the old Communist regime as worse, minus 45, a position 13 points lower on the heaven/ hell scale than the current regime.
- *Compliant (approve of both Communist, new regimes: 23 percent).* Given a history of authoritarian pressures to bow to the powerful, it is not surprising that some people will endorse both old and new regimes.

The mean rating on the heaven/hell scale is almost identical for the Communist regime (plus 46) and the current regime (plus 43).

- *Reactionaries (approve of Communist regime, dislike new: 19 percent).* This group is the mirror image of the democrats. The mean rating given the Communist regime on the heaven/hell scale is plus 58 and for the new regime it is minus 45.

Within post-Communist countries, democrats who positively prefer the new regime and reject the old are usually the largest group. But only in the Czech Republic are they a majority. The views of democrats tend to be reinforced by the skeptics, for even though skeptics give a negative rating to both old and new regimes, they usually regard the current system as a lesser evil. The compliant, people inclined to say yes to all institutions of authority, are certainly not against democracy, but their commitment appears shallow. Reactionaries, just under a fifth of society, are significant in number, but they are also very much a minority.

The critical issue is the direction in which individual attitudes toward the regime change. Democratization requires a gradual increase in the percentage approving the new regime. If everyone became more positive about the regime, the population would be divided into *leaders* (those who became democrats as soon as the new system was introduced) and *laggards* (persons slow to endorse the new democratic regime, but doing so eventually). Attitude changes in Germany, Austria, and Spain appear to have followed a leaders and laggards model (Figure 3.2 above). But this theory requires reactionaries in post-Communist societies to make a big turnaround.

The alternative is a *polarization* of public opinion into two conflicting camps, one favoring and the other against the regime. A simple extrapolation of current positions would predict polarization. As the skeptics gradually join the democrats, this would create a majority supporting the new regime, but a movement of compliants toward the reactionaries would increase the minority against it. Polarization was the position in the Weimar Republic of Germany and in the Fourth French Republic until it collapsed. If the polarization thesis is correct, opinions for and against the regime in future will be more divided than today.

Because five years is a very long time in the politics of post-Communist regimes, the *New Democracies Barometer* assessed hopes and fears by asking people how they expect the political and economic regimes to rate in future. Hopes greatly outweigh fears (cf. Figure 5.3). Central and Eastern Europeans are very positive about the political future: 79 percent give a positive rating to the regime as they expect it to evolve. This is almost double the proportion approving the old Communist regime. Similarly, people are optimistic about the future economy; its positive rating is up 32 points from the current economy.

Whether polarization occurs depends upon the movement of people who have been reacting against the current regime. The *New Democracies Barometer* data show that skeptics expect their initial reservations to be overcome in future, with a majority coming around to endorsing the new regime. Reactionaries too turn out to be converts to the idea of democracy, even though lagging behind others. Instead of expecting the future to be even worse than the present, reactionaries reverse their position. The average reactionary is 37 points more in favor of the regime in the future than today, resulting in a majority of reactionaries eventually giving positive, even if grudging, support. In the future, differences are likely to occur between a majority who are definitely in favor of the regime and a minority who are lukewarm or neutral supporters.

part III

THE POLITICS OF REPRESENTATION

6

MOBILIZING POPULAR SUPPORT

Political parties are necessary for representative government because parties formulate policies, nominate candidates, and conduct election campaigns, and the winners participate in government. Opposition parties use Parliament and the media to publicize what the government is doing wrong and what government ought to do. Parties reduce the multiplicity of opinions held by millions of voters to a choice between a few alternatives. An individual's vote is not an endorsement of everything that a party promises but a preference for a group that *more or less* represents his or her outlook. The greater the number of parties in a system, the greater the diversity of outlooks—economic, religious, ethnic and other—that can be represented, But the more a party concentrates its appeal on a single group or issue, the smaller its vote is likely to be. The bigger a party's share of the vote, the more likely it is to represent diverse and even conflicting opinions among its supporters.

Parties want a lot of votes, but in a democratic party system no party can win all the votes. Appealing to one group can result in a party writing off other support; for example, a party cannot win votes from both sides on an issue such as abortion. Proportional representation ensures a party a significant number of seats in Parliament even if it does not finish first in popular preferences (see Chapter 8). It can win sufficient seats to participate in a coalition government with as little as a tenth of the popular vote. Given that a party can do well by mobilizing votes from one section of the electorate, to whom does it appeal?

In Europe parties normally address their appeals to organized social groups and interests. It is easier to solicit votes from people who identify with a church or a trade union than to convert people to support a cause that they have never heard of. Catholic parties were started with the support of clerical authorities, and before an election bishops would issue pastoral letters calling on communicants to support the Church's party. In Britain most "members" of the Labour Party are not individuals but "ghost" members whose unions automatically affiliate millions to the Labour Party by sending checks from union headquarters. Parties target groups through programs identifying themselves with specific interests in society. Each party's election manifesto reaffirms its appeal to established supporters. Party discipline does not allow individual candidates the leeway to appeal to local interests, as do members of Congress in the United States (see Budge et al., 1987; Bogdanor, 1985). A party's program does not change every time a party changes its leader.

Lipset and Rokkan (1967) identified classic dimensions of social cleavage in European party systems. Two dimensions—religion and national identify—concern *cultural* values. Cultural divisions between Catholics and Protestants date back to the sixteenth-century Reformation, and conflicts between clericals and anticlericals about church influence on social policy arose in the nineteenth century. A second cultural dimension concerns national identity. In societies that were relatively homogeneous, centralization in a modern state produced a nation-state identity. In multinational states, it produced reactions against central authority from peripheral ethnic groups. *Differences in economic interests* are the second major dimension of party cleavage. Differences between urban and rural interests reflected conflicts between the food-producing countryside and manufacturing centers, and have often overlapped with differences between a traditional or religious rural population and secular urban dwellers. Within cities, there are class differences between manual workers in industry and the nonmanual middle class.

Social cleavages from the past remain relevant in party politics today, for once a party becomes established individuals can identify with it through thick and thin. If the regime is not disrupted, party identification can be lifelong and transmitted from one generation to the next through political socialization. At any one election, the great majority of votes are cast for parties that have been contesting elections before the average elector was old enough to vote, or even born (cf. Bartolini and Mair, 1990). For example, the British Conservative and Liberal parties can trace their origins to the early nineteenth century, and the German Social Democratic Party, founded in 1871, has survived the fall of four German regimes.

If the four basic cleavages of religion, national identity, and agrarian and class interests were equally important, there would be parties representing each of the 16 logically possible combinations of cultural values and economic interests. But this does not happen. The link between social cleavage and party appeals is contingent. Lipset and Rokkan (1967: 26) caution, "Cleavages do not translate themselves into party oppositions as a matter of course." Political entrepreneurs must mobilize potential support by organizing a party that can attract popular support. No effort is made if there are very few voters in a category (for example, peasants in urban areas) and if a country is homogeneous, having a common ethnic identity, religion and language, distinctive parties cannot organize along these lines. In a homogeneous society, parties tend to organize around economic interests. This is largely the case in Britain and Scandinavia. But European countries such as Belgium and Switzerland are not culturally homogeneous, and in countries such as France, Germany, and Italy, historic cultural conflicts about religion remain significant today.

When new political differences arise in society, political entrepreneurs in established parties can adapt an established party to deal with fresh concerns of their supporters. If traditional appeals decline, a party can try to broaden its appeal by using television to emphasize its leader's personality and stress its competence in managing government rather than its position on historic cleavages. But playing down traditional policies risks splitting a party—if some supporters remain firmly committed to policies that new leaders wish to abandon as out of date electoral handicaps. Occasionally, entrepreneurs can launch a new party—for example, the ecology movement has created an awareness of the environment and green parties are now found in most European countries.

Once mobilized by a party, voters tend to stay mobilized. Hence, the first two sections of this chapter focus upon historic cleavages of religion, national identity and economic interests. Since party competition is inherently dynamic, the third section looks at the way in which new parties emerge and how old parties adapt, decline, or split in response to changes in the electorate. The concluding section shows how differences in social structure and political history have produced two major types of party competition in Europe today: a one-dimensional system reflecting economic interests and a two-dimensional system in which religion and economic interests are both important.

TRADITIONAL CULTURAL CLEAVAGES

Cultural characteristics may unite *or* divide a society. Since it is normal for a European country to have a state religion, there are societies in which virtually everyone belongs to the same church, whether the Catholic Church in Ireland or the Lutheran Church in Scandinavia. But even where nominal religion is the same, there can be a political cleavage between churchgoers who accept clerical influence in public policy and anticlericals who reject the influence of bishops. Many European countries are today virtually homogeneous in language, national identity, and race. They are nation-states because national identity and state boundaries are the same. However, where divisions exist, then even Catholic and Socialist parties can divide on linguistic lines.

Religion and Anticlericalism

When the Reformation pitted the Catholic and Protestant churches against each other, religion was a matter of public policy, not individual conscience. Subjects were expected to adopt the religion of their ruler, and those who did not were denied political and civil rights. Until well into the nineteenth century in Britain, Roman Catholics and Jews could not vote and an atheist could not sit in Parliament until 1869. The introduction of compulsory education created a new church-state dispute between religious authorities demanding the right to control what was taught in the schools and those who wanted schools to be secular institutions free of clerical influence.

After the defeat of Fascist regimes in World War II, the Catholic Church sought to promote Christian parties as a democratic, pro-church alternative to the anticlerical left. Since the Catholic Church has workers as well as middle-class members, Catholic parties are not especially pro-business. The parties are described as centrist in economic policy, supporting trade union rights and also defending private enterprise. On social issues parties endorse welfare state maternity benefits and children's allowances but oppose abortion through a national health service. In Italy the cross-class Christian Democrats were the largest single party at every election until massive corruption scandals led to collapse in 1994.

Today, the great majority of European countries still have parties that appeal for votes by supporting *or* opposing church doctrines (Figure 6.1). The classic cleavage between a pro-Catholic and anticlerical parties is found in Austria, Belgium, France, Italy, Luxembourg, and Spain. In these six countries the chief anticlerical group is a social democratic party concerned with economic interests too; in countries such as Germany, the Christian Democratic Union (CDU) was formed jointly by Protestants and Catholics after the failure of an earlier Catholic Center Party. Catholic support remains particularly important for the CDU. The Free Democratic Party (FDP) opposes the state enforcing church morality and is willing to form a governing coalition with Social Democrats. Because the FDP also favors antisocialist economic policies, it also joins government coalitions with the CDU.

Divisions among Christian churches are politically salient in the Netherlands. It has Protestant versus Catholic cleavages as well as clerical versus anticlerical divisions. The classic Dutch party system had a Catholic party, three different Protestant parties, and two major anticlerical parties. Secularization led to the merger of the largest Protestant party and the Catholic party into a single Christian Democratic Appeal in 1979, but smaller denominational parties continue to exist. After the 1994 Dutch general election, a cross-class government of liberals and labor was created, notwithstanding economic differences, because the parties shared a common anticlerical heritage.

Scandinavian societies are secular societies. The tradition of the state Lutheran Church is not to take an independent line in politics. Because the great majority of voters there are indifferent to religion, there is neither a large anticlerical nor a large clerical party, and small parties of committed Protestants have little political impact. Religion is a matter of political indifference in Britain too. In Greece and Ireland religion has been a basis for national unity prior to independence. Ireland is unique because the pervasiveness of Roman Catholicism makes all parties respectful of church interests in education (religious instruction in the schools is consistent with Catholic doctrine), health (abortion is unconstitutional) and related matters. No Irish party proclaims secular policies and Catholics divide their votes among all the parties.

Complementary or Conflicting Identities

Everyone has a multiplicity of identities relating to gender, race, religion, age, nationality, hobbies, and so forth. Thus, it is normal for many identities to exist in society, and to do so in ways that are complementary rather than a source of political conflict. Few identities become politically salient; this can happen only if political entrepreneurs seek to mobilize support along lines of an identity that divides the population—and they secure a positive response from a substantial portion of the electorate. If an identity belongs to a minority, then by definition such a group cannot become a dominant party in a political system. If everyone in a society shares an identity, then it cannot be the basis for political divisions.

Language and national and territorial identities are potentially the most potent sources of political cleavage. A common language is necessary if govern-

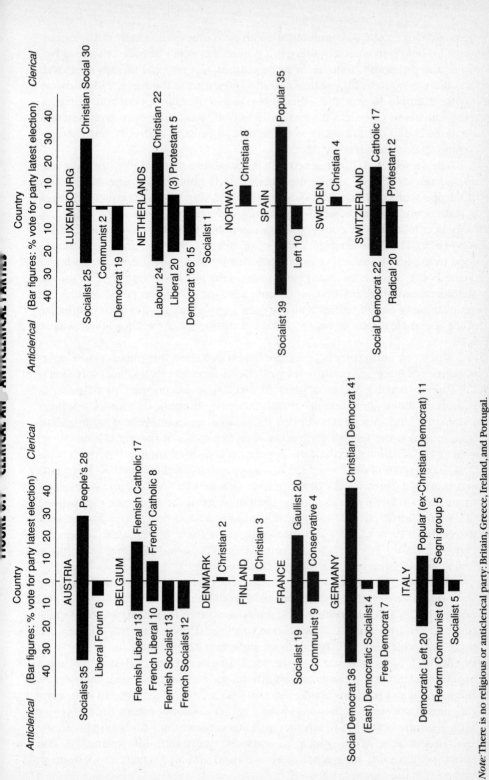

Note: There is no religious or anticlerical party: Britain, Greece, Ireland, and Portugal.

Source: Classified by the author on basis of 1995 election or nearest date previous.

ment and citizens are to communicate with each other. When more than one language is spoken in a society, there is a potential conflict between the state language and the home language of some citizens. If a national identity is shared, then there is no basis for political division. If territory is the basis of identity—as it is for example, in Scotland—then it is possible to make special administrative arrangements to cater to a distinctive identity. However, if groups with different identities live in the same city, as is the case in Brussels and in Belfast, then accommodation is much more difficult.

When a society is homogeneous in language and national identity, these cultural characteristics cannot be the basis for party competition. The major states of Europe were multinational states until World War I, but subsequent changes in state boundaries and forced population movements have resulted in the majority becoming almost completely homogeneous in identities (cf. Rose and Urwin, 1975). The Scandinavian societies of Norway, Sweden, and Denmark are good examples of uniformity in national identity. So too are the Netherlands and Luxembourg. France, Germany, and Austria also meet this criterion, as do the Mediterranean societies of Greece and Portugal. When everyone speaks the same language and identifies with the same community, parties must emphasize other social cleavages in order to make a distinctive appeal for votes (Figure 6.2).

When one nationality is by far the largest in a state, this puts pressure upon minorities to integrate, because they can never form an electoral majority. This is the case in Finland, where a party of Swedish-speakers often participates in Finnish coalition governments to advance the interests of Swedish-speakers *within* the Finnish state. The United Kingdom is an example of a multinational state in which the English form more than five-sixths of the population (Rose, 1982a). The remaining sixth of the population is divided among those with Scots (less than a tenth of the United Kingdom population), Welsh (less than 5 percent) and another 3 percent with Ulster or Irish identities. In Scotland and Wales, most parties are all-Britain parties and the great majority of the electorate support one or another British party. Three-quarters or more of Scots do *not* vote for the Scottish National Party and in Wales, nine-tenths do not vote for the Welsh Nationalist Party (McAllister, 1982). National distinctiveness is limited to giving a disproportionate share of the vote to the British Labour Party.

Where two groups each form a substantial part of the population and identity conflicts are intense, then cooperation is different. This is the case in Northern Ireland, where pro-British Protestants constitute two-thirds of the population and pro-Irish unity Catholics form one-third. Unionist parties compete for Protestant votes; they disagree about how best to maintain the Union with Britain. Irish Nationalist parties—the Social Democratic and Labour Party and a republican Sinn Fein—compete for Catholic votes. Parties that seek votes across the national and religious divide win less than a tenth of the vote. In both communities, there are also divisions about whether the ballot box or the bullet—or both—are the best ways to advance national causes. Sinn Fein is allied with the Irish Republican Army, which pursues the unification of Ireland, as one spokesperson said, "with a ballot in one hand and an Armalite (an automatic weapon) in the other."

FIGURE 6.2 ETHNIC, REGIONAL, AND NATIONALIST PARTIES

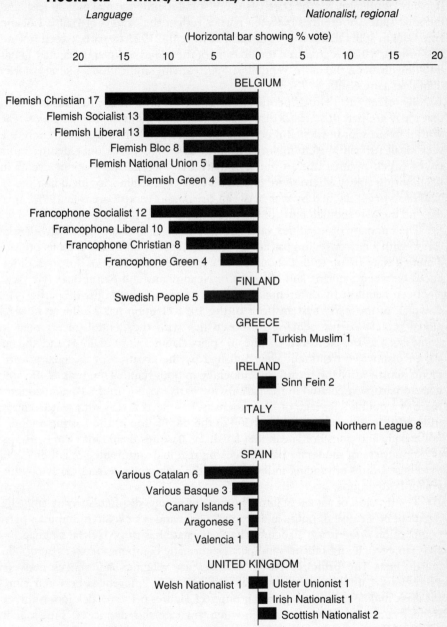

Language   *Nationalist, regional*

(Horizontal bar showing % vote)

20	15	10	5	0	5	10	15	20

BELGIUM

Flemish Christian 17
Flemish Socialist 13
Flemish Liberal 13
Flemish Bloc 8
Flemish National Union 5
Flemish Green 4

Francophone Socialist 12
Francophone Liberal 10
Francophone Christian 8
Francophone Green 4

FINLAND

Swedish People 5

GREECE

Turkish Muslim 1

IRELAND

Sinn Fein 2

ITALY

Northern League 8

SPAIN

Various Catalan 6
Various Basque 3
Canary Islands 1
Aragonese 1
Valencia 1

UNITED KINGDOM

Welsh Nationalist 1   Ulster Unionist 1
Irish Nationalist 1
Scottish Nationalist 2

Note: There is no noteworthy linguistic or ethnic party in Austria, Denmark, France, Germany, Greece, Luxembourg, the Netherlands, Norway, Portugal, Sweden and Switzerland.

Source: Classification by the author by 1995 election result or nearest date previous. Parties with less than 5 percent of the total vote included where they obtain significant support in the region where they contest seats.

In the 26 counties of the Republic of Ireland, there is no difference about nationality or religion, for the post-1918 War of Independence makes it an Irish and Catholic state. Differences between parties reflect the origins of Fianna Fail and Fine Gael in splits that led to civil war following the 1921 treaty between Ireland and Britain, which recognized the division of the island of Ireland. Fianna Fail has traditionally been the more "republican" party, giving unification a higher priority than does Fine Gael.

Historically, the Greek people were scattered around the Aegean in places that today are part of states as distant as Egypt, Turkey, and the former Yugoslavia. Within its present borders, Greece is almost completely homogenous. There is a very small Turkish Muslim minority in northeast Greece. National identity influences Greek politics due to the sensitivity that Greeks show about events in neighboring states where there is a significant Greek minority, including the island of Cyprus (divided by war between Greek and Turkish areas in 1975), Albania, and the Macedonian parts of the former Yugoslavia and of Bulgaria.

The intensity of identities varies between and within states. In Italy identification with a city or region has always been strong, for cities and regions predate a unified state by up to one thousand years (see Putnam, 1993). However, differences between Sicilians and Milanese or Neapolitans and Florentines have usually been manifest by differential patterns of voting for nationwide parties. The downfall of the party system prior to the 1994 election has produced new regional protest parties seeking to loosen ties with the central government in Rome, such as the Northern League. In Spain, claims from Catalonia and Andalusia for distinctive treatment were satisfied by the creation of regional governments shortly after the return to democracy. In both regions the bulk of the vote goes to parties integrated in the nationwide party system. In the Basque country there is a double cleavage of high intensity. Basque is a very different language from Spanish but a substantial portion of the population of the Basque region is not Basque and does not speak that language. Basques divide into three groups: (1) supporters of moderate parties seeking regional autonomy, (2) adherents of extremist groups advancing independence through violence, and (3) sympathizers for both groups.

The division of a society into a number of groups distinguished by language need not be a cause of political division. Switzerland is a classic example of party competition *integrating* a society. The Swiss state has three official languages—German, French and Italian—and parties normally compete for votes across linguistic lines. The principal party cleavages are religious differences between Protestants, Catholics, and secular groups, and class differences between working-class, middle-class and agrarian groups (cf. Figures 6.1–6.4). Belgium is the extreme example of what can happen when language and identity become salient. After generations of cross-linguistic cooperation between class and religious parties in a form similar to Switzerland, Belgian parties started dividing along linguistic lines in the 1960s (Dewachter, 1987). Its "national" elections are effectively two elections: in one, Flemish parties compete for the support of Flemish speakers; in the other, Francophone parties compete for the votes of French speakers. This is true not only of parties that are aggressively nationalist but also of Catholic, Socialist, Liberal, and Green parties.

COMPETING ECONOMIC INTERESTS

The twentieth century has seen the rise of party competition along economic lines. In every European country today, at least one party successfully appeals for votes on economic or class grounds. But economic interests are translated into party support in different ways with varying success. Scandinavian countries have agrarian parties that reflect conflicts between urban and rural interests that predate the Industrial Revolution. Parties differ in their ability to mobilize electoral support from the class to which they appeal; in Britain the Conservative Party has usually been more successful in mobilizing middle-class support than the Labour Party has been in mobilizing working class votes. In France class and religion are crosscutting influences, giving French Socialists middle-class support because the party is anticlerical, and in Germany manual workers who attend mass tend to vote Christian Democratic (Figure 6.3).

Divisions Within the Middle Class

When few manual workers had the right to vote, there could not be electoral competition between the middle class and the working class. Instead, electoral competition occurred among those who had the right to vote and, in economic terms, were better off than most of the population.

Political differences arose between urban interests that welcomed modernization, and rural landowners and peasants upholding traditional ways. German intellectuals coined the phrase: "Cities make for freedom." There remain economic differences today, for farmers want higher prices for food products whereas urban workers want lower food prices. This conflict is specially salient in the European Union, for the bulk of its spending goes on farm subsidies. Agrarian parties have made attractive partners in coalition governments, since their interests are narrow and, if satisfied, will support a variety of coalition policies. Today, farming interests are usually advanced by pressure groups that lobby ministers; this is notably the case in France. Even where agrarian interests are numerically large, as in Greece, Ireland, and Portugal, agrarian groups lobby all parties rather than form their own distinctive rural party. In Denmark, Finland, Norway, and Sweden agrarian parties have changed their name to appeal to urban residents who favor the rural environment.

Liberal (sometimes called radical) parties were created to represent the secular middle class and promote political reform in opposition to conservative groups of aristocrats, landowners, and some urban interests. Historic differences remain relevant today in the two types of middle-class parties, the liberal and the conservative. While both are antisocialist, they differ in their commitment to the market and in their stance on moral issues; liberals are permissive and conservatives are not.

Historically, liberalism is as much about individual freedom of conscience (removal of disabilities of minority religions and privileges of the state church) as it is about economic doctrines. Today, the *liberal parties* of Europe vary in out-

FIGURE 6.3 CLASS PARTIES

Working class   Country   Middle class

50 40 30 20 10 0 10 20 30 40 50

AUSTRIA

Socialist 38   People 28

BELGIUM

French Socialist 12   Flemish Liberals 13

Flemish Socialist 13   French Liberals 10

BRITAIN

Labour 34   Conservative 42

DENMARK

Social Democrat 35   Conservative 15

Left Unity 3   Radical 5

a-Liberals 23

FINLAND

Social Democrat 28   National Coalition 18

Left Alliance 11   a-Centre 20

Rural 1

FRANCE

Socialist 19   Conservative 4

Communist 9   Gaullist 20

Extreme left 2   Union French Democracy 19

GERMANY

Social Democrat 36   Free Democrats 7

GREECE

Socialist 47

Communist 4

IRELAND

Labour 19

Democratic Left 3

a = Originally an agrarian party.

Source: Classification by the author by 1995 election result or nearest date previous.

look. The British Liberal Democrats emphasize not only individual freedom but also social welfare policies. Many continental liberal parties give more emphasis today to choice in the market (see Kirchner, 1988: chs. 16–17, 19).

Liberal parties differ substantially in political success. Liberal parties tend to poll the most votes in Switzerland, France, and Britain. But shares of the vote can be misleading, for the British Liberal Democrats have not been in office since World War II, because a sixth of the vote is insufficient to win many seats in

FIGURE 6.3 *Continued*

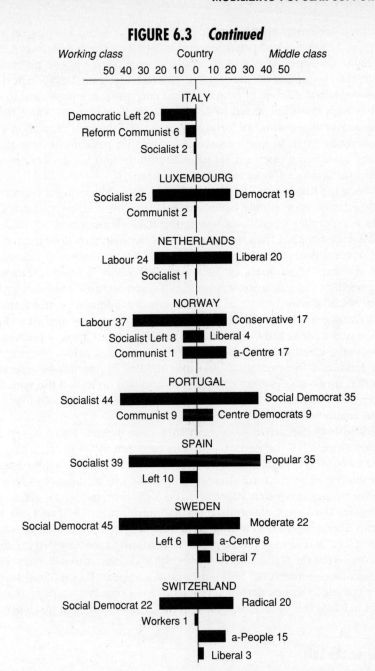

Working class   Country   Middle class

50 40 30 20 10   0   10 20 30 40 50

ITALY

Democratic Left 20

Reform Communist 6

Socialist 2

LUXEMBOURG

Socialist 25   Democrat 19

Communist 2

NETHERLANDS

Labour 24   Liberal 20

Socialist 1

NORWAY

Labour 37   Conservative 17

Socialist Left 8   Liberal 4

Communist 1   a-Centre 17

PORTUGAL

Socialist 44   Social Democrat 35

Communist 9   Centre Democrats 9

SPAIN

Socialist 39   Popular 35

Left 10

SWEDEN

Social Democrat 45   Moderate 22

Left 6   a-Centre 8

Liberal 7

SWITZERLAND

Social Democrat 22   Radical 20

Workers 1

a-People 15

Liberal 3

Britain's first-past-the-post electoral system. In proportional representation systems, by contrast, a liberal party can participate in a coalition government with a sixth of the vote, or even less. In the extreme case of the German Free Democrats, they have alternated holding office as the junior coalition partner of the Christian Democrats or of the Social Democrats.

Conservative parties have historically stood for order in a society in which all classes and interests had privileges and obligations. Conservative parties oppose socialist doctrines of economic equality; they often oppose political and economic reforms of liberal parties. The German Christian Democratic Union promotes the social market, in which private enterprise is encouraged to make profits, but high taxes are levied to fund social welfare benefits. The CDU also supports conserving traditional economic practices through regulation rather than allowing free rein to market forces. For example, regulations normally prevent shops from being open on Saturday afternoons and Sundays because this would impose "antisocial" hours on small shopkeepers.

In France the historic role of General de Gaulle, a philosophical conservative with little interest in economic issues, remains relevant in divisions among non-Socialists. For decades after World War II, the Radicals preferred to collaborate with the Socialists rather than the Gaullist right because they doubted the commitment of conservative Gaullists to the republic. Clerical versus anticlerical differences also kept them apart. In 1974 and 1981 Valéry Giscard d'Estaing was elected president running against both Gaullist and Socialist candidates. After a decade of Socialist government, in 1993 the two anti-Socialist parties formed an electoral alliance and won a landslide parliamentary majority against a divided opposition of Socialists and Communists. In 1995 Jacques Chirac, a Gaullist, won the presidential election in competition with the Gaullist prime minister and a Socialist candidate. In Scandinavia multiple middle-class parties—conservative, liberal and center—successfully contest seats and win up to half the vote. When their strength in Parliament is great enough, anti-Socialist parties join together in bourgeois coalitions.

The British Conservative Party combines both "liberal" and "conservative" tendencies. Since 1945 the party has usually been led by moderates who were prepared to conserve welfare state measures as well as older middle class and business interests. The electoral strategy of appealing to working-class as well as middle-class voters was often successful (cf. McKenzie and Silver, 1968). However, Margaret Thatcher, Conservative Prime Minister from 1979 to 1990, was a free-market liberal with a very strong commitment to economic change. She was more interested in rewriting public policy to conform to the "laws" of the market than in conserving the status quo. However, she was conventionally conservative in opposing more integration of Britain in the European Union. Thus, Margaret Thatcher combined in her person divisions in the Conservative Party that have remained to haunt her successor, John Major (cf. Crewe and Searing, 1988).

Divisions on the Left

The political logic of socialist or left parties has been simple. Manual workers can best advance their interests through collective political action because as individuals they lack the capital to prosper in the marketplace. It is thus in their material interest to vote for socialist parties. Since manual workers have outnumbered the middle class, a socialist party could hope to be permanently in office if it successfully mobilized the working-class vote.

The theory has turned out to be half right. In almost every European country parties appealing to working-class interests today win between a quarter and a half the vote. But the political impact has been limited because that vote is divided between as many as three parties:

1. *Social democrats or labor parties:* pragmatic about policies and ready to compromise.
2. *Left socialists,* uncompromising adherents of socialist doctrines and often breakaways from social democratic parties.
3. *Communist parties* linked with Moscow until electoral pressures drove them toward Euro-Communism, a pro-democratic stance emphasizing independence of Moscow.

Divisions between Social Democrats and Communists have been most significant in Italy, where the Communists have been stronger than Social Democrats throughout the postwar era. The resulting polarization of electoral politics resulted in anti-Communists always winning a majority of seats in Parliament. Socialists and Social Democratic parties joined in governing coalitions with the Christian Democrats, marginalizing the Communists outside government. In the 1994 election the anti-Communist coalition collapsed. The Party of the Democratic Left, founded by ex-Communists, came second in the popular vote; it had to compete with Left Socialists and with Social Democrats too. In France, Communists have always been a well organized party and their backing has been necessary for a Socialist such as François Mitterrand to win the absolute majority of votes necessary to be elected president. According to the tactical situation, French Socialists have also made alliances with anticlerical centrists.

The connection between left parties and trade unions has historically taken three different forms (Beyme, 1980).

1. A single trade union movement and a high level of union membership in both middle- and working-class occupations. This is the Scandinavian model of unionization; it is also found in Austria. A broad coalition creates tensions—for example, between well-paid and low-paid union members.
2. A single trade union movement in which a quarter to a third of the labor force belongs to unions. The British Labour Party was created by trade unions and is principally funded by unions. Even though unions control votes in most party committees, they cannot dictate Labour Party policy for this would be electoral suicide, since most voters are not trade union members. Moreover, unions disagree among themselves about what is in their political interest.
3. A low level of trade union membership and unions divided between Communist, Socialist and Christian trade unions. This has been the pattern in France and Italy for most of the postwar period.

Political divisions on religious issues add *and* subtract electoral support for the left. Religious parties compete for votes by stressing cross-class solidarity among a community of believers, while middle-class voters opposed to clerical influence are ready to support Socialist parties as bastions of anticlericalism.

Political divisions arising from civil war have been more important than economic interests in defining party cleavages in Greece and Ireland. Guerrilla resistance to Nazi occupation during World War II was followed by a civil war between Greek Communists and anti-Communists, which the latter won. The colonels' coup of 1967 brought the royal house back into politics; it then produced a reaction in favor of democracy. Today, the two major parties, PASOK, nominally a Socialist party, and New Democracy, anti-Socialist, compete for office by mobilizing clients more than classes (cf. Diamandouros and Gunther, in press). In Ireland, the Irish Labour Party has tried to emphasize class interests but has come third in popular votes. As a third party, Labour can sometimes extract advantage as a coalition partner alternating between governments led by Fine Gael and Fianna Fail.

Where there is no major cultural cleavage, social democratic parties are often the largest national party. In Sweden and Norway social democratic parties have been the largest during the postwar era, usually governing alone or as the dominant partner in a coalition. In Austria, Germany, and Britain social democrats are one of the two major parties, alternating power with a large opponent. Portugal is distinctive in that a party calling itself Social Democratic has succeeded in winning more than half the vote—but it is not socialist in its policies and ideology (see Gunther and Montero, in press).

The Socialist faith in a permanent electoral majority was based upon assumptions not realized anywhere in Europe. The traditional working class base is now contracting, due to the shift from industry to services increasing middle-class employment and reducing industrial employment. Social changes have produced cleavages cutting across traditional class structure. In the postwar era the real family income of the average European household has risen by several hundred percent. Home ownership gives families a financial asset and makes mortgage payers very sensitive to interest rates. The expansion of further education has created opportunities for children from families of below-average means to attend university and gain middle-class jobs. A more educated electorate is better able to arrive at a definition of economic interests and political values independent of peer group pressure in a factory or slum street.

Less than a quarter of Europeans now match the prototype definition of a class voter, with a manual occupation, limited education, union membership, and lower income or the middle-class alternatives. Three-quarters of the electorate in Britain, France, and Germany have a mix of middle-class and working-class characteristics (Dalton, 1988: 176). The tendency of individuals to combine attributes of different classes reflects changes in the middle class too. While union membership has contracted in declining traditional industries, growth in union membership has occurred among teachers, bank clerks, and civil servants.

The loosening up of traditional class alignments has not abolished economic differences between voters. Even though income has risen, it has not become equal. There remain differences of economic interests between those with above-average and below-average incomes. The terms "left" and "right" are still used to refer to differences between left parties promoting government action on behalf of organized labor and the poor, and parties on the right, acting on behalf of business interests and all who want to reduce taxation and take more responsibility for their own welfare (cf. Dalton et al., 1984; Papadakis and Bean, 1993).

CHANGING WINE, CHANGING BOTTLES, OR BOTH?

Even though economic, religious, language, and national identity are well established, it is dangerous for party leaders to assume that their past support will continue in future. The world in which parties compete for votes is subject to continuous change, eroding old bases of support and presenting new opportunities for winning support.

One cause of change is the turnover of generations through birth and death. Voters whose party loyalties were formed by the depression of the 1930s, World War II, or hardline confrontations between church and state are now a shrinking or small proportion of the electorate. Many historic cleavages in society have little relevance for younger voters. Second, political institutions are changing. In Southern Europe democratic regimes have replaced authoritarian systems and West European Communist parties were destabilized by the collapse of Communism in Eastern Europe. Third, the structure and values of society are changing. The old pyramid of class is giving way to a "diamond-shaped" class structure with a large middle mass; church attendance is falling, and education is becoming much more widely diffused. There are some signs of postmaterialist or postmodern cultural values (cf. Inglehart, 1990). Increased skepticism among Europeans is creating doubts about values in religion and science and in politics (Therborn, 1995: 275 f.).

Political leaders must respond to change or risk losing votes and seats. Politicians have three alternatives: (1) Those dissatisfied with the existing party system can offer new wine in new bottles, starting parties that will appeal for votes on fresh dimensions of cleavage; (2) leaders of established parties can offer new wine in old bottles, adapting their appeal to new issues while keeping their organization intact; (3) alternatively, leaders of established parties may ignore social changes and continue to pour out old appeals from old bottles.

New Bottles for New Voters

Countries moving from authoritarianism to democracy give substantial scope for new parties to emerge because the old regime's party is likely to be discredited. Portugal is an extreme case, for there had been no free elections there for nearly half a century prior to democratization. All the Portuguese parties competing in elections today were created in the 1970s, except for the Communists. The popular election of a president created a basis for division into two groups, but around personalities rather than policies or interests. In Spain, even though there had been no free elections for four decades, both Socialists and Communists man-aged to keep organizations intact, partly in exile; they emerged as significant par-ties following the death of Franco. The problem of creating new parties has arisen on the right, for Franco's Falangist Party had no place in a democracy.

The *green* parties that have appeared in virtually every country of Europe since the 1970s are the one clear-cut example of a new dimension emerging in European politics (Figure 6.4). Green parties give priority to protecting the envi-ronment from the impact of modern science and technology, opposing the pol-lution caused by automobiles and industry, and both civil and military uses of nu-clear energy. This opens a gulf between "post-modern" green parties and "modern" class parties, for the economic interest parties give higher priority to economic growth and reducing unemployment than to protecting the environ-ment for its own sake. (cf. Mueller-Rommel, 1989).

Initially, ecological activists promoted their views through pressure groups and direct action. Parties were formed when established party leaders paid little attention to their demands. Forming a party requires a group to have positions on a wide range of subjects, such as health care, unemployment, or foreign pol-icy. In doing so, green parties either become more like other parties, appear ex-treme (e.g., pacifist) or alienate many voters (e.g., proposing big boosts in taxes on gasoline and energy). Even concentrating upon environmental issues threat-ens splits between members prepared to make compromises with government in order to secure improvements in the environment (e.g., a reduction in pollu-tion) and those who want a complete ban on many everyday activities that inci-dentally create pollution, such as automobile traffic in city centers. Germans di-vide these two green tendencies into "realos" (realists) and "fundis" (fundamentalists).

The electoral fortunes of green parties show the difficulties of creating a new party with a new appeal. The median green party wins only 4 percent of the national vote. The "strongest" green vote is 10 percent; to win this share takes two green parties in Belgium and three green parties in France. In a proportional rep-resentation electoral system, a small percentage of the vote can be enough to win seats in Parliament—but it is insufficient to take part in government. More-over, once in Parliament green MPs are forced to take stands on many issues out-side the immediate scope of environmental policy and conduct their internal de-bates in the full glare of critical competitors. In Germany, what started as a green party has become a "multi-colored rainbow" (Dalton, 1993: 298).

The greens are not the only party to be an outgrowth of an interest group. In a few countries parties of pensioners have been formed to put electoral pressure on governing parties. However, this strategy threatens to backfire, for their vote reveals weakness. Parties claiming to represent pensioners win as little as 1 per-cent of the national vote, and a very small percentage of the vote of older people. Few old people vote for a party claiming to represent them for their party loyal-ties became established earlier in their lifetime. In four-fifths of countries there is no party organized to represent pensioners. Pensioners exert their political influ-ence primarily as pressure groups lobbying all the established parties.

Protest or "flash" parties spring up unexpectedly in response to a crisis within a major party—for example, a big scandal as in Italy, or because estab-

FIGURE 6.4   NEW DIMENSIONS OF PARTY CLEAVAGE

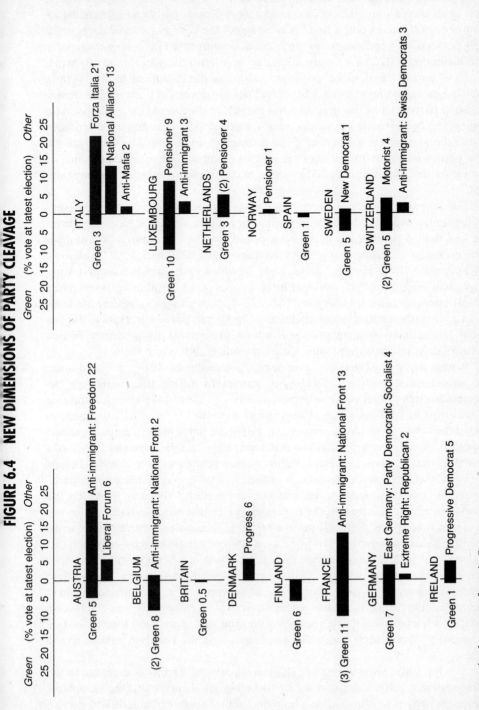

Green (% vote at latest election)   *Other*

25 20 15 10 5 0 5 10 15 20 25

AUSTRIA
Green 5
Anti-immigrant: Freedom 22
Liberal Forum 6

BELGIUM
(2) Green 8
Anti-immigrant: National Front 2

BRITAIN
Green 0.5

DENMARK
Progress 6

FINLAND
Green 6

FRANCE
(3) Green 11
Anti-immigrant: National Front 13

GERMANY
Green 7
East Germany: Party Democratic Socialist 4
Extreme Right: Republican 2

IRELAND
Green 1
Progressive Democrat 5

Green (% vote at latest election)   *Other*

25 20 15 10 5 0 5 10 15 20 25

ITALY
Green 3
Forza Italia 21
National Alliance 13
Anti-Mafia 2

LUXEMBOURG
Green 10
Pensioner 9
Anti-immigrant 3

NETHERLANDS
Green 3
(2) Pensioner 4

NORWAY
Pensioner 1

SPAIN
Green 1

SWEDEN
Green 5
New Democrat 1

SWITZERLAND
(2) Green 5
Motorist 4
Anti-immigrant: Swiss Democrats 3

No new party wins 1 percent of vote in Greece.

Source: Classification by the author.

125

lished parties have ignored an issue important to a significant group of voters, such as an increase in taxes or in immigrants. A protest party can gain media attention even if it wins only a small percentage of the vote, because of the novelty of its personalities and issues. The problem that confronts a protest or flash party is to maintain its fledgling organization and hold onto the votes it initially wins.

New parties tend to be populist, making a direct appeal to the people against established institutions and individuals in power. They are against the established party system, but that does not mean that they are against a democratic regime. The opportunity to use elections to gain support channels their activities within the system, even when they claim to reject much of it. The total vote for new parties is low in almost every European country. Hence, the emergence of protest parties is best interpreted as a sign of the responsiveness of the party system.

Protest parties take many forms (see again Figure 6.4). Although every European country today has some immigrants from alien cultures or races, they average less than 3 percent of the national population and two-thirds of countries have no *racist, antiimmigrant party* winning votes (cf. Ignazi, 1992; Husbands, 1981). Among these parties, the Austrian Freedom Party gets the biggest vote, more than one-fifth of the national total. It does so by combining propaganda against immigrants from Turkey and Balkan Europe with attacks against the long-serving incumbents in a grand coalition of moderate parties. In France, the National Front protests against several million immigrants from former French colonies in North Africa, and wins more than one-eighth of the vote.

A new party can claim to be moderate, protesting against established interests or extremist lurches by established parties. In Ireland the Progressive Democrats launched their party in protest against the alleged high-handed running of government by Fianna Fail. In Italy, many new parties entered Parliament in 1994 when the old system collapsed. An anti-Mafia party made the most explicit appeal to "good government." *Forza Italia* was based on the personal appeal of a rich industrialist, Silvio Berlusconi, who became prime minister in 1994. In East Germany the Party of Democratic Socialism is a unique regional protest party, formed by ex-Communists to exploit grievances about the way in which the Bonn government has treated the region since German reunification.

From time to time protest groups resort to street demonstrations or arms. The novelty of their methods of protest—a sit-in or a mass march—may gain media publicity. Such groups measure their impact in minutes on prime time television news and column inches in the press rather than in votes. The student protest movement of 1968 was a unique example of a Europe-wide protest movement capturing headlines everywhere. In Germany extremist left-wing groups such as the Baader-Meinhof gang and the Red Army Band took to assassination to publicize their cause. The result was a public backlash against terrorism.

Survival is the great test of a flash protest party, for its abrupt entrance to the party system is a reminder that it can also make an abrupt exit. One alternative for a new party is to consolidate a hold on a few seats in Parliament, and survive as a minor party. A second alternative is for a party to become established within the existing party system. The Dutch D '66 party is exceptional in continuing to win votes long after its founding as a protest party in 1966. A third course is to split. For example, when the Freedom Party of Austria's leader, Jorg Haider, became identified with extremist and even neo-Nazi views, some of his supporters broke away to form the Liberal Forum as a centrist protest against Haider's extremes. The fourth alternative is collapse; the Poujadist party is a textbook example. Campaigning on behalf of the "little people"—that is, small businesses and artisans—Pierre Poujade won more than a tenth of the French vote in 1956; by the next general election, the party's disputes had so weakened it that it secured hardly any votes and quickly disappeared.

New Appeals in Old Bottles

A puzzle of European party systems is that notwithstanding many changes in European politics and society in the twentieth century, a substantial number of parties have persisted in name for generations. Their support appears to be "frozen" (cf. Lipset and Rokkan, 1967: 50). There is also substantial continuity in the aggregate vote for different "families" or blocs of parties appealing to a particular economic or cultural interest (see Bartolini and Mair, 1990; Rose and Urwin, 1970). How can this be?

Parties survive if they adapt; the older they are, the greater the pressure to change in order to continue winning votes (see Rose and Mackie, 1988). One time-honored method of adaptation is to alter policies and programs. Conservative parties have survived by not being conservative; that is, they do not defend the status quo against all forms of change but accept changes introduced by other parties, such as welfare state policies. Leaders of social democratic parties have adapted by following working-class voters "up market" as their traditional electoral base has contracted (cf. Kitschelt, 1994: 5 ff.).

A second strategy is to reduce the emphasis placed on policies and programs, and stress instead vague values about which the electorate is united. Parties may then compete on the grounds of which is most competent to produce peace and prosperity (Stokes, 1963). Leaders can point to their record in government to justify claims to competence or use parliamentary debates and the media to challenge the competence of their opponents. Votes can also be sought by projecting the personality of a leader as caring, tough or whatever opinion polls show is desired by the majority of the electorate. The replacement of policy debates by personalities projected through the media is often described as the Americanization of European politics. Parties that abandon programs and policies relevant to historic cultural and economic divisions are "catch-all" parties, seeking to garner votes from all parts of the electorate without regard to logical or ideological consistency (Kirchheimer, 1966: 190; see also Wolinetz, 1991).

A symbolic change in name is a third way in which a party can adapt. In response to a marked reduction in the farm population, agrarian parties in Scandinavia have adopted the ambiguous title of Centre Party in an effort to broaden their appeal to include urban dwellers as well as farmers concerned with agricultural subsidies and rural roads. The right-wing Swedish party signaled a move toward the center by changing its name to the Moderate Unity Party. Everywhere in Europe, Communist parties have changed their name after the collapse of the Communist Party of the Soviet Union.

Organizational change is a fourth form of adaptation. Merger is intended to combine the support of two parties threatened with decline. In the Netherlands falling church attendance faced both Catholic and Protestant parties with a loss in votes. In 1979 the three parties merged to form the Christian Democratic Appeal. In the 1994 election the new party was the second largest, with 22 percent of the vote. But this was less than half the vote won by the three separate religious parties in previous decades, when religious denominations had more followers and churchgoers tended to vote as a bloc for their own church's party.

A fifth alternative is that parties can split. This often accompanies a major change in policies or name or a merger. Big changes create conflict between members committed to traditional policies and symbols, and leaders wanting to alter in pursuit of electoral success (see Rose and Mackie, 1988). In most continental countries a left-wing Socialist party has split off from a socialist party when it moved closer to the center. When the British Labour Party lurched left in the early 1980s, this caused the formation of a Social Democratic Party as a centrist breakaway. It fought two elections in an electoral alliance with the Liberals and then merged with it to form the Liberal Democrats. It was not until after the left-leaning Labour Party had lost four successive elections that it began to move back to the center ground, and under Tony Blair as leader has even endorsed policies introduced by Margaret Thatcher.

In an ever changing political environment, disappearance is the final alternative. This happens when a party is closely identified with a regime that collapses—for example, the Nazi Party of Hitler's Germany. It can happen to a breakaway party that fails to win much electoral support. Italy is unique among European democracies in seeing an established party system collapse because of corruption without the regime also collapsing, as a consequence of corruption that came to light in 1992. The Christian Democratic Party, the largest party throughout the postwar era, disbanded before the 1993 election, and in 1994 its successor won less than half its normal vote. The second largest party, the Communists, changed its name and policies and saw its vote drop too.

A systematic examination of the hundreds of parties that have competed for votes in modern Europe emphasizes the difficulties of parties persisting in name and organizational form. Of all parties that have taken at least 1 percent of the vote at one election, 42 percent have failed to fight as many as three elections. Among those that have survived for three elections, only one in three have remained intact since their foundation (Figure 6.5). Parties that are familiar names in the textbooks are familiar because they are the minority that have adapted. Persistence in name is evidence of programmatic change.

Of parties that have altered, 22 percent have merely undergone minor changes, such as a splinter group leaving. Another fifth have been transformed by significant mergers or splits. A small number of parties have passed a visible inheritance to a successor party. For example, in Ireland parties using the label Sinn Fein have emerged and disappeared, each an heir to the Republican tradition of

FIGURE 6.5   ALTERNATIVE CAREERS OF POLITICAL PARTIES

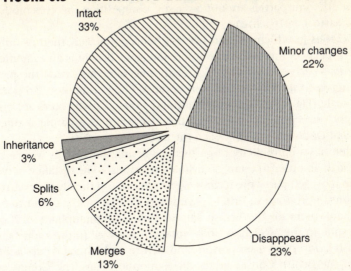

Source: Richard Rose and Thomas T. Mackie "Do Parties Persist or Fail? The Big Trade-Off Facing Organizations." In Kay Lawson and Peter Merkl, eds., *When Parties Fail* (Princeton: Princeton University Press, 1988), table 20.1. Calculated for all parties in 19 Western nations contesting at least three elections and securing at least 1 percent of the vote at one of them.

achieving Irish unification through linking votes and the armed force of the IRA. Political parties have maintained continuity by following the rule laid down in Lampedusa's account of life in Sicily, *The Leopard:* "If things are going to stay the same, there will have to be some changes made."

VARIETIES OF PARTY SYSTEMS

Political parties can be studied in isolation but their votes rise and fall in competition with each other, and all cannot succeed equally. Election results produce losers as well as winners, for what one group of parties gains at election time, another group must lose.

The two major dimensions of party competition in Europe today are religious and economic interests. Even though some countries are relatively free from religious cleavages, where they have existed the effects are long-lasting. How voters place themselves along these two dimensions of party competition can be analyzed with data from the 1990 European Values Survey, which asked about a wide range of values (Knutsen, 1995). A factor analysis of replies to questions about economic equality, state ownership of firms, and state versus individual responsibility for welfare produces a left/right scale of economic interests. A question about belief in God places voters on a religious scale. Data about voters for each party can be aggregated to place each party on left/right and religion scales. The distance between the parties on an 11-point scale shows the extent to which party competition is polarized by voters holding extreme views. If supporters of different parties are not far apart, competition involves moderate pluralism (cf. Sartori, 1976: ch. 6).

In societies in which religion has not been politicized, there is only one dimension of party competition: economic interests. Britain is an example of a traditionally two-party system in which economic interests divide the parties. The distance between the Labour and Conservative voters is limited, 2.5 points on an 11-point scale (Figure 6.6). Both Labour and Conservative voters are on average to the right on economic issues and the electorate as a whole is tilted to the right. Liberal Democrats fall between the two larger parties.

Sweden has a multiplicity of parties dispersing themselves widely along the left-right scale in order to establish distinctive appeals. The distance between voters for the most left party, the former Communists, and the Moderate Unity party, is 3.5 points, more than in Britain. Swedish Social Democrats tend to be less to the left than voters for the British Labour Party. The multiplicity of "bourgeois" parties results in the Moderate Unity voters being well to the right (and fewer) than British Conservative supporters, and Centre and Liberal voters being just to the left of the British Conservatives on economic issues. The Greens appear in the center of the party system on economic issues, because the environmental issues that the party promotes are on a different dimension, where the greens occupy an extreme position.

Party competition along two dimensions of economic interest and religion produces four quadrants. However, no religious party in Western Europe is to the left on economic issues. Three groupings are commonly found: (1) economically left and anticlerical; (2) economically right and pro-clerical; and (3) economically right and anticlerical (Figure 6.7). In France the Communist Party is very left on economic issues and also anticlerical. The Gaullist RPR (Rally for the Republic) is the furthest in the other direction on both issues and the average voter for the UDF (Union for French Democracy) is very close. In the two-dimensional French party system there is not a "center" in the simple sense. Socialist and Green voters are closer to the Gaullists on economic issues but closer to Communists in anticlericalism. National Front voters are to the right on economics but anticlerical; they are distinctive in antiimmigrant views, which they seek to introduce as a third dimension in French party competition.

In Germany both religion and economic interests are politically salient, but the distance between political parties is not so great as in France (see again Figure 6.7). This is shown by the closeness on the economic dimension of the two largest parties, the Social Democrats and the Christian Democrats; they are only one point apart. The difference between their voters on religion is nearly twice as great. Christian Democrats are the middle party on economic issues; the Free Democrats are most to the right. But on religion, Christian Democrats are at one extreme. The German Greens are distinctive among German parties in being the most anticlerical and the least to the right. On religion German differences are moderate by comparison with France, for in Germany there is no equivalent to the strongly left-wing and anticlerical French Communist voter.

Party competition is dynamic, not static; the dimensions of party competition can change. For example, the greens have introduced a new, albeit relatively

FIGURE 6.6   PARTY COMPETITION IN ONE DIMENSION: ECONOMIC LEFT-RIGHT

(Vote latest national election)

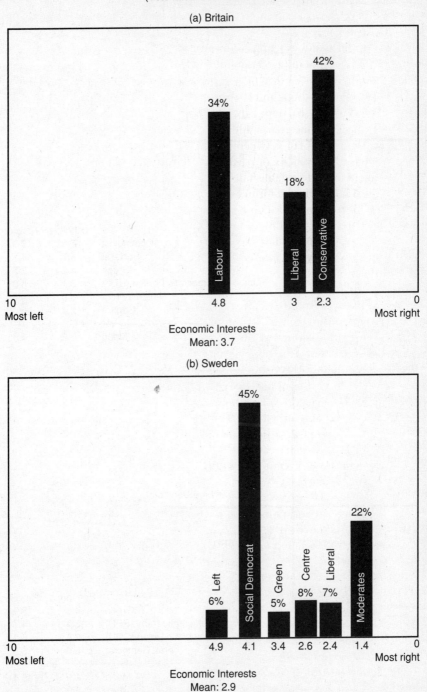

(a) Britain

34%

42%

18%

Labour

Liberal

Conservative

10
Most left

4.8

3   2.3

0
Most right

Economic Interests
Mean: 3.7

(b) Sweden

45%

22%

Left

Social Democrat

Green

Centre

Liberal

Moderates

6%

5%

8%   7%

10
Most left

4.9   4.1   3.4   2.6   2.4   1.4

0
Most right

Economic Interests
Mean: 2.9

Source: Oddbjorn Knutsen, "The Impact of Old Politics and New Politics Value Orientations on Party Choice: A Comparative Study," *Journal of Public Policy,* 15, no. 1 (1995), 1–63.

FIGURE 6.7 PARTY COMPETITION IN TWO DIMENSIONS

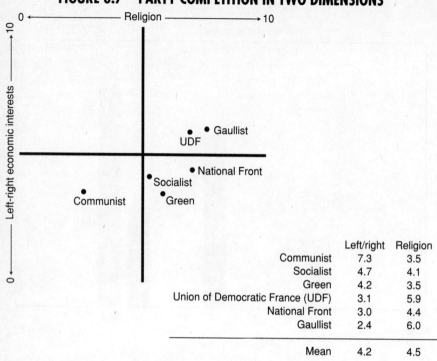

	Left/right	Religion
Communist	7.3	3.5
Socialist	4.7	4.1
Green	4.2	3.5
Union of Democratic France (UDF)	3.1	5.9
National Front	3.0	4.4
Gaullist	2.4	6.0
Mean	4.2	4.5

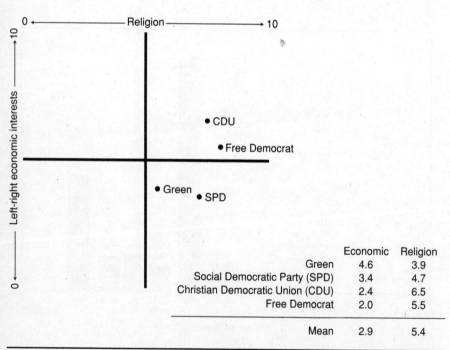

	Economic	Religion
Green	4.6	3.9
Social Democratic Party (SPD)	3.4	4.7
Christian Democratic Union (CDU)	2.4	6.5
Free Democrat	2.0	5.5
Mean	2.9	5.4

Source: Responses to questions about economic interests and belief in God in European Values Survey, 1990, as factor analyzed by Oddbjorn Knutsen "The Impact of Old Politics and New Politics Value Orientations on Party Choice: A Comparative Study," *Journal of Public Policy,* 15, 1 (1995), 1–63.

minor, environmental dimension. Change also arises when there is a gap between the positions that party leaders take and the preferences of their average supporter. Changes in party programs and voters" placement of themselves on a left-right scale show a decrease in the distance between the average voter and the programs of his or her party (Klingemann, 1995). Insofar as differences remain, this is due to party programs being more centrist than a party's voters. While partisans want their party to take more clear-cut positions, party leaders are inclined to steer toward the center, because that is where there are usually more votes to be won.

chapter 7

MOBILIZING DEMOBILIZED VOTERS

Representative government assumes that individuals trust the parties they vote for to reflect their views in the national capital. In a civic culture, not only are voters free to choose between parties, but they also believe that the party they identify with can be trusted to represent their views in government (Almond and Verba, 1963: 123 ff.). Lipset and Rokkan's (1967) classic formulation of the emergence of a modern party system similarly presupposed a high degree of individual trust in unions, farmers' groups, business associations, churches, and masonic lodges mobilizing their members to support parties.

But what happens if voters have a generalized distrust of parties? In France there has been *incivisme,* as many electors were socialized into an uncivil, antiparty mentality (see Converse and Dupeux, 1966; Gunther et al., 1988: ch. 3). In such circumstances an election may be democratic in Joseph Schumpeter's (1952) sense of offering voters a choice between competing elites. However, when the choice offered is between more or less distrusted parties, then voters can only be negatively represented, voting to turn the rascals out or keep the less unsatisfactory alternative in office.

Communist regimes had the perverse effect of demobilizing voters because of their incessant insistence on support for the party-state. Many reacted to Communist efforts at mobilization by becoming "negatively integrated" in the political system. Party propaganda made people apathetic or anti-party. The legacy of that is that in post-Communist societies people now appreciate the *freedom not to participate* in party politics (see again Table 5.2, p. 96). Free elections remain valid, even if there is a "missing middle" of trusted parties, but the outcome is not representative government as it is understood in established democracies.

Post-Communist societies are halfway to the creation of a representative party system, for the preconditions have been met. Two rounds of fair and free elections have been held since 1990, and parties have multiplied (White, 1990; Wightman, 1995). The first free election produced many surprises to the losers, and sometimes to winners too. Many parties that fought the first post-Communist elections of 1990 won few votes and have since merged, split, or disappeared.

In post-Communist societies the starting point for the electorate is the experience of socialization into distrust of The Party. The starting point for politicians is the prospect of freely creating parties—but not being sure where to start. Political entrepreneurs can appeal for support on democratic or undemocratic grounds, and they may address real problems of the economy and real economic divisions within the population or offer populist solutions that ignore economic constraints. The second section of this chapter shows the great variety of parties that have been created. The response of the mass of the electorate has been skeptical at best, and often negative. People socialized in a party-state are unlikely to trust parties or identify with parties, and their votes will not be an expression of positive commitment. The evidence for this is presented in section three. The consequence is a "floating party system," in which there is a great deal of instability in the names of parties and uncertainty about how those elected can and do represent the views of those who have voted for them.

SOCIALIZATION INTO DISTRUST: THE COMMUNIST LEGACY

For two generations after 1945, politics in Central and Eastern Europe was the politics of the Communist Party. The party used its organizational network to control the major institutions of government *and* the major institutions of civil society. The party articulated the "objective" truth of Marxism-Leninism. While Marxist-Leninist doctrines were subject to frequent reinterpretation, they were not subject to a popular referendum or free elections. Critical decisions about government were made by the elite of the Communist Party. Since the ideology of Communism was internationalist, national parties were also expected to follow the vanguard party of the working class, the Communist Party of the Soviet Union. The Communist practice of "democratic centralism" was far more centralist than democratic.

The ruthless elimination of organizations that might challenge Communist authority was given a high priority. In the 1940s political parties and trade unions were dissolved or turned into Communist satellites. Professors who did not follow the party line were dismissed. Private enterprises were taken over by the party-state. The press, book publishers and broadcasting became mouthpieces for the party line. Churches were subject to subtle and not so subtle pressures. Controlling these institutions gave the party great patronage powers. It was also consistent with the party's totalitarian ideology. As the inquisitor proclaimed in Arthur Koestler's *Darkness at Noon,* "There is no salvation outside the party."

Socialization by the party was carried on in school and in party youth organizations. Having a party card was often necessary to get a good job, enter a profession, or gain promotion. It also brought material benefits (White and McAllister, 1994: table 4). Party membership, attendance at meetings, and making references to the scientific principles of Marxist-Leninism were rituals in which many people participated as an outward show of party loyalty. This did not mean that people making such statements believed what they said. For many "it was mere lip service and a source of personal embarrassment" (Berglund and Dellenbrant, 1991: 4). Instead of producing Marxist-Leninist ideologues, the party's efforts produced cynicism.

Unfree Elections, Apathy, and Distrust

Whereas in Spain Franco's authoritarian regime dispensed with national elections, Communist regimes periodically held elections that had some but not all the attributes of elections in established democracies. Elections were of two types: endorsement of a single candidate by acclamation and ballots offering a limited choice between candidates approved by the party (Pravda, 1986; Furtak, 1990). Where choices between two candidates were possible, both could be members of the Communist Party or one a party member and another nominated by a satellite organization within the Communist network. Even when the result was a foregone conclusion, individuals were expected to vote. The choice was between casting a preprinted ballot endorsing the party's candidate and conspicuously crossing out the party's choice in front of party officials conducting the election. Communist officials took elections by acclamation seriously. In the Soviet Union, for example, between 1946 and 1984 they reported an average turnout of 99.97 percent, with 99.74 per cent of all ballots cast in favor of Communist candidates (Furtak, 1990: 37).

Why have elections when the result is a foregone conclusion? The official doctrine was that elections were "hard" evidence of popular support for the regime. Dissidents viewed elections as demoralizing critics by forcing them to run the risks of public opposition or making a hypocritical show of compliance. "Elections buttress the regime—not by legitimizing it but by prompting the population to show that the *illegitimacy* of its 'democratic practice' has been accepted and that no action to undermine it will be forthcoming" (Zaslavsky and Brym, 1978: 371).

Communist efforts to mobilize support for an unpopular regime produced more mass apathy than commitment. Intellectuals could become "internal émigrés," concentrating upon abstruse questions of no concern to party commissars, such as the musicology of the Italian Renaissance. Retreat into the study of pure mathematics was popular, for unlike history and philosophy, there was no party line on mathematics.

On occasion, alienation erupted into overt demonstrations of dissent, such as strikes and mass demonstrations. Only in Poland were demonstrations organized by nationwide institutions independent of the party, the Solidarity trade union movement, and the Catholic Church. Attempts at reforming the regime by politicians were crushed by Soviet troops in Hungary in 1956 and in Czechoslovakia in 1968, and by martial law in Poland in 1981. Harshness in the repression of protests discouraged frequent repetition.

Dissident groups could discuss ideas contrary to party doctrines—provided that the group was small and intimate enough to prevent infiltration by the state security police. Even if the police knew, such activities could be tolerated as long as they did not constitute a public challenge to authority. Attending church or listening to rock music were minor forms of dissent, involving identification with values that the party scorned. Even when dissidents exercised pressure on the Communist Party to alter course, as was increasingly possible in the 1980s, they could not organize an independent party. The totalitarian outreach of the Communist Party was such that many pressures for change initially came from reform

TABLE 7.1   TRUST IN PARTIES

Respondents asked to indicate trust in political parties on a seven-point scale: positive, 5–7: neutral, 4; low, 1–3.

	Positive	Neutral	Low	Difference High-Low
		(% respondents)		
Bulgaria	11	16	73	−62
Czech Republic	24	38	38	−14
Slovakia	16	25	58	−42
Hungary	11	23	65	−54
Poland	7	22	71	−64
Romania	19	17	63	−44
	—	—	—	—
Mean	15	24	61	−46

Source: Paul Lazarsfeld Society, Vienna, *New Democracies Barometer III* (1994).

groups within the party. Notwithstanding this, the Communist party was seen not as legitimate but rather as a representative of Soviet forces (see Berglund and Dellenbrant, 1994: 28 ff.; Waller, 1994).

Distrust of political parties is a significant part of the legacy of Communism. When the New Democracies Barometer asked people to say whether they trusted or distrusted parties, less than one in six expressed trust (Table 7.1). In Poland the percentage trusting parties was down to seven percent. Countries differ only in the degree to which parties are distrusted. Overall, three-fifths actively distrust parties, and another quarter are neutral. Only one in six electors positively trusts political parties. Distrust in parties is much greater than in other institutions of government and civil society, such as the courts, the police and churches (see Rose and Haerpfer, 1994: questions 48–62).

CREATING PARTIES IN UNCERTAIN CIRCUMSTANCES

Free elections in post-Communist societies have created a quandary for politicians and for voters. The choice is no longer between the Communist Party and dissidents, a conflict that could be framed in "a language of philosophic and moral absolutes, of right against wrong, love against hate, truth against falsehood" (Garton-Ash, 1990: 51 f.). Instead, elections offer the opportunity to choose between a wide range of non-Communist, anti-Communist, and ex-Communist groups.

To create a party requires organization by political entrepreneurs. Former Communist activists are the biggest pool of experienced political entrepreneurs. With the collapse of the Communist regime, such individuals must create new institutions to mobilize popular support or leave party politics. Dissidents are a second source of leadership. But dissidents normally could not organize mass organizations under the Communist regime; they were "more like tribes than parties, being held together by friendship ties" and opposition to the Communist regime. They often did not share a common positive set of beliefs (see Lomax, 1995: 185 f.; Markus, 1991: 247). Political amateurs outside politics during the Communist regime have been a third source of party leadership. While free of the past, they are often ignorant of many everyday features of party politics.

Given discontinuity between regimes, politicians have two alternatives: (1) to create parties based on historic cleavages that existed prior to the Communist takeover in the 1940s, or (2) to try to mobilize support afresh (see Cotta, 1994: 105 ff.). The Lipset-Rokkan (1967) model of the creation of parties emphasizes the durability of cultural and economic cleavages. In Germany and Austria, which achieved democracy with interruptions, parties often persisted from one regime to the next. However, the legacy of four decades of Communist rule left much greater discontinuities in Central and Eastern European countries because the Communists were strongly committed to eliminating or controlling institutions of civil society that could be used as a basis for independent party organization. The intensity and duration of Communist repression of institutions of civil society has resulted in great uncertainty about the interests and values that voters would like to see represented.

Free elections have demonstrated the truth of the old political adage: "There is only one way to say no, but there are many ways to go forward." The dozens of parties fighting elections include parties of ex-Communists and dissidents; parties that hark back to pre-1945 cultural traditions, emphasizing religion and national identities, or radical right or fascist appeals; parties that emphasize current economic interests of the market, social democracy, or farmers; and new parties proclaiming green values or new personalities. While many different appeals have been tried, they have not met with equal success (Table 7.2).

1. The Failure of Dissident Movements as Electoral Parties   The absolutes of life under Communism discouraged debate about what government ought to do; the central thesis of dissidents was that the Communist regime was illegitimate and should be rejected. Nor was there much opportunity for organization. As long as a dissident group was small, members could know (and trust) each other. Expansion risked infiltration by agents of the state police and disbandment, loss of jobs, and jail. Since movements could not contest elections, they held street demonstrations and strikes in which masses of people responded more or less spontaneously to a call for protest. Olson (1993: 642) describes the groups as "above parties and politics." In Czechoslovakia the Civic Forum movement had the slogan, "Parties are for Party (that is, Communist) members; the Civic Forum is for all."

The collapse of Communist parties represented victory for dissidents—and the fulfillment of their original mission. Critics of the regime were now to be found everywhere, including reform-minded Communists who had not publicly protested under the old regime but sometimes tried to alter the party from within. Dissidents who had not compromised with the party differed about whether or not to welcome converts to their cause. When civic movements

TABLE 7.2 PARTIES IN POST-COMMUNIST SYSTEMS

	Bulgaria (1994)	Czech Republic* (1992)	Slovakia (1994)
		(Parties and % share of vote at latest election)	
1. Dissident movement	Union Democratic Forces 24	Civic Forum 6	Public Against Violence (ceased)
2. Ex-Communist	Socialist 43	Left 14	Common Choice 10
Historic culture			
3. Religion	—	Christian People 6	Christian Democrats 12
4(a). Nationalist	—	—	Slovak Nationalists 5
4(b). Ethnic minority	Turkish Rights, Freedom 5	Moravians 6	Hungarian Coalition 10
5. Radical right	—	Republican 6	—
6. Personalist	Business: Grachev 5	—	Movement Dem. Slovakia: Meciar 35 Workers 7
Economic interests			
7. Liberal market		Civic Democracy 30	Democratic Union 8
8. Social democrat	—	Social Democrat 6	—
9. Agrarian	Agrarian Union 6	Liberal Social Union 6	Others
10. Small, other	Monarchist 1 Others 16	Pensioners 3 Others 17	13

*1992 Czech result: election to Czech National Assembly.

Continued

TABLE 7.2 *Continued*

Hungary (1994)   Poland (1993)   Romania (1992)
(Parties and % share of vote at latest election)

	Hungary (1994)	Poland (1993)	Romania (1992)
1. Dissident movement	—	Solidarity 5	Democratic Convention 20
2. Ex-Communist	Socialist 33 Workers 3	Democratic Left 20	Social Labour 3
3. Religion	Democratic Forum 12 Christ. Democrat 7	Fatherland 6	—
4(a). Nationalist	—	—	Rom. Natl Unity 8
4(b). Ethnic min.	—	Germans 1	Hungarian Union 7
5. Radical right	Justice (Csurka) 2	Indepen. Poland KPN 6	Greater Romania Party 4
6. Personalist		BBWR: Walesa 5 X: Tyminski 3	Dem. Natl. Salvation 5—Iliescu 28** Natl Salvation Front—Roman 10**
7. Liberal market	Free Democrats 20 FIDESZ: Young Democrats 7 Republicans 2	Democratic Union 11 Liberal Democrats 4 Union Real Politics 3	—
8. Social democrat	Social Dem. 1	Union of Labor 7	—
9. Agrarian	Smallholders 9 Agrarians 2	Peasant 15 Agrarians 2	Agrarian 3
10. Small, other	Others 2	Others 11	Others 17

**Both Iliescu and Roman were formerly in the Communist Party.

Source: Classified by the author from 1995 election or nearest date previous. For more detailed discussions see Bulgaria (Karasimeonov, 1995); Czech Republic (Olson, 1993; Kostelecky, 1995); Slovak Republic (Olson, 1993); Hungary (Rady, 1994); Poland (Vinton, 1993; Jasiewicz, 1994); Romania (Shafir, 1992).

sought to develop a party for post-Communist politics, they failed. This was spectacularly demonstrated in Poland. Solidarity's leader, Lech Walesa, could not win half the national vote in the country's first presidential election, by 1993 Solidarity was an also-ran party, and in 1995 Walesa was defeated by an ex-Communist in his bid for re-election. In Czechoslovakia the linked Czech and Slovak protest movements, Civic Forum and Public Against Violence, successfully contested the 1990 election, but the two parties both disappeared before the 1992 election that led to the breakup of the state. Only in Bulgaria and Romania do civic movements still poll a substantial amount of votes, but this is as coalitions opposed to strong parties of ex-Communists.

2. From Communist to Ex-Communist Parties   For Communists, old party ties are both an asset and a liability. It is an asset because Communists have skills in organizing and manipulating political organizations, and a network of contacts in every institution in which the party had a presence under the old regime. But identification with the old regime is a liability, since only a small fraction of the electorate wants to return to the past. In these circumstances, many Communists who were full-time party workers in the old regime have left party politics to seek profits in the marketplace. Their capital includes the network of contacts they have with ministries and major industries, and sometimes state assets they bought cheap through a process described as *nomenklatura* privatization. Others have remained in party politics, but they have abandoned the Communist Party name and many of its doctrines.

For those people who joined the Communist Party for ideological reasons, the key word in describing them remains "Communist." But for people who joined for opportunistic reasons the key word is *ex*-communist. They should respond opportunistically to competitive elections, following Joseph Schumpeter's (1952: 282 f.) dictum that in the electoral marketplace politicians behave like garment manufacturers, changing policies in response to changes in consumer taste. Ex-Communists thus need to lean over backward to pay tribute to freedom in order to reassure voters that they truly have changed their practices. Concurrently, they can emphasize continuing priority for social welfare rather than market values (cf. Kitschelt, 1995). In Hungary, the leader of the Socialist (that is, ex-Communist) Party, Gyula Horn, campaigned successfully against an ineffectual conservative government with the slogan, "Let the experts govern." In Bulgaria the Socialist (that is, ex-Communist) Party has flourished by dispensing patronage in the countryside (see Karasimeonov, 1995).

The electoral success of ex-Communist parties varies by election and by country. In the first free elections of 1990, ex-Communists were usually unsuccessful (cf. White, 1990). In the second round of free elections, parties of ex-Communists have capitalized on the swing against the government of the day to increase their vote. In Bulgaria, Hungary, and Poland, parties of ex-Communists have gained government office, although sometimes with as little as 20 percent of the popular vote. In Romania ex-Communists are prominent in both governing and opposition parties. The passage of time has reduced fears of voters that ex-Communists would bring back a Soviet-style regime—and in any event the Soviet Union has ceased to exist.

TABLE 7.3   VALUES OF EX-COMMUNISTS
AND NON-COMMUNISTS COMPARED

	Ex-Communist	Communist in family	Non-Communist	Difference (%)
Approve	%	%	%	%
Communist political regime	48	38	36	12
Current political regime	60	61	63	3
Future political regime	77	81	78	1
Past economic system	68	59	54	14
Current economic system	34	39	44	10
Future economic system	69	73	72	3
More freedom now to speak	82	85	85	3
Return to Communist rule	18	14	14	4

Note: Respondents were asked if they or any member of their family had belonged to the Communist Party or an associated organization. Answers were pooled from Bulgaria, Czech Republic, Slovakia, Hungary, Poland, and Romania.

Source: Paul Lazarsfeld Society, *New Democracies Barometer III* (1994).

At the mass level the critical question is: How Communist are voters for ex-Communist parties? The 1994 New Democracies Barometer asked people about their own and their family's ties to the old Communist Party. We can thus compare the political values of the 16 percent who said they had been members of the party or an affiliated organization, the 18 percent reporting someone in the family in the party, and the 64 percent without a family affiliation to the party.

Ex-Communists are not ideologues; they are similar to non-Communists in their basic political views (Table 7.3). A majority of non-Communists and ex-Communists are in agreement about endorsing the present regime, optimism about the political future, and disapproval of the old regime. A majority of both groups also agree about giving a higher rating to the old economic regime and a negative rating to the economic system in transition and they are optimistic about the future of the economy. An overwhelming majority in both groups appreciate the greater freedom to speak out that they enjoy today. Four-fifths agree that they do not want a return to Communist rule. The differences, between communists and non-communist are limited, and greater about evaluations of the past. Differences between party members and nonmembers are usually insignificant when evaluations are made about the present and future (see Rose, 1996).

The responses of ex-Communists to the incentives of electoral competition have enabled their parties to be successful in competition with parties having stronger claims to social democratic origins. A latterday Schumpeter might argue that ex-Communists have not changed: "Once an opportunist, always an opportunist." However, when in office ex-Communists must learn to govern in a world in which they can no longer depend upon Moscow to help, or know that an election is won before the ballots are printed. Like governments elsewhere in the world, ex-Communists face the constraints placed upon small countries by their bigger and richer neighbors. To get foreign money to deal with economic problems, ex-Communist governments must seek loans from such agencies as the International Monetary Fund and the World Bank. Such institutions are prepared to offer some assistance—but only if satisfied that the recipients are promoting the market economy not a return to the command economy.

For *cultural cleavages* identified by Lipset and Rokkan to persist from pre-Communist to post-Communist regimes, a number of conditions must be met (Cotta, 1994). Prior to the Communist takeover, there should have been a lengthy period of democracy; the majority of adults having the right to vote; parties having been well organized nationwide; and the gap between pre- and post-Communist regimes less than the lifespan of the average voter. In Central and Eastern Europe, none of these conditions are met. In Czechoslovakia, democratic government existed prior to World War II, but there was a gap of more than half a century between free elections—and national divisions have disrupted the old federal state.

It could be hypothesized that even though Communist regimes systematically sought to subordinate or eliminate loyalties to religion and ethnic or national identities, these nonetheless remain as potential sources for mobilizing voters today. However, when one looks at the percentage of people in post-Communist societies who go to church or who identify with ethnic minorities, the potential appears limited (Table 7.4).

3. The Weakness of Religion and Religious Parties   Today, religion is unimportant in the lives of most people in Central and Eastern Europe, and so too are church-related parties. A majority profess a nominal identification with the state religion, but less than a third report attending church at least once a month. Those parties seeking votes with a Christian label win a tenth of the vote or less (see again Table 7.2, pp. 139–140). The Hungarian Democratic Forum has done slightly better because it appeals not only to churchgoers but to conservative voters generally. In Poland, the one country where there was mass commitment to Catholicism, the inclusiveness of the church's membership has made it

TABLE 7.4   POTENTIAL FOR ETHNIC AND RELIGIOUS FRICTION

	Churchgoers*	Ethnic minorities (% country's population)	Gypsies
Bulgaria	10	10	3
Czech Republic	18	5	NA
Slovakia	49	13	1
Hungary	21	4	4
Poland	78	3	NA
Romania	36	10	2

*Attend church once a month or more often.

NA: Data not available; numbers small.

Source: Paul Lazarsfeld Society, *New Democracies Barometer III* (1994). Ethnic minorities, gypsies: various censuses.

unable to create a single party representing the diverse nonreligious interests of Catholics in Polish society. The Polish Catholic Church remains significant as a pressure group lobbying on issues of particular church concern, such as abortion, an issue that divides the Polish people.

4. *The Weakness of Nationalist and Minority Ethnic Identity*   As long as Czechoslovakia was a single country, Slovak nationalists could use nationalism as an appeal against the "Czech-dominated" government in Prague. But since Slovakia has become an independent country, Slovak politicians have had to find new grounds for appealing for votes. In a country in which nine-tenths or more of the population is of the same nationality, as is the case in Bulgaria, the Czech Republic, Slovakia, Hungary, and Poland, it is not possible for a party to make a distinctive appeal for votes by claiming to be the party for all Poles or for all Hungarians. People who share a common nationality can disagree about much else.

In pre-Communist days political entrepreneurs could appeal for support from the dominant nationality by offering a defense against real or imagined threats from neighboring countries or minorities within the country, such as Jews. The Holocaust and the movement of state boundaries and peoples at the end of World War II has greatly reduced the potential for friction between nationalities. It has also warned politicians of the dangers of whipping up extreme nationalist sentiments. Only in Romania do racist parties win votes by claiming to be "more nationalist" than other parties and promise to restore Romania's greatness at the expense of minorities. The combined vote of racist parties there is similar to that of the racist French National Front.

Ethnic parties appealing to a minority identity within a country can be found in nearly every post-Communist country, but such parties face a dilemma. In order to have a distinctive appeal, ethnic parties must stress the problems of a minority, such as Hungarians in Slovakia or Romania. In Bulgaria the constitution bans the formation of ethnic parties; hence, Turks have organized as the Movement of Rights and Freedom. But when ethnic groups constitute less than a tenth of the country's population, ethnic parties are limited in the votes they can hope to win. Gypsies are fewer in number and exceptionally difficult to organize politically. Because ethnic parties are small, they also do not stimulate a reaction by the national majority (for details on minorities, see Bugajski, 1994). The problems of ethnic division that have erupted into violence in parts of the former Yugoslavia are atypical of the majority of countries of Central and Eastern Europe.

5. *Personal Parties*   The term "charismatic leader" is often misused as a description of any party leader who wins an election. Strictly speaking, the term describes a leader with a following so strong that it can overturn established institutions of a regime. Lenin was such a leader, and so too was Charles de Gaulle. In post-Communist societies, only Vladimir Meciar of Slovakia could claim this accomplishment. This ex-boxer was initially a major figure in the Slovak movement, Public Against Violence; he broke with it in 1991 to found his own party, the Movement for a Democratic Slovakia. Initially Meciar campaigned for greater Slovak autonomy from Prague and greater subsidies from federal funds to support ailing industries. The result was the breakup of Czechoslovakia, and Meciar became the first prime minister of an independent Republic of Slovakia (see Butorova and Butora, 1995: 122 ff.).

An alternative form of personalistic leadership is based on patronage distributed to clients who are loyal to individuals rather than impersonal parties or laws of the regime. Romania had a tradition of personalistic politics prior to the advent of Nicolae Ceauşescu, who combined it with Communist ideology to exercise personal rule in a totalitarian manner. Ceauşescu's death meant the end of one-party politics but not of personalistic politics. The initial move to overthrow Ceauşescu came from Communists and ex-Communists. The movement then split, leading to the formation of parties clustered around different leaders. Romania has a directly elected president, thus offering a major opportunity for personal voting. In 1992 Ion Iliescu, an ex-Communist, was elected president with the backing of the Democratic Party National Salvation Front created to support his candidacy after he was unable to gain control of a party to which both he and his rival, the prime minister, Petre Roman, both belonged (cf. Nelson, 1990; Eyal, 1993).

Post-Communist countries differ in whether the head of state, the president, is popularly elected (cf. McGregor, 1994: table 2). Where this occurs, as in Bulgaria, Poland, and Romania, a two-ballot system enables a large number of individuals to run in the first ballot with or without a party endorsement. The run-off second ballot reduces the choice to two, thus forcing different parties to coalesce for or against one choice. In Poland, the Solidarity leader, Lech Walesa, won election as president in 1990, but he took only 40 percent of the vote in the first ballot, before winning the run-off second ballot against a complete unknown. Furthermore, Walesa could not secure the election of a Polish Parliament favorable to his views or create a party winning a substantial vote. In 1995 he failed to win re-election.

6. *Liberalization and Liberal Parties*   Because the command economy was a political creation, imposed by the party-state, dismantling the command economy is a political act too (cf. Kornai, 1992). The term "liberalization" is used to describe an increase in the market's role in determining supply and demand for goods and labor through the price system. It reflects the links in post-Communist societies between classic political values of liberalism, such as freedom of speech and representative government, and a reduction of the role of the state in the marketplace.

Liberal parties are found in almost every post-Communist country; they are liberal in the style of Margaret Thatcher or University of Chicago neoclassical economists—that is, they are market-oriented. The most electorally successful market-oriented liberal party is the Civic Democratic Party in the Czech Republic, led by Vaclav Klaus. In Poland liberal parties promoting the market claimed that their measures subsequently produced economic success (see Sachs, 1993), but in the 1993 election only one such party, the Democratic Union, was able to retain any seats in Parliament, and it took only a tenth of the vote.

7. *Social Democratic Parties Versus Ex-Communists*   In Western Europe social democrats and Communists have often been enemies because they compete for votes from the same people. Everywhere except in Italy, social democrats have been far more successful in winning votes (see again Figure 6.3, p. 118). In Communist systems, such competition could not exist. Insofar as social democratic ideas were expressed, this was done by reform Communists speaking out within the party. In post-Communist countries, social democrats have had little electoral success, winning less than a tenth of the vote and sometimes failing to win seats in Parliament. Insofar as they are anti-Communist, pro-market parties can claim to be even more anti-Communist in rejecting an active role for the state in the economy. Insofar as social democrats promote welfare through the state, they compete with ex-Communist parties claiming that they created a welfare system when in power (cf. Waller, 1995). To note that social democratic values are promoted by other parties—for example, personal freedom by liberal parties and welfare benefits by ex-Communists—spotlights the difficulties that social democrats are having in establishing a distinctive appeal.

8. Urban/Rural Differences   The proportion of Central and Eastern European living in small towns and rural areas is higher than in most Western European countries, but this does not create a politically salient cleavage between rural and urban dwellers. Except in Poland, Communist regimes collectivized agriculture, treating farming as if it were a factory enterprise and turning peasants into workers guaranteed a low but steady wage on a collective farm. The system was notoriously inefficient, creating chronic shortages of food and leading urban dwellers to cultivate vegetable gardens in order to have a secure source of food outside the state system (cf. Pryor, 1992; Rose and Tikhomirov, 1993).

Agrarian parties are found in most post-Communist countries, and their share of the vote is similar to that of Scandinavian agrarian parties (compare Figure 6.3, p. 118 and Table 7.2, pp. 139–140). But this represents a low level of success, for in Central and Eastern Europe the potential agricultural vote is much greater than in Scandinavia. Only in Poland, which retained a large peasant sector under Communism, do agrarian parties take most of the rural vote, albeit it is divided among three different parties. Following the 1993 election the Polish Peasant Party took the prime ministership in a coalition government with ex-Communists.

Every party contesting an election must have some sort of economic policy, but it is misleading to label differences in post-Communist countries as class differences along West European lines, for the social, economic and political context is very different. In post-Communist systems a party that espouses policies deemed left in the West, such as maintaining state ownership of enterprises to keep people in work, is conservative—that is, seeking to keep in place practices from the command economy. Nor is debate about economic policies a matter of marginal adjustments in taxing and spending. Amidst the wreckage of a Communist economy, economic issues raise fundamental issues with the urgency conveyed by the Leninist question: What is to be done?

There remain big differences in standards of living between households in Central and Eastern Europe. In part these reflect influences also found in Western Europe, such as education; in part they reflect the pathologies of a party-state and its aftermath, offering some people opportunities to get rich quick in the transition to the market economy (cf. Rose and McAllister, 1996). Differences between those who are better off and worse off can be expected to go along with differences in political priorities between those who favor the collective provision of welfare and those preferring individual responsibility.

When *New Democracies Barometer III* asked a battery of questions about economic issues in 1993, the people of every country were divided, as would happen in Western European countries too. A majority favored the state taking responsibility for welfare and favored a secure job rather than making money; a majority also endorsed private ownership of major enterprises and people being paid according to their achievements rather than income equality. Factor analysis showed that answers to these questions were sufficiently consistent to justify combining them into a scale measuring collectivist as against individualist attitudes toward social welfare (for details, see Rose and Makkai, 1995).

- *Individualists* (44 percent of total). In this group people react against their experience of Communist policies; they reject three or four collectivist alternatives. Individualists are the largest group in Central and Eastern Europe. In the Czech Republic 64 percent are classified as individualists. However, they are not an absolute majority overall.
- *Ambivalent* (29 percent). Because individuals do not reason with ideological rigor, the second largest group is ambivalent about collective action, tending to favor a secure job and state responsibility for welfare, and private enterprise and differential incomes. In Poland the largest group of the population is ambivalent.
- *Collectivists* (26 percent). Democracy does not preclude collective action to promote individual welfare, and social democratic parties give it priority. In post-Communist societies 25 percent are clearly in favor of collective welfare, endorsing three of the four propositions. The proportion is as high as 44 percent in Bulgaria.

There appears to be *a party system in the heads of voters,* for the great majority have clear and conflicting economic preferences. But in political terms, parties have yet to gain sufficient trust from voters to stabilize party support.

All parties in Central and Eastern Europe today are new. Even those derived from Communist organizations have been refounded and renamed. Yet new parties in the Western European sense are relatively few. Green parties have appeared but won few votes. Idiosyncratic parties have also emerged—for example, the Beer Lovers' Party in Poland. It won seats in Parliament in 1991, but by 1993 the froth was off the party and it lost its seats. The striking feature of the first two elections in post-Communist countries is not the emergence of new parties, democratic or undemocratic, but the appearance on the ballot paper of dozens of parties with labels that combine terms familiar in Western Europe (cf. Table 7.2 and Figures 6.1–4).

A DEMOBILIZED ELECTORATE

A stable party system requires stable partisans—that is, people who not only vote for a party but also identify with it and trust it. However, the experience of four decades of Communist party indoctrination has produced a demobilized electorate, in which most people do not do this. In such circumstances, free elections register the negative and transient preferences of antiparty voters.

Uncommitted and Antiparty Voters

When election day came people who had not previously had a chance to express their views freely were ready to cast a ballot. The turnout at the first free elections was as high as 95 percent in Czechoslovakia and has remained high since. Only in Poland has turnout dropped as low as it is in the United States. But the meaning of these votes is very different than in a society with an established party system.

Party identification is the anchor that holds people to a particular party through thick and thin. When party identification does not exist, then the vote of an individual is cast by default for whatever group happens to appear the lesser evil, or is temporarily preferable. It will help a party gain seats in Parliament—but voters will feel no obligation to support the party thereafter. The party can thus suffer a dramatic loss of votes at the next election.

A lifetime of being told that "the party knows best" has led the majority of Central and Eastern Europeans *not* to identify with any political party: four-fifths or more in Poland and Hungary do not identify with any political party. By contrast, in an established party system such as that in Britain, four-fifths do have a party identification (Figure 7.1).

Negative party identification is often stronger than positive party identification. When the New Democracies Barometer has asked people whether there is any party they will never vote for, more people are likely to name a party that they are permanently opposed to than a party with which they now identify. In the extreme case of Romania, the number of people naming a party they would never vote for is twice as many as those naming a party that they would support. In Bulgaria, where party ties are relatively strong, so too is hostility against parties. More Bulgarians can identify a party that they would never vote for than one they support. Rejection is divided almost equally between the Socialist Party, the coalition Union of Democratic Forces, and the Movement for Rights and Freedom, the party of the Turkish minority.

Because the vote of every individual is equal, an election cannot register the degree of commitment or distrust felt by individual electors. The views of those who do not turn out to vote are completely ignored. The votes of individuals who are alienated and cast a negative vote or apathetic electors who register a transitory choice have their votes count just the same as those who are positively committed to the party for which they vote.

When public opinion surveys ask people in post-Communist societies how they would vote if an election were held that week, the largest group is usually the "don't knows." In *New Democracies Barometer III,* covering six countries of Central and Eastern Europe, an average of 26 percent say they did not know how they would vote. In Hungary the don't knows were 43 percent only six months before its general election. There is substantial evidence that the don't knows are not trying to keep an established party preference secret but are those who have difficulty in identifying a party they would like to support (cf. Carnaghan, 1994). Don't knows result in the "largest" party in a post-Communist society having little support.

Among those naming a party when asked how they would vote, preferences are scattered among more than a dozen different parties. The typical party contesting elections in post-Communist countries today is supported by less than 4

FIGURE 7.1   IDENTIFICATION WITH PARTIES
IN POST-COMMUNIST COUNTRIES

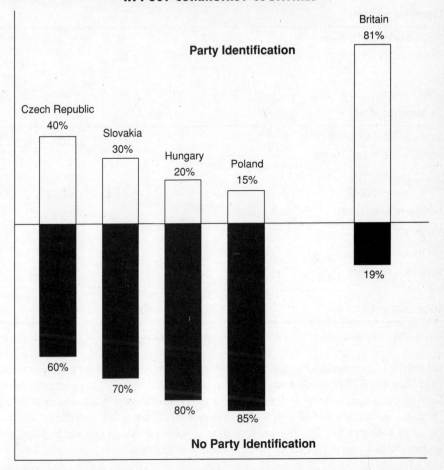

Source: Paul Lazarsfeld Society, Vienna, *New Democracies Barometer III* (1994). Britain: *Gallup Political and Economic Index* (London: Gallup Poll No. 396, August 1993), p. 7. Bulgaria and Romania omitted because question not asked in a fully comparable way.

percent of the total electorate (cf. Table 7.2, pp. 139–140). Across six countries, the most frequently named party claims the support of only 22 percent of electors. The fragmentation of the vote persists on election day. In Poland the "biggest" party in the 1993 election, the ex-Communist, took only 20 percent of votes actually cast. Even if this leads such a party to be described as the "winner," it remains the case that three-quarters of those who vote cast ballots against the party coming first, and an even larger proportion of the electorate is uncommitted to the so-called winning party.

If a mobilized voter can be defined as a person having a party identification and trusting parties, then three-quarters of post-Communist electors can be said to be *demobilized* (Table 7.5). The largest bloc in the electorate are uncommitted voters, who have no party identification and distrust parties—yet are

TABLE 7.5   DEMOBILIZED ELECTORS PREDOMINATE

Committed partisans	Czech	Slovak	Hungary	Poland	Mean
Votes, has ID, trusts parties	13	9	2	2	7
Votes, has ID, no trust in parties	23	20	12	12	17
	—	—	—	—	—
Total Partisan	36	29	14	15	23
Uncommitted voters					
Votes, no ID, distrusts parties	36	41	39	64	45
Votes, no ID, trusts parties	9	5	5	4	6
	—	—	—	—	—
Total Uncommitted	45	46	44	68	51
Anti-party non-voters					
No ID, no trust, no vote	14	22	33	17	21
No ID, trusts, no vote	2	2	3	1	2
ID, no trust, no vote	3	1	6	—	3
	—	—	—	—	—
Total anti-party	19	25	42	18	26

Source: Paul Lazarsfeld Society, Vienna, *New Democracies Barometer III* (1994).

nonetheless prepared to name a party they would vote for if an election were held that week. The second largest group consists of actively anti-party electors, lacking even a transitory preference for a party, and usually without any trust in parties. The backbone of a stable party system, committed partisans, are the smallest category, accounting for less than a sixth of the electorate in Hungary and in Poland, and divide their votes among many parties.

CONSEQUENCES OF A DEMOBILIZED ELECTORATE

The object of free elections is to give people a choice between political elites competing for control of government. In every post-Communist country this condition has been met: People now have a very large choice between parties. In Romania 74 parties contested the first free election, and in Poland 67 different parties did so, with 29 parties winning seats in the Polish Parliament. President Walesa described the result as "excessively democratic" (quoted in Webb, 1992: 166). Elsewhere in Central and Eastern Europe the number of parties contesting elections ranged from 45 in Hungary to a "low" of 21 and 22 in the Czech Republic and Slovakia respectively (McGregor, 1993: table 2).

But free elections "can delegitimate just as easily as they legitimate" (White, 1990: 285); they only support the consolidation of democracy if the great majority of the electorate votes for parties that are committed to maintaining a democratic regime. Given the history of Central and Eastern Europe in the first half of this century, such an outcome could not be taken for granted when the first elections were held in 1990. An election offering a free choice between many parties measures the weakness or strength of popular support for undemocratic parties.

The first condition of consolidating democracies in post-Communist countries is that the vote for undemocratic or antiregime parties is low. As Table 7.3 shows, people who vote for parties of ex-Communists are not voting for a return to the Communist regime. Ex-Communists now have a personal interest in defending political freedoms, for they are obvious targets for the restriction of rights under an illiberal regime. Nor is there anywhere a Fascist or National Socialist (Nazi) party securing support on the scale that such parties could claim before World War II. Parties of the radical right receive few votes. For example, at the 1994 election in Hungary the Justice and Life Party, founded as a breakaway from the governing party by an anti-Semitic right-wing leader, Istvan Csurka, failed to win any seats in Parliament. In Romania, virulent nationalist and radical right parties win upward of one-eighth of the vote. In no Central or Eastern European country has an antidemocratic party won the quarter of the vote that Vladimir Zhirinovsky's extreme nationalist party took in the December 1993 Russian parliamentary election.

A second condition of consolidating democracy is that parties alternate in office as the result of elections and votes in Parliament. Conservative and ex-Communist parties full of suspicions and rancor toward each other have exchanged places as government and opposition in Bulgaria, Hungary, and Poland, and in Slovakia Vladimir Meciar, the most successful of the personalistic politicians, has not used his personal authority to ignore the rules of the game when the rules dictate that he leave office.

Free elections voting parties in and out of office are evidence that the transition to democracy has started in post-Communist countries. But the absence of committed partisans shows that party systems have yet to become stable. A stable party system requires a large proportion of the electorate to identify positively with parties; the absence of stable parties is an obstacle to representative government.

A Floating Party System

In a stable party system some electors will be floating voters, moving between established parties as their preferences and the performance of parties changes. For the moment, post-Communist countries have a "floating party system," for parties lack mass membership, established organizations and commitment from voters and many of their members of Parliament (Lomax, 1995: 185).

At the time of the first post-Communist elections, neither politicians nor voters were sure about what parties stood for, how much or how little support they had nationally or what they would do if elected. In Poland, 29 parties won seats in Parliament; in the Czechoslovak Federation, 22 parties did so; and in Hungary, 14 parties did. In Bulgaria the first election results registered only five parties winning seats, but that was because the Union of Democratic Forces, one of the two largest parties, was actually a coalition of 15 different groups.

Once in Parliament, individual MPs have shown a weak sense of party identification. This creates difficulties in committee assignments, organizing party whips for voting on contentious bills, forming coalition governments, and developing a party's program for the next election. MPs of the same party are often on opposing sides of an issue. Party discipline is not always a virtue for individuals socialized in reaction to a Communist regime. Inexperience in parliamentary procedure creates difficulties in conducting debates and deliberating about policies (e.g., see Agh, 1994; Olson, 1993: 646 ff.). Negotiating about the rewards of office creates conflicts between ambitious people in the same party, and making difficult decisions in office creates additional tensions.

The unsettled state of parties during the first Parliament results in the parties contesting the second election changing due to failures in the first election, splits in Parliament and the governing coalition, and the emergence of new parties and alliances. In Poland, 22 of the parties that had held seats in their own name in the first Parliament did not win any seats in their own right in the second election. Most of the survivors did so through merger or forming tactical alliances. In Hungary, four parties disappeared during the first Parliament and six new parties emerged at the second election.

A demobilized electorate and a floating system of parties results in very large interelection shifts in votes. This can be shown by an index of volatility, which sums the changes in each party's share of the vote in two successive elections on a scale ranging from a minimum of 0 to a maximum of 200 (Figure 7.2). In Czechoslovakia the index approached this maximum, for the party structure was transformed by the collapse of Czechoslovakia and the emergence of new parties in the two successor states. In Romania the index is 126 because the National Salvation Front, an anti-Ceauşescu coalition of ex-Communists and non-Communists, won 66 percent at the first parliamentary election. It subsequently split; the remnant of that coalition took only 10 percent of the vote at the second election. Elsewhere, volatility has primarily been due to big rises and falls in support for parties fighting both elections.

At the initial stage of transition, volatility in post-Communist countries is much higher than in other European countries that have abruptly moved from authoritarian regimes to democratic elections. Even though Spain had been almost 40 years without free elections, volatility in Hungary or Poland has been more than twice as high as in Spain's first democratic elections. It is also more than twice as high as in Portugal, where parties were absent for an even longer period. Volatility in post-Communist countries is also higher than in the early days of the Federal Republic of Germany or Austria.

Elections in established democracies show a much lower degree of volatility than in post-Communist countries. In a normal election in an established democracy, the index of volatility can be as low as 10. In Germany the index fell from 52 points at the start of the Federal Republic to 16 points for the 1994 election, which included disturbances arising from reunification with East Germany. East German volatility has been much lower than in other post-Communist countries because of the presence of "ready-made" parties with which East Germans could vicariously identify through West German television.

FIGURE 7.2   VOLATILITY IN PARTY SUPPORT BETWEEN ELECTIONS

Index of Volatility
(minimum, 0; maximum, 200)

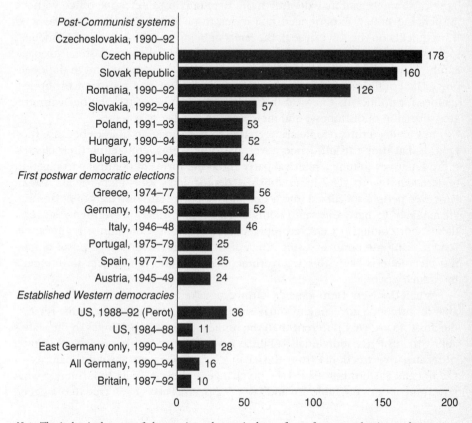

Note: The index is the sum of changes in each party's share of vote from one election to the next.

Source: Calculated by the author from official results.

Trusted Representatives—the Missing Middle

In a country of tens of millions of people, democratic government must be representative government. This requires politicians who understand how to advance the interests of their supporters, and parties that can organize individual MPs to give direction to government. But if MPs are amateurs in the world of government and parties are undisciplined and floating, there is a missing middle. Individuals can vote and governors can govern, but it is difficult for voters to know how to hold the government of the day accountable from one election to the next.

Volatility in parties and in popular votes has created a big turnover among members of Parliament. In Poland, 69 percent of MPs elected in 1993 were new to the job: in Hungary, 64 percent of the MP selected in 1994 were new; When the majority of MPs are inexperienced in representing voters, committee work, parliamentary debate, and influencing government, the connection between how people vote and how the country is governed is reduced.

Political amateurs who have entered Parliament by accident through the collapse of Communism may do little more than occupy an elective office without influencing policy. Experienced politicians from the old regime or those who learn quickly on the job can seek the fruits of being an MP—increased influence, income, and status—or the even greater benefits of being a minister. Patronage can be dispensed to create a network of clients within a party and in the economy. . The confusion caused by the transition to the market creates many opportunities for politicians to award themselves material benefits. Such behavior creates suspicion of dishonesty and increases the distrust of voters.

In a civic culture, people are prepared to participate in politics because they believe that they can influence government by voting, contacting their elected representatives, joining a political party and other forms of political participation undertaken by activists in established democracies (see Parry et al., 1992). However, people socialized into a Communist party-state distrust politicians and are unlikely to have the same confidence in their ability to influence government. Shortcomings of elected representatives in post-Communist regimes will tend to reinforce popular suspicions. A distrustful and demobilized post-Communist electorate is likely to see government as alien and not subject to influence by ordinary people.

When the New Democracies Barometer asked if ordinary people are better able to influence government today than under the former Communist regime, the answers are very different than the replies given about changes in the state's ability to influence individuals. Whereas a big majority see themselves as gaining many negative freedoms from the change of regimes, an absolute majority of Central and Eastern Europeans see no change in their inability to influence what government does (cf. Table 7.6 and Table 5.2 p. 96). This is even true in the Czech

TABLE 7.6   POST-COMMUNIST CITIZENS DOUBT THEIR INFLUENCE ON GOVERNMENT

Q. *Do you think our present political system, by comparison with the Communist, is better, the same, or worse in enabling ordinary people to influence what government does?*

	Better (%)	Same (%)	Worse (%)
Czech Republic	29	52	18
Slovakia	15	59	26
Hungary	27	59	14
Poland	29	55	15
Romania	36	49	14
	—	—	—
Mean	27	56	17

Source: Paul Lazarsfeld Society, *New Democracies Barometer III* (1994). Bulgaria omitted as question not asked in a directly comparable way.

Republic where a freely elected government replaced a regime resting on Soviet bayonets. Romanians are most likely to see regime change as increasing their influence on government; that is a reflection of conditions under the Ceauşescu regime rather than a positive endorsement of the new regime. A quarter of Slovaks feel that they have had their influence on government reduced, a reminder that creating a nationalist government does not of itself make the government in Bratislava responsive.

Competition between parties at free elections is evidence that democracy exists in post-Communist countries, but until there are stronger links between voters and party leaders representative government has yet to be institutionalized. The missing middle in post-Communist political regimes has not produced a South American–style plebiscitarian system in which a president is popularly elected once every four years to exercise power over ministries and bureaucrats. In post-Communist countries the president is often distrusted, especially if he seeks to act independently of elected representatives (cf. chapter 9, in this book; O'Donnell, 1994). The result is a reduction in the representativeness and responsiveness of government.

chapter 8

FROM REPRESENTATION TO GOVERNMENT

The choice of voters is only the first step in forming a representative government. Converting votes into seats in Parliament is the second critical step, and there is more than one way to do this. Forming a government that is supported by Parliament is the final step. At each step in the process of creating a representative government, there is more than one alternative that is compatible with democracy (Rose, 1983).

Today, no one seriously opposes the principle that all men and women have the right to vote. But there are fundamental differences of opinion about *how* votes should be converted into seats in Parliament. Proportional representation (PR) is the usual method of electing members of Parliament in both Western and Eastern Europe. The intent is to award seats in Parliament to parties in keeping with their shares of the popular vote; this is said to be fair. PR also encourages more parties to contest elections, since a party can win a number of seats in Parliament with as little as 5 percent of the popular vote. In a PR election there is usually not a "winner" in the sense of one party gaining an absolute majority of parliamentary seats. The normal consequence of a PR election is the formation of a coalition government.

The first-past-the-post (FPTP) electoral system used in Britain and the United States declares the candidate with the most votes in a constituency the winner, whether he or she has an absolute majority or a plurality of votes. If only two candidates contest a seat, one candidate necessarily wins an absolute majority. But when three or more candidates contest a seat, the winning candidate's plurality can fall short of half the vote in the district. First-past-the-post is a system of disproportional representation; it tends to manufacture a majority of seats in Parliament for a party that wins less than half the national vote. For example, no British party has won as much as half the popular vote since 1935, yet in 13 of the 14 general elections of the past half century one party has won an absolute majority of seats in Parliament. The first-past-the-post system fixes responsiblity for government squarely upon a single party.

The winner-take-all character of single-party majority government contrasts sharply with parties sharing power in a coalition government. Hence, the debate about electoral systems is not only about the fairest way of awarding seats in Parliament but also about the best form of government (for reviews, see Blais, 1991; Lijphart, 1984; Sartori, 1994). Having one party in control of a cabinet is justified as a means to the end of *accountable and effective* government. A single-party government is deemed more accountable because it is easy for voters to know which party to credit or blame for what government does. A single-party government is expected to be more effective because it does not need to conduct inter-party negotiations to reach agreement about major issues.

But one person's idea of effective government may appear to critics as an "elective dictatorship." The case for coalition government rejects the assumption that one party necessarily has the best policies. It endorses *consensus* policies, since "all who are affected by a decision have the chance to participate in making the decision" (Arthur Lewis, quoted in Lijphart, 1984: 21). The creation of a consensus is a time-consuming process and can require many compromises, or it may even lead to Washington-style gridlock. But proponents of coalition government regard the time spent in discussion and bargaining as time well spent to ensure that a wide variety of alternatives are considered, and there is a broad base of support for whatever course of action is decided.

The institutions for converting votes into seats and control of government are much the same in established democracies and post-Communist countries (cf. Kuusela, 1994). Hence, in this chapter it is possible to make direct comparisons about such matters as the degree of proportionality in many different political settings. But the context in which procedures operate is different, as later chapters will demonstrate. Generalizations about countries in which free elections have only operated for a few years must be tentative.

After explaining the mechanics of PR and first-past-the-post electoral systems, the first section shows that all electoral systems achieve a substantial measure of proportionality and some PR systems are actually less proportional than some first-past-the-post systems. In forming a government, the subject of the second section, the decisive issue is not the number of parties in Parliament but the size of the largest party. Coalitions differ greatly in the extent to which one party dominates the group. Competition between parties is the essence of democracy; this implies that no single party monopolizes control of government. The concluding section shows that while parties differ in the amount of time they spend in government, in the great majority of European countries there is no long-term monopoly in control of government.

TRANSLATING VOTES INTO SEATS

In parliamentary democracies the choice of an electoral system determines how votes are counted. Before the introduction of universal suffrage, most countries used a first-past-the-post electoral system. Almost everywhere in Europe, the broadening of the franchise was accompanied by the adoption of proportional representation. Traditional elites saw this as guaranteeing their retention of some seats in Parliament when the electorate was expanded and raising the threshold for a "left" majority in Parliament. Liberals and social democrats often backed proportional representation as a means of ensuring "one person, one vote, one value." In post-Communist countries, some form of proportional representation has invariably been adopted (see McGregor, 1993).

The First-Past-the-Post System

The logic of the plurality system is simple: The candidate with the most votes becomes the member of Parliament for a constituency, whatever the frontrunner's share of the vote. The percentage of the vote needed to win a seat reflects the number of candidates contesting a seat. If there are three or more candidates in a parliamentary constituency, then the winner *may not* have a majority of the votes. In the extreme case of a hard fought five-candidate contest in the Scottish constituency of Inverness in 1992, the winner took the seat with only 26 percent of the vote. In American presidential elections, third-party candidates have won sufficient votes to result in Bill Clinton, Richard Nixon, John F. Kennedy and Harry Truman each being elected president with less than half the popular vote.

The proportionality of the election outcome in a first-past-the-post ballot is also influenced by how a party's vote is spread between constituencies. A party that finishes a close second in a seat "wastes" more votes than does a party that finishes a poor third. The 1992 British election shows how the relation between seats and votes varies between parties (Table 8.1). The Conservative and Labour parties won a greater share of seats than votes. Due to the presence of three or more candidates in every constituency, with 42 percent of the popular vote the Conservatives won an absolute majority of seats in the House of Commons. The Conservatives won a third of their seats with less than half the vote. Labour did well because it concentrated its vote in winnable seats. In hundreds of seats where it had little chance of victory, Labour often finished in third place behind both Conservative and Liberal Democratic candidates, thus minimizing its "wasted" votes.

The Liberal Democrats did worst from the fast-past-the-post system, winning only 3 percent of the seats in the House of Commons with 18 percent of the national vote, because the party's vote was spread evenly throughout Britain. If

TABLE 8.1   THE FIRST-PAST-THE-POST SYSTEM: A BRITISH EXAMPLE

	Conservative	Labour	Liberal Democrat	Scot National	Welsh National
Votes and seats in the 1992 election					
Candidates	645	634	632	72	35
MPs	336	271	20	3	4
Votes per MP	41,809	42,657	299,950	209,666	38,500
Disproportionality					
% share MPs	52	42	3	0.5	0.6
% share vote	42	34	18	2	0.5
Difference, % seats-votes	+10	+8	−15	−1.5	+0.1

Note: Table excludes votes for miscellaneous minor parties and all votes and seats of Northern Ireland parties.

Source: Prepared by the author.

seats had been allocated in proportion to votes, with almost six million votes the Liberal Democrats would have won 116 seats. By contrast, the Welsh Nationalists concentrated their vote in rural Welsh areas where a substantial percentage of voters speak the Welsh language. In consequence, the party won *more* seats in the House of Commons than would have been awarded by a strictly proportional distribution of seats. Like the Liberal Democrats, the Scottish Nationalists spread their support evenly. Its candidates are much more likely to finish second than first, and the party thus won fewer seats than its share of the popular vote.

In the great majority of countries the electoral system is not altered by partisan control of government. France is distinctive in that governing parties have often altered the method of electing MPs according to calculations of partisan advantage. For example, thanks to a winner-take-all electoral system, in 1981 the Socialist Party won 56 percent of the seats in the French National Assembly with only 37 percent of the popular vote. When its support slumped, it introduced proportional representation prior to the 1986 election, so that even though the Socialists lost their majority in Parliament the party was not wiped out.

Normally, the French use a two-ballot version of the first-past-the-post system. In the first ballot a candidate must win more than half the vote to be elected to Parliament. Since half a dozen candidates often contest a seat, this rarely happens. In the second ballot, candidates failing to receive a stipulated share of the vote cannot stand, and also-rans can bargain about throwing their support to a potential frontrunner. This makes it possible to form a coalition against an extremist Communist or racist candidate. Whereas in the 1986 PR election the anti-immigrant National Front party won 35 seats with 10 percent of the vote, the two-ballot FPTP election of 1993 awarded the National Front no seats even though its share of the popular vote increased.

Proportional Representation: Sharing Seats More or Less According to Votes

The object of a PR system is clear: to award seats in Parliament in proportion to each party's share of the popular vote. However, the operation of such a system is more complicated than a first-past-the-post system, and there are significant differences between European countries in the mechanics of their systems (for a short introduction, see Mackie and Rose, 1991: 509 f.; for a very detailed exposition, see Taagepera and Shugart, 1989).

In a PR ballot the critical choice is between parties rather than individual candidates. The first requirement is that each voter must endorse a *party list* to establish each party's share of the total vote. The choice of individuals to represent the party in Parliament is usually determined by how the party caucus ranks candidates on the party list. The party's first seat will go to the candidate placed first on the list; the second seat won will go to the candidate placed second on the list and so on down the line. The candidate placed last on the list has no hope of winning a seat. The list system enables the party organization to place individuals in Parliament who might not be telegenic but could serve the party's interests there. It also enables a party to balance its ticket between competing factions within the party or to alternate top positions in the list between women and men (Rule, 1987; see also Figure 9.1, p. 183). Some PR systems allow voters to alter the party's ranking of candidates on a party list, but usually this does not alter who is awarded seats.

Multimember constituencies are a second requirement of proportional representation. If only one candidate is to be elected from a district, as is the case in Britain, it is impossible to distribute seats in proportion to votes. However, in a multimember district with ten seats, as many as ten parties could win representation. As a general rule, the more seats in a multimember district, the greater the degree of proportionality. The number of seats in a district varies greatly between PR systems. In Ireland the average constituency has only four seats, thus discouraging smaller parties. By contrast, in the Netherlands the whole country is a single constituency within which 150 seats are shared out. Within a country, there are substantial differences between districts in the number of MPs returned. In Spain the smallest constituency elects two members to Parliament, and the largest, Madrid, elects 33 members. Because a multimember district has representatives from several parties, in Parliament a district's MPs vote on opposite sides, because they vote their party whip, not their district.

The *threshold for representation* is a third critical requirement. The *constituency threshold* is the minimum quota of votes needed to be sure of receiving a seat. Methods of calculating quotas and awarding seats differ between PR systems. The quota can be determined by dividing the number of votes cast by the number of seats plus one. In a five-member seat with 100,000 votes, the quota is thus 16,667. If five seats were awarded parties on the basis of each having won at least 16,667 votes, the remaining votes, a maximum of 16,665, would be less than the votes of the winners. A party winning just over one-sixth of the vote should win one seat and a party with one-third of the vote in the district should receive two seats.

The *national threshold* is the minimum number of votes a party must win in order to participate in the national sharing out of seats. A national share out is necessary because parties sometimes fail to win a quota of votes to be awarded a seat in a multimember constituency and winning parties may accumulate "leftover" votes if their actual vote in a constituency exceeds a quota. For example, if five parties each won 18,000 votes in a five-member constituency and a sixth party won 10,000 votes, then each of the winning parties would contribute to the national pool a remainder of 1,333 votes surplus to the quota of 16,667, and the sixth party would contribute 10,000 votes. In the Netherlands, a party can be awarded one seat in Parliament with as little as two-thirds of 1 percent of the national vote. Most countries require a higher threshold; it is 4 percent of the national vote in Norway and Sweden and 5 percent in Germany. A high threshold prevents the proliferation of small parties. The Netherlands has eight parties in Parliament that would not be represented in the Norwegian or Swedish Parliament because they secure less than 4 percent of the national vote, the threshold there.

The 1994 election for the Swedish Parliament illustrates how PR can distribute 349 seats almost exactly in proportion to votes cast. Sweden is divided into

38 multimember constituencies returning an average of just over eight MPs. There is also a national constituency with 39 members to top up the number of MPs of parties that had wasted votes at the district level. The electoral law requires a party to win at least 4 percent of the national vote or at least 12 percent in one constituency to share in the national distribution of seats. More than eight parties nominated candidates and seven won seats in Parliament (Table 8.2). Proportionality was exact for the Center Party and correct to within one-tenth of 1 percent for three more parties. The "biggest"' deviation from pure proportionality was the 1.0 percent bonus of the largest party, the Social Democrats, and an underrepresentation by 1.6 percent of the New Democrats, who won no seats because they failed to cross the 4 percent vote threshold needed to claim a share of seats.

Since a multimember district has MPs representing up to half a dozen different parties, nearly every elector in the district will have an MP of her or his party choice. Advocates of constituency representation regard it as a disadvantage not to have one MP responsible for servicing the district. Germany maintains a link between a constituency and MP by electing half the members of the German *Bundestag* from single-member districts by the first-past-the-post system. To achieve proportionality, the other half of the seats are awarded by proportional representation to parties that win at least 5 percent of the national vote or three single-member seats.

Ireland is distinctive in combining proportional representation with an American-style primary in which voters can choose between candidates of the same party. It does this through the single transferable vote (STV) system of proportional representation. Each voter lists candidates in order of preference from first to last. If the voter's first choice has votes surplus to the quota required for election, these are transferred to the elector's second choice. If after transfers of votes an elector's first choice does not have sufficient votes to secure the quota

TABLE 8.2 DISTRIBUTING SEATS BY PR: SWEDEN AS AN EXAMPLE

1994 election	Votes (%)	Seats (%)	Difference Seats-Votes (%)
Social Democrats	45.3	46.4	+1.1
Moderates	22.4	22.9	+0.5
Center	7.7	7.7	0
Liberals	7.2	7.4	+0.2
Left Party	6.2	6.3	+0.1
Greens	5.0	5.1	+0.1
Christian Democrats	4.1	4.0	−0.1
New Democrats	1.2	0	−1.2
Others	0.9	0	−0.9

Source: Calculated by the author.

for a seat, the vote is transferred to the elector's second choice, and so on. Instead of lobbying a party caucus for a top place on the party list, Irish candidates canvass voters for first preference votes in competition with other members of their own party. In principle, an STV ballot avoids the normal PR requirement of voting for a party list. In fact, most Irish voters follow party lines in assigning preferences to candidates.

Degrees of Proportionality

Debates about electoral systems usually imply a difference in kind between first-past-the-post and proportional representation systems. However, no democratic system could grossly repress all expression of popular preferences. The proportionality of electoral systems is a matter of degree. While the first-past-the-post system accepts a degree of distortion as the price of manufacturing an absolute majority for the biggest party, it does not deny representation to most voters. Nor do PR systems aim at 100 percent proportionality. Setting a threshold of 4 or 5 percent of the vote to qualify for seats accepts a little disproportionality in exchange for preventing the proliferation of very small parties in Parliament.

The fit between votes and seats can be measured by an index of proportionality. It is calculated by summing the difference between each party's share of seats and its share of votes; dividing the total by two since the underrepresentation of some parties must be matched by the overrepresentation of others; and subtracting the result from 100. If an electoral system were totally proportional, the index would be 100 and if it were totally disproportional, the index number would be 0. The higher the numerical value, the greater the degree of proportionality.

The index of proportionality averages 94 percent for PR systems in Western Europe; the range around the mean is very low (Table 8.3). Denmark comes within 1 percent of having an electoral system that is perfectly proportional. The Netherlands aims at perfect proportionately but falls three points short because of a proliferation of minuscule parties and the rounding-off effect among parties qualifying for seats. Spain produces the least proportional PR result, with an index of 88 percent. This shortfall is due to Spanish constituencies often electing fewer members of Parliament than there are parties contesting the seat. Spain is also unusual among PR systems in sometimes manufacturing a majority for a party that wins only two-fifths of the popular vote, the Socialists led by Felipe Gonzalez.

Among first-past-the-post systems, average proportionality is lower, 79 percent, but there is a 32-point range between the most and the least proportional system. The U.S. House of Representatives achieved a proportionality index of 91 percent in 1992. In Canada the very strong regional division of party support and the collapse of the governing Conservative Party produced an index of proportionality of 77 percent in 1993. The new Italian electoral system, used for the first time in 1994, elected most voters by a first-past-the-post method that succeeded

TABLE 8.3   PROPORTIONALITY IN ELECTORAL SYSTEMS:
A DIFFERENCE OF DEGREE

Proportional Representation (PR)	Index of Proportionality (%)	First-Past-the-Post (FPTP)
Denmark	99	
Sweden	98	
Germany, Netherlands	97	
Sweden, Austria	98	
AVERAGE, Western Europe PR	94	
Ireland, Norway	94	
Finland	93	
Belgium, Luxembourg, Portigal	92	
Switzerland	91	US House of Representatives 1992
Greece	90	
Spain	88	
Slovakia	87	
	86	Australia
Bulgaria	85	Italy*
	83	United Kingdom
Romania	81	
Czech Republic	80	
AVERAGE Post-Communist	79	*AVERAGE, FPTP*
Hungary	78	
	77	Canada
Poland	66	
	59	France

*One-quarter of seats allotted by proportional representation; index of proportionality for FPTP seats only, 78.

Source: Calculated by the author from 1995 or most recent election results.

in squeezing smaller parties; the index of proportionality was raised due to the distribution of a quarter of the seats by proportional representation. France has the most disproportional first-past-the-post system; in the 1993 Assembly election the French system was only 59 percent proportional. In a bipartisan fashion it penalized the left parties, which won only 15 percent of the seats with 31 percent of the vote, and the extreme right National Front, which won no seats with 13 percent of the vote. The Gaullist Rally for the People won more than twice as many seats as votes and the Union for French Democracy did almost as well. Together, the two parties forming the government claimed 82 percent of the seats in the National Assembly with only 40 percent of the vote.

When post-Communist countries drafted election laws in a hurry before the first free elections in 1990, each chose a form of proportional representation. But because none of the party leaders had much idea about the size of their support and dozens of parties sought votes with erratic degrees of success, the result has been a much lower level of proportionality than in Western Europe or even than that found in many first-past-the-post systems. The average degree of proportionality is only 79 percent, and Slovakia is the one country to approach the degree of proportionality found in Spain. Before the 1993 election in Poland the law was changed to require a party to win a minimum of 5 percent of the national vote to secure PR seats in Parliament. Because a third of the popular vote was cast for parties that failed to reach this threshold, the index of proportionality in Poland was only 66 percent.

Failure to achieve proportionality in post-Communist countries reflects the inexperience of politicians forming parties that have little popular support, and the uncertainties of demobilized voters unsure about which parties are and are not likely to win seats. Larger parties welcome this. In the 1994 Hungarian election, the ex-Communists won an absolute majority of seats with less than a third of the popular vote and after the 1993 election in Poland ex-Communists and Agrarians formed a coalition government with two-thirds of the seats in Parliament, even though together they won only 36 percent of the popular vote.

The pursuit of pure proportionality is like chasing after a will-o'-the-wisp, for no system guarantees complete proportionality. The difference in the average index of proportionality in the PR systems of Western Europe and first-past-the-post systems is 15 percentage points. Moreover, there is some overlap across systems. While no FPTP system is as proportional as the most fine-tuned PR system, the U.S. House of Representatives is as proportional as three West European systems. Moreover, the first elections in post-Communist countries have produced outcomes no more proportional than is normal in FPTP systems.

TRANSLATING SEATS INTO GOVERNMENT

All democratic systems are multiparty systems, and most have more than two parties. In a parliamentary system, the government must have the confidence of a majority of MPs. The only way a single party can be sure to have the confidence of Parliament is if it wins an absolute majority of seats. But this is only likely to happen under very limiting conditions; two parties share the great majority of seats between them, and a first-past-the-post electoral system manufactures a majority for one of them. This is normally the case in Britain. Even before the last election result is declared, the leader of the party winning a majority in the new Parliament is preparing to spend the weekend in the prime minister's home at 10 Downing Street.

There are differences in the number of parties that win seats in PR and FPTP systems. As many as a dozen different parties can win seats in Belgium, the

Netherlands, Spain, and Switzerland. However, simply counting the number of parties in Parliament can be misleading, for many parties are very small. The *effective* number of parties is determined by their relative size (see Laasko and Taagepera, 1979; Sartori, 1976: ch. 4; Mueller-Rommel and Pridham, 1991). In Britain, the presence of nine parties in Parliament is less important than the fact that two parties normally win more than nine-tenths of the seats in the House of Commons. By contrast, in the 1994 election in the Netherlands, no party won as much as one-quarter of the seats.

When no party has an absolute majority, this normally leads to a coalition government. The pact between coalition partners reflects their relative parliamentary strength, the degree of harmony or inconsistency between their policies, and the ambition of individuals and parties for office. Parties opposing each other on a given cleavage, whether class or religion, will find it more difficult to work together in a coalition than parties that emphasize different cleavages. For example, a market-oriented conservative party and a social democratic party would find it difficult to collaborate on economic issues, whereas a Catholic party finds compromise with either party easier because it is ideologically in the middle on economic issues (cf. Bogdanor, 1983; Laver and Schofield, 1990). The formation of a coalition involves bargains about which parties are to be included and how many ministries and which ministries each party gets. Ideological characteristics of parties shape coalition negotiations. An agrarian party would be much more interested in heading the ministry of agriculture than defense, a Catholic party more interested in education and social welfare, and a social democratic party in the ministry of labor (see Budge and Keman, 1990: ch. 6).

If a coalition government is to be sure of the confidence of a majority of MPs, the coalition should command a majority of seats in Parliament. If politicians were opportunists solely motivated by a pursuit of office, then a coalition need consist of no more than 50.1 percent of MPs to be guaranteed a majority. But insofar as coalition government is about creating and maintaining political consensus, a coalition is likely to consist of more than the minimum number of MPs. The number of parties in a coalition varies between countries and even from election to election within a country.

It is not necessary to have the support of parties with a majority of MPs in order to govern; minority governments occur in a number of European countries (Strom, 1990). A government representing a minority of MPs can survive as long as opponents are divided about how to vote on issues of confidence. In Norway and Sweden, social democratic parties benefit from left socialists and communists being loath to combine with right-wing parties to vote against a social democratic minority government. In Denmark, where the party system is highly fragmented, minority government is normal. A positive vote of confidence is not needed to take office in Denmark and a majority vote is required to dismiss a government and put another in its place. Minority governments rely upon what the Danes call a "jumping majority." In 1973 a Liberal government lasted for two years, even though it had only 12 percent of the seats in Parliament. Like an American president facing an opposition Congress, a minority government can carry legislation by introducing bills that attract votes from a shifting majority of MPs; participation in the majority "jumps" from bill to bill.

FIGURE 8.1   TYPES OF MAJORITY AND COALITION GOVERNMENT

(Postwar pattern in 14 countries)

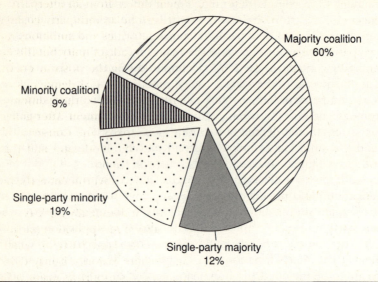

Source: Calculated by the author from Jaap Woldendorp, Hans Keman, and Ian Budge, eds., "Party Government in 20 Democracies," *European Journal of Political Research*, 24, no. 1 (1993): 20–106. Data refer to the whole postwar period in 14 countries examined in Chapter Six; Greece, Portugal, and Spain are excluded because they were not democracies throughout the postwar period.

Across Western Europe, more than two-thirds of governments are majority coalitions with an absolute majority of seats in Parliament (Figure 8.1). Whereas single-party governments hold an average of half the seats in Parliament, coalition governments are supported by an average of three-fifths of MPs. Often, coalition governments have far more than the minimum required for a majority. In Austria, for example, the two largest parties, the Socialists and the People's Party, normally govern together with two-thirds to nine-tenths of the seats in Parliament. More than a quarter of governments have only a minority of votes in Parliament. Single-party minority governments are normally headed by a party that is only a few short of an absolute majority—for example, the Social Democrats in Sweden or Fianna Fail in Ireland. A minority coalition is typical of Denmark, where party fragmentation is high, and it was often found in Italy too, when the Christian Democrats were large enough to be able to command a jumping majority. Single-party government, the norm for Anglo-American theories of party government, is found in only one-eighth of governments in Europe.

Making a Party Government

The simplest form of party government is single-party government. In recent decades only three European countries have had two parties that are each big enough to govern on their own. Britain is the best known example. Greece, even though it holds elections by proportional representation, also has two parties large enough to govern on their own. Even though Spain has many parties, one party has usually been able to win a majority of seats.

By definition, a single-party government differs from an interparty coalition, but the larger the party, the more likely it is to be an intraparty coalition of factions and tendencies with different political priorities and ambitions. A common party label and desire for office can maintain a facade of unity, but this facade can hide major intraparty disputes. For example, during the postwar era the British Labour Party has been divided between moderate social democrats and an aggressively socialist left wing. When the party was in office, these differences were usually repressed for the sake of holding on to government. After going into opposition in 1979, they erupted in a split in the party. The Conservative government of John Major is divided between economic moderates and Thatcherites and between those for and against the European Union.

Alternation between single-party and coalition government is the practice in Norway, Sweden, and Portugal. One party is pivotal; if it does well at an election it is large enough to dominate government and if it does badly there is a vacuum in government that can be filled only by a coalition of opposition parties. In Sweden and Norway social democratic parties are the large party on which government pivots. Even if it does not have an absolute majority, it may count on the backing of small left or ex-Communist parties to support its major policies. The alternative is a "bourgeois" coalition of three or more anti-Socialist parties. In Portugal a nominally Social Democratic party currently holds an absolute majority of seats; there is no comparable unity among its opponents. Among post-Communist countries, Hungary and Bulgaria have each alternated between a government dominated by an ex-Communist party and coalition governments.

A two-party coalition has one dominant party or a balanced partnership. Having only two parties limits the number of party leaders who must be consulted and given places in the cabinet and the compromises that must be made. Germany is a textbook example of a dominant partnership, for the largest party in Parliament, whether the Christian Democrats or Social Democrats, holds more than two-fifths of the seats. To take office, the dominant party strikes a coalition bargain with the Free Democrats, a party with less than a tenth of the seats. Most two-party coalitions are balanced, having parties similar in strength. In France the anti-Socialists are divided into two parties almost equal in size: the Gaullist Republican movement and the more centrist UDF (Union for French Democracy). In Poland ex-Communists and an agrarian party have tried to govern as more or less equal partners.

In a fragmented party system, three or more parties form a big coalition and usually have a majority of votes in Parliament. Big coalitions extend from Finland and Denmark through Belgium, the Netherlands, Switzerland, and Italy to the Czech Republic and Slovakia. The composition of a coalition of three or more parties turns as much on the party left out as on that included: a large coalition may be against the left or against the right or, occasionally, anticlerical. In a big coalition, no one party is likely to dominate the Cabinet.

Empirically, there can be no debate about the relative frequency of single-party as against coalition. Coalition government is the norm. A third of European countries have not known a single-party majority government in the postwar era.

The chief difference between countries is in the size of the governing coalition. A big coalition of three or more parties characterizes six countries (Belgium, Denmark, Finland, Italy, the Netherlands, and Switzerland). In an additional five countries, a two-party coalition is the norm (Austria, France, Germany, Ireland, and Luxembourg). Alternation between coalition or single-party majority government is the rule in Norway, Sweden, and Portugal. Single-party government is found in only three countries (Britain, Greece, and Spain). A free choice of government has not existed long enough in post-Communist countries to establish stable national patterns. One thing is clear: the normal practice is coalition government. Elections are about which parties and how many are necessary to form a coalition.

Competing for Reelection

Participation in government makes a party more prominent. Whether governing parties are more likely to win or lose the next election is affected by what happens while they are in the spotlight. One familiar theory is that incumbency is a liability, because government faces tough problems and must make hard and sometimes unpopular decisions. The alternative theory is that governing parties can use control of office to increase their vote by manipulating the economy to appear favorable at election time (the "political business cycle") or by exploiting the assets of office, such as media publicity (cf. Katz and Mair, 1995).

When the government of the day faces the electorate, two-thirds of the time its vote goes down. This is true for both single-party governments and coalitions (Rose and Mackie, 1983: 117 ff.; updated by the authors). This tendency is not due to economic recessions condemning parties to lose support, for it is evident in periods of economic boom as well as periods of gloom.

The arithmetic of competition is very different when there is a coalition government. Whereas in a two-party system any increase in the share of votes of one party decreases the share of the other, in a party system with half a dozen or more parties, two-thirds can see their votes go down and a third rise or vice versa. Furthermore, in a multiparty system, even if a party's vote remains the same in aggregate, it can simultaneously win votes from one direction while losing support in another.

When several parties form a coalition government, electoral competition is not only a contest between a government and opposition party but also a contest in which governing parties *jostle* with each other for votes. The outcome of a general election can see all coalition partners win votes, all lose votes, or jostling can result in one coalition partner's vote going up while another's goes down. In 64 percent of postwar elections, some coalition partners saw their vote rise while that of other coalition partners fell. In a third of contests, all the coalition partners had their vote fall. It is very rare for all partners in a coalition to have their vote rise.

Losing votes does not mean that the governing parties lose office. Parties hold office because they win more seats than their opponents; hence, they normally enter an election with seats surplus to a majority. When some coalition partners gain seats and others lose seats, there may be no change in support for the coalition overall. Even if a governing party loses votes and seats, it can still hold onto enough to retain a majority against its opponents. In a coalition, if one party does badly, it may be dropped from the coalition and another added in its place. The most common postelection outcome in a coalition system is that all the parties in government remain in office; this occurs in 46 percent of coalition elections. Second is a coalition reshuffle, in which some partners remain in office and others leave. The least likely election outcome, occurring after 15 percent of elections, is that all partners in the coalition lose office.

Coalition governments do not fit Schumpeter's model of democratic accountability through competition between a clearly identified governing and opposition party. Voters are offered a choice of half a dozen or more parties that might participate in a coalition government. Even if an election causes a breakup in the governing coalition, the next coalition is likely to have in it some parties that have also participated in the outgoing government.

HOW MUCH COMPETITION FOR OFFICE?

Each election gives some parties a share in government and leaves others in opposition. Hence, at any one point in time some voters are not represented by the government of the day. If all voters are to be represented in government at least some of the time, there must be alternation of parties in office. A party system in which one party always won would assume attributes of a one-party state. It could even lead opposition parties to engage in extraparliamentary opposition, as happened in Northern Ireland, where a Protestant majority in the electorate always produced a Unionist government until street demonstrations and killings led to the suspension of its elected Parliament in 1972.

Competition or Monopoly?

The critical question for democracy is whether a series of elections results in sufficient changes of government over a period of time to prevent one party or group of parties from having a monopoly of office. There is no hard and fast measure of how much is "enough" alternation between governing parties. Over a quarter century we would expect democratic competition to reward each of the two largest parties in the system with substantial periods in office, and neither party to be in office all the time. A review of the past quarter century of party competition in Europe shows a variety of patterns, the great majority of which are competitive (Table 8.4).

In six countries *two-party competition* occurs. In Britain, the classic model, the government of the day has three times been turned out of office by the electorate. The relatively long tenure of the Conservatives has not been due to unfairness in the system but by the British Labour Party veering to the left for a decade. In 1983 it produced an election manifesto later described by one of the party's leaders as "the longest suicide note in history." In Germany power has alternated almost equally between the two largest parties too. Notwithstanding recent experience of authoritarianism and regime change, Greece, Portugal, and Spain have also changed office between two big parties. France and Germany are distinctive in a third party participating in government for a significant time too.

TABLE 8.4 UNION OF FRENCH DEMOCRACY

Parties by % vote:	Biggest	Second	Third
		(number of years in office, 1968–1992)	
Two-Party Competition			
Britain	Conservative 18	Labour 7	Liberal 0
Germany	Christian 12	Social Democrat 15	Free Democrat 23
France	Gaullist 15	Union of France Democratic 15	Socialist 10
Spain*	Socialist 12	Popular 7	Communist 0
Portugal**	Social Democrat 12	Socialist 7	Center 5
Greece*	New Democrat 12	Socialist 9	Communist 1
Competing Coalitions			
Norway	Social Democrat 16	Conservative 8	Christian Center 8
Sweden	Social Democrat 18	Moderate 6	Liberal 7
Denmark	Social Democrat 12	Conservative 14	Liberal 16
Ireland	Fianna Fail 16	Fine Gael 12	Labour 10
Luxembourg	Catholic 21	Socialist 15	Liberal 15
Netherlands	Christian 25	Labour 8	Liberal 18
Belgium†	Catholic 25	Socialist 13	Liberal 11
Monopolistic Tendency			
Italy‡	Catholic 25	Communist 0	Socialist 16
Austria	Socialist 23	Peoples 8	Freedom 4
Finland	Center 20	Social Democrat 24	Swedish 23 National 6
Monopoly			
Switzerland	Liberal 25	Social Democrat 25	Catholic 25 Peoples 25

*Democratic elections for 19 years of this period in Spain and Greece.

**Democratic elections for 18 years of this period in Portugal.

†All groups include both Flemish and French parties.

‡Party system collapsed before 1994 election.

Sources: Calculated by the author principally from Jan-Erik Lane et al., eds., *Political Data Handbook: OECD Countries* (Oxford: Oxford University Press, 1991); T.T. Mackie and R. Rose, *International Almanac of Electoral History* (Washington, DC: CQ Press, 1991).

There is *competition between coalitions* in seven countries. In three Scandinavian countries social democrats are the pivot. If the party does well in an election, it holds office on its own or dominates a coalition. The alternative is an anti-Socialist coalition, usually led by a conservative party. In Ireland a decision about coalition pivots on the Fianna Fail party, but the alternative, a coalition government led by Fine Gael, is based on historical differences about Irish unity rather than on class differences. In the Benelux countries Christian parties are the pivot of coalition government, as each is big enough to make it difficult to be excluded from office. The alternative coalitions thus are a Christian-Social Democratic bloc that excludes the conventional pro-business parties, or a Christian-bourgeois coalition that excludes the pro-trade union parties. In such circumstances a party that is third in size may spend more time in government as a partner of the biggest party than does the second-largest party.

A party that is almost always in office shows *monopolistic* tendencies. In the quarter century under review, the Italian Christian Democrats were always the largest party in Parliament and held most positions in the cabinet. Italian coalitions differed in the Christian Democrats' choice of partners. But corruption scandals have broken the Christian Democratic Party; its successor, the Popular Party, went into opposition in 1994, when a new era of competitive coalitions appears to have emerged. In Austria, the Socialist Party has held office almost continuously since 1970, governing on its own for 13 years, in a coalition with the Freedom Party before it turned extremist, and since 1986 in coalition with the second largest party, the Catholic People's Party. In Finland, the fragmentation of parties requires the formation of coalitions with numerous parties; thus, three Finnish parties have been in office for at least four-fifths of the period.

Switzerland is unique in that government is in the hands of a *monopolistic cartel*. Four parties—liberal, social democratic, Catholic, and a centrist agrarian group—have formed a coalition government after every election since 1959. After the 1995 election the four parties collectively held 81 percent of the seats. The monopoly is an extreme example of consensus government, requiring agreement between all the major groups—economic, religious, and linguistic—that go to make up Switzerland (cf. Kerr, 1987: 124 ff.). The cartel can claim approval by a big majority of voters; those who want a change are left to vote for a variety of small protest parties seeking to represent ecologists, motorists, fundamentalist Protestants, and so forth.

Exclusion is the complement of monopoly. Among more than a hundred parties winning a significant share of the vote in the past quarter century, only two have been excluded from office for the whole period. In Italy, Communists were excluded because of the extreme polarization in Italian politics during the Cold War and the ability of the Christian Democrats to make shifting alliances with other parties, including social democrats. The British Liberal Democrats have been excluded from office because the party wins few seats in the British first-past-the-post electoral system (see again Table 8.1, p. 158). The Liberals' solution, the adoption of proportional representation, would exchange underrepresentation in government for overrepresentation, because the centrist Liberal Democrats would hope to be the perennial coalition partner of either a Conservative or Labour prime minister, as the Free Democrats have done in Germany.

Overall, the dominant pattern of government in Europe is alternation in office between a social democratic and religious party or, in the absence of a religious cleavage, between a social democratic and an economically conservative and pro-market liberal party. At any one election, the multiparty systems of Europe offer voters a far wider choice of parties than is available in the United States. This is even true of the election of the president in France. The leading candidates do not trail around the provinces of France seeking support in local primaries nor do they emerge from a party caucus. The president is elected after two ballots. In the first ballot many candidates can enter; the second ballot is a run off between the two candidates with the most votes in the first. In the 1995 French presidential election, nine candidates divided the vote. In the first ballot the "winner," Lionel Jospin, a Socialist, had only 23 percent of the vote. The runner-up, Jacques Chirac, with 21 percent of the vote, eliminated from the runoff the prime minister, Edouard Balladur, who finished third with 19 percent. In the second round contest between Jospin and Chirac, Chirac was able to win by forming an anti-Socialist alliance.

European voters are likely to have their views represented in government because coalition governments are based on parties with differing views and command more popular votes than does the normal single-party government. The reshuffling of coalitions and alternations in control of government results in almost every party with ten percent of the vote spending a significant period of time in government. Only Switzerland might be described as an exclusive "cartel" of parties. In the course of time small changes in votes lead to changes in the coalition controlling government. In post-Communist countries there has not been time to establish long-term patterns. In place of the monopoly that the Communist Party enjoyed for four decades, today dozens of parties compete for votes, and the chief complaint about coalition governments (cf. Holmes, 1995) is that they represent too many conflicting views.

chapter 9

LEADERSHIP AND ACCOUNTABILITY

Every government consists of leaders and followers; a democracy is distinctive because leaders are meant to be accountable to followers. Accountability is most evident in a general election. It can also be exercised by members of Parliament questioning or voting no confidence in the government of the day. Successful political leaders internalize the sense of accountability. Before taking decisions, they ask: Who will support what I propose to do? How can I convince others to do what I would like done?

In a parliamentary system, effective leadership rests with the prime minister and the cabinet. Collectively, this small group of politicians is responsible for what is done by the government of the day. Individual cabinet members are ministers in charge of ministries or departments of state, such as finance, foreign affairs, welfare, and industry. The prime minister has a unique position as the chair of the cabinet; this makes him or her first among equals in government. The prime minister and cabinet are not directly elected; they hold office only as long as they retain the confidence of a majority of MPs. In France, which has a strong directly elected president, relations with the president are also important.

Parliament is a representative assembly; its members individually and collectively voice popular demands and criticisms of the government of the day. MPs tend to be closer to the views of ordinary voters than cabinet ministers, for they are not caught up in the responsibilities and routines of running a government department. Doing so makes ministers aware of the difficulties of implementing popular demands voiced by MPs. There is inevitably tension between MPs voicing demands about what government ought to do and ministers responsible for what government can do.

Accountability is the link joining Parliament and cabinet. The cabinet must regularly account for its actions to Parliament. The cabinet can expect a sympathetic hearing from MPs who belong to the party or parties forming the government. But parliamentary sympathy can be withdrawn if the government makes a mess of policies, or if a minister is unconvincing in defending a controversial policy in Parliament, forcing a minister or even the prime minister to resign and leading to the formation, without a general election, of a new cabinet capable of maintaining the confidence of Parliament. The interests and ambitions that bind together coalitions are shifting too. A cabinet can collapse by losing the confidence of Parliament.

The combination of collective cabinet government *and* accountability to a popularly elected Parliament is a distinctive feature of parliamentary democracy. The prime minister is not the chief executive officer of government, but the captain of a cabinet team in which every member is expected and expects to make a contribution. Parliament cannot make government decisions but, unlike Washington, the legislature can dismiss the executive by withdrawing confidence. The link pulls two ways: MPs loyal to their party will vote for a particular government bill that is disliked by themselves and their constituents if voting against the bill would result in their party losing office. By contrast, the absence of accountability to the electorate through Parliament was a hallmark of Communist systems; the government was accountable to the party, not the people, in accord with the Marxist-Leninist doctrine of "democratic centralism" (Roeder, 1993).

Today, many people may think that the prime minister is powerful because she or he represents the government on television. But the political behavior of a prime minister is subject to the constraints of office. Many constraints are institutional, thus accounting for significant differences between countries in the capacity for leadership. Hence, the first section of this chapter examines the office and roles of the prime minister and cabinet colleagues. The second section outlines the functions of Parliament: to represent voters and constituencies; to revise but not make laws; and to hold the executive accountable and if very dissatisfied to dismiss the prime minister and cabinet without a general election. Post-Communist countries have established parliamentary forms of government similar to Western Europe. However, the regimes there have not yet had time to institutionalize procedures. This is shown by tensions between prime ministers and heads of state and Parliament. Furthermore, as the third section emphasizes, given the legacy of the past, most post-Communist voters today reject the idea of a strong leader; they want most power in the hands of a representative Parliament.

PRIME MINISTERS AND CABINET COLLEAGUES

At the top of government is a head of state. In a modern monarchy, a king or queen is the hereditary head of state but not the head of government; this is the job of a prime minister accountable to Parliament. Eight European countries have a hereditary monarch: Denmark, Norway, Sweden, the three Benelux countries, Britain, and Spain. Most European states are a republic with a president as the ceremonial head of state. In Germany, Greece, and Italy, the presidency is filled by a legislative vote. In Switzerland the office rotates annually among members of the Federal Cabinet. The president is popularly elected in five states: Austria, Finland, France, Ireland, and Portugal.

Today, the monarch's role is primarily symbolic. In a democratic era, gaining office by accident of birth is a handicap greatly limiting political influence; elected politicians are aware of this. Scandinavian monarchs are symbols of modern ways of living, riding bicycles and undertaking everyday pursuits. The Belgian king is a symbol of national unity in a country in which the primary identity of individuals is to their language community, Walloon or Flemish. The president of the Republic of Ireland is a symbol of the country's independence from the British Crown. In Northern Ireland the British queen is a positive symbol to British Protestants and a negative symbol to Catholics who want a united Ireland. A king or queen who is involved in politics becomes a divisive symbol, and risks the repudiation of the monarchy. Many former monarchies have become republics because a particular monarch became involved in political controversy. Since the end of World War II, national referendums in Greece and Italy have dismissed monarchs in favor of a republic (Rose and Kavanagh, 1976).

The constitution can authorize a head of state to undertake limited political functions. In countries where democratic institutions have been introduced after dictatorship, the head of state can be a protector of the integrity of the constitution. In Germany, the power to decree an emergency in the event of a crisis rests with the president of the Federal Republic, not the prime minister (Dalton, 1993: 65 ff.). The German president also has a moral role to play, reminding Germans of the crimes of Hitler's Reich, and offering assurance to its victims that Germany has changed. As the head of the regime replacing the Franco dictatorship, the Spanish king, Juan Carlos, mobilized support for the new democratic constitution. Right-wing opponents had difficulty in campaigning for an authoritarian regime against a King who supported democracy (cf. Hermet, 1988). The head of state may appoint a person to negotiate the formation of a coalition. In Italy the president of the republic may be directly involved in the search for a politician who can put together a coalition government (see Laver and Schofield, 1990: 64, 208 ff.). The president of Finland also has foreign policy responsibilities.

France is unique in giving a directly elected president a major role in government. The president is elected for a fixed seven-year term independent of the National Assembly. The Fifth Republic's Constitution gives the president powers in foreign affairs, the authority to appoint the prime minister and senior civil servants and the right to call referendums and a parliamentary election. Moreover, the Constitution gives the executive branch far more power to impose its views on a reluctant Parliament than is available in other parliamentary systems. Since the vote is fragmented between many parties, the president can claim to be president of "all the people." As long as the president and the majority of MPs belong to the same coalition of parties, the president heads a stable majority government and the prime minister and cabinet have less authority. But since parliamentary elections must be held every four years, these sometimes produce divided government. The constitution forces the president and prime minister to live together (*cohabitation*)—but they do so uneasily (Hayward, 1993).

Prime Ministers: Office, Role, and Personal Inclinations

The accountable leader of government is described in English as the prime minister or premier, emphasizing that he or she ranks first in government. The titles used in other languages differ; for example, the German and Austrian premiers are called chancellor. In Ireland, the head is the *Taoiseach;* the word means chief, an image from days of clan leadership. In Spain the premier's title can be translated as president of the government.

The office exists before a particular individual enters it, and remains after each departs. It confers powers and responsibilities, and it also institutionalizes constraints. A prime minister is not chosen to govern as she or he would like, but to lead within the law and the expectations of party, cabinet colleagues, and Parliament.

The importance of individual personality tends to be exaggerated. Most students of politics are familiar with big names such as Konrad Adenauer, Charles de Gaulle and Margaret Thatcher. But few remember the "little names" of politics, such as Kurt-Georg Kiesinger (German chancellor, 1966–1969), Alain Poher (acting president of France for three months in 1969), or Sir Alec Douglas-Home (prime minister of Britain for a year in the early 1960s). In Italy dozens of politicians have been prime minister since 1945, many several times. The holder of the post is not only identified by name but also by number, such as Fanfani III or Andreotti VI. Even if a politician succeeds in being prime minister for many years, he or she does not thereby become a well-known leader. Few Europeans would recognize the name of Pierre Werner, prime minister of Luxembourg for 20 years, or Pierre Dupong, prime minister for 11 years.

A prime minister has three major responsibilities. The first is party leadership, a necessary condition of gaining office. The second—managing a cabinet—is a condition of keeping office. The third is to influence policy, including hard choices on which the government's fate stands or falls.

Party is both a resource and a constraint. The support of a party enables an individual to become prime minister. The need to keep the party, or a coalition of parties, satisfied with his or her performance is a constraint. MPs almost always owe their place in Parliament to party endorsement rather than individual vote-getting efforts. To gain office, an ambitious politician must spend years working in the ranks of the party. In Britain, many leaders start their career by becoming an officer in a university Conservative or Labour club. This gives experience in public speaking and also in committee intrigues. After 10 to 20 years as an active party member, a person may be selected by a constituency to stand for Parliament where the party has a big majority. In a PR system, an individual enters Parliament by having her or his name placed high on its candidate list. In Germany each party offers two routes to the top: service in the federal Parliament in Bonn and in *Land* (regional) governments; the average German leader spends 20 years in a combination of such offices before heading government. For most of his or her political career, an aspiring prime minister is disciplined by the party rather than cracking the whip over it (see Rose, 1991b: ch. 6).

A party usually chooses its leader at a convention or a parliamentary caucus in which the views of party workers matter most. The choice is not made through American-style primaries in which everyone in the electorate is eligible to vote. To rise toward the top, an aspiring MP must be recognized as skillful by senior politicians in the party, display an understanding or aptitude for problems of government, and be popular with workers in the party organization outside Parliament. A quarter-century or more of work in the party makes party members aware of the strengths and weaknesses of candidates for the party leadership.

In the multiparty politics of Europe, election campaigning is less significant than in the American presidential system. The logic of a PR ballot encourages voters to cast their vote for parties not individuals. The prime minister is not chosen by the national electorate but by the party or parties that form the cabinet. Since most governments are coalitions, the breakup of a coalition rather than election defeat is the immediate threat to a prime minister's hold on office.

The media's need to personalize stories and the desire of the prime minister to promote himself or herself as indispensable produces publicity. But publicity cuts two ways. When the government appears successful, the prime minister is usually popular, but when it is unsuccessful, the prime minister is unpopular and there is intense media speculation about the governing party or coalition withdrawing confidence (see Rose, 1991b: ch. 13). The speculation is fueled by the concern of MPs that an unpopular leader may cause the party to lose seats at the next election; it is also stimulated by ambitious politicians who hope to succeed to the prime ministership. In Britain a prime minister is equally likely to lose office because of a loss of confidence by the governing party or through a general election.

Managing the cabinet is essential to remain in office. Making a cabinet is a political art, for there is intense rivalry between individuals, factions, and party leaders about who gets what jobs. A prime minister's task is to create a coalition broad enough to ensure the support of a majority in Parliament. Even if a majority of MPs belong to a single party, a prime minister must still dispense patronage carefully in order to balance different factions and interests within the party. The power to appoint and dismiss cabinet ministers gives a prime minister influence on the careers of ministerial colleagues.

Patronage is the glue that holds a government together, for those who enjoy office have a stake in maintaining it. Countries differ in the patronage powers of a prime minister. In Britain, the prime minister has the unchallenged right to appoint and dismiss a hundred members of the majority party in Parliament to posts as ministers. In making cabinet appointments a prime minister aims first to include some potential enemies to prevent them publicly attacking the government of the day, for the convention of collective responsibility binds a cabinet minister not to express disagreement in public. Second, the prime minister must have some colleagues who are personally loyal or dependent on him or her, thus ensuring support for the leader's position in cabinet. A third consideration is representativeness in terms of gender or region. Margaret Thatcher entered a Conservative cabinet as the token woman in an all-male cabinet—and then demonstrated she was twice the politician of her cabinet colleagues.

Competence is a final consideration. A prime minister who believes the government's reputation stands or falls on economic success cannot afford to have an incompetent minister of finance. To put the direction of government in the hands of experts, a French president may name senior civil servants to ministerial posts, including that of prime minister. An MP who takes a ministerial job must resign from Parliament; this then makes the minister depend upon the president or prime minister for their place in national politics.

In the formation of a coalition government of three or more parties, the prime ministership can be one of the jobs up for grabs in negotiations. In the Netherlands, the Dutch prime minister has no power to appoint or to dismiss ministers. Each party in the coalition decides which individuals will represent it in the cabinet (Andeweg, 1991). In Italy, the prime ministership is offered to a politician on condition that he accepts a prearranged sharing out of posts in the cabinet (cf. Hine and Finocchi, 1991).

Politicians named to ministerial office often have multiple qualifications. The most important is party. More than five-sixths of ministers have been a member of Parliament, elected to a regional government, or held a party office. In a quarter of cases, ministers have started their career in policy making as a civil servant, and then transferred to electoral politics in order to lead from the top rather than give advice from behind the ministerial chair. In some countries up to half the ministers have been officers of interest groups such as trade unions or business associations, giving them strong ties with groups affected by the ministry they head (see Blondel and Thiebault, 1991: 181 ff.). The presence in the cabinet of ministers who have had two careers provides a mixture of political and subject-matter expertise.

When individuals hold office as party representatives, they can be more secure than the prime minister. The tendency of parties to "capture" particular ministries closest to their interests means that a particular minister need have little fear of losing office if a coalition collapses. The average cabinet minister is in office more than half again as long as the average prime minister. In countries such as Italy where prime ministerial turnover is high, a cabinet minister can be in office more than three times as long as the prime minister (see Blondel and Thiebault, 1991: 120). Ministers may welcome the collapse of a cabinet if it offers opportunities for promotion, including the prospect of becoming prime minister.

To be more than a passenger on the ship of state, a prime minister must influence *policy*. As the only member of the cabinet who can speak for the government as a whole, a prime minister has a special role to play in foreign relations, negotiating with other heads of government at meetings of the European Union and with Washington. International dealings are usually welcomed by prime ministers, as they are issues of major importance and expand their potential for deciding in intergovernmental negotiations what they think is in the national interest. Problems crop up in national politics that require a statement when there is not time for a cabinet to deliberate. In such circumstances, the prime minister can speak on behalf of the government as a whole. Usually, the prime minister will consult with ministerial colleagues with the most knowledge and political involvement in the problem area.

Being on top of government is a liability because there is not time enough in the day for a prime minister to keep informed about all the affairs of state from agriculture through justice to social security. Furthermore, there are cabinet ministers concentrating full time on each of these policy areas. In a coalition government, a prime minister often lacks the political clout to intervene in a ministry headed by an important politician in another party. Noninvolvement is sometimes an advantage, for when things go wrong—for example, if there is an airplane crash or corruption is uncovered—the prime minister can be insulated from responsibility and let the minister responsible take the blame.

The limits of time compel a prime minister to practice "management by exception." Exceptional issues are those that determine a government's political fate; a prime minister wants to make decisions that can decide whether or not he or she stays in office. The decision may be of major importance to the country as a whole—for example, whether to give priority to reducing inflation or unemployment. Or the problem can be a matter of internal cabinet politics—for example, a clash of personalities between two leading cabinet ministers.

To be effective in policy making a prime minister must act in a politically favorable environment (see Rose, 1991a: 21 f.). In smaller European democracies a leader's best hope of being effective is to address issues that are domestic, such as education, rather than international trade, which is largely determined over the national government's head by what happens in the international economy. If a prime minister takes initiatives while ignoring the prevailing political environment, he or she is vulnerable as an unfavorable environment can frustrate initiatives. For example, when the French Socialist Party took office in 1981 it enacted left-wing economic policies to promote economic growth and full employment. Because these measures went against the prevailing trends in the international economy, the initiative was abandoned. Some prime ministers see environmental constraints as leaving little scope for action. In such circumstances, a prime minister may wait until the environment is favorable in order to appear successful as a free rider on events. However, when the environment is unfavorable, doing nothing has risks. A prime minister who does not react positively to growing signs of national dissatisfaction is likely to leave office a political failure.

The career of Winston Churchill illustrates how changes in the policy environment sometimes make an individual appear a failure and sometimes an effective leader. Following a brilliant early career, Churchill fell out with the dominant Conservative Party leadership after 1929 because he espoused causes that they rejected, such as the maintenance of the British Empire in India and rearmament against Hitler. Many MPs feared that the unpredictable Churchill might break up the Conservative Party. But because Churchill was right about Hitler's threat, the prospect of Nazi invasion, and Britain under siege in 1940, after years in the political wilderness he was seen as the one person who could succeed (cf. Kavanagh, 1974).

Constraints of Cabinet Collegiality

The logic of cabinet government is collegial government—that is, policy making by a small, face-to-face body with no single member dominating. Collegiality brings together many minds and many interests. Collegiality also imposes constraints. A prime minister cannot be described by the American corporate title of chief executive officer. The authority to execute laws is usually vested in government departments and their ministers or in the cabinet. When the prime minister chairs the cabinet, he or she is dealing with about 20 individuals, each of whom has considerable detailed knowledge about the policy area for which their department is responsible, and some of whom also have considerable influence in party matters. Even though each minister may individually be a lesser political figure than the prime minister, collectively they are a big obstacle to prime ministerial government.

Switzerland represents the extreme in collegial government. Since only one person can hold the top post at a time, the presidency of the Federal Council, the post equivalent to the prime minister, rotates each year between the four parties that have governed Switzerland in coalition for generations. The coalition reflects a Swiss desire for consensus through sharing representation among different religious, linguistic, and economic interests. A cabinet minister usually retains the same post until he or she reaches retirement age. The result is a high degree of continuity and consultation between politicians who have no choice but to govern together (see Baylis, 1989: ch. 2).

The limits of time prevent a cabinet from reviewing all the problems of government when a dozen or two dozen ministers meet together only a few hours a week. Most business is done in cabinet committees or informal caucuses of ministers who are partisan allies or have common interests about an issue (cf. Mackie and Hogwood, 1985). In Sweden ministers meet for lunch daily without civil servants or an agenda to discuss issues confronting them. The pressures of work, including international travel, have reduced attendance at lunches but they remain important for informal coordination on political matters (Larsson, 1994: 173 f.).

The cabinet's importance is due less to what is decided at meetings and more to what is decided between meetings by individuals who enjoy political influence because they have their hands on major departments of state and the political backing of their party. Each minister is a politician with his or her own ideas, interests, and ambitions. Within a department, an individual cabinet minister has more time and authority than in a collective meeting, and detailed knowledge about policies provided by expert civil servants in the bureaus into which a ministry is divided. But since a minister's time is limited, he or she can expect to initiate only a handful of new policies during the life of a Parliament. Some do not even try, relying upon civil servants and interest groups to negotiate consensus policies for which they can take credit as free riders (cf. Headey, 1974).

In a coalition government the division of ministries between parties strengthens the tendency to view problems as narrowly specialized. Ministries such as agriculture and defense have little in common with each other (cf. Rose, 1987). A minister of industry will tend to identify with business, and disagree with proposals from the minister of labor. When ministers see their political careers depending upon success in promoting their own ministry's interests, this intensifies conflicts. Ministries are joined together by conflicts about government policies—for example, disputes between the finance ministry and big-spending social welfare ministries about whether priority should be given to social programs or tax cuts.

Striking a balance between competing policies is a unique responsibility of a prime minister, for she or he has a much broader view of government than any individual minister. The German Constitution seeks to formalize this responsibility by authorizing the chancellor to set general guidelines for policy while assigning each cabinet minister full personal responsibility for departmental policies (Mayntz, 1980). In the business of government, the line between the two responsibilities is drawn by politicians, not lawyers.

Collegiality is a matter of degree, and it varies within a country and from issue to issue. At any given moment, relations between a prime minister and his or her colleagues in the cabinet depend upon the issue at hand; the interests in play; the political strength or weakness of ministers and parties in a coalition; and individual personalities. There is no point in debating whether the realities of parliamentary government reflect prime ministerial rule, cabinet government, party government, or civil service dominance (cf. Laver and Shepsle, 1994); the critical issue is: Under what circumstances and to what extent is each important?

Differences in the Political Roles of Prime Ministers

Even though every government has a single head, differences in formal and informal political institutions influence what a prime minister can and must do. Being at the center of government is important only if government is centralized, and if the office at the center is able to exercise influence that can overcome the pressures directed at the center. The first major factor affecting the prime ministership is whether or not there is a coalition government. A second factor is whether or not the institutions of government are centralized—for example, whether they are unitary or federal. Combining these two dimensions produces a fourfold typology of alternative prime ministerial roles (see Rose, 1991a: 19). Because these characteristics are persisting institutional features of a political system, cross-national differences are greater than within-country differences arising from variability in the personalities and political goals of individual incumbents of the prime ministership.

- *Centralized leader:* In Greece the centralization of authority inherent in single-party government of a unitary state is further strengthened by the legal and institutional powers of the prime minister, harking back to an earlier era of dictatorship (Koutsukis, 1994: 274). A similar concentration of authority in theory gives a British prime minister exceptional scope for action, but a tradition of collegiality and consensus makes it unusual for this potential to be exploited. Margaret Thatcher was unusual, and controversial within her own cabinet, because she wanted to lead from the top rather than to consult.
- *Bargainer:* If one party dominates government, a prime minister can use the powers of office to take initiatives, but the outcome of an initiative reflects a process of bargaining rather than command and control. In Norway, for example, a Social Democratic prime minister is engaged in incessant discussions with politicians who have important positions in the party organs that have placed him in the most important formal post within a unitary state (Olsen, 1980: ch. 6). Because one party dominates coalition government in Germany, the chancellor is in a relatively strong position when bargaining with other political leaders in a federal system. Helmut Kohl is a German chancellor who has excelled in *Kuhhandel* (Dealing in cows, the German word for horse-trading).
- *Juggler:* In a broad multiparty government a prime minister must keep all parties together; if one is dropped the coalition falls apart. In such circumstances, a prime minister must devote lots of time to juggling the elements of a fragmented coalition. This can be true even if power is formally centralized. In authoritarian Spain, General Franco was nominally a

dictator, but he was compelled to juggle the influence of the army, the Catholic church, and the fascist Falange Party (see Alba, 1980). The Netherlands is formally a unitary state but fragmented coalitions give the prime minister virtually no influence on individual ministers and little on cabinet discussions (Andeweg, 1991).

- *Symbol:* A prime minister with little or no influence on government departments is a figurehead. Italian prime ministers have usually been condemned to such a role because of the institutional weakness of the office and political vulnerability as a leader of fragile coalitions. In Switzerland the annual rotation of the office of prime minister symbolizes the country's commitment to collective consensus under a symbolic leader (cf. Steiner and Dorff, 1980).

PARLIAMENT: REPRESENTATION AND ACCOUNTABILITY

The prime function of Parliament in a democracy is to represent the diverse views of society to the cabinet; it does not itself govern. The word *parliament* derives from the old French word for speaking. It is apt, for Parliament is often described as a talking shop. It might even be described as a shopping mall, so diverse are the parties and interests that set out their views there. A second function of Parliament is holding the government of the day accountable; it has the power to dismiss government by withdrawing confidence. A third function, law-making, is relatively unimportant, for laws are drafted by administrators in ministries, which is where experts and interest groups concentrate their lobbying.

Multiple Representation

The simplest form of democratic representation would be a Parliament with a single chamber to which MPs are elected on the basis of one person, one vote, one value. However, unicameral (that is, single-chamber) Parliaments are found in less than half the countries of Western Europe; all of these countries are small in population and have a relatively uncomplicated social structure (Table 9.1). Formally, single-chamber Parliaments appear close to the voters, for they average less than 25,000 electors per MP. However, since these countries use proportional representation with multimember districts, MPs often do not represent a constituency in which they know many voters personally. MPs see themselves as representing a party or functional interest, such as farmers, churchgoers, or schoolteachers, rather than a geographical district.

The majority of Parliaments have two chambers representing different political constituencies. The lower house is always popularly elected; the second chamber or upper house is usually *not* popularly elected. Popular election makes the lower house more important politically. The upper chamber usually represents regions and in federal states regions have significant political powers in their own right. The German upper chamber, the *Bundesrat,* consists of members appointed by the governments of each *Land* (the German equivalent of American states); until early in the twentieth century, American senators were similarly chosen by the legislature of each state. Because *Land* representation is territorially based, the difference in the number of Bundestag members, from three to six, does not reflect interregional differences in population as great as 25 to 1 between Bremen and North Rhine-Westphalia. In Switzerland and Spain the great majority of members of the upper house are popularly elected by region; the number of representatives is determined by administrative geography, not by the population.

The Irish Senate is unique among upper houses in having members chosen to represent five functional interests in society: agriculture and fishing; labor; industry and commerce; public administration; language, culture and literature. Members are chosen from separate lists by an electoral college of members of the lower chamber, the Senate, and local government. In addition, university graduates elect six members and the prime minister appoints eleven senators. The

TABLE 9.1   THE STRUCTURE OF PARLIAMENTS

Unicameral (Single Chamber)	Number of MPs	Electors per MP	Women as % MPs
Denmark	175	23,000	33
Finland	200	20,000	34
Greece	300	26,000	6
Luxembourg	60	3,600	20
Norway	165	20,000	39
Portugal	230	31,000	9
Sweden	349	12,000	40

Bicameral (Two Chambers)	Lower Chamber			Upper Chamber	
	Number of MPs	Electors per MP	Women as % MPs	Number of members	How chosen
Austria	183	29,000	21	64	Regions
Belgium	150	47,000	12	71	Ethnic regions: co-option
Britain	651	66,000	9	1183	Hereditary; nominated
France	577	64,000	6	321	Regions
Germany	672	91,000	26	79	Regions
Ireland	166	14,000	12	60	Nominated; corporatist
Italy	630	73,000	15	315	Elected
Netherlands	150	71,000	31	75	Region
Spain	350	83,000	16	256	Regional elections
Switzerland	200	21,000	18	46	Regional elections

Sources: Adapted from T. T. Mackie and Richard Rose, *International Almanac of Electoral History* (Washington, DC: CQ Press, 1991). Women MPs: Inter-Parliamentary Union, *Women in Parliament, 1945–1995* (Geneva: IPU, 1995).

British House of Lords is unique in retaining a feature of predemocratic assemblies of estates of the king's realm: individuals who inherit a title such as duke, earl or lord can sit there. In the past generation the House of Lords has added men and women nominated as peers or peeresses for life on the basis of their own achievements, including service to the governing party. The hereditary basis of the chamber makes it weaker than the House of Commons.

The rise of feminism has introduced a new issue, the representation of women. Even though women are now a majority in the electorate in every European country, relatively few women are MPs. Instead of organizing a separate political party, feminist groups have lobbied established parties to increase the number of women candidates given winnable positions on the ballot. Throughout Europe, the representation of women in Parliament is increasing from its very low base, and some parties are taking special measures to promote women candidates. Very striking cross-national differences remain between countries (see again Table 9.1). In four Scandinavian countries women on average constitute 36 percent of MPs, whereas in Britain only 9 percent are women and in France 6 percent.

What explains this great variation in the representation of women? A multivariate statistical analysis identifies institutional and sociocultural obstacles to more women gaining seats in Parliament (Figure 9.1; Rule, 1987). The single most important influence upon the election of women is the use of the party list in proportional representation systems. Because it requires party headquarters to rank candidates in order of priority for claiming seats, centralization effectively enables a party to determine most of the individuals who represent it. A party can use gender as an important factor in deciding the placement of individuals on the list, and even take affirmative action to place women high on the list to reduce past underrepresentation. By contrast, in single-member first-past-the-post districts on the British model, candidate selection is decentralized. Local parties usually prefer to adopt male candidates and national party headquarters do not want to impose their own choice. In order to increase the representation of women, the British Labour Party is currently trying to resolve the dilemma between local choice and national party direction by negotiating agreements with constituencies to exclude men from the short list of prospective candidates interviewed at the local selection conference.

Germany offers a particularly good illustration of the importance of the electoral system for the representation of women, since it elects some MPs by single-member districts and some by the party list method of proportional representation. Four times as many women are elected on the party lists as are chosen by single-member districts. Similarly, in France MPs are elected from single-member districts and are overwhelmingly male, whereas French members of the European Parliament are elected by proportional representation and 30 percent are women.

The socioeconomic position of women in a society also influences chances of gaining seats in Parliament. In countries in which women are more active in the labor force they are also more likely to become MPs. High labor force participation is also linked with full employment in a society. Just as educated men have a better chance of becoming MPs than uneducated men, so too the level of education of women helps raise the number of women MPs. Ideological and cultural

FIGURE 9.1   INFLUENCES UPON THE ELECTION OF WOMEN MPS

(% of variance explained)

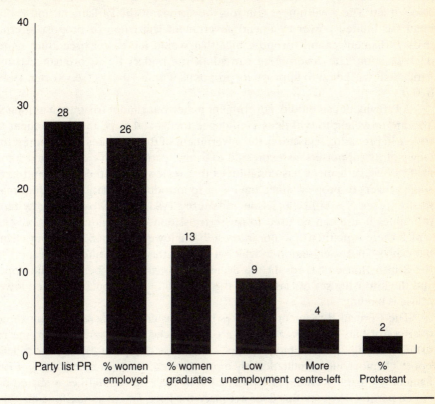

Source: Derived from Wilma Rule, "Electoral Systems, Contextual Factors, and Women's Opportunity for Election to Parliament in 23 Democracies," *Western Political Quarterly*, 40, no. 3 (1987), Table 1. Total variance explained: 82 percent.

factors, such as the strength of center or left parties and of Protestantism rather than Catholicism, are secondary influences upon the number of women MPs in a country's Parliament.

Revising Rather than Making Laws

The approval of Parliament is needed for legislation; usually approval is a formality. Success rates for government legislation run at the level of 90 percent or higher (cf. Inter-Parliamentary Union, 1986: ch. 9). Defeat on a major piece of legislation could cause the government to resign or even force an election in which the political fortunes of MPs as well as cabinet ministers would be at stake. If party leaders demand support, the party whip normally produces it. As a British cabinet minister has argued, "It's carrying democracy too far if you don't know the result of a vote before the meeting!" (quoted in Rose, 1989b: 121).

In France, the Constitution of the Fifth Republic makes it difficult for Parliament to prevent the government of the day from carrying out its policies. In many areas, the government (that is, the executive) can issue decrees with the force of law. The government controls the agenda of the Parliament, and Parliament has limited power to amend government legislation or propose alternatives. Parliament cannot propose bills that would increase expenditure or reduce taxation. The government can adopt the budget by an ordinance if the Parliament has failed to approve its proposals within 70 days (see Keeler, 1993: 520 ff.).

A Parliament can modify government policy, but cannot frustrate it as long as MPs are unwilling to withdraw confidence totally and force the government to resign. In preparing legislation, the government of the day takes into account the views of its supporters, as expressed in formal parliamentary debate and informally. Every Parliament has committees that review government bills and have some powers to propose amendments or to introduce legislation on minor matters (e.g., see Norton, 1990; Olson and Mezey, 1991). In a two-chamber system, the upper house can be used to revise legislation or introduce minor bills for which there is neither time nor interest in the lower chamber. The upper chamber can also delay legislation to which it objects; this is the principal "weapon" of the British House of Lords. In the event of a disagreement between the upper and the lower houses of Parliament, the decision of the popularly elected lower house is binding.

The German Parliament illustrates how consultation operates. About three-quarters of bills enacted each year are introduced by the government; the remainder, usually about minor matters, come from groups of MPs or the federal upper chamber. Bills simultaneously move through specialist committees of Parliament and party working groups. The job of chairing committees is shared between parties. However, this does not place the government at risk, for a majority on each committee consists of MPs in the governing coalition. Ministries participate in committee meetings, which are held in private. "The ministry representatives are not a witness but active participants in committee discussions . . . becoming virtual nonvoting committee members" (see Dalton, 1993: 335 ff.). In the major parties, MPs vote the party whip at least 99 percent of the time. Many noncontroversial or popular bills are supported by opposition MPs as well as by the governing parties. Approval of the *Bundesrat* is required for the enactment of most laws. This compels the government to take regional interests into account and, if the partisan composition of the upper house differs from the lower, to adopt a more bipartisan approach too.

The Italian Parliament has long been an example of an assembly that plays "too active" a part in the legislative process. Italian deputies are ready to put forward little laws (*leggine*), pork barrel measures providing benefits to their own region or to a very narrowly defined interest group. However, the Parliament balks at dealing with major bills, which are often controversial. In response, the Italian government uses emergency powers to enact decrees that do not require parliamentary approval and are valid for a short period of time (cf. di Palma, 1977; Hine, 1993: 174 ff.). The frequent use of emergency decrees implies that nearly every week is an emergency in Italy!

Accountability of the Executive

The confidence of Parliament makes it easy for ministers to act in the expectation that MPs will endorse what they do, but the power of Parliament to withdraw confidence makes ministers vulnerable to pressures that do not confront a president elected for a fixed term of office. The need for continuous confidence encourages government to be attentive to the opinions of MPs. A politically alert prime minister will treat changes in the mood of MPs as symptoms of underlying dissatisfaction in the country. For example, a government may become so committed to fighting inflation that it loses sight of rising popular discontent with unemployment. If a prime minister senses increased discontent in Parliament, he or she is likely to alter policy rather than risk losing office.

While it is constitutionally correct to say that the government of the day is accountable to Parliament as a whole, in fact it is accountable to a majority of Parliament. Most cabinets are accountable to a coalition of parties; this requires maintaining support through both intraparty and interparty politics. Since each partner in the coalition is sensitive to its own MPs, the influence of MPs upon the government of the day is strengthened, although it can pull a coalition government in conflicting directions (cf. Warwick, 1994).

To reduce instability from frequent changes in governing coalitions, the German Constitution requires a constructive vote of no confidence to remove the government of the day. The lower house of the German Parliament must not only vote no confidence in the current government but also express confidence in a successor government. It is very difficult for this to happen, since it requires opposition MPs of several parties to combine with at least one party or faction of the governing coalition to agree to a successor. Only once in four decades has such a vote succeeded in removing the German government.

Democracy assumes that every government's term of office should end with the electorate evaluating its performance. The maximum life of a Parliament is normally four or five years. An election can be held before the Parliament's term ends if the government of the day loses the confidence of Parliament or no new alternative government can be formed. In Britain the governing party can call an election at any time of its choice before the end of its five-year term if it judges this enhances its chances of reelection. Even with this advantage, the British government of the day has lost almost half the elections fought since 1945.

Politics within government can cause it to terminate without a general election being called. Internal dissension in the governing coalition, with or without a formal vote of no confidence in Parliament, causes two-fifths of governments to leave office (Figure 9.2). Instead of an election, the government's resignation leads to the search for a new cabinet with some outgoing members hoping for a better post in the new government. The call of an election marks the end of two-fifths of all governments. It is the normal practice for the end of government in only four countries in Europe: Britain, Sweden, Norway, and Austria. A fixed date for elections introduces predictability to the lives of politicians; it also increases the chances of a reshuffling of coalitions between elections.

FIGURE 9.2   HOW GOVERNMENTS END

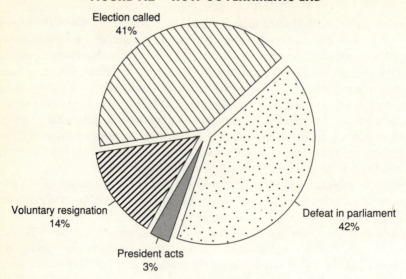

Source: Calculated from "Political Data 1945–1990: Party Government in 20 Democracies," *European Journal of Political Research* 24, no.1 (1993), 5, 116. The data cover 13 of the countries listed in Table 9.1, excluding Switzerland, which has a permanent coalition, and Greece, Portugal, and Spain, which were not democracies throughout the period.

Even when a party has an absolute majority in Parliament, voluntary resignation can occur due to the prime minister being ill. A change of prime minister gives the governing party a chance to renew its leadership. In 1990 Margaret Thatcher was unpopular with the British electorate and many MPs thought they would do better with a different leader. She faced a challenger in a ballot of Conservative MPs and failed to get a vote of confidence. Conservative MPs then elected John Major as their leader and he became prime minister. In Germany internal pressures are more likely to lead to a change in the Christian Democratic chancellor than to a breakup of a coalition (cf. Schmidt, 1983).

In France and Finland, the prime minister and cabinet are accountable to a directly elected president as well as Parliament. In Finland, the large number of parties in a governing coalition enhances the standing of the president. In France, if the Parliament and presidency are in the hands of the same party, the president can claim to be the elected leader of the country and treat the prime minister as the deputy leader. If the two offices are in the hands of competing parties, the president has an incentive to bring down a prime minister who may subsequently be a challenger for the office of the presidency.

REORGANIZING POWER IN POST-COMMUNIST REGIMES

Democratic centralism was the basic organizational principle of Communist regimes. The key term was centralism, for power was in the hands of those who controlled the Communist Party. Democratization has made the government accountable to Parliament rather than to the central committee of the Communist Party, and has increased representation through free elections. But post-Communist governments must also be effective in the face of unprecedented economic problems. The tension between representation and effectiveness is expressed in the triangle involving Parliament, the prime minister and the president.

Contenders at the Center

The starting point of democratization is the election of a Parliament with the power to hold the government accountable. These conditions have been met throughout Central and Eastern Europe. Proportional representation ensures that a broad range of parties are present in Parliament. The ratio of electors to MPs is well within the range in Western Europe. Three Parliaments have only a single chamber, thus avoiding conflict with an upper house. Insofar as there is a potential for conflict, it is with an elected president (cf. Table 9. 2).

Ironically, the shortcomings of Parliament often constitute a check upon the government of the day. In post-Communist societies, MPs are inexperienced in procedures. Rules for debate, scrutinizing bills, and investigating executive actions must all be developed from the beginning. Many choices facing the government of the day are unpalatable—for example, whether to accept more inflation or more unemployment. Inexperienced MPs may be surprised to face demands to vote for measures that ordinary voters will dislike. In reaction against the excessive discipline of the Communist Party, it is difficult for many parties to enforce party discipline making MPs vote as a bloc. In turn, this makes it difficult for the government of the day to predict whether a policy it is considering will be supported in Parliament. Stephen Holmes argues: "Democratization will succeed in Eastern Europe only if the parliaments of the region manage to combine legitimacy with effectiveness, public acceptance with successful strategies of economic reform." (1993: 24; cf. Agh, 1994; Holmes, 1995; Liebert and Cotta, 1992).

TABLE 9.2 PARLIAMENTS AND PRESIDENTS IN POST-COMMUNIST COUNTRIES

	Number of MPs	Electors per MP	President
Bulgaria	240	29,000	Popular election
Czech Republic	200	39,000	Parliament elects
Slovakia	150	25,000	Parliament elects
Hungary	386	20,000	Parliament elects
Poland	460	61,000	Popular election
Romania	341	50,000	Popular election

Note: All elections involve proportional representation; in Hungary the system combines single-member seats with PR. Bulgaria, Hungary, and Slovakia have a unicameral Parliament; the Czech Republic, Poland, and Romania elect an upper chamber.

Source: Derived by the author from David M. Olson, "The Parliaments of New Democracies: the Experience of Central Europe," in *World Encyclopedia of Parliaments and Legislatures,* ed. George Kurian. Washington, DC: CQ Press, forthcoming.

In post-Communist systems, the prime minister and cabinet depend upon the support of Parliament and coalition government is the rule. Because the parties forming the coalition are new, the commitment of partners to the coalition can be weak. As in Western Europe, coalition governments often fall due to internal dissension. In the first four years of accountable government, Poland had five prime ministers drawn from four different parties, and Bulgaria has had five different governments. The Czech Republic is exceptional; Vaclav Klaus has maintained himself in office without interruption since the breakup of Czechoslovakia. Hungary is distinctive in that its mixed system of PR and single-member seats produces very disproportional outcomes; in 1994 it manufactured an absolute majority of seats for the ex-Communist Socialist Party, which won only a third of the popular vote. Moreover, to reduce the risk of governmental instability, the Hungarian constitution requires a German-style constructive vote of no confidence to remove one government and replace it with another. The only changes in prime minister to date in Hungary have been due to a general election or ill health.

The president is directly elected in Poland, Bulgaria, and Romania, and must win half the vote in a two-ballot run off system of direct election. An elected president can thus claim more popular support than a prime minister leading a party with less than a third of the popular vote. In the Czech Republic, Slovakia, and Hungary, the president is chosen by Parliament; this enhances the influence of MPs over the government. Hungarians were sufficiently concerned about too much power being in the hands of one person that a national referendum rejected a proposal to have a strong, directly elected president. In the Czech Republic and Hungary, writers who were dissidents in Communist days, Vaclav Havel and Arpad Goncz, were chosen as president; this has enhanced the moral status of the office without making it the prize of party.

In every post-Communist country the president has some political responsibilities (cf. *East European Constitutional Review*, 1994: 58–94; McGregor, 1994). All presidents are responsible for nominating the prime minister, subject to confirmation by parliament. Presidents also have the power to dissolve Parliament and call a general election. Most have some powers to use in case of a national emergency and can propose legislation. Only the Polish president has American-style veto powers. No Central or Eastern European president has the power to ignore or overrule Parliament, as Boris Yeltsin has done in Russia.

In the unprecedented situation of a new regime, presidents can try to "stretch" their powers by setting precedents. The security of a fixed-term office gives a president considerable leeway for acting without regard to the concerns of a prime minister in charge of an insecure coalition government. The president can criticize publicly the actions of the prime minister and cabinet. There is usually no common party loyalty to inhibit such criticism, and party and personality differences encourage friction. An election can change the political complexion of Parliament, forcing a president to "cohabit" with a prime minister of an opposing party, as happened to Lech Walesa in Poland in 1993, when ex-Communists won office. No president has been successful in seeking constitutional authorization for a French-style presidential regime. In Poland, Lech Walesa publicly attacked the "Sejmocracy" (dictatorship of the Polish Parliament, the *Sejm*) (Vinton, 1992). He did not gain additional powers for the presidency, and in 1995 was defeated in an attempt to secure re-election.

A prime minister is under pressure from three different directions. First, urgent problems related to the economy and to foreign and domestic policy need resolution. Second, MPs in Parliament and cabinet colleagues can criticize actions without regard to party discipline, thus jeopardizing the ruling coalition. Third, a president can believe that government policies would be harmful to the country or even unconstitutional, and thus seek ways of voiding them. Baylis (1994: 4 f.) describes the result thus:

> Presidents find their prestige and popularity vastly outweigh their formal powers and their actual political influence. They thus seek to find ways of converting their assets of prestige into "real" power over policy, often utilizing the ambiguities in constitutional and legal provisions to do so.
>
> Prime ministers, on the other hand, find themselves with considerable formal power but limited legitimacy, and frequently discover that the more they exercise their power in areas of controversy, the more their legitimacy tends to erode. Incursions by presidents into what prime ministers regard as their areas of responsibility seem particularly to threaten the success of their policies and with it their credibility, if not the actual maintenance of their parliamentary majorities. Accordingly, they fight back.

Parliament holds the decisive vote in resolving tensions. An alliance between president and Parliament can lead to a vote of no confidence in the prime minister. But the prime minister and MPs can make common cause when a president threatens to encroach upon their powers, rebuffing a president such as Lech Walesa, who sought to "stretch" his powers beyond what MPs regard as acceptable in a parliamentary system.

Representation and Effectiveness: What Eastern Europeans Think

The new Parliaments of post-Communists often voice inconsistent and sometimes unrealistic demands. But in doing so they represent the collective views of those who elect them, for in the unprecedented circumstances of transformation there is much confusion and uncertainty about what can and what should be done. Whatever their shortcomings, the new Parliaments are firmly supported by public opinion. When the New Democracies Barometer asked people whether they would welcome the suspension of Parliament, an average of 74 percent opposed the suspension of Parliament (see Mishler and Rose, 1994: table 1). In every country a big majority favors keeping a popularly elected Parliament.

While the job of MPs is to voice popular demands about what government ought to do, the job of leaders in the executive branch of government is to see that government acts effectively. The need for effective government is palpably clear in post-Communist states. Yet when the New Democracies Barometer asked whether people think a strong leader could do more for the country than all the discussions in Parliament, three-quarters rejected a strong leader in principle. This reflects the starting point for new democracies of Central and Eastern Europe; there is a tradition of dictatorships being too effective.

FIGURE 9.3   REPRESENTATION BEFORE LEADERSHIP IN POST-COMMUNIST SOCIETIES

(% preferring:)

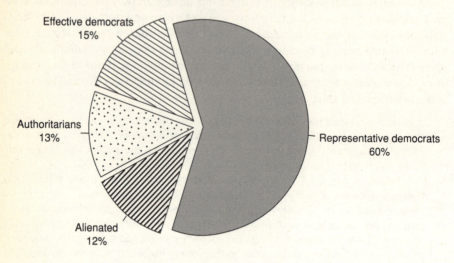

Representative democrats: Support Parliament without strong leader
Effective democrats: Support Parliament and strong leader
Authoritarians: Support strong leader without Parliament
Alienated: Reject both Parliament and strong leader

Source: Calculated from Paul Lazarsfeld Society, Vienna, *New Democracies Barometer III* (1994). Cross-tabulation of answers to questions about approving or disapproving of suspension of Parliament and approving or disapproving of strong leader making decisions instead of Parliament. Countries included Bulgaria, Czech Republic, Slovak Republic, Hungary, Poland, and Romania.

People can endorse strong leadership because of a desire for a dictator in place of representative institutions or to make democracy work more effectively by altering the balance between MPs and the leader of the government of the day. The commitment of Central and Eastern Europeans to democratic as against dictatorial leadership can be measured by combining answers to two New Democracies Barometer questions: whether a person would approve of the suspension of Parliament, and whether a person would approve of a strong leader.

After decades of living with propaganda about Communist leaders, people give first priority to a strong Parliament and distrust giving more powers to leaders; three-fifths are democrats who put representation first (Figure 9.3). An additional 15 percent are reform-minded democrats who would support increased powers for a leader in hopes of increasing effectiveness—but not if it meant abolishing Parliament. Authoritarians who want a strong leader in place of Parliament are a small minority in every country surveyed, an eighth of the total. There is also a small group that is completely alienated, wanting to get rid of both Parliament and strong leaders. In the struggle for power at the center of post-Communist states, three-quarters of the people are on the side of representative government.

In established democracies, strong leadership is meant to complement representation, not undermine it; the most respected American presidents have been individuals successful in combining representation and effectiveness. Yet members of Congress often complain that the White House is trying to become too strong. Disagreements about how best to combine representation and leadership are not a denial of democracy; they are an integral part of democracy at work. In response to the experience of Communist rule, the great majority of Central and Eastern Europeans give greater priority to representation than to strong leadership.

part

IV

MAKING PUBLIC POLICIES

10

GIVING DIRECTION
TO PUBLIC POLICY

Governing is not so much about choosing as it is about steering; the word *government* originates from the ancient Greek word, *kybernan,* the person who steers a ship (Deutsch, 1963). But even though the ship of state has only one tiller to steer by, there are many different hands trying to give it direction (see Rose, 1987a). At the center of government, no single person, whether prime minister or president, can be informed about all the activities of the state. The direction of public policy cannot be decided by a single decision or a single act of will. A cabinet has up to 20 ministers, a Parliament has hundreds of members, and government can employ millions of people. A politician who thinks that a television talk is sufficient to govern is a passenger on the ship of state. A politician who thinks that rational analysis is sufficient to determine what government does risks being blown off course or shipwrecked when there is a change in the political climate.

A nation's capital is meant to centralize authority, but the offices of central government are scattered throughout many buildings. Intragovernmental politics is of primary importance. Government is not a single organization but a multiplicity of institutions engaged in a multiplicity of activities. The adoption of a government policy requires agreement between different public agencies about what ought to be done, who will be responsible for implementing the policy, approval by the Cabinet, enactment by Parliament, and the appropriation of public funds. Much of the time and effort devoted to making policies is invested in one group of ministers and civil servants trying to win the agreement of other groups of ministers and civil servants.

Giving direction to government is not a military operation in which elected officials command subordinates to follow their orders. The prime minister and cabinet have the legitimate authority to lay down policies, but they have neither the numbers nor the technical expertise to deliver such things as defense or health services themselves. The vast majority of public employees delivering policies are civil servants or people not thought of as bureaucrats, such as elementary school teachers and hospital nurses. Cooperation is needed between politicians with the political legitimacy to determine goals and civil servants with the expertise to design and deliver public policies consistent with these goals. The ideal public policy is one that expresses the political values of elected governors and can be administered easily and effectively by civil servants.

If we asked "Where is government?" in the days of a traditional monarch, there would be one answer: in the palace of the king. The rise of representative government made Parliament an important forum in which issues of principle could be debated and laws enacted. The growth of social policies has made government responsible for delivering a multitude of services such as education and health care wherever people live. Since the majority of Europeans today live outside the national capital, most employees of government are hundreds of miles distant from the office of the prime minister and the buildings of Parliament (Rose, 1985).

In an era of big government, the distinction between state and society becomes fuzzy, for public policies not only maintain the security of the state but also influence the social and economic well-being of society. The deeper government goes into society's problems, the more it must take into account the dispositions of those it seeks to influence. To manage the economy, government must secure the cooperation of business and labor; it cannot issue commands as did the leaders of Communist states. Every modern European state routinely deals with interest groups that offer views about how policies should be delivered and what government ought to do. In some European countries the relationship has been formalized in corporatist institutions in which public policies are negotiated between public officials and private sector interests.

Giving direction to government involves much interdependent activity. The first concern of this chapter is outlining the primary resources of the state—laws, money, expert knowledge, and electoral support—which must be brought together to make a policy. Second, agreement must be arrived at between ministers and civil servants who depend on each other. The former have legitimate authority to make decisions but often lack the technical expertise of civil servants. The third section examines the state's relations with organized interests in society, of particular importance for economic policy making. In post-Communist societies, there is great need to change the way in which government is directed, but, as the concluding section shows, the Communist legacy is an obstacle to change.

MANY SIGNALS FOR MANY AGENCIES

Government can give direction by using a variety of resources. It has a monopoly of legislation and taxing powers, it employs experts in many fields, and it has the legitimacy of popular election. But to develop and implement a particular policy is not easy, for every policy requires combining diverse resources in distinctive ways. For example, environmental policies rely upon laws and expert knowledge, health programs require money and expert knowledge, and social security pensions require money above all (Rose, 1989c: 63 ff.).

Multiple Signals Guiding Policy Makers

The unique resource of government is *law* (Rose, 1986). A few laws, particularly the criminal code, prohibit antisocial actions; others, such as laws about compulsory vaccination, seek to compel people to act in a specified way. Laws that command or prohibit individual actions are relatively few in society today. Many laws simply state conditions under which individuals can act. For example, if a business wants to market food products, laws specify what steps must be taken to en-sure that the product meets public health standards. Many laws regulate the be-havior of government employees, for a bureaucrat is expected to act in accord with the law. Laws also confer benefits upon individuals. For example, social se-curity laws entitle individuals to a pension of a specific value. A claimant does not have to canvass a politician for a pension or accept an arbitrary ruling by a low-level official; entitlements are calculated according to rules that a claimant can read too. Compulsory education laws ensure that every child receives an educa-tion. Laws also create entitlements to health care. Statutory entitlements en-shrined in acts of Parliament thus determine spending for three of the most costly policies of government (cf. Chapter 11).

Expert values are important in determining the education actually delivered in the classroom. Since education is free and compulsory, pupils and parents are not customers but recipients of the services recommended by specialist producers, classroom teachers, educational administrators, and pedagogical experts in teacher training institutions. Experts are only subject to intermittent direction by politi-cians. In health care, the state sets out rules determining entitlement to health care and finance, but doctors use their medical expertise to prescribe the health care that each individual receives. Experts may also be influential by organizing as inter-est groups within government and within the governing party. In Sweden, public employees are union members linked to the social democratic party in power for most of the past half century. In consequence, social services have been criticized for being more responsive to producers than to individuals receiving public service and Swedish Social Democrats have had to launch a major program to make public employees more "client-oriented and responsive" (Pierre, 1993: 397).

In economics textbooks, the *market* is meant to make producers responsive to individual consumers, who can take their money elsewhere if they are dissat-isfied. But in the public sector this is usually not possible, for a person dissatisfied with government policies must still pay taxes. To reject public education means paying twice for schools, once through taxes and once through tuition fees. In some European health systems, people pay for part of the cost of services—for example, medicines or a private room in hospital. Such practices can be criti-cized, however, as unfair to those who do not have the money to pay or as un-dermining the obligation of the state to treat all its citizens the same. Market-ori-ented governments such as the Thatcher administration endorsed intellectual arguments for introducing more charges for public services. They emphasized that services described as "free" to recipients are in fact costly in terms of public finance. But even pro-market politicians bow to political arguments against re-pealing free access to services financed by taxation; hence, charges tend to be lit-tle used by governments to finance services (Rose, 1990)

The voice of the *electorate* rarely influences policy directly, for it can only be authoritatively stated at a referendum. European countries do not hold referen-dums on taxing and spending issues, as is done by many American cities and states. In Switzerland, the one European country where referendums are fre-quent, there is no provision for voting on tax increases or bonds that finance public roads or other capital investment (cf. Butler and Ranney, 1994). Politicians believe that they themselves should decide what government ought to do. Elec-tion is deemed sufficient to validate their claim to know what the public wants or ought to want, or will accept once it is put into effect. Issues such as crime control, an emotive electoral issue in the United States, are normally treated as matters for decision by experts. In Britain MPs voted to abolish capital punishment even though public opinion polls showed a big majority in favor of the retention of hanging as a punishment for murder.

Managing Intra- and Intergovernmental Relations

Government is a collective noun that describes organizations differing in form, in function, and in accountability. Whether a state is federal or unitary, there inevitably is interdependence between ministries in the national capital and the agencies that deliver services nationwide. Much of the effort invested in giving direction to public policy must be devoted to managing relations within and between different public sector organizations.

To monitor the actions of local officials in a unitary state, Napoléon created prefects, high-ranking officials resident in the administrative centers of local and regional government throughout France. Prefects were given substantial formal powers and were expected to be tutors of local officials; that term emphasizes the center's view of local authorities as pupils needing central instruction. The prefect system has subsequently been imitated in countries following the French model of administration. In fact, prefects have acted as brokers between local and central authorities rather than simply as agents of central control, for their reputation rests on their ability to maintain peace by preventing disputes between elected local officials and the center (cf. Machin, 1977; Tarrow, 1977). In Britain, the national government has sought to use the power of the purse to control local authorities and functional agencies by imposing many restrictions on spending. However, this strategy is politically vulnerable if services deteriorate—for example, if education spending does not increase proportionally when there is an increase in young people of college age and in the proportion wanting further education.

During the Thatcher-Reagan era, a new philosophy of public management emerged (see Aucoin, 1990). Public choice theories treat politicians as captives of bureaucrats running agencies for their own benefit rather than according to the priorities of elected representatives (cf. Niskanen, 1971; Dunsire and Hood, 1989). It prescribes that politicians should reclaim the power of giving direction to government. Cutting public employment and increasing the number of political appointees in agencies are two recommendations for doing so. A managerialist approach sees public agencies as needing reform to focus more attention upon the recipients of public programs. It seeks to make civil servants more cost-conscious and more "customer"-conscious and less concerned with procedures. It endorses payment by results, provided that civil servants produce results specified by politicians. It also endorses contracts with private sector companies to deliver services, if this is cheaper and more efficient.

In theory new public management doctrines could improve services delivered to individuals while at the same time reducing costs. In practice, a major attraction is its rationale for leapfrogging over problems of intergovernmental politics by purchasing services from profit-making companies, or entirely abandoning responsibility for providing some services, such as housing. The prescriptions are being tried out, but the results of experiments have yet to uphold claims made by the rhetoric of new public management.

Political bargaining between public agencies is continuous, but the relationship differs in federal as against unitary systems. In a federal system relationships are *inter*governmental. Regions as well as central government have powers entrenched in the constitution and incentives to make the most of their powers. In unitary states, the relationships are *intra*governmental because local and intermediate authorities are not "governments" in the constitutional sense. Yet local and regional governments still have influence because they deliver services that central ministries cannot or do not want to deliver. Whereas functional agencies depend on central government for money and legal authority, central government depends upon functional agencies for expertise and the delivery of services.

Central government is peripheral when it comes to delivering public services. Education, health care, social services, police protection, and other community services cannot be delivered at offices in the nation's capital. Teachers, doctors, social workers, and police must work locally. Few national governments want to burden themselves with responsibility for the routine delivery of everyday services from one end of the country to the other. National health services illustrate the peripheralization of central government. When a person is ill, the immediate need is not a speech by a minister or a letter from a civil servant in the ministry; it is for treatment by a local doctor or hospital. Even if health care is financed by central government, crucial decisions about medical treatment are in the hands of medical experts on the spot.

The division of employees between public sector organizations indicates the unimportance of central government in service delivery (Figure 10.1). Local and

FIGURE 10.1   EMPLOYMENT IN THE PUBLIC SECTOR

(% of all public employees)

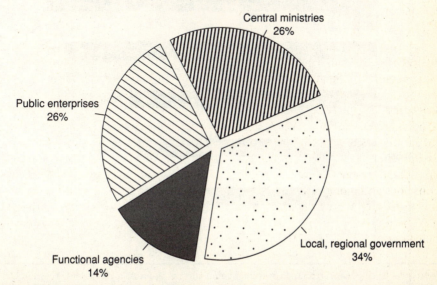

Source: Average for France, Germany, Italy, Sweden, and United Kingdom, calculated from Richard Rose, *Public Employment in Western Nations* (New York: Cambridge University Press, 1985), Table 1.9.

regional government normally count for more than a third of all public employees. This is true of unitary states such as Sweden and Britain as well as the German federal system. Central ministries on average account for only one-quarter of public employees. In Britain and Sweden, central government employs less than a fifth of all workers in the public sector. Even in France, where education is a centralized service, central government employs less than half of all public sector workers. Public enterprises trading in the market account for about a quarter of public employees. The percentage in functional agencies is relatively low, but because health care is usually delivered by functional agencies it is growing steadily.

Tension arises between public agencies because central government is chiefly responsible for raising money through taxation while other parts of government spend the money delivering services (Figure 10.2). Central government collects more than 90 percent of tax revenue in Italy, Britain, and France. The centralized collection of social security and unemployment benefit taxes makes it possible to maintain uniformity in paying pensions and unemployment benefit. But three-quarters of public sector employees do not work for central government ministries. In every European country the central government's control of revenue is much greater than its control of personnel; in Britain it is almost seven

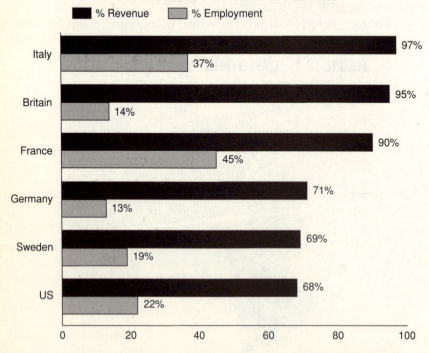

FIGURE 10.2 CONTRAST IN CENTRAL GOVERNMENT REVENUE-RAISING AND SERVICE DELIVERY

■ % Revenue   ▢ % Employment

Country	% Revenue	% Employment
Italy	97%	37%
Britain	95%	14%
France	90%	45%
Germany	71%	13%
Sweden	69%	19%
US	68%	22%

Source: Public employment: central government ministries, as reported in Figure 10.1. Revenue: Organization for Economic Cooperation and Development, *Revenue Statistics of OECD Member Countries, 1965-1992* (Paris: OECD, 1993), 196.

times greater. While the central government has the power of the purse, lower-tier agencies have their hands on the delivery of most public policies.

Each level of government faces a dilemma. Advocates of local government claim it is superior because it is closer to the average household and delivers services on the doorstep. Since each vote counts more when the electorate is a city, a ward, or a small commune rather than the nation, local councillors can also claim to be closer to the people than MPs (cf. Tables 4.2 and 9.1 in this book, and Dahl, 1994). Especially in poor cities and regions, local governments do not want to do without the tax revenue that central government collects and transfers to them. This makes it possible for local authorities to spend more on delivering services than they collect in taxes. However, the transfer of money from central government is usually accompanied by central controls.

Drawing responsibility closer to the center increases the formal power of the center but also threatens to overload it with parochial concerns. Central government can pay the piper and call the tune, but central officials do not have their hands on the pipes that actually play the music. Furthermore, it attracts political blame when things go wrong—for example, when a local fire department fails to prevent a disastrous fire or an epidemic breaks out in a hospital. The capacity of central government to determine what is done varies with the degree of discretion in the hands of those who deliver a service. In policing, much discretion is left with the officer in a patrol car. In fields such as environmental pollution, precise technical rules and regulations can be established when delegating powers of inspection. In the health services, neither central nor local government can control the independent expert judgment of doctors.

INTERDEPENDENCE OF MINISTERS AND CIVIL SERVANTS

Politicians and civil servants are recruited in different ways to play different yet complementary roles in the policy-making process. As elected officials, politicians are primarily concerned with the ends of policy. Politicians have the legitimate authority to decide political goals, what government *ought* to do. Civil servants are administrators expert in the means of policy. Based upon their expertise and experience, they offer advice on what government *can* do. The two groups are interdependent; both are involved in giving direction to public policies (Rose, 1987a).

Notwithstanding differences in perspective, politicians and civil servants can sometimes come to the same conclusion. Table 10.1 illustrates two ways in which this can happen. If politicians consider a goal desirable and civil service experts consider it technically feasible, a policy is doubly desirable. For example, politicians may want to cut taxes and economic experts may consider this good for the economy and easy to administer. Alternatively, a pressure group may lobby for legislation that politicians consider unpopular and civil servants think impractical; its demand can be dismissed as doubly undesirable.

Politicians face a hard choice when they enunciate a goal that is politically desirable, such as cutting taxes to create a preelection economic boom, and experts advise that this is technically inadvisable because it is likely to stimulate

TABLE 10.1 CONTRASTING OUTLOOKS OF POLITICIANS AND CIVIL SERVANTS

	Advice of Civil Service Experts	
	Feasible	**Impractical**
Desirable	Doubly desirable	Technically dubious
Politician's Assessment of Goals		
Undesirable	Politically awkward	Doubly undesirable

Source: Derived from Richard Rose, *Ordinary People in Public Policy,* (Newbury Park, CA: Sage Publications, 1989), 85.

inflation. Such advice does not prevent politicians from doing what they would like to do—but if the experts are right, the consequence may be unwelcome afterward. Alternatively, experts can advise politicians to take actions for good technical reasons, but the results can be politically awkward—for example, raising taxes to reduce inflation before an election. Here again, the government of the day can reject the advice, but if inflation follows, the experts cannot be blamed for lack of foresight.

Differences Among Civil Servants

Throughout Europe, civil servants are recruited in similar ways: There is an emphasis upon formal educational qualifications and security of employment. Within every civil service there is a fundamental division in the jobs to which civil servants are recruited: the great majority are routine, while a few are intimately concerned with policy making.

Most civil servants are *bureaucrats or technicians* dealing with routine activities of government, to which formal rules and regulations can readily be applied—for example, the registration of individuals for social security, the collection of taxes, and the payment of social security benefits. Rules are designed to ensure that every public employee acts the same in similar circumstances so that every citizen is treated equally. Bureaucratic routines are not unique to the public sector; a private sector telephone company has rules about the installation of telephones, assigning numbers, and sending out bills. The routines of bureaucracy are mechanisms for control by higher civil service and political superiors. They are most effective as control mechanisms when officials delivering services have little discretion—for example, in quoting post office charges for different types of letters. When ordinary people deal with government, they normally deal with bureaucrats.

Higher civil servants deal with nonroutine problems of concern to ministers; often the topics are politically controversial. While most ministers are good at voicing political demands and defending policy choices, they have little detailed knowledge about the feasibility of policies. Ministers need advice about the means to achieve their desired goals. Higher civil servants are responsible for preparing policy options and advising ministers about the drawbacks and attractions of each alternative. Higher civil servants normally have much more knowledge of a department's programs than do their ministers, because they have spent more time working in the department and have qualifications in law, economics, public health, or other relevant fields. Advice about the means of policy can influence the choice of ends. Higher civil servants constitute only 1 percent of the civil service, but they are disproportionately important because they have direct access to ministers faced with major political problems (cf. Suleiman, 1984)

The boundaries of the civil service are broad; for example, in many continental countries university professors are civil servants whose appointment is a matter for ministries or even ministers. In most countries, higher- as well as lower-ranking civil servants are allowed to belong to political parties and, if they choose, to run for Parliament. In countries with long-standing coalition governments, some ministries can be regarded as "socialist," with the top civil service jobs in the hands of "red" supporters of that party, and other ministries as "liberal" or "Catholic" because of the political loyalties of civil servants. Britain is among the minority of countries in which higher civil servants avoid identification with any political party; they are meant to be bipartisan, giving professional advice to Conservative and to Labour governments. The continental practice of allowing party membership is likely to increase commitment of civil servants to policies that their party promotes; it may also reduce their detachment. The British procedure tends to encourage skepticism and reduce commitment.

Civil services differ in their history and form. In Britain responsibility for civil administration was initially in the hands of the local nobility and gentry; the English civil service was not created until after Parliament had established its supremacy. In France a strong bureaucracy was introduced before democracy. The absolutist French monarch wanted officials who would prevent the nobility from frustrating what was decided in Paris. France today retains the classic goal of a hierarchical administration promoting the Napoleonic goal of "uniformity of action on a grand scale that will give immense results" (quoted in Cassese, 1990: 358). The *École Nationale d'Administration (ENA)* trains the elite of the French higher civil service, creating an old boy network of graduates of ENA, self-confident technocrats who believe that they have the expertise to make policy (Rouban, 1993). Graduates of ENA occupy top posts in the civil service; the prime minister is often a graduate of ENA, and two graduates, Valéry Giscard d'Estaing and Jacques Chirac, have become president of France.

The Federal Republic of Germany is heir to the Prussian tradition of legalistic administration, emphasizing formal procedures. Historically, the absence of a strong political class has given higher civil servants more scope for influence; the legalistic tradition is being moderated by the rise of democratic politicians (cf. Mayntz, 1984). A survey of European civil servants found that the proportion of German higher civil servants thinking legalistically was twice as great as in any other country (cf. Aberbach et al., 1981: table 4.3) In Italy the higher civil service is primarily staffed by law graduates from Southern Italy. To prevent promotion depending upon personal or partisan favoritism, strict rules emphasize promotion by seniority. Since officials have little opportunity to rise faster by substantive achievements, there is little incentive for initiative (cf. Cassese, 1984).

Interdependence of Policy and Administration

The growth of government has transformed public administration. In the mid-nineteenth century the responsibilities of the British Foreign Office were so few that the foreign minister could read all the letters from ambassadors and write his own letters in reply (see Parris, 1969). As government has increased the range and volume of its activities, it has become more difficult for ministers to be informed about what is happening with every program for which they are responsible. Politicians increasingly depend upon civil servants to act in their name.

The increased dependence of politicians upon expert higher civil servants is sometimes said to make the latter the real rulers, saying "Yes, Minister," when they mean "perhaps," and indicating agreement "up to a point" when they disagree. A civil service that moves slowly because it is skeptical of political initiative can prevent change, particularly if ministers lack political direction, expert knowledge, or interest in departmental affairs. However, civil servants can only act without consulting ministers when the issue at hand is of little political concern and there is a politically acceptable response to make.

Political controversies force ministers and civil servants to produce a response in the name of the ministry, because the reputation of everyone in the department is at stake. When problems are politically controversial, the influence of higher civil servants is confined in three ways: by the insistence of politicians on imposing their value preferences to direct or to veto choices; by popular demands or outcries; and by pressure groups imposing conditions for cooperation and support (see Page, 1992a). Many obstacles to a particular minister achieving an objective arise from conflicts within the government of the day. In a coalition government, there can be disputes between parties to the coalition. Even within a single party, disagreements can arise between ministers in charge of government departments with different policy priorities—for example, road building and environment, or spending on health care and cutting taxes.

Within government, we can distinguish individuals according to the strength of their *political will*, the capacity to mobilize partisan and popular support for policy goals; and their *policy expertise*, the capacity to develop programs effective in achieving goals. The ideal democratic politician is a *policy entrepreneur*, an individual with well-defined political goals and sufficient expertise to identify measures that can achieve them. If a politician enunciates goals without knowing how they can be attained, he or she is an ideological *zealot*, strong on will but without any practical idea about how to achieve ideological goals. Politicians who lack both expertise and will are *passengers on the ship of state*.

The ideal civil servant is a *technician*, capable of developing programs that can achieve the goals of the government of the day, whatever its partisan composition. However, this ideal is difficult to attain, for experts can disagree on professional grounds, and such disagreements can parallel disagreements between parties. This is most evident in economic advice, for there are as many "parties" in economics as there are in Parliament. When their adherents offer conflicting advice, politicians are forced to choose between competing experts (Rose, 1989c: ch. 5).

TABLE 10.2   ROLES OF HIGHER CIVIL SERVANTS AND MEMBERS OF PARLIAMENT

	Civil servants	MPs	Difference
	(% mentioning relevance; six-nation average)		
Partisan	7	66	59
Advocate	21	66	45
Technician	72	26	46
Policy maker	74	72	2
Trustee	53	54	1

Source: Derived from J. Aberbach, R. Putnam, and B. Rockman, *Bureaucrats and Politicians in Western Democracies* (Cambridge: Harvard University Press, 1981), Table 4.3. Average of answers from elite surveys in Britain, France, Germany, Italy, the Netherlands, and Sweden. Roles not endorsed by a majority of either civil servants or MPs are omitted.

A prime minister is responsible for combining political will and expertise. Able politicians acquire a degree of technical expertise, especially if they hold office in the same ministry for a number of years, and senior civil servants are often sensitive to the crosscurrents of party politics. In some European countries the minister has a *cabinet* of advisors who are drawn from personal, party, and civil service networks. In France, prime ministers are likely to have spent more of their career as leading civil servants than as politicians running for office (see Rose, 1991b: table 6.3).

A comparative survey of elected MPs and higher civil servants in six European countries found the groups differing in complementary ways (Table 10.2). Two-thirds of MPs saw their role as setting political goals, representing party principles, and advocating action in a specific policy area. More than two-thirds of civil servants saw themselves as technicians, concerned with the complexities of making and delivering policies. There is also an element of common ground, since more than two-thirds in both groups saw themselves as policy makers, thinking about ways in which government can respond to pressing problems in ways that reconcile conflicting political interests. A majority of both groups also see themselves as trustees of the public interest, exercising judgment independent of electoral pressures or pressures from interest groups.

Changing Direction

Politicians who win elections can claim the legitimate right to give direction to government. But a question remains: How? The administration of Margaret Thatcher illustrates the scope and limits of action. On entering office in 1979, Thatcher gained control of a highly centralized government and had an absolute majority in the House of Commons. A badly split opposition enabled her to win three successive elections. As the longest-serving British prime minister of the twentieth century, she had an exceptional amount of time, 11 years, to put policies into effect.

Political will distinguished Margaret Thatcher from other postwar British prime ministers and from many leaders in other countries. Many politicians, such as her predecessor Harold Wilson, have regarded office as itself the principal reward; she saw office as an instrument for achieving political goals. Thatcher was determined to introduce changes in government, regardless of what was said by opponents, experts or critics within her own party and cabinet (see Young, 1990; Kavanagh, 1990; Metcalfe, 1993). She described herself as a conviction politician, explaining that the prophets in the Old Testament did not follow the opinion polls but asked other people to follow them because of a conviction of the righteousness of their cause.

The first step in changing the course of government was to change personnel, a shift that went well beyond the conventional rotation of parties in office. Thatcher was not satisfied with a cabinet representing the Conservative Party, for she correctly reckoned that many in the party did not agree with her strongly held views about the market and the need for radical reforms. The critical question in making appointments was "Is he or she one of us?"—that is, a person sharing the same ideological convictions. Instead of relying upon career civil servants or bipartisan commissions of experts, Thatcher turned to management consultants and investment bankers for advice on how to implement market policies that she had already decided upon. To make her administration more Thatcherite, the prime minister turned to younger civil servants whose chances for rapid promotion depended upon showing that they could do what she wanted (cf. Ranelagh, 1991; Rose, 1988).

Laws remove discretion from institutions outside government. A series of industrial relations acts imposed obligations upon trade unions, such as requiring honest elections for top posts and ballots on whether or not to call a strike. When Labour-controlled local governments proved unwilling to reduce expenditure, laws imposed spending controls. When this was insufficient, new acts of Parliament were introduced to abolish local authorities in London and elsewhere, and their powers were transferred to nonelected bodies. A local government tax, a poll tax on residents, was introduced in place of a centuries-old property tax on houses. Since laws had been unable to make many nationalized industries profitable, new laws were enacted authorizing the sale of public enterprises to the private sector.

The Thatcher administration showed that it is easier to achieve policy goals that depend on laws than to produce big changes in public expenditure. Big-spending social programs continued to spend big sums of money. Will was insufficient to prevent expenditure on entitlements to social security, health care, and education authorized by laws inherited from predecessors (see Rose and Davies, 1994). The government's budget powers could only limit the rate of increase in expenditure. Economic problems such as unemployment continued or worsened. Thatcher's will at times became dangerously willful, as the prime minister ignored professional advice about the difficulties of implementing some convictions. When the poll tax forced on local government turned out to be a political disaster, she became politically vulnerable. Support was also lost from cabinet colleagues and MPs who found her "overbearing." In consequence, Conservative

MPs failed to show sufficient confidence in a vote on the party leadership in 1990, and she resigned as leader.

In most European countries it would not be possible to govern as Margaret Thatcher did, because coalition government makes it impossible for a single individual to insist on policies. Dialogue rather than monologue is the normal mode of decision making in a coalition government. Action requires consensus—and this requires compromise. An earlier British prime minister was fond of quoting a veteran politician's remark that when he was young he talked a lot about his conscience, but when he got older he realized it was his conceit that made him think he knew better than anyone else. Consensus politics is not a recipe for inaction, but it is a recipe for gradual change. Whatever the will of a few strong personalities, a policy cannot be adopted until doubters agree on the desirability of the goal and the feasibility of the proposed policy.

INTERDEPENDENCE OF INTEREST GROUPS AND THE STATE

Public policies do not exist in a vacuum: We can conceive of government as a producer of policies and the individuals and organizations that collectively constitute society as consumers. There are producers and consumers in the private sector of the economy too. Interdependence arises when both government and the private sector are partners in an exchange (Table 10.3). The private sector produces many goods and services that are sold to public agencies, ranging from hospital equipment to boots and shoes for soldiers. Likewise, the public sector produces goods and services on which the private sector depends, such as an educated labor force. Many products, such as bus services, are produced by both the public and the private sectors. Individuals consume goods and services from both the public and private sectors—for example, supplementing social security benefits with private insurance. To treat the public sector and the private sector as if they were two separate and unrelated worlds is unrealistic.

Every European country has a mixed economy, and almost all states contribute far more to the mix than does government in the United States. In buying and selling goods and services, the public and private sectors interact. Even

TABLE 10.3 INTERDEPENDENCE OF PUBLIC AND PRIVATE SECTORS

	Consumer		
	Private	**Both**	**Public**
Producer			
Private	Sporting events	Computers	Hospital equipment
Both	Bus services	Pensions	Military hardware
State	Education	Roads	Training civil servants

Source: Prepared by the author.

goods that we normally think of as products of the private sector, such as the food we eat, would not be produced in the same quantity or sold at their current price in the market if agricultural subsidies were withdrawn.

The interdependence of the public and private sectors is most evident in the making of economic policy. Government ministries concerned with promoting investment, full employment, and stable prices—for example, the ministries of finance, trade, industry, agriculture, and employment—depend upon cooperation from the private sector to achieve their policy goals. Business enterprises want government to spend more money on public infrastructure, such as roads and high-tech education, reduce taxes on profits of firms, and reduce regulation of businesses. Specific industries, such as automobile manufacturers or the oil industry, lobby for special benefits. Trade unions want higher wages and lower prices, better state social services and benefits mandated upon employers by legislation, tighter regulation of health and safety at work, and special benefits for organized labor.

Because government, business, and unions need the help of each other to achieve some of their goals, there is continuous interaction between particular government ministries and interest groups affected by the ministry's policies. The relations can take either of two main forms: corporatism or pluralism. In every society, both are found, but the relative weight given each varies between countries (see Lijphart and Crepaz, 1991).

Incorporating Interests in Policy Making

The constituent elements of a corporatist state are associations representing organized interests; they are not individuals (see Schmitter, 1974; Cawson, 1986). In a *corporatist* system of interest groups the state grants monopoly privileges to interest groups representing manufacturers, retailers, industrial workers, and farmers. By restricting the formation of new organizations, those recognized by the state gain the advantages of a cartel. Corporatist philosophies are thus inconsistent with American-style antitrust legislation. Membership in a corporatist institution may be a necessary condition of a firm carrying on its business, or an individual holding a job. Monopoly greatly facilitates elite bargaining. It also reflects the roots of corporatism in Catholic theories of the organic nature of society and fascist theories about mobilizing subjects to do what the state deems necessary.

Corporatism makes pressure groups insiders in the policy process. They are given the right to participate in formal and informal institutions deciding and implementing policies. Government uses corporatist institutions to put pressure on business and labor organizations to deliver the support of their members for measures that the government of the day deems in the public interest. Corporatist institutions give interest groups an opportunity to influence policy before it is made and to influence what is often most important to their members, how public policies are delivered.

Two different types of corporatism can be distinguished. The classic form is *state corporatism;* the state takes the initiative in encouraging institutions to organize, grants monopoly privileges, and creates institutions that incorporate groups into the policy process. Regimes as diverse as Franco Spain and Sweden have sought to encourage organization under state auspices. *Societal corporatism* refers to systems in which organizations have a significant degree of independence from the state—for example, being created before gaining recognition from ministries. Organizations of employers and workers may cooperate with each other independently of the state. If cooperation leads to the exclusion of the state, this becomes a form of private interest regulation. For example, press and advertising agencies claim that their rights of free speech should not be subject to government regulation, can band together to "police" their industries to prevent abuses of freedoms leading to legislation introducing government regulation (cf. Lehmbruch and Schmitter, 1982; Streeck and Schmitter, 1985; Williamson, 1989).

Austria is a classic example of corporatism. Before World War II, the doctrine was promoted by very conservative Catholics as an alternative to Marxist class conflict. After 1945, conservative and social democratic parties agreed to establish formal chambers of business, labor, and agriculture to cooperate in promoting economic reconstruction through a corporatist partnership involving negotiations between them. Membership in a relevant organization affiliated to a chamber has been compulsory. Today close links between interest groups and parties and a coalition government of Socialists and the pro-business People's Party draws parties and interest groups close together in peak negotiations, and the country's small population encourages groups to act collectively to advance interests in the international economy (cf. Marin, 1987; Katzenstein, 1985).

Corporatism assumes that public policies on behalf of the economy are best made by discussions among elites. Government officials are only one among several elites participating, and they can claim no special rights by virtue of representing the electorate as a whole. The concentration of power in elite hands makes corporatism consistent with authoritarian regimes as well as Scandinavian democracies. Corporatism insulates interest group leaders from pressures by their followers. Compulsory membership makes it impossible for individuals to leave a union or firms to leave a business association if they are dissatisfied with an agreement. If partners in corporatist institutions have difficulties in enforcing agreements on wages or prices, the force of law may be invoked to ensure compliance. Policy making is removed from open debate in Parliament. Election results are also diminished in importance, for whatever the parties in government, interest groups remain the insiders.

Corporatism is about the organization of producers; consumers are neglected or completely ignored. This is illustrated by the common European practice of retail firms and unions of shop workers agreeing to restrict shop opening hours to times that suit their convenience, closing by six o'clock, half a day on Saturday and all day Sunday. The fact that shops are closed when it is most convenient for many people to shop is irrelevant, for corporatist policies are meant to satisfy producer interests, not those of consumers.

If individuals cannot be compelled to join groups, corporatist bargaining is difficult because leaders cannot deliver sufficient followers to make agreements stick. If there are no conflicting interests, then there is no point in having a corporatist triangle. In AIDS policy, for example, public health officials seek to prevent the spread of the disease; they do not negotiate between proponents and opponents of AIDS. When there is a conflict of principle, as is the case with abortion, it is not possible to establish a corporatist institution bringing together Catholic and pro-choice groups to agree about the content and implementation of abortion policies.

For decades after World War II, a majority of European states relied upon some form of corporatist institutions to deal with the risks of inflation and unemployment and to promote investment. The strategy appeared to offer a way of maximizing political benefits and minimizing the costs of managing the economy. Corporatist economies were treated as closed economies, and small nations were described as particularly likely to be corporatist in order to maintain their position in world markets. However, the development of a single market in Europe and the internationalization of economic transactions has created new pressures upon national economic institutions—public, private, and corporatist. It is much more difficult for national agreements to be effective when capital and goods are mobile across international boundaries and labor is not (cf. Goodman, 1992; Kurzer, 1993).

Pluralist Competition

In the Anglo-American tradition, individuals are the basic unit in the political system. The *pluralist* sees interest groups as organized by their members to serve their interests, not to serve the state. Groups may therefore advance demands that are in conflict with goals of the government of the day and civil servants in ministries. The national interest, which the state seeks to define through corporatist institutions, is regarded as no more than the by-product of the clash of conflicting interests of individuals and groups. In a pluralist system, public policy emerges as the by-product of competition between many groups. Whereas corporatism starts from the assumption that the state should exert pressure on organized interests, pluralism emphasizes group pressures upon the state, viewing government as little more than an umpire registering the strength of competing groups (Bentley, 1949: 208).

Membership in pluralist interest groups is voluntary, not compulsory. The political incentive to join is that an individual or enterprise can gain increased influence (see Parry et al., 1992: 422). Pluralism promotes competition between groups for members. The state takes a laissez-faire attitude; it does not try to create organizations monopolizing the representation of a particular interest. It may even welcome intergroup competition as a means of preventing any one from becoming too powerful. A clear line is drawn between government and interest groups; business and labor each retain the right to act against the pleas of government officials if they see this as in their particular interest.

Britain is a pluralist alternative to corporatism, for government attempts to use organized labor and business to manage the economy have repeatedly failed. One reason is that membership in British interest groups is usually voluntary. Interest groups are numerous and sometimes compete: trade unions, for example, tend to be organized by skills rather than by industry, leading to competition between unions about wage claims in a factory. The absence of corporatist cooperation is demonstrated by the failure of successive Conservative and Labour governments to prevent inflation through wage and price controls. In the 1980s the Thatcher administration ignored unions and many business groups too, because the prime minister did not want to negotiate government policy with nonelected groups. The economy was managed through measures the government could determine, such as monetary policy, high interest rates, and increased unemployment.

In every system of interest group representation, there are substantial inequalities between groups. Some are inherent in the character of groups; for example, banks have more money and trade unions have more votes. Others reflect the character of a policy area: Producers are easier to organize than consumers. Conflicts can exist within the labor movement—for example, between Social Democratic, Communist, and Catholic trade unions in France and Italy—and everywhere they are found between banks that loan money and manufacturers that borrow money.

In a pluralistic system, some groups will choose to influence public policy as "insiders" and others as "outsiders" (Walker, 1991: 9; Maloney et al., 1994). Insider groups have regular access to government ministries and higher civil servants, cooperating with government of their own choice. Outsider groups are more visible publicly, using the media and public debates in Parliament to call attention to their demands. But going public is usually a sign of exclusion from private deliberations inside ministries. In a pluralistic system, outsider groups can put a topic on the political agenda that the state has ignored. The green movement has publicized problems that government once regarded as of no importance,.

Within a country, the organization of interests is likely to vary from one policy sector to another, thus creating what is sometimes described as *sectoral corporatism.* Agriculture is corporatist everywhere in Europe, for government and agricultural groups bargain as insiders in annual reviews of farm subsidies. But feminist, gay, and lesbian interest groups are outside the corporatist structure, for they organize on behalf of their members, not official agencies. From country to country, the capacity of groups to influence public policy varies too. In the extreme case of France, the state tends to dominate rather than negotiate as an equal with interest groups. Many major French businesses are state-owned, and trade unions are divided and weak. French higher civil servants and ministers are confident of the state's authority, and lobby groups to do what the government of the day has decided upon. Hayward argues (1983: 68) that in France "the executive is so powerful that the peak organisations are more like pressured groups than pressure groups" (cf. Keeler, 1987).

Interest groups, whether corporatist or pluralist, can be seen as participants in policy networks (van Waarden, 1992; Jordan and Schubert, 1992). Policy networks involve government ministries and private sector interest groups. Some participants in a policy network are freelancers, such as academic experts. Even if there are no formal negotiations between groups, interdependence makes each aware of the others. Outsider groups can become part of a network if their demands make an impact on insiders. Policy networks are not corporatist because they are informal institutions without any power to bind groups legally. It is an empirical question whether, in a given sector of public policy, the pattern of interest group–government relations is pluralist or corporatist.

CHANGING DIRECTORS IN POST-COMMUNIST EUROPE

Interdependence presupposes that leaders of different institutions recognize the right of others to an independent existence. Whereas corporatist and pluralist models accept a civil society in which many organizations are independent of the state, this was not the case in Communist regimes. All parts of society were meant to be manifestations of a single organization, the party, and trade unions and business enterprises were meant to represent the interests of the party-state rather than their members. The Communist drive to bring everything under the control of the party had an unintended consequence: It encouraged people to distrust institutions that claimed to represent them.

To make post-Communist governments more representative requires changes in the direction of government. It also requires the "privatization of society" through the growth of institutions of civil society independent of the state.

Changing People and Turning People

In post-Communist societies free elections have brought new parties and people into government, but the continued presence of people from the old regime is an inertia force supporting old policies and practices. The problem facing new governors is, in the words of a former dissident: "When we were forming the new structures, we had to hire people from the old structures. Our supporters—the people who came to rallies and street demonstrations—didn't know anything about how to run a country" (Dietz, 1994: 873; cf. Derlien and Szablowski, 1993). New leaders have faced two problems: What to do about the officials who gave direction to the old regime? Insofar as new appointments are to be made, where can new leaders be found?

Personnel policies are people policies. Newly elected governors know many people anxious for appointment to top jobs in government. However, zeal for office is not proof of expertise. In post-Communist societies new entrants to office are normally inexperienced in giving direction to large bureaucracies. This is true whether they were outsiders opposing the old regime or too young to have held any official position before 1989. Newcomers to high office must learn how to govern by a process of trial and error. When a new minister or civil servant makes a mistake, critics clamor for his or her resignation and claim the job for themselves. The result is a rapid turnover in political offices. This can be followed by ex-Communist parties winning office, as the Hungarian Socialists did in 1994, with the campaign slogan, "Let the experts govern." Yet after entering office, ex-Communists started disagreeing with each other, for they were accustomed to facing political challenges with the resources of a one-party command economy rather than governing a market economy with a democratic Parliament.

In East Germany the problem of changing directors had a unique solution: integration in a ready-made state, the Federal Republic of Germany. With the end of an independent Communist state, some ministries of the former German Democratic Republic (GDR) were no longer necessary, such as foreign affairs, and agencies responsible for planning a nonmarket economy. Older GDR officials were pensioned off (Derlien, 1993; Koenig, 1993). Ministries in Bonn could take over responsiblity for national policies. To fill the vacuum at the level of regional and local politics and administration, some West German politicians and civil servants have taken posts in East Germany and are paid bonuses, referred to by the imperialist term "jungle money" (*Buschgeld*). Because they are outsiders, East Germans have criticized these officials as "carpetbaggers" and in the 1994 election the ex-Communist Party of Democratic Socialism, running on a protest platform, gained a fifth of the East German vote.

Importing outsiders is not possible outside East Germany. New governors have had to come to terms with the inheritance of officials who were members of the *nomenklatura* system, which conferred privileges on individuals who served the party-state. Because the Communist Party was a mass membership party, it could not make a high level of ideological commitment a condition of membership. That would have made the party like a religious sect composed of a small number of "true believers." Many people joined the Communist Party from necessity, not conviction. Surveys have found that opportunism not altruism was more important in leading people to join (see White and McAllister, 1994: table 4). Many people who held in the old regime professional posts that required technical qualifications as well as a party card could claim that their professional skills remain of use, for example, in public health or in aircraft control.

There are disagreements within post-Communist societies about whether those responsible for acts of the old regime should be prosecuted under existing laws or under new laws designed to secure "backward-looking" justice (Elster, 1992: 15). Opponents of the old regime, who often suffered many indignities, can resent seeing those who prospered in those days continuing to prosper now. But since the Communist regime compelled so many people to serve it, any attempt to punish all who did so would affect a large number of leaders throughout society. Moreover, lawyers argue that people should not be punished for actions that were not illegal when they were undertaken. The upshot has been that only a small percentage of Communists have been removed from government posts, usually those at the top of ministries or in strategic security posts.

Changing the direction of government not only requires new directors but also turning many who served the old regime into officials responsive to elected leaders and to citizens. The problem is not unique to post-Communist countries. After World War II, Germany had a problem of de-Nazification in a society in which millions had held Nazi party cards. Then as now, the collapse of the old regime gave individuals who joined the party to secure a job an impetus to discard their nominal allegiance. The introduction of a new regime offers incentives for individuals to adapt to new procedures of government. There remains, however, a major difference between post-Nazi Germany and post-Communist countries. In Germany, even if officials were deficient in democratic values the many who had been trained in pre-Nazi days were experienced in administering a *Rechtsstaat*. In post-Communist societies, by contrast, higher civil servants have never worked in a rule-of-law state or in a market economy. The problem of reorientation is therefore much greater (see reports in the periodical *East European Constitutional Review*).

Misrepresentation and Representation of Group Interests

In Communist regimes formal organizations were intended to represent the party-state to their members rather than group interests to the state. Trade unions, agricultural groups, and professional associations were licensed by the state and controlled by the same party apparatus that controlled ministries. The idea of a private (that is, civil) society was just as much alien as that of a private sector in the economy. In such circumstances there could not be a plurality of free and independent interest groups competing for influence. Nor could corporatism operate, for even though Communist institutions were monopolies in their field, they were not trusted by their members. Between trusted face-to-face groups and the abstraction of the nation there was, in the words of a Polish sociologist, "a huge vacuum" (quoted in Wedel, 1986: 116; see also Shlapentokh, 1989: 6 ff.).

The legacy of Communism is distrust in major institutions of society. Individuals are now free to show whether major institutions of society represent or misrepresent their views. When the New Democracies Barometer asked people in post-Communist societies whether they trust a variety of institutions, a majority consistently said they do *not* trust the institutions named; the only difference is in the size of the percentage lacking trust (Figure 10.3). Distrust is highest for political parties; 85 percent indicate no trust in these crucial institutions of a representative democracy. In addition, four-fifths do not trust trade unions or Parliament. Among state institutions, an average of 75 percent distrust civil servants, more than two-thirds distrust the courts and police, and more than half distrust the army.

Distrust in post-Communist societies is much higher than in the established democracies of the European Union. There an average of 59 percent trust state institutions, compared to 34 percent in post-Communist societies. Trust in Parliament and in trade unions is more than twice as high in Western Europe and, although no comparable data are available, trust in political parties is likely to be higher too. The graphics in Figure 10.3 almost certainly understate the contrast between the two parts of Europe, for even if a Swede or a Briton does not trust the courts or Parliament, by any objective standard they are more trustworthy than institutions that were part of a Communist regime for four decades.

In post-Communist societies the first requirement is to *create* business enterprises, trade unions, television stations, publishing houses, and universities independent of the state. Such free institutions make it possible for exponents of different ideas and policies to compete. Civil institutions are also important in providing political parties with money, organizational support, and members.

The privatization of state-owned enterprises is important politically as well as economically, for private enterprises and free trade unions can decide which parties to support or oppose, and what demands they want to press on government (cf. Agh, 1993). Allowing new businesses to open creates a nationwide network of small businesspersons who can promote activities at the local level and in rural areas; divesting the state of the ownership of farm land is especially important. Until large-scale privatization occurs, state enterprises remain political as well as economic organizations, lobbying within ministries for grants from the public treasury to finance what are often loss-making activities.

Every post-Communist regime has taken steps to transfer state property into private hands in order to create a market economy, but there has been no common or consensual way to privatize without a private sector. Whereas privatization in a market economy is simply about the transfer of ownership through established market mechanisms, in post-Communist countries privatization is occurring simultaneously with the establishment of stock exchanges, commercial banks, and commercial law. Methods of privatization differ between countries and even within countries. There may be several bidders for a shop in the main square of a large city but none for a steel mill losing lots of money each week.

The first problem is politically charged: Who ought to own the state's property? Former owners may launch a claim for restitution. If the principle of restitution is endorsed, there are disagreements about how far back claims can extend. For example, treating 1945 as the date for determining property rights would repudiate the legality of actions by the Communist regime but recognize expropriation during Nazi occupation. There are disputes about privatizing

FIGURE 10.3 TRUST IN INSTITUTIONS HIGHER IN WESTERN THAN POST-COMMUNIST EUROPE

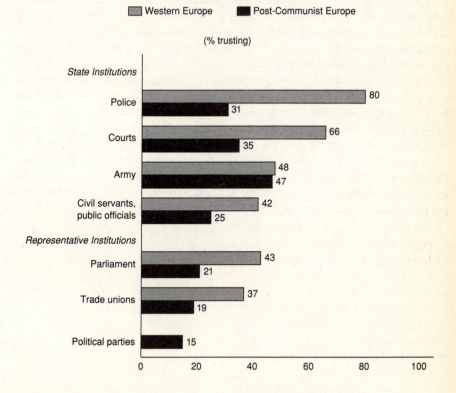

Western Europe   Post-Communist Europe

(% trusting)

Source: Post-Communist countries: Paul Lazarsfeld Society: *New Democracies Barometer III,* Vienna: (1994): mean for Bulgaria, Czech Republic, Slovakia, Hungary, Poland, and Romania. *Western Europe:* World Values Survey, 1991, average for Austria, Belgium, Britain, Denmark, Finland, France, West Germany, Ireland, Italy, the Netherlands, Portugal, Spain, and Sweden.

through selling shares to highest bidders at auction, and whether foreigners should be allowed to bid for firms or land. Spreading ownership widely can be encouraged by giving everyone vouchers that can be converted into shares. Whatever the economic arguments, there are political advantages in spreading ownership among the general public. Workers and managers in an enterprise may claim that inasmuch as they have invested a lifetime of effort in a firm, they have a right to become part owners. By the time post-Communist governments took office, there was some *nomenklatura* privatization, Communist officials transferring profitable assets to themselves at favorable terms before resigning public office.

A second problem is to assess the market value of enterprises that had operated in a nonmarket economy in which the target was to fulfil bureaucratic plans rather than achieving profits, and indebtedness to state banks was not a concern (cf. Winiecki, 1988). Many enterprises have been part of a ministry or giant state-owned cartels. Before they can be sold, each must become an independent legal enterprise with its own shares, rules of governance, statement of profit or loss, and balance sheet.

Once privatization occurs, a third problem becomes evident: There is a shortage of capital and of capitalists, including people who undertake the everyday activities of management in a market economy, such as accountants, bankers, corporate lawyers, and marketing and export managers. People with such skills were not required in Communist regimes.

Changing direction in post-Communist regimes involves acts of deconstruction and innovation. The first—taking power from institutions and individuals who had exploited office under the Communist regime—has been accomplished to a substantial extent. The second—creating trustworthy and effective institutions—is long-term. Anyone with a knowledge of the creation of market economies in Western Europe—a process requiring more than a century— should not be surprised that this cannot be done overnight in post-Communist societies. It is equally important to understand that time is also needed to create the trustworthy institutions of a civil society.

chapter 11

PUBLIC POLICY AND WELFARE

The resources of government are not buried or burned; they are spent to do things. Yet the question—What does government do?—does not permit a simple answer, for public policies are not all the same. This is true whether one thinks of the purposes, the costs, or the political justification of policies as different as defense, agriculture, and education.

Politics is first of all about purpose and power. The policies that express the purposes of the European state have developed in a similar pattern (Rose, 1976). First came the *essential activities,* necessary by definition: defense, foreign affairs, taxation, and law enforcement. These activities were undertaken at the end of the eighteenth century by Napoléon in France and by the American government of George Washington. Achievements that today appear obvious, such as the routine collection of taxes, were a major advance by comparison with the premodern state (Tilly, 1975).

The state's administrative and fiscal resources were then used to promote *economic development,* supporting transportation, communication, industry, trade and agriculture programs. In the nineteenth century governments built canals, roads, and railways, established post, telegraph and telephone services, and promoted industry and trade. In countries such as France and Prussia, state action reflected an ideology of national interest that justified state monopolies instead of free markets. Even supporters of the laissez-faire doctrine of nonintervention by the state recognized that the industrial revolution required a framework of law, property rights, sound money, and order, a point that has been rediscovered by post-Communist regimes.

In point of time, *social programs* for individuals have come most recently. In the late nineteenth century, the state took responsibility for public health and primary education. In the 1880s in Prussia, Bismarck introduced the first social security measures offering protection against industrial injury and sickness. By 1914, richer European states had taken the initial steps toward ensuring income for the elderly and the unemployed, and health care too. By the outbreak of World War II, the foundations were laid for the social security, health, and education programs that today claim the largest share of public expenditure and public employment. The cumulative legacy of past commitments has "locked in" programs that provide major benefits for the majority of European citizens at important stages of life. Collectively, these measures are described as the welfare state (for a detailed history, see Flora and Heidenheimer, 1981; Baldwin, 1990).

It is doubly misleading to confine the study of public policy to social welfare programs. First, social welfare was not the initial concern of the state nor is it the sole concern today. Historically, defense, public order, and a sound national currency have been the first priorities of the state; a substantial part of public resources continues to be devoted to defense and economic programs today. Second, the state is not the sole source of welfare. In contemporary society the market and not-for-profit institutions also provide pensions in old age, health care, and schools. The family also has a major impact upon how much children actually learn at school, and an individual's choice of diet and life style is critical for health.

Every European today lives in a big economy with a big government. The first section shows how economic growth has enabled government to increase taxing and spending, sometimes painlessly and sometimes painfully. Since the first priority of government is to maintain order and security, this is addressed in the next section. Every European government is involved in managing the economy, but there are national differences in economic philosophies, and divisions within nations too. The third section shows how changes have occurred in the priorities of economic policy in response to changes in rates of inflation and unemployment. The importance of the state in providing social benefits, such as education, social security, and health, is half the story of the concluding section. In a civil society, institutions independent of the state also make an important contribution to individual welfare.

BIG GOVERNMENTS WITH GROWING ECONOMIES

The size of government depends upon the political values of governors and the country's economic resources. Economic growth has been a necessary condition for the growth of government in the past half century. But it has not been a sufficient cause. The scale of public expenditure is also affected by how much national governments consider is "enough" spending and "too much" taxation.

Economic Growth and Growth in Public Expenditure

The great increase in wealth in post–World War II Europe has been the consequence of compounding seemingly small annual rates of growth over five decades. From 1950 through 1964, the wealth of the average European OECD country grew by 4.9 percent per capita each year; this almost doubled the gross domestic product per person. Growth in the next decade was 4.2 percent. By 1974, the average economy was producing almost three times as much per person as in 1950, and in Germany almost four times as much. Even Britain, the slowest growing major economy in Europe, doubled its standard of living.

The annual rate of growth slowed down after the first oil shock in 1973. In the 1980s growth averaged 2.3 percent a year. But because this rate was applied to a much wealthier economy, in absolute terms European economies have been growing more than in the earlier period. The national product per capita in Europe today is more than four times as great in real terms as it was in 1950 (Figure 11.1).

FIGURE 11.1 ECONOMIC GROWTH AND GROWTH IN PUBLIC SPENDING SINCE 1950

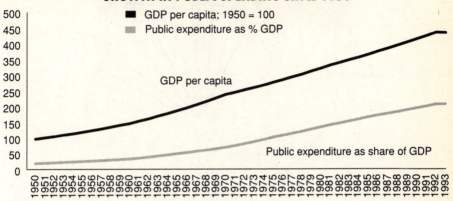

Sources: OECD data as reported in *OECD in Figures 1994,* 24 f., 40 f.; Jan-Erik Lane, David McKay and Kenneth Newton, *Political Data Handbook: OECD Countries* (Oxford: Oxford University Press, 1991), 61, 71.

Most Europeans today enjoy a higher standard of living than did their parents and a much higher living standard than their grandparents. Consumer goods that 40 years ago were the privilege of a relative few, such as an automobile or a refrigerator, are now fixtures in the majority of European households. Consumer goods that did not exist in 1950, such as color television, are also now commonplace. Instead of being tenants in small flats or old-fashioned houses, the majority of Europeans can now afford to buy a modern house. While incomes are not equal, low living standards are now the experience of a limited minority of the population.

An expanding economy increases the value of the tax base—that is, the economic activities that are the object of taxation. Government relies upon a multiplicity of sources to raise revenue (Figure 11.2) the chief taxes are as follows:

- *Expenditure taxes:* The value-added tax (VAT) is the largest single source of tax revenue in Europe. It is a tax that is levied upon each step in the manufacture and sale of goods and services. Economists endorse this tax on expenditure as an encouragement to saving. Tax officials like it because the burden of record keeping and collection is placed on firms. VAT can add more than 20 percent to the price of everyday necessities, such as clothes. Since the tax is a percentage, revenue rises with inflation. Sales taxes on gasoline and tobacco are much higher in Europe than in the United States, reflecting government efforts to discourage the importation of these raw materials. Alcohol taxes tend to be low in wine-producing countries; in Scandinavia they are very high in an attempt to discourage drinking.
- *Income tax:* Before World War II, the majority of European workers paid no income tax because their income and public expenditure were both low. Income tax was popular with social democrats because it was a means of redistributing welfare from rich to poor. Today, the amount of revenue required to finance big social programs requires the average

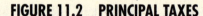

FIGURE 11.2   PRINCIPAL TAXES

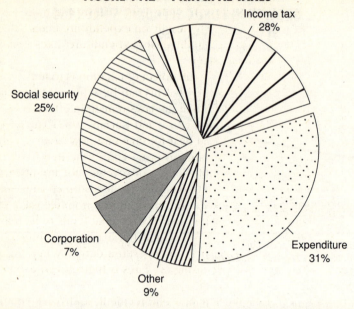

Income tax
28%

Social security
25%

Corporation
7%

Other
9%

Expenditure
31%

Source: OECD in Figures 1994: (Paris: OECD, 1994) 42 f. Mean contribution to tax revenue in 17 European countries. The principal expenditure tax is a value added tax.

wage earner to pay a significant portion of his or her income in taxes. If income tax is withheld from wages, it is a very easy tax to administer, because employers are responsible for deducting the tax from wages and paying it to the tax authorities. Income tax is much more difficult to collect from the self-employed and peasants, who are disproportionately numerous in Mediterranean countries.

- *Social security tax:* Earmarking social security taxes for a popular benefit, income security in old age, makes this tax more palatable politically. It is also easier to levy because employers as well as employees contribute; in Italy and Spain the employer contributes four times as much in social security taxes as does the employee. Social security taxes produce almost as much revenue as the income tax.

- *Corporation taxes:* Taxes on the profits of corporations account for relatively little revenue. The principal contribution of firms to revenue is to act as tax-collecting agencies, routinely paying government large sums of money deducted from wages for income tax and social security; employer contributions to social security; and value-added taxes. Revenue from levies on the gross cash flow of firms is four or five times greater than taxes on profits.

The relative emphasis given taxes varies between European countries. Sweden is an example of a country that depends heavily on income tax, a tax that falls more heavily upon the well-to-do, consistent with social democratic preferences. France, with a level of taxation higher than the average in Europe, raises less than one-seventh of its revenue from income tax, which is not deducted prior to payment of salaries. Two-fifths of revenue comes from social security taxes paid by employers directly to the state. Less wealthy and more rural countries such as Greece and Portugal rely heavily on expenditure taxes, which avoid attempts to collect income tax from individuals. Expenditure taxes assume that if people spend money they must earn it.

From a politician's point of view, the object of taxation is to maximize public revenue while minimizing electoral costs. This can be achieved by relying upon the force of political inertia, the fact that tax laws remain in effect from one year to the next without need for renewal (Rose and Karran, 1987). The government of the day does not face the political heat for enacting new taxes. It can collect up to half the national product by administering taxes inherited from its predecessors. This guarantees a predictable source of revenue, for tax officials know how to collect established taxes, and taxpayers are accustomed to paying them. Since inflation and economic growth both push up the nominal value of the income and sales that constitute the tax base, tax revenue tends to be buoyant, increasing faster than the economy grows overall. But inasmuch as public expenditure is even more buoyant, most governments run a deficit. When the political costs of introducing new taxes or raising tax rates is high, governments borrow money to finance the resulting deficits.

Because education, health care, law enforcement, and many other public policies are labor-intensive, the growth of government spending has been accompanied by a growth in public employment. The great majority of public employees provide benefits directly to citizens and communities; they are not shuffling papers or staring at computers. Public employees differ greatly in their skills and salaries, ranging from university professors and air force generals to collectors of garbage and swimming pool attendants. They differ too in the organizations that employ them (see again Figure 10.1).

At the beginning of the 1950s, public employees averaged 17 percent of the labor force in major European countries. By the 1980s, the proportion rose to 30 percent. Growth did not occur evenly; it followed changes in policy priorities. The big increase has been greatest in workers in two major entitlement programs, health and education. Each is labor-intensive; more education requires hiring more teachers, and more health care requires more doctors, nurses, and hospital workers. To some extent, expansion has been offset by cutbacks in defense personnel; the total of uniformed and civilian defense personnel is about half what it was during the height of the Cold War (Rose, 1985a: 11 f.).

Whereas taxes usually claim less than half the national product, government enacts 100 percent of the laws (Rose, 1984: ch. 3). Laws have been especially important in the growth of the welfare state when they guarantee individuals entitlements to expensive social benefits. A decision about whether a person receives a pension is not at the discretion of a politician or clerk; it is determined by a social security act. So too are entitlements to health care and education. When people live longer, the amount of money spent on pensions and health care goes up. Entitlement legislation binds government to continue providing services, whatever the election result, unless politicians are prepared to face the political controversy of repealing a measure.

Laws can regulate some forms of behavior without any significant expenditure of public funds. Many European countries have a history of legal regulation of economic activities dating back to medieval guilds. Laws can grant advantages to businesses and benefit workers—for example, increasing the number of paid holidays that firms must grant. Pressures from environmental groups have led every country to enact laws to control environmental pollution; however, national political institutions have resulted in substantial differences in the particular laws enacted (cf. Vogel, 1986; Fernandez, 1994). The European Union relies much more on laws and regulations than upon expenditure to promote a single market (see Chapter 13).

Costs and Benefits of Growth

Economic growth increased the value of public policy throughout Europe. Young Europeans enjoy more years of education than their parents and far more than their grandparents; older Europeans receive pensions with a greatly enhanced purchasing power; and people of all ages have a much higher standard of health care than a generation ago.

Economic growth has financed a portion of the big increase in public expenditure chronicled in Figure 11.1. When the economy grows, economic growth can produce a fiscal dividend of more tax revenue while still leaving some money for increased take-home pay. If the size of the national product doubles, public spending can double too without any increase in tax rates. Insofar as this happens, it is possible for governments to deliver what Hugh Heclo (1981: 397) has described as "policy without pain." In the postwar era, the public expenditure of every government in Europe has grown faster than the national economy. This has increased average national expenditure from 22 percent of the national product in 1950 to more than double that today. In the extreme case of Sweden, the share of the national product allocated by government has almost tripled from a starting point in 1950.

The actual amount of money that a government spends on public policies reflects three primary considerations: (1) the size of the economy; (2) political preferences for high taxes and high levels of expenditure or lower taxes and lower levels of expenditure; and (3) the purchasing power value of money spent.

There are big disparities between European countries in the average value of gross domestic product per capita. After controlling for differences in purchasing power, Switzerland ranks a clear first and Greece last among European OECD countries (Table 11.1). Everything else being equal, a rich country will spend more on public policy. However, everything else is not equal: tax effort, the readiness of governments to levy taxes, also varies between countries. Seven European countries allocate more than half their national product through public expenditure, while four claim less than two-fifths in taxes. Britain and Sweden have economies that produce similar purchasing power resources per capita, but the Swedish government spends half again as much as the British government. Even though Switzerland ranks first in GDP per capita, it ranks twelfth out of 17 countries in the purchasing power value of per capita public expenditure, due to low taxes and public spending.

Because of differences in tax effort and national product, the cash value of public expenditure varies greatly across Europe. The three richest countries—

TABLE 11.1   PUBLIC EXPENDITURE IN RELATIVE AND ABSOLUTE TERMS

	GDP per capita (PPP $)	Public expenditure (as % GDP)	Public expenditure per capita (PPP $)
Denmark	17,813	57.2	10,189
Belgium	18,195	55.2	10,044
Sweden	16,590	59.8	9,920
Luxembourg	21,929	45.0	9,868
Netherlands	17,023	55.3	9,414
Norway	17,756	52.9	9,393
Germany	20,435	44.4	9,073
France	18,590	48.5	9,016
Italy	17,482	51.3	8,968
United States	23,215	36.4	8,450
Austria	18,096	45.7	8,270
Finland	14,545	56.2	8,174
Switzerland	22,268	35.0	7,793
United Kingdom	16,340	39.7	6,487
Ireland	12,391	41.9	5,192
Spain	12,853	38.8	4,987
Greece	8,303	47.1	3,911
Portugal	9,786	39.3	3,845

Source: OECD in Figures 1994, (Paris: OECD, 1994) 24 f., 40 f. Data are for 1992.

Switzerland, Luxembourg, and Germany—rank twelfth, fourth, and seventh respectively in public expenditure per capita. Even though Switzerland has an average national product more than half again that of Finland, public expenditure is higher in Finland because tax effort is much higher. Denmark ranks seventh in the value of its national product per capita but first in the value of its public expenditure because of an unusually high tax effort. Portugal and Greece spend as large a share or larger of their national product on public expenditure as Britain, but a much lower living standard in Mediterranean countries means that much more money is spent on public services in Britain.

ESSENTIAL TASKS: MAINTAINING ORDER AND SECURITY

The purposes of government cannot be reduced to the amount of money spent, and this is especially true in the state's concern with its essential tasks of maintaining internal order and security against external threats. If a government does not succeed in these two goals, the regime will fall and be replaced by another, or the state will be overrun by a foreign army.

Order is a fundamental concern of every government, small or large. Order is most easily maintained when citizens voluntarily obey the law and abstain from antisocial crimes and illegal acts. In such circumstances, there is no need for a large police force. England has been an outstanding example of a society in which self-control has minimized the role of the police. The most striking feature of the traditional English "bobby" is that he or she patrols without a gun. As is the case elsewhere in Europe, the crime rate is rising in England. Nonetheless, after controlling for differences in population, the murder rate remains one-sixth that of the United States. Nor does England have a tradition of using military or paramilitary forces to maintain domestic order. The premier branch of the armed services has been the Royal Navy, defending the island against invasion by sea.

The challenge to order can come from political forces as well as from antisocial criminals. This is illustrated by the history of Ireland, North and South, where more than a century of revolutionary activity to secure independence from Britain has left a tradition of armed insurrection, and in Northern Ireland local paramilitary groups, both Catholic and Protestant. As a consequence, Northern Ireland has never been subject to policing in the English style; it has always had uniformed paramilitary groups in reserve or in the streets in attempts to maintain order there. A quarter-century of armed violence after 1969 involved four principal armed groups—the British Army, the all-Protestant Royal Ulster Constabulary; the Catholic-led Irish Republican Army; and Protestant paramilitary groups—each advancing political goals, legal or illegal, through the use of force.

In France political authority, since the Revolution has been challenged in the streets. There is a centralized police force to protect the regime against public disorder, as well as a police force to deal with "nonpolitical" crimes. Responsibility for protecting the regime is divided between the Ministry of Defense and the Ministry of the Interior. The Gendarmerie Nationale of the defense ministry is organized along military lines and stationed in barracks. It can be called into action in the streets of Paris or the back roads of France in the event of riots. The national police force under the Ministry of the Interior has a security division, the Companies Républicaines de Sécurité (CRS) to control street demonstrations. Demonstrators normally confine themselves to barricading public roads or throwing things at law enforcement officers. Police are disciplined to make baton attacks but not to use firearms; few deaths result from these clashes, but injuries can easily occur (cf. Roach and Thomaneck, 1985; Guyomarch, 1990). Italy and Spain, where there is a similar history of insurrection, have security forces similar to the French system (cf. Roach and Thomaneck, 1985).

Size matters when defense against external threats is the issue. Small countries cannot match the military force of big countries, whatever proportion of their national product is spent on defense. For example, Norway has only one-twentieth the population of contemporary Germany, and 3 percent the population of Russia. Small countries seek to defend themselves by entering into military alliances, such as the North Atlantic Treaty Organization (NATO), or by pursuing an active policy of neutrality. In the postwar era the NATO has been the bulwark of defense for most European countries (see Chapter 14). Sweden and Switzerland have maintained an active, almost aggressive policy of neutrality, offering their services as brokers to both sides during two world wars and staying aloof from military alliances. Since the Republic of Ireland gained its independence, it too has followed an active policy of neutrality rather than joining a military alliance with the United Kingdom.

Big European countries can mobilize substantial defense forces. Britain and France are each nuclear powers; Germany has wealth and technology but because of its history of militarism it no longer seeks to maintain a large and powerful army. Large European states spend a lower proportion of their national product on defense than does the United States (Sivard, 1993: 43). Britain spends 4.0 percent and France 3.6 percent, whereas the United States spends 5.6 percent of its GDP on defense. This does not reflect a lesser priority for defense in Europe, the front line of the Cold War, than in a country on the other side of the Atlantic. Even if Britain or France were to spend as big a share of their national product on defense as does the United States, with less than a quarter of the U.S. population, their national defense forces would be only a quarter the size of the United States.

ALTERNATIVE APPROACHES TO MANAGING THE ECONOMY

The goals of economic policy can be simply stated: to promote economic growth, full employment, stable prices and benefits from international trade. The means to achieve these ends are disputed. Differences in political values lead to differences in the priority given such goals as fighting inflation or unemployment. Differences in economic theories lead to disagreements about the policy most likely to achieve a given goal. Thus the management of the economy is not a technical subject but rather a subject caught up in party politics, as some theories favor social democratic goals while others favor goals of antisocialist parties (cf. Ricketts and Shoesmith, 1990). The Swedish Nobel Prize Committee in Economics has recognized the "multiparty" nature of economics by balancing prizes for economists favoring social democracy and planning, such as Gunnar Myrdal and the Soviet economist Leonid Kantorovich, with prizes for proponents of market forces, such as the Chicago monetarist, Milton Friedman, and the Austrian opponent of planning, Friedrich von Hayek.

Competing Economic Philosophies

The oldest economic philosophy is nationalism or mercantilism. A wealthy nation was seen as good for the king, generating tax revenues and expanding a nation's power. It was also good for those who supported the king. In nineteenth-century Germany industrialization was seen as a means to military power. A mercantilist state actively sought to control economic activities. It promoted tariffs to protect national industries against foreign competition, even if this meant higher prices for domestic consumers, granted monopoly rights in tobacco, and recognized cartels in fields such as steel. As the most powerful institution of society, the state promoted industrialization by developing transport, communications, currency, foreign markets, and colonies. The contemporary French version of mercantilism can be described as *dirigiste* (directing), since the state claims the power to direct or control important elements of the economy. As the then French prime minister Edouard Balladur explained, the state's role is to civilize the market: "What is the market? It is the law of the jungle, the law of nature. And what is civilization? It is the struggle against nature." (Gowers and Buchan, 1993).

In the *social democratic tradition* the state enables people without capital to use their vote to secure benefits not available through the market or even as members of trade unions. Social democrats have differed about the extent to which the state should own industry. In Britain Labour governments promoted state ownership, but in Sweden large firms have been left to make profits under private ownership, and the profits are then heavily taxed. Social democrats favor a high level of expenditure on social policies benefiting the majority of the population, and levying high and progressive taxes to finance these policies.

The *social market philosophy* is Catholic in origin; it rejects both socialism and capitalism in favor of a noneconomic moral philosophy that is collectivist. The state and church are seen as partners, with the state responsible for the material welfare of workers as well as for securing private property. The social market doctrine is found in Catholic parties in the Benelux countries. It is also important in Germany, where the Christian Democratic Union seeks votes across class lines by espousing social policies involving a high level of public expenditure and taxes.

The *free-market philosophy* favors the private sector over governmental decision making. It is much weaker in Europe than in the United States, because Americans assume that the state ought to be weak and individual choice is preferred to collective choice. In Europe both these assumptions have been rejected by conservatives and social democrats. Economic individualism is strongest in Britain, the home of the eighteenth-century philosopher of the markets, Adam Smith. As the world's first industrial country, it benefited from free trade in the market. Free-market doctrines of economic individualism were revived by Margaret Thatcher as prime minister.

Keynesianism and After

Between the two world wars, a variety of economic philosophies gave priority to fighting inflation by tight control of the money supply, even when there was a great depression. In reaction, for more than a quarter century after World War II the chief priorities were economic growth and full employment. These political policies relied heavily upon the economic theories of John Maynard Keynes (Hall, 1989).

In simple terms, *Keynesian theory* prescribed that when the economy was growing slowly and a rise in unemployment threatened, government ought to run a deficit, spending more than it raised in taxes in order to stimulate extra demand in the economy. This was seen as producing economic growth and full employment. If such measures led to a rise in prices, making inflation the bigger problem, then the inflationary pressures from high levels of demand could be reduced by squeezing consumer expenditure and public spending by running a budget surplus. Each Keynesian prescription had a cost: stimulating employment and growth threatened to boost inflation, and antiinflation measures threatened recession and increased unemployment. Keynes assigned the government of the day the task of striking the balance, deciding how much inflation it would trade off for full employment, or how much unemployment it would accept in order to reduce inflation.

The political attraction of Keynesianism has been great, for it offers a justification for spending more on public policies when times are bad and when times are good extra tax revenue is generated that can finance more public expenditure too. Proponents have given less attention to the prescription to reduce demand when inflation threatens. In effect, politicians practiced "one-eyed Keynesianism," running deficits when Keynesian theories prescribed doing so, and often running deficits when Keynesian theories prescribed the opposite. In the quarter-century of economic boom from 1951 to 1975, the nominally conservative Italian government ran a budget deficit every year, Sweden ran a deficit seven years in every eight, and Britain, France, and Germany ran deficits two-thirds of the time (Rose and Peters, 1978: 138 f.).

The turning point in economic policy making came in 1975, shortly after the first crisis due to a big boost in oil prices engineered by the Organization of Petroleum Exporting Countries (OPEC). In that year, in almost every European economy there was contraction rather than growth. Contrary to Keynesian theories, both inflation *and* unemployment started to rise. The result was "stagflation," a combination of very low, almost stagnant economic growth and high rates of inflation and unemployment.

The political impact of increased inflation and unemployment differs (Figure 11.3). Inflation is cumulative; each year's price increase is added to that of the previous year. In the 1960s, inflation averaged 3 percent a year in Europe, and the cumulative consequences were tolerated. But in the five years beginning 1973 inflation averaged above 10 percent annually, producing a 61 percent increase in prices. During the 1980s, inflation rates were less high but remained almost three times those of the early 1960s. In the 1990s inflation rates have fallen to their lowest level in Europe in two decades, but the cumulative effect continues to devalue long-term savings.

Unemployment rose along with prices, but the nature of the increase is very different. In the 1960s the 2.8 percent average unemployment rate was due to people taking time to look around for a new job when moving from one to another, or from being a student to being an employee. The unemployment rate almost doubled by the mid-1970s, as people who lost a job found it took longer to get another job. In the 1980s, even though the economy continued to expand, employment in Europe failed to grow and unemployment averaged above 9 percent. Today it averages about 10 percent. Rates of unemployment once deemed politically "intolerable" have become accepted as normal.

Inflation affects the prices that everyone pays and the value of all wages. Since progressive income and social security taxes take a substantial chunk of increased wages, a 10 percent increase in wages may leave a worker with only a 6 percent increase in cash in hand. Governments initially gained extra tax revenue from inflation, and the decline in the value of money made it easier to deal with the national debt. But then financial markets began to demand interest on government bonds that took inflation into account, rates of up to 12 or 15 percent.

FIGURE 11.3 UNEMPLOYMENT AND CUMULATIVE INFLATION SINCE 1960

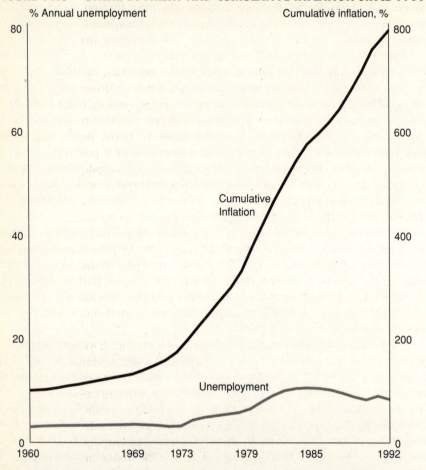

Sources: Calculated from *OECD in Figures 1994,* (Paris: OECD, 1994) 12 f., 22 f.; OECD, *Economic Outlook,* No. 51 (June 1992), tables R11, R19; *OECD Historical Statistics, 1960–89,* (Paris: OECD, 1991) tables 2.15 and 8.3.

High interest rates squeeze consumers, people with home mortgages, and investment in new equipment. Governments came under pressure from voters opposed to rapidly rising prices and to high interest rates used to combat inflation.

Whereas inflation affects everyone who spends money, unemployment directly affects a limited proportion of the population, those without a job. In the welfare state unemployment benefits cushion the immediate effect of losing income. The effect is also cushioned since most unemployed people live in a household in which at least one other person is employed. The duration of unemployment is critical; a person without work for a month suffers only a small drop in annual income and temporary anxiety. A person unemployed for a year or more is seriously hampered by loss of income and by difficulties in reentering the work force. Politically, unemployment has been tolerated because long-term unemployment directly affects a limited minority of the population. The majority are insiders in the labor force, working all year. Even though people in secure jobs may sympathize with the unemployed or feel uncertain how secure their own jobs now are, such concerns are usually less than their anxieties about inflation.

Monetarist theories associated with Milton Friedman of the University of Chicago have gained influence as inflation has risen. Monetarism prescribes that the state fight inflation by controlling the money supply. If the central bank does this, inflation is expected to fall, encouraging investment and subsequent economic growth. Whereas Keynesian policies to boost public expenditure made economics a "happy" science, monetarism places a political squeeze on elected politicians. The short-term consequences can include a rise in interest rates and unemployment and even a contraction in the economy. Yet a government faced with annually accelerating rates of inflation and a crisis in the foreign exchange value of its currency may feel driven to turn monetarist. In Britain, Labour governments gained trade union support by increasing public expenditure on welfare policies, but the policies were abandoned when inflation rates rose. Monetarist policies were adopted as part of the conditions of International Monetary Fund loans in 1967 and in 1976 (see Burk and Cairncross, 1992). In France a social democratic government entered office in 1981 expecting to use the state's powers to promote economic growth, but it made a U-turn as inflation rose.

In response to the common problem of stagflation, governments have responded differently. Because of past experience with hyperinflation, Germany has been a leader in keeping prices relatively stable. The German central bank, the *Bundesbank* in Frankfurt, is much more independent of influence by elected politicians than the Bank of England, the Bank of France or the Bank of Italy (cf. Goodman, 1992). Laws entrench its independence and obligate the *Bundesbank* to give first priority to fighting inflation. An incidental consequence of doing so is that Germany has had a below-average rate of economic growth. German reunification in 1990 complicated the situation, creating a temporary economic boom with inflation reaching a "high" of 4 percent in a year. It has also landed the federal government with massive bills to finance changes in the former command economy of East Germany.

Sweden has long been an example of a country combining economic growth and full employment. A social democratic government cooperated with trade unions to encourage workers to change jobs and retrain for new occupations in order to maintain economic flexibility. A buoyant economy financed high and rising social benefits, and led to more than one in three Swedish workers being in the public sector. However, for the past two decades both social democratic and antisocialist governments have faced increasing economic difficulties. For a decade after 1982, the Swedish economy grew at a rate of only 1.6 percent, the second worst in Europe. Prices rose at a rate higher than that in Italy or Britain. Between 1990 and 1993, the Swedish economy actually contracted each year. Unemployment has remained below the European average, but if those without employment currently being paid for participation in "re-training"' programs are counted as unemployed, the Swedish figure is above the European average (cf.

Ramaswamy, 1993; Freeman et al., 1995). Since 1976, control of office has swung between social democrats and an antisocialist coalition as Swedish voters have sought to recover the steady economic growth of the past.

Structural Adjustments

Today, most European governments have decided that structural economic adjustments are needed in response to long-term changes in markets, technology, and international competition. Whereas Keynesian and monetarist philosophies assume that an economy is basically sound and government need only make marginal changes in policy to maintain a market equilibrium, structural adjustment policies diagnose fundamental faults in the economy requiring state action to promote restructuring. For example, if a shipbuilding industry is unable to compete with shipbuilders in other countries, then policies will be adopted to finance the transition of the workforce and employing organizations into other activities where they may be competitive. If a workforce has insufficient skills and education to adapt to producing high-technology microelectronic products, the state may invest money in training youths and retraining adults. A multiplicity of strategies can be employed to promote structural change.

One strategy of structural adjustment is negative: subsidizing the closure of firms or industries whose products are no longer in demand. This was easy enough in an era of full employment, for a boom economy generated money to subsidize declining industries, and coal miners who became unemployed when antiquated mines were closed could find well-paying jobs elsewhere—for example, in the automobile industry. But now automobile manufacturers have come under pressure from Japanese imports to produce more efficiently and shed labor. Subsidizing a loss-making industry is now more difficult because of alternative claims on tax revenue. Simultaneously, finding new jobs for workers in growth industries is more difficult.

Privatization of state-owned firms is a second strategy. The logic of privatization is that of economics textbooks: a firm in the private sector is able to make profits and this should make it more efficient. Privatization has led to restructuring state enterprise into firms that investors would want to buy. The transfer of firms to private ownership has led some to become more efficient by increasing productivity, investment, and profits and decreasing employment. But since many state-owned enterprises, such as electricity, gas, telephones and water, are public utilities, privatization can lead to the introduction of new forms of state "interference," regulatory agencies limiting prices so that newly privatized utilities will not extract monopoly rents (see e.g., Vickers and Yarrow, 1988; Moran and Prosser, 1994).

"Backing winners" is a third strategy, seeking to promote growth by the government providing cash, tax relief, monopoly rights, or other forms of assistance to enterprises producing new products promising jobs and wealth in the decades ahead. This is consistent with the *dirigiste* philosophy of economic nationalism. In theory, building up new enterprises complements structural policies designed to close down or contract declining industries. But civil servants are not venture capitalists, experienced in identifying new opportunities in the market, and the priorities of ministers are political, not economic. For example, it made political sense for the French and British government to develop the supersonic Concord aircraft; this yielded jobs for ministers' constituents and prestige for governments. However, it has never made commercial sense, for while the Concord flies faster than the speed of sound it cannot generate enough revenue to pay for the billions spent in developing the aircraft.

Investing in people is a fourth adjustment strategy. The theory is that a well-trained and sophisticated workforce will adapt to whatever demands are made by firms capable of making profits in a competitive economy. Most European countries maintain extensive programs teaching vocational skills in schools and in "sandwich" courses in which youths divide their time between learning technical subjects in special vocational institutions and learning on a job directly related to their vocational training. In Germany more than four-fifths of young people who leave school without going to university secure a vocational qualification through a dual system of classroom instruction and on-the-job apprenticeship under the supervision of a *Meister* (master worker or worker). Occupations covered range from servicing airplanes through selling clothes to such basic manual skills as mending holes in roads (see Hamilton, 1990). To adjust the labor force also requires teaching new subjects to people having a qualification that is becoming obsolete or wanting to upgrade their skills by retraining as adults; for example, a typist may want to learn to use computers and a mechanic to become an electronics technician.

Making Europe a single market is a fifth strategy to change the structure of national economies. In the 1980s the member states of the European Union concluded that it was unrealistic for national governments to think solely in terms of promoting growth in a national context. In 1987 they agreed to the Single European Act, setting out procedures for establishing a single market for the free movement of goods, services, labor, and capital throughout Europe by the end of 1992. The single market now has a population much larger than the United States (see Chapter 13). Market mechanisms rather than bureaucratic rules are supposed to provide a dynamic economic stimulus to countries within the single market. There are also political pressures from some governments in the EU to use the single market to promote state direction of the economy and social market philosophies.

WELFARE FROM THE STATE

Every European state spends a substantial portion of its revenue on social welfare programs, but the evolution, current policies, spending levels, and political justifications of programs differ (see e.g. Esping-Andersen, 1990: ch. 1; Baldwin, 1990). Charity provided the earliest justification for state action to assist the very poor and destitute. This led to the development of *residualist programs* to provide public benefits to individuals too poor to provide for themselves. This is the logic of Medicaid in the United States, which finances health care for people of working age who cannot afford it. Targeting programs requires means testing, an assessment of individual and household income and assets. It also makes programs much less costly than providing benefits to everyone. Critics describe means testing as subject to error, socially stigmatizing, and politically divisive.

Compulsory *social insurance programs* in limited respects resemble private insurance, because payments are made to social insurance funds financing pensions in old age and health care, and only those making contributions are entitled to receive benefits. Social insurance programs differ from private-sector insurance in that contributions are compulsory. Moreover, employers and employees each must make contributions. Furthermore, the state sometimes makes contributions too. If the contributions provide only limited or deteriorating benefits, as can happen in an inflationary era with pensions, the state can step in to provide additional funds to raise social security pensions in line with inflation and/or in keeping with economic growth. It would be more accurate to describe such programs as programs funded by a combination of earmarked taxes (that is, compulsory employer and employee contributions) and general taxation. Effectively, the insurance element is used to exclude people who do not contribute to such funds. Residual programs provide benefits to those who have not made payments to social insurance funds.

Universalist programs avoid the problems of having two sets of programs, one for those regularly in work and another for the temporarily or long-term poor. Benefits are given everyone in society, whatever their income. Primary and secondary education are familiar examples of universalist programs. Social democrats, especially in Scandinavia, regard social benefits as a right of all citizens, and therefore argue that they should be provided to all through universalistic programs (Titmuss, 1958). Concern with equality can also justify making the state the primary or even sole provider of a service. Universalism offers a broad political base of support, since everyone benefits. The inclusion of the middle class, however, reduces the redistributive element, especially as middle-class people are more adept at making use of public services such as university education (cf. Goodin and LeGrand, 1987). Universalist programs also dramatically increase costs.

The Big Three: Education, Health, and Social Security

The earliest social program, *education,* is universalist; the state guarantees every child free education and makes it compulsory. Initially, the guarantee covered a minimum of elementary education; fees were charged for secondary education and universities were few or very small. Between the two world wars, scholarships opened a path to secondary and technical education for bright youths from families of average or below-average income. After World War II, free secondary education became available throughout Europe. In the 1960s new universities and colleges were founded and old ones expanded to offer places to a much increased number of qualified youths. In Europe today university tuition fees are very low, and there are hardly any private universities. Entrance standards are high, normally requiring competence in both mathematics and at least one foreign language. The expansion of free university education has benefited a minority of working-class youths and a disproportionate number of youths from middle-class families.

Prior to the establishment of free public education, churches were a major provider of education, and in most European countries the state funds some church-run schools and in some there is compulsory teaching of religious doctrines. Liberals have emphasized a scientific approach to education in which skepticism rather than doctrinal faith is encouraged and young people study subjects appropriate to a modern society rather than entry to a religious seminary. In France the battle between church and anticlericals continues; state schools are a stronghold of anticlericalism. In Italy, the Vatican gained influence in the schools by a concordat with Mussolini in 1929. In the Netherlands, three separate school systems—Protestant, Catholic and secular—have existed. In England there is compulsory non-denominational Christian worship in schools. It is today challenged by the presence in schools of Hindu and Muslim children of immigrants.

Universal education does not mean everyone gets the same education. In every European country two different types of secondary education have evolved: an academic secondary school qualifying youths for university entrance, and vocational schools emphasizing education in subjects leading to an apprenticeship, a job, or full-time attendance at a technical or business school. Such "streaming" is criticized on political grounds as socially divisive, since youths are selected for separate schools in their early teens, and are likely to end up in different occupations and social classes. In the 1950s the Swedish social democratic government introduced comprehensive secondary education, with students of all abilities studying in the same school, as is normally the case in American school systems. Britain followed the same path under the 1964 Labour government. German social democrats tried to promote the adoption of comprehensive schools but failed, in part because education is the responsibility of *Land* governments, which can be controlled by different parties, and partly due to popular opposition to merging very different types of schools under a single roof (for more details, see Heidenheimer et al., 1990: ch. 2).

Public *health* measures were initiated in the nineteenth century because booming cities needed pure water and effective sewage disposal to prevent epidemic diseases. Today, every European state has a health service ensuring care for all its citizens without test of means or age. The organization of health systems differs from country to country (cf. Saltman, 1988; *Health Affairs,* 1991). In Britain everyone is eligible to use the national health service without paying an earmarked tax into a sickness fund; health care is financed from general tax revenue. Doctors are self-employed, but their remuneration is determined by the state. Patients make no payment for a visit to a doctor, and state-owned hospitals make no charges to patients. Many European countries have corporatist systems; individuals or employers are compelled to make payment into health funds related to their industry or employment, and the funds finance and organize health care. In France the funds pay a fixed sum for treatment; doctors bill patients for a supplementary amount (Godt, 1989). Insofar as taxes or contributions to health funds are related to income, the system is redistributive. Insofar as the middle classes are more sophisticated users of the health system, it is not.

TABLE 11.2   HEALTH EXPENDITURE AND HEALTH CONDITIONS

	Britain	France	Germany	Sweden	US
Health expenditure as % GDP					
Public	5.5	6.7	6.1	6.7	5.9
Private	1.1	2.4	2.4	1.9	7.5
Total	6.6	9.1	8.5	8.6	13.4
Public expenditure as % of the total	83	74	72	78	44
Health outcomes					
Infant mortality (per thousand)	7.4	7.3	7.1	6.1	8.9
Life expectancy in years: women	79	81	79	80	79
Life expectancy in years: men	73	73	73	75	72

Source: OECD in Figures 1994, (Paris: OECD, 1994) 44–47.

The national priority given health expenditure, as measured by spending as a percentage of national gross domestic product, varies between European countries, and differences do not reflect national income (Table 11.2). Britain has consistently spent well below the European average on health care, because the British Treasury keeps tight controls on all forms of public expenditure, including that of hospitals and payment to doctors. In Britain free provision is universalist; there is very little private expenditure on health services supplementing or substituting for the national health service. French public expenditure on health is a fifth more than it is in Britain, and private expenditure is more than double that of Britain. No country in Europe spends as large a share of its national product on health care as does the United States. The United States is doubly distinctive: the private sector spends more on health than is spent by the public sector in Europe, and total health expenditure, both public and private, is half again or double the rate in European countries. When allowance is made for America's higher level of GDP per capita, trans-Atlantic differences in total and private health expenditure are greater still (cf. Tables 11.1, 11.2).

Health demonstrates a fundamental proposition of public policy: *input does not necessarily equal output.* There is no correlation between public and/or private spending on health care and health outcomes within Europe. Germany spends much more per person on health care than does Britain, but the life expectancy of women is the same in both countries. France spends much more on health care than does Britain, and its infant mortality rate is only better by a rate of 1 per 10,000 births. The United States spends half again or even double the amount of money on health as do European countries, yet the health of Americans is actually *worse* than in Europe. Infant mortality is higher in the United States, and life expectancy for women is lower or the same. Differences in health outcomes reflect differences in national environments and individual lifestyles. The biggest inequalities in health outcomes are found within countries and relate to gender. Everywhere women live longer than men, and in France women live eight years longer.

Social security programs were created because no one can live without a money income in a modern society, and people who are too old to work, or are unemployed or without a breadwinner in the household lack a weekly wage. Before World War I, social security programs were selective, and focused on better paid manual workers rather than those most likely to be in need. Since 1945, social security programs have expanded to provide universal coverage, sometimes through a single state fund and sometimes through corporatist funds covering different occupations or industries as well as farmers (Gordon, 1988; Kohli et al., 1991).

Social security benefits are redistributive in two ways. Insofar as current taxation contributes to pensions, payments are redistributive between the old and those of working age. When everyone is paid the same pension regardless of contributions on previous earnings, pensions redistribute income between classes. Yet paying a flat-rate pension means that on retirement well-paid individuals may suffer a big drop in income. Hence, most European countries now accept that income differentials during a working lifetime should be maintained in retirement. This is done through earnings-related pensions outside or inside the state system.

Whereas Scandinavian societies pay high levels of social security benefits to everyone, Britain emphasizes a residualist approach. The state pension is less than a quarter of average earnings, and thus approaches the poverty line. However, there is not widespread poverty, for most retired Britons have multiple streams of income from savings accumulated during their working lifetime, occupational pensions, and private pensions. The fifth of older Britons solely dependent upon social security payments claim means-tested supplementary benefits to pay rent and to meet additional short-term or long-term needs that cannot be financed with an ordinary pension.

The combination of social programs has made the state the source of the majority of incomes in European countries today (Figure 11.4). A third of all incomes are social security benefits paid to individuals who are not in work, such as pensioners, the unemployed, single-parent mothers, and others unable to work. Up to a fifth of incomes are paid public employees. The greatest number of public employees are in programs delivering education and health care, two of the major social benefits of the welfare state. Together, 52 percent of individuals with a regular income receive it from the state; less than half receive their primary income from employment in the private sector.

WELFARE IN THE MIXED SOCIETY

The state is only one source of welfare (Rose, 1986a). Total welfare in the family is the sum of goods and services obtained from three different sources, including the market and the household:

FIGURE 11.4   GOVERNMENT PROVISION OF PRIMARY INCOMES

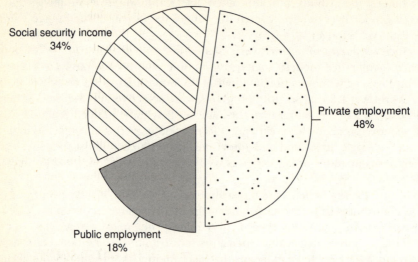

Social security income 34%

Private employment 48%

Public employment 18%

Source: Derived from Richard Rose, *Public Employment in Western Nations* (New York: Cambridge University Press, 1985), Table 1.17, average for Britain, France, Germany, Italy, and Sweden.

Total welfare in the family = State + Market + Household

To ignore the role of the household in producing welfare simply because family members do not pay each other for their services, is to imply that the unwaged work of women in the home is of no value and the care that parents give children or adults give each other when sick is valueless because it is not paid for. To deny any role to the market in the provision of welfare is to reject a basic assumption of civil society—namely, that individuals have a right to turn to institutions other than the state for their well-being.

The Welfare Mix Varies by Program Area

A contemporary European society is best described as a *mixed society,* because individual welfare depends upon combining all three streams of resources (Figure 11.5). We cannot say that the state, the market, or the household is most important, because the significance of each varies from one area to another. The household is most important in caring for children and the elderly. Even though children spend time each week in school or public preschool facilities, they spend even more time at home. Every European state provides social services for the elderly but most care is given by an elderly couple looking after each other or by relatives, friends, and neighbors. The market is most important in providing food; individuals choose their own diet and meals are normally prepared at home, not in municipal kitchens or government canteens. Education is the only welfare service in which the state approaches the position of monopoly provider. Yet education expenditure has its limits. The best-paid teachers and the newest buildings will be of little effect if the home does not encourage children to make an effort to learn.

Responsibility for welfare is often divided between two or three sectors of society. Incomes may come from the state or the market and children rely on parental income. The market is the usual source of housing, yet almost half of housing maintenance is a do-it-yourself activity, and public housing or housing subsidies give shelter to some. State and market usually deal with ill health; positive health requires that individuals look after themselves. When people are ill, they are more likely to stay home and be cared for by other members of their family than to go to an expensive hospital. When people drive, their transportation combines a car and gasoline bought in the market with the use of public roads and their own "self-employment" as a driver.

In a mixed society, the state still has a significant role to play. Public programs provide major benefits to people at all major stages of the life cycle, starting with prenatal care for mothers: free education for children and vocational training, unemployment benefits, retirement pensions, health care, and death benefits paid to survivors.

FIGURE 11.5   SOURCES OF WELFARE IN THE MIXED SOCIETY

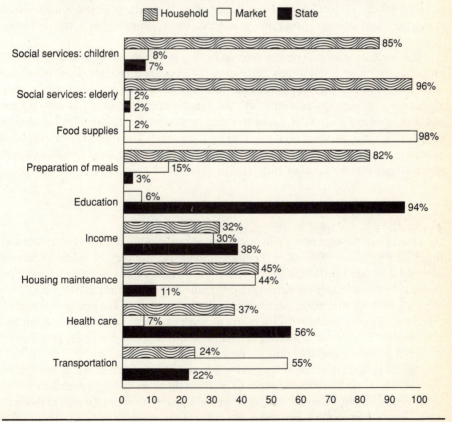

Source: Derived by the author from Richard Rose, "The Dynamics of the Welfare Mix in Britain," in R. Rose and R. Shiratori, eds., *The Welfare State East and West* (New York: Oxford University Press, 1986), Table 4.9.

The great majority of families are regularly in receipt of major public services. In Britain 90 percent receive at least one major benefit, such as a pension, education for children or hospital treatment, and the average family receives 2.3 benefits. In Scandinavian societies, where welfare benefits are more numerous and entitlement is easier to establish, the proportions are higher still (see Rose, 1989c: 23 ff.). The abolition of public programs for education, health care, and income in old age would not produce big savings in the budget of the average family. Instead of paying for services through taxation, people would have to buy these services or do without education or health care or security in old age. Whether an individual is a net gainer or loser in balancing the value of benefits against taxes can be a function of where an individual is in the life cycle.

At any given moment, taxation and public expenditure are "churning" a substantial portion of the national product. With one hand, the state takes money in taxes, and with the other it dispenses social benefits. In the accounts of the average family there is also a great deal of churning. The average British household pays the equivalent of 45 percent of its initial income in direct and indirect taxes. But its income is effectively increased by 34 percent through benefits in cash and in kind. The 11 percent difference between taxes paid and benefits received finances collective public services such as roads, police, environmental protection, and defense, programs that serve the community as a whole rather than identifiable households (Rose, 1989c: 100).

The welfare state can be considered both a problem solver *and* a creator of problems, because it combines high levels of benefits and high taxes, generous entitlements to benefits and lack of choice. Individuals satisfied with public policies can regard benefits as well worth the taxes paid, but individuals who do not like how they are treated by social workers or how their children are being educated can do little to alter such services by their votes. The only choice offered is to accept a standard state service or do without it, because most families cannot afford to pay for private education and private health care.

Program Priorities

Looking at public expenditure in aggregate is misleading, because the total combines very different types of programs. Ordinary people are not much interested in sums that add up to billions or trillions in national currency. People are concerned about spending on particular programs that benefit themselves and their families, such as education, health, and social security. Nor are politicians and interest groups concerned with spending in aggregate. A minister of education and teachers fight for more spending on schools, and defense ministers and service groups lobby for more spending on defense.

Social programs account for two-thirds of public expenditure in Europe today (Figure 11.6). The biggest slice, 44 percent, goes in cash payments to the elderly, unemployed, disabled, and other groups unable to work. Health and education each account for more than 10 percent of public spending. In popular language, these goods and services are normally regarded as "good" goods; they are not what politicians complain about when attacking government "waste."

Interest paid on borrowing to finance current and past deficits now ranks fourth in importance. Historically, deficits reflected the cost of past wars. Today, deficits reflect the unwillingness of governments to raise taxes high enough to finance all that is spent on social policies. The rising cost of deficits also reflects higher interest rates due to inflation. Defense spending ranks fifth, ahead of spending on domestic public order. The remainder of public expenditure is divided among a very large number of relatively small economic programs to promote or protect industry, trade, and agriculture; environmental measures; housing; transportation; and the cost of administering government itself.

The tendency for public expenditure to grow reflects three principal causes. Population growth is one major influence (Rose, 1984: ch. 7). The greater the number of people entitled to receive a benefit, the more money government must spend. The biggest spending programs—social security, health care, and education—especially benefit the young and the old. Spending on social security and health care for older people goes up automatically as advances in health care prolong life. If more children are born, there are more youths entitled to a free, compulsory education.

Second, labor-intensive services such as health care and education can increase productivity at the same rate as in industry. Insofar as public sector wages rise without a compensating increase in productivity, this increases the relative cost of education and health care. This phenomenon is not confined to the public sector. For example, such services as haircuts have become more expensive

FIGURE 11.6   PUBLIC EXPENDITURE BY PROGRAM
(Average share of public expenditure in 17 European countries)

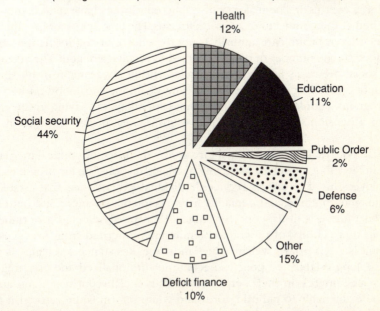

Health
12%

Education
11%

Public Order
2%

Defense
6%

Other
15%

Deficit finance
10%

Social security
44%

Source: Derived by the author from *OECD in Figures 1994,* (Paris: OECD) 40 ff.; OECD, *Economic Outlook* No. 56 (December 1994), annex Table 32.

relative to the cost of color television sets or computers. The pressures of the relative price effect may be met by government limiting pay increases for public employees or capping the total amount spent on a program, but doing so invites political controversy.

Rising standards of public provision are a third reason for increased spending on social programs. Medical and hospital standards have improved greatly and become more costly since the introduction of national health services. When more youths decide voluntarily to stay on at secondary school or enter university, the result is not only a better educated population but also a more costly education system. When societies become wealthier, people want government to provide new services. For example, Europeans have turned from wanting more jobs in "smokestack" industries to demanding environmental policies promoting cleaner air and water.

The idea that government grows inexorably in all its activities is false. To understand public expenditure, we must break up the total into major program headings: in this way we can identify programs that grow a lot, those that are changing little, and the few that may be contracting (see Rose, 1985b: 14 ff.). Defense has *reduced* its share of the national product by almost half since the height of the cold war in the 1950s. In the same period, the claims of social security on the national product have more than doubled and that of health has trebled. Education expenditure and the payment of debt interest have doubled their share of the national product too.

At the start of the twentieth century, every government in Europe had great scope for choice, because few social programs existed. Today, most major programs are virtually "uncontrollable." A modern state cannot disband its defense or police force overnight. The majority of public employees have tenure; they cannot be fired at the command of a few politicians. The amount of money spent on social security or health care annually is not the choice of politicians; it is chiefly determined by the number of people entitled to receive a benefit. The accumulation of social programs has created agencies within government disbursing social benefits, and their staffs are strategically positioned to lobby on behalf of their programs. People today plan household spending and saving in the expectation of a pension in old age, and provision for health care throughout their lives.

Public policies today are carried forward by the force of political inertia, embodied in laws that authorize programs, agencies responsible for programs, public employees hired to deliver services, individual expectations that established programs will continue, and demands from recipients for more and better services. Today there is little scope for choice. Each newly elected government is locked in to a century of program commitments inherited from predecessors. The result is ". . . a frozen welfare state landscape. Resistance to change is to be expected, long established policies become institutionalized and create groups with a vested interest in their perpetuation. Thus social security systems are not likely to be amenable to radical reform, and when reform is undertaken, it tends to be negotiated and consensual" (Esping-Andersen, 1994: 23).

chapter **12**

GETTING BY IN POST-COMMUNIST SOCIETIES

The economies of Communist states were command economies based on political power rather than the marketplace calculations of producers, consumers, and investors. The state not only guaranteed jobs and welfare services but also made decisions about what goods and services were produced and their price, thus determining what people could and could not buy. In a party-state money was not a proper measure of value, for many goods and services were allocated to those with the priceless advantages of a high position in the Communist Party's *nomenklatura* or personal connections in a factory or shop (Rose and McAllister, 1996). The collapse of the Communist system destroyed the power of the commanders of the command economy. But institutions of the market do not emerge spontaneously. Meanwhile, people still require education, health, and money to buy basic necessities.

In post-Communist societies policy makers have inherited the unprecedented challenge of transforming a command economy into a market economy while simultaneously converting the political system from a strict authoritarian regime into a consolidated democracy. There are pressing problems of inflation, fears of unemployment, organizing the privatization of enterprises in the absence of a private sector, and protecting the welfare of those whose lives are being disrupted by the economic transformation. Simultaneously, it is necessary to create institutions of a market economy that took generations to evolve elsewhere, starting with laws of property and contract, a commercial banking system, a stock exchange, bankruptcy procedures, and an effective system of tax collection.

Households immediately face the challenge of getting by—that is, sustaining themselves from day to day and week to week on whatever resources are at hand. In a market economy, most people are able to get by on the wages they earn. In post-Communist societies, this is not yet possible. In the welfare states of Western Europe, public policies help people whose earnings are insufficient to get by. People in post-Communist societies do not trust the state, and the state does not have the tax revenue to finance social welfare for everyone.

To cope with problems of transformation, individuals can fall back on skills developed to cope with the pathologies of the command economy (cf. Grossman, 1977; Katsenelinboigen, 1977). As in a market economy, people combine state and nonstate resources, but the choices available are very different—*the official economy,* with activities recorded in government statistics and tax records; the second or shadow *uncivil economies,* where payment is in cash and "private" means there is no official record or tax; and *social economies,* in which households produce things for themselves and exchange help with friends, relatives, and friends of friends without any money changing hands (see Rose, 1992a).

> *Total welfare in the family = Official + Uncivil + Social economies*

The continuing significance of unofficial and social economies means that standard statistics of gross national product and public expenditure give an inadequate or misleading evaluation of conditions in Central and Eastern Europe. Official statistics of the old regime did not give a fair picture of how people lived because producers reported success in achieving targets in the national plan by inflating or inventing accomplishments. Specialists in the field have long debated: How small was the Soviet economy? (e.g., see Winiecki, 1988; Aslund, 1990). Converting national currencies into dollars has been especially misleading, for exchange rates were fixed by the Communist regime to give national economies an artificial advantage. Estimates of gross product per capita in U.S. dollars can differ by 300 or 400 percent—or more (Marer et al., 1992: 45).

The stressful legacy of Communist rule is not easily expunged. Because the state has been viewed as inefficient or corrupt, people do not rely solely on it for their welfare. Uncivil and informal social economies remain important today in enabling the majority to get by. Even though living standards of people in post-Communist societies are not as high as Sweden or Germany, they are not as low as in the average developing country in the United Nations. In the postwar era, Central and Eastern European societies became industrialized, urbanized, and well educated, and they achieved a higher level of gender equality in participation in the labor force than most Western European countries. The challenge facing post-Communist societies is to accelerate progress in order to catch up with the living standards of the least affluent countries of the European Union, such as Greece and Portugal, and to make further progress thereafter.

THE STARTING POINT: A STRESSFUL ECONOMY

To describe post-Communist countries as societies in transition is politically convenient, because it implies predictability—we know both the starting point and the destination, a modern market economy. Transition is simply a matter of ensuring that the necessary steps are taken to achieve the goal. This goal-oriented approach, ignoring inherited difficulties, is sometimes described as "market Bolshevism" because, like the classic Marxist-Leninist prescriptions for achieving Communism, it ignores the "mere" problems of transition.

A realistic model of change must accept as the starting point the legacy of more than four decades of a nonmarket command economy. The idea of transition is derived from development economics. In a developing country three types of economies operate simultaneously. There is a modern market sector producing raw materials for export—for example, oil, and some goods and services to support such activities. There is an informal second economy, mostly found in cities, in which people earn just enough money to live on. The third economy is found in rural areas, where people subsist with very little money changing hands, producing what they consume (Thomas, 1992). In such a context, modernization is about increasing the proportion of economic activity that takes place in the already established modern market sector.

In post-Communist societies the fundamental problem is the absence of a modern market sector; the command economy had a pervasive and negative influence. Whereas in a developing country policy makers are trying to expand the market sector, in post-Communist societies the challenge is to *create* a market economy. The pervasive changes required are better described as transformation rather than transition. They involve a substantial amount of what Schumpeter (1952: ch. 7) described as "creative destruction."

A Stressful—Not a Modern—Economy

A modern society has a complex set of institutions that operate rationally according to calculations based on empirically observed predictable cause-and-effect relations. It is a civil society in which the state respects the rule of law, and economic and social institutions are able to operate independently of the state.

The command economy of a Communist state was undoubtedly complex. It was also effective in creating heavy industries that could manufacture both civil and military goods. But it was not a market economy in which goods and services were bought and sold at prices reflecting supply and demand. It was a bureaucratic command economy in which decisions were determined by power and ideology: "Transactions are not necessarily monetized and, even if they are, the subordinated individual or organization is financially dependent on its superior" (Kornai, 1992: 33 f.). In a narrow sense, the institutions could be described as functional, since they functioned to produce benefits for those in command of the system. However, economies can function in many different ways, and command economies did not function as modern economies do. In *The Distorted World of Soviet-Type Economies,* Winiecki (1988) describes the system as "pseudo-modern," because of its reliance upon nonmarket mechanisms. Another author (Z: 1990: 298 ff.) has described it as "surreal," because of the contrast between ideology and reality.

The command economy was a *stressful* system; stress arose from uncertainties about whether goods and services would be produced according to the plan, by "informal" or even formally illegal methods or not produced at all. In contrast to a modern economy (see Table 12.1), a stressful system is opaque rather than transparent. Unrealistic plan targets encouraged deceit and exaggeration of output to make it appear as if everything was working all right—at least on paper. The rule of law had little meaning; the most efficient markets involved cash-in-hand transactions or an exchange of favors as a reward for people breaking rules. Industrial managers took their cues from plans determined through political processes; who you knew was more important than what you could sell.

TABLE 12.1   A COMPARISON OF MODERN AND STRESSFUL ECONOMIC SYSTEMS

	Modern	Stressful
Operation	Complex	Complex
Signals	Prices	Bureaucratic, political, or personal commands
Openness	Transparent	Opaque
Lawful	Yes	Rigidity tempered by favors, bribes
Cause-and-effect relations	Rational, calculable	Uncertain
Output	Efficient	Inefficient
Effective	Yes	Usually but not always

Source: Compiled by the author; for a discussion, see Richard Rose, "Getting by Without Government: Everyday Life in Russia," *Daedalus,* 123 no. 3 (1994), 41–62.

There was no way within the command economy in which consumers could signal their preferences to planners. In the absence of market prices, shoppers needed to curry favor with shopkeepers or engage in barter and corruption; factory managers had to do the same to get supplies to keep a factory going. In extreme cases, factories were not adding value but subtracting value, as their output was worth less than the materials, labor, and equipment used to produce it.

To get anything done in a stressful society, it is necessary to invest more time and energy than in an efficient system. As well as producing goods and services, the uncertainties of the system produce stress. A stressful system offers a perverse example of Weber's (1972: 126) dictum: "Power is in the administration of everyday things." It shows that weakness is in the stressful administration of everyday things.

Agriculture illustrates how demodernizing the system was. The collectivization of agriculture under Stalin substituted factory farms for peasant farming. Confronted with massive resistance by peasants, the state relied upon coercion, terror, and famine to achieve collectivization. East and Central European farmland was normally collectivized too. Even where there was very rich agricultural land, the new system was incapable of producing food efficiently. People learned not to rely upon the official economy to deliver food to shops. The majority of urban residents had a small plot of ground near their home where they could grow potatoes and some vegetables. In a stressful economy, most people growing food are not farmers but factory and office workers or retired people. They do not grow food for sale, as in a modern market economy, but in order to have things to eat (Rose and Tikhomirov, 1993).

By the material standards of Western Europe, the standard of living in Central and Eastern Europe is low, but by that of developing countries on other continents it is relatively high. Consumer goods taken for granted in Western Europe are present—but not to the same extent. Across six Central and Eastern European countries the New Democracies Barometer finds that the proportion of households with a color television set ranges from 84 percent in the Czech Republic to 28 percent in Romania.

The State: Providing and Corrupting Welfare Services?

Communist regimes followed the Prussian tradition of seeking to "buy" support for an authoritarian regime through an implicit social contract. Workers were offered full employment, health care, education, and a rising standard of living in exchange for political quiescence. The strategy assumed: (1) Without a rising level of welfare there would be political discontent; (2) a command economy could deliver increased social benefits satisfactory to recipients; and (3) workers would be politically quiescent in exchange for a rising living standard. These assumptions were also endorsed by some Western social scientists (see the quotations in Cook, 1993: 5 ff.). But critics of the system argued that social benefits appearing progressive to Western social democrats "within Eastern Europe were perceived as part and parcel of the totalitarian state project of forcing work out of reluctant citizens for purposes which seemed to benefit only the privileged party state apparatus" (Deacon, 1993: 182).

The state provision of education, health care, and pensions were generous by the standards of the national product of Central and Eastern European countries, and abnormally high in comparison with welfare provision by West European countries at a similar stage of their economic development.

A modern welfare state must not only offer a high level of benefits but do so honestly and efficiently. Scandinavia can have a massive welfare system because the state there approaches the ideal of a modern, rational, bureaucratic instrument of governance (cf. Allardt, 1986). But trust in the state is not found in every advanced industrial society. In Italy the state has been riddled by corruption.

Social welfare in Communist regimes was administered by the dictates of a distrusted party state. Public officials sometimes demanded money (including hard currencies) to admit children to a good school, for medical treatment, or for housing. Ideological tests could be used for admission to universities and jobs. A study of the use of connections at the start of transformation found two-thirds of Czechs and Slovaks and one-third of Bulgarians used bribes (Rose, 1993: 234 ff.). The higher level in Czechoslovakia reflects the fact there was more money there. Such "tips" were not only used to obtain consumer durables in short supply, which is not necessary in a market economy, but also to obtain social welfare services that were meant to be provided free. In such circumstances, "health care ceases to be a free service, since different patients have different incomes and a different inclination towards tipping; access to health services was not equal" (Adam, 1991: 11).

The party-state did not have to worry about popular dissatisfaction with welfare services for it was not subject to competitive elections. Nor did it have to worry about a taxpayer's revolt, for the state's control of the economy made it unnecessary to collect large amounts of tax revenue from individuals and private enterprises. The state could determine in the plan the division of revenues between enterprises and the public budget.

GETTING BY IN A MULTIPLICITY OF ECONOMIES

Official statistics showed the economy in Central and Eastern Europe contracting by a quarter or more at the start of transformation, producing wages of $25 to $50 a week. Yet most people continue about their everyday lives without showing destitution, and some have money to spend for visible pleasure. How do people live on $25 to $50 a week? The answer is: "They don't." Hardly anyone gets paid in dollars in post-Communist societies. People are paid in forints, zlotys, koruns, and other national currencies, which have a much greater purchasing power for everyday necessities than is suggested by the overvalued foreign exchange rate of the dollar.

Today as in the old command economy, virtually every household draws upon resources from a multiplicity of economies, social and uncivil as well as official; the median household is involved in four of the nine economies (cf. Table 12.2). Basic necessities such as food, housing, and clothing can be produced in unofficial or uncivil economies ignored by national and international statistical agencies.

The two *official* economies are legal and monetized. Nearly every household has at least one cash income from employment or a state income-maintenance grant such as a pension. But 98 percent of households also are active in *social* economies, which are officially unrecorded and no money changes hands. These activities include growing food, do-it-yourself work on a house, and exchanging help with friends or friends of friends. Some of these activities can also be found

TABLE 12.2   PARTICIPATION IN NINE ECONOMIES

	NDB mean (% households in each economy)
Official economies: Monetized, Legal	(96)
1. Member of household has regular job	75
2. Receives pension, welfare benefits	39
Social economies: Nonmonetized, alegal	(98)
3. Household production of food, housing	64
4. Exchange help with friends, neighbors	67
5. Gets/gives free favors	18
6. Queuing more than an hour a day	9
Uncivil economies: Monetized, illegal	(40)
7. Job in second, shadow economy	19
8. Pays, is paid as a connection	20
9. Uses foreign currency	12

Source: Analysis of data in *New Democracies Barometer II* (1993) mean for Bulgaria, Czech Republic, Slovakia, Hungary, Poland, and Romania.

in a market economy, but they are usually hobbies or acts of friendship rather than adopted from necessity. In an economy in transformation, growing food is not a leisure pastime but a way of ensuring that a family has enough to eat. *Uncivil* economies produce a money income that is untaxed and unreported. Two-fifths of households are involved from time to time in "cash only" transactions. Such earnings are not so widespread as anecdotal evidence suggests. Even though the supply of "shadow" economy workers is large, the demand is limited when many people lack the money to put cash in the hands of willing workers.

Just as investors in market economies diversified their assets, so households trying to cope with transformation combine activities into different portfolios (cf. Rose, 1993b). When the New Democracies Barometer asked people in post-Communist societies to identify the two most important economies for their household, 55 percent retreat from modernization, having a *defensive* portfolio, relying on a nonmonetized social economy as well as the official economy. Even though this is often rational at the household level, it contradicts macroeconomic strategies for long-term growth of investment in the official economy. Becoming *enterprising* is the choice of 19 percent of households; this group combines a money income from the official economy and another from an uncivil economy. This portfolio is individually rational, but discourages investment in enterprises employing thousands of people, for such firms cannot be run as fly-by-night activities. The *vulnerable* are distinctive because they rely solely upon the official economy. Whatever their current standard of living, this group is specially at risk in transformation. Paradoxically, *marginal* households are less at risk, because they subsist on the fringes through social economies; money is least important to this tenth of society.

Since money economies are not the only economies in post-Communist societies, a family's ability to cope cannot be assessed by its income in the official economy. Coping is best measured by a household's ability to mobilize resources from a multiplicity of economies to meet its basic needs through the year without borrowing money or spending savings. If a household can do this, it is getting by on a basis that can be sustained indefinitely.

Two-thirds of people in Central and Eastern Europe are able to get by thanks to activities in a multiplicity of economies (Figure 12.1). In the Czech Republic as many as 77 percent are able to do so. Only in Bulgaria are less than half able to get by. Of those who get by, little more than one-fifth do so on the basis of earnings in a regular job; almost twice as many do so by relying on a portfolio of economies. In a market system, involvement in a multiplicity of economies is of very limited importance. For example, in Austria 72 percent earn enough from their regular job to get by, more than double the proportion in post-Communist societies. Additional economies boost the proportion of Austrians getting by only 11 percent.

People can get by at different living standards. A wealthy family can spend all its money on luxuries and a middle-class family may be in financial difficulties if it is paying for private education for its children. Even in prosperous market economies, at any given moment some households have difficulties in getting by—for example, a student may need a summer job to pay off debts contracted during the academic year.

FIGURE 12.1   MULTIPLE ECONOMIES HELP FAMILIES GET BY

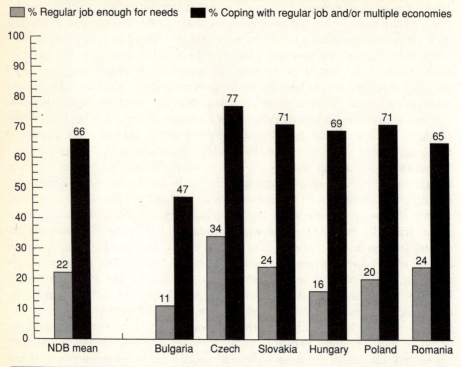

☐ % Regular job enough for needs   ■ % Coping with regular job and/or multiple economies

Source: Paul Lazarsfeld Society, Vienna. *New Democracies Barometer III* (1994).

Whatever the nature the economy, every family needs food, clothing and a home with heat and light. Lacking such necessities makes a family destitute. To measure destitution in economies in transformation, the third New Democracies Barometer asked people whether they have been without these necessities in the past year and if so, how often. Responses across six Central and Eastern European countries show that while many people may experience some form of hardship at least once in a year, few regularly do so (see Figure 12.2; Rose, 1995a).

Doing without is a matter of degree. To be destitute, a family must often be short of food, wear threadbare clothes, and have to sit in cold or unlit rooms. If this does not happen, households are adapting to the challenges of transition. Even if people are not living as well as they would like, they are not destitute. A third important group consists of those who sometimes do without and sometimes have enough to meet basic needs. Because they bounce in and out of trouble, this group can be described as resilient.

The difficulties of transformation are real but are not producing widespread destitution. More than two-thirds of Central and Eastern European households are adaptable. They are getting by and rarely or never doing without basic necessities. An additional quarter are resilient; difficulties are temporary. If people go without meat for dinner one Sunday, they may have meat the following week, and if clothes become worn they are patched. People who get into difficulty be-

FIGURE 12.2   ADAPTABLE, RESILIENT, AND DESTITUTE HOUSEHOLDS

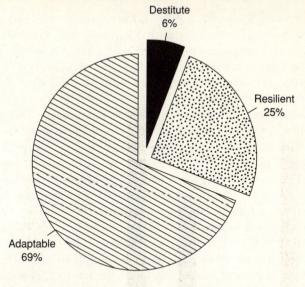

Destitute: Often doing without food, clothing, or heat and electricity.
Adaptable: Getting by and not destitute.
Resilient: Sometimes borrowing or spending savings but not destitute.

Source: Paul Lazarsfeld Society, Vienna, *New Democracies Barometer III* (1994) mean for Czech Republic, Hungary, Poland, Romania, Slovakia, and Slovenia.

cause of being unemployed find another job, meanwhile borrowing money, relying upon help from family and friends or uncivil economies. Those who frequently do without necessities are a minority of a minority, 6 percent of all households.

MAKING PROGRESS AND CATCHING UP

Money is a very "soft" measure of welfare in post-Communist countries. If we are interested in how people are living, health, education and signs of destitution can be directly measured without making misleading assumptions about the purchasing power of currencies. Census data indicates how much or how little progress has been made over the years, and it makes possible comparisons across Europe of literacy, infant mortality and gender equality in employment. Insofar as there is a gap between Eastern and Western Europe, rates of change indicate whether countries currently lagging behind are likely to catch up sooner or later or not at all. Comparing achievements on different social indicators guards against the mistaken assumption that a country doing badly in one area is doing badly on every count (for a full discussion of concepts and data in this section, see Rose, 1994).

Progress and Catching Up: Education

Literacy is essential for working in an industrialized society and secondary education for working in a contemporary modern society. At the end of World War II, there were parts of Mediterranean Europe where some older people were not literate, and the same was true in Eastern Europe. Today, this is no longer the case. Virtually 100 percent literacy has been achieved from the West of Ireland and the South of Italy to the Black Sea.

The postwar era has seen free secondary education become standard in every European country, East and West. In Communist societies education was distinctive because of what pupils were encouraged or compelled to learn, and what they could not study. First, there was a heavy emphasis upon mathematics, science, and engineering as part of national plans to upgrade the economy. The prototypical graduate was an engineer rather than a business school product. Second, learning a foreign language was often compulsory; the language was Russian, the common language for dealings between Poles, Hungarians, and Romanians as well as with Moscow. It was difficult to be taught English or German in schools, for these were languages enabling people to learn what the party did not want them to read or hear about. Third, the teaching of social sciences and humanities conformed to a Marxist-Leninist mold. Even in East Germany, where classics of social science could easily be read in German, the party aggressively discouraged people doing so.

If we compare educational attainments across Europe today, the big differences are not between societies but within societies. In each country, the aptitudes and inclinations of youths differ, resulting in some youths achieving a much higher or different standard than others; the same is true in the United States (cf. OECD, 1993: 151 ff.).

Making Progress but Lagging Behind: Infant Mortality

Health is a basic concern of individuals everywhere, and public policies directly affect health care. Infant mortality is a classic measure of health care, for it directly measures a fundamental social concern, human life, and the ability of an infant to survive for a year after birth reflects the health of the mother and health policies generally.

In the postwar era, great progress has been made across Europe in reducing infant mortality. Since 1950, infant mortality has fallen by more than five-sixths in such relatively wealthy countries as France and Germany and in poor OECD countries such as Portugal (Figure 12.3). In Central and Eastern Europe infant mortality has fallen dramatically too. It was 117 deaths per thousand in Romania in 1950 and in Poland 108 deaths; by 1993 the rate had fallen by four-fifths in Romania and seven-eighths in Poland. Within a national context, every ministry of health in Europe can claim credit for great progress.

There has been convergence within Western Europe, as infant mortality has been falling faster in countries where it was previously highest. In Portugal, the country with the worst record in 1950, infant mortality fell by an average of 6 percent annually over three decades, almost double the rate of improvement in Sweden. Whereas in 1950 the difference in infant mortality between the two countries was 74 deaths per thousand, today it is less than five deaths per thousand.

Progress in reducing infant mortality in both Western and Eastern Europe has reduced the absolute gap but not the relative differences. In 1950 infant mortality in what were then Communist societies was two-thirds higher than the average for Western Europe. By 1993 the absolute gap between the two groups of countries had fallen from 40 to 6 deaths per thousand. However, the relative gap had risen slightly.

The transformation of Communist societies has interrupted but not reversed the downward trend in infant mortality. Since 1989, infant mortality rates have remained steady or even risen slightly in at least one year in most countries. But over half a dozen years the pattern shows continued improvement. The Czech Republic today has as low a level of infant mortality as the United States. Across

FIGURE 12.3   LONG-TERM PROGRESS IN REDUCING INFANT MORTALITY

(Deaths per 1000)

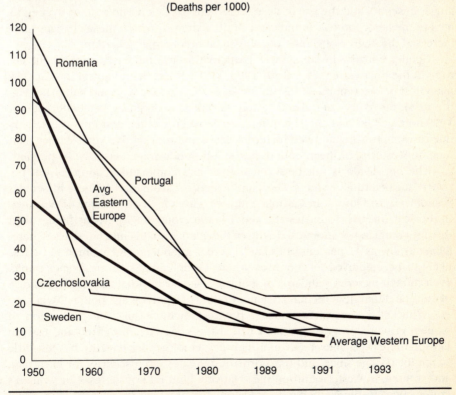

Sources: Calculated from Richard Rose, *Comparing Welfare Across Time and Space* (Vienna: European Center for Social Welfare Policy and Research, European Center Eurosocial Report 49, 1994), Table 2; *OECD in Figures 1994,* 40f; and UNICEF, *Crisis in Mortality, Health and Nutrition* (Florence, Italy: International Child Development Center Regional Monitoring Report No. 2, 1994), 104.

six countries, the mean level of infant mortality is now 14 deaths per thousand. This was the average rate of Western Europe in 1980 (cf. UNICEF, 1994: 104).

Gender Equality in the Labor Force: Post-Communist Societies Ahead

In command economies everyone had a job, but that did not mean that everyone was fully employed at their place of work. Firms hoarded labor; more people were employed than needed for efficient production. Strict wage controls reduced the incentive for workers to change jobs or work consistently. No one could be paid the market rate for the job, for there was no market! The reality was "overemployment" (e.g., see Gregory, 1987; Hanson, 1986). These conditions are an important qualification in comparing employment in a command economy with a market economy.

Whatever the economy, the percentage of women in paid employment has risen greatly across Europe in the postwar era, due to a reduction in the population living in rural areas where women were often unpaid farm workers; a reduction in family size; and an increase in the education of women. Concurrently, the proportion of men age 15 to 65 in employment has fallen, as young males stay longer in school and the age of male retirement has fallen. The ratio of women to men in the labor force is an indicator of the extent to which these changes have increased the degree of gender equality in labor force participation.

Gender equality in labor force participation has increased throughout Europe in the postwar era (see Rose, 1994: 31 ff.). It has been highest in East Germany; just before reunification, half the labor force was female and half male (Figure 12.4). Across six Central and Eastern European economies the gender ratio in 1990 averaged 86 percent. The difference between women and men was largely due to women being allowed maternity leave and retiring five years earlier than men. In Western European countries, the ratio on average was less, 70 percent.

The big divide is not between market and command economies but between sociocultural systems. The employment of women is highest in secular Scandinavia, and lowest in Catholic cultures with a high percentage of peasants. In the Scandinavian countries, the gender ratio averages 89 percent, higher than that for command economies. However, the gender ratio is much less elsewhere, falling as low as 47 percent in Ireland. There is a tendency for women to be less likely to be employed in countries where Catholicism is strong. For example, even though material standards of living are similar in Britain and Italy, because of cultural differences the Italian gender ratio is 18 percentage points lower.

While all countries have made progress in increasing the proportion of women in work, progress has not been at the same rate. In Central and Eastern Europe the early achievement of a high degree of gender equality has left little scope for change since, and transformation creates job insecurity for both men and women. In Western Europe the relatively high rate of increase in women's employment in the Netherlands holds out the prospect that it may soon attain the average for post-Communist countries. But the relatively low rate of progress in Austria and Germany implies that such a level will not be reached for a generation (cf. Rose, 1994: table 12).

FIGURE 12.4 GENDER EQUALITY IN LABOR FORCE PARTICIPATION

(Employed women as % employed men)

(Black bars are Post-Communist societies)

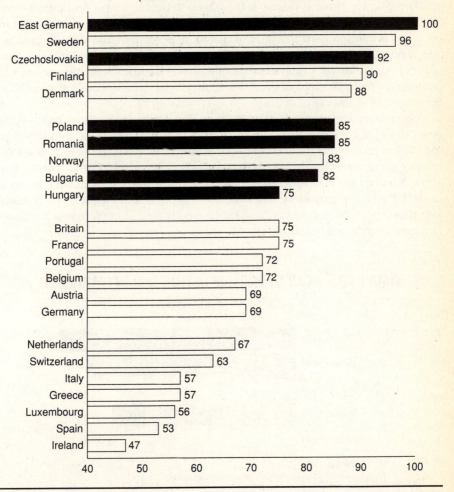

Source: Richard Rose *Comparing Welfare Across Time and Space* (Vienna: European Center for Social Welfare Policy and Research, European Center Eurosocial Report 49, 1994), tables 8, 9.

Car-Ownership Across Time and Space

A car is a good indicator of material well-being; along with a house, it is the single biggest purchase that a family normally considers. Buying a car costs many months wages; running a car is a continuing expense for a household too. Before and after World War II, cars were luxury goods in Europe; people traveled by public transportation or bicycle. In Britain only one family in seven owned a car in 1951. The spread of car ownership has been a major indicator of rising affluence across Western Europe, and in Central and Eastern Europe too.

If we compare car ownership in post-Communist countries with Britain to-day, every country lags behind (Figure 12.5). In Britain more than two-thirds of households have at least one car, and no post-Communist country is this prosperous. The country coming closest is the Czech Republic, where 58 percent have cars. The average level of car ownership across six Central and Eastern European countries is a third below Britain, and falls to 29 percent in Romania. The gap between post-Communist countries and Western Europe is increased if the quality of cars is taken into account. In post-Communist countries some people are still driving cars manufactured in the Communist era to uncompetitive standards far below that of market economies.

Comparing car ownership across time and space shows how many years post-Communist countries are behind Western countries. In the Czech Republic the current level of car ownership is that of Britain in 1981. The Central and Eastern European mean for car ownership today is at the level of Britain in the late 1960s. Yet even the poorest country, Romania, is ahead of car ownership in Japan in 1971. These comparisons emphasize that it is possible for a country that ranks low at one point in time to catch up subsequently by making progress at a faster rate than countries that initially are better off.

FIGURE 12.5 CAR OWNERSHIP IN TIME-SPACE COMPARISON

(% households with cars)

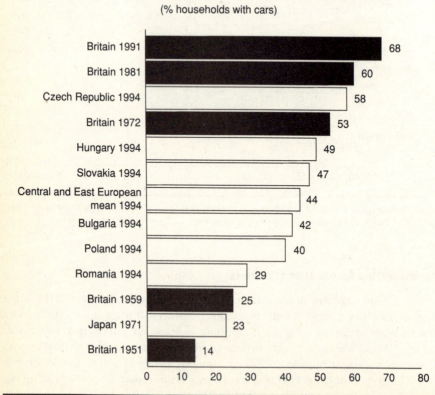

Source: Paul Lazarsfeld Society, Vienna, *New Democracies Barometer III* (1994). For Britain and Japan, government statistics.

The peoples of post-Communist countries know that materially they lag behind Western Europe—and they also know that they would like to catch up. Goals such as car ownership are attainable; the great rise of car ownership in Western Europe in the past generation gives evidence of this. But catching up also takes time. Standing in queues for hours to buy goods in short supply in a command economy has taught people patience. In that system it was often necessary to wait years to buy an inadequate car or obtain a cheap television set at a high price. When the third New Democracies Barometer asked Central and Eastern Europeans how long it will be until they are economically satisfied, among those with an opinion, the median answer was six to ten years. The largest group, two-fifths of the total, consists of people who don't know how many years it will be before they become economically content.

The time it will take Central and Eastern European countries to catch up depends upon the goal. On average, post-Communist societies are ahead on gender equality in labor force participation, even on education, and behind in infant mortality and car ownership. If the goal is fixed, such as achieving 100 percent literacy, then every country can catch up with the leaders, for once everyone is literate a country can go no further. However, if a goal is a moving target, such as gross domestic product per capita, if all countries improve at the same rate, then significant differences will remain. If evaluations are made in terms of the top-ranking country, then one will always be ahead of all the others. Yet we do not say that the German economy has "failed" because GDP per capita is less than Switzerland, nor should we say that countries in which living conditions are improving, such as Portugal and the Czech Republic, are "failing." In short, where a European country ranks depends upon the criterion used for ranking as well as its absolute achievement.

The countries selected for comparison also affect the prospect of catching up. Comparisons within OECD Europe spotlight big differences between Northern and Southern European countries (cf. Table 2.2, p. 53). By definition, half the countries must be below the median country. It is even more unreasonable to expect Central and Eastern European countries to match overnight the achievements of high-ranking countries such as Sweden or Germany. For post-Communist societies, the level of well-being of less prosperous European Union countries such as Portugal or Greece is more immediately relevant. Post-Communist countries differ too in their achievements. On most measures of social well-being, a realistic target for Bulgarians or Romanians is to catch up with Czechs or Hungarians.

The time dimension is critical too. If current living standards in Central and Eastern Europe are compared with Western European countries a decade or two ago, when they were already described as affluent industrial societies, then most post-Communist countries have already reached the standard of an OECD country. Given time, Central and Eastern Europeans can improve their welfare in the future, by maintaining or improving their rates of progress.

part V

INCREASING INTERDEPENDENCE

chapter **13**

ORGANIZING EUROPE: FROM INTERDEPENDENCE TO UNION?

In contemporary world politics, interdependence is a fact of life, and this is especially true for the states of Europe. National capitals are only an hour or two apart in flying time, whether by civil or military aircraft, and chemical works in one country can create air pollution in another. Comparative politics arrays states in parallel for analysis; parallel lines never meet. The politics of interdependence is about what happens when nominally sovereign states interact with each other (cf. Keohane and Nye, 1977; Rose, 1991; Evans et al., 1993).

A key question is facing European states today: What are the terms of interdependence? Two world wars were fought in the belief that the alternatives were dominance or submission. The European Union (EU) originated in the political desire of French and German leaders to prevent the outbreak of yet another war. In 1951 France proposed to Germany the creation of a European Coal and Steel Community to promote economic cooperation. It was, according to French Foreign Minister Robert Schuman, "a leap in the dark" (Milward, 1984: 1). This step has been followed by many more, as European states have come to cooperate in dealing with problems that they lack the power to resolve on their own. The epigram of the Spanish intellectual Ortega y Gasset sums up the thoughts of proponents of European Union: "Spain is the problem, Europe is the solution" (quoted in Perez-Diaz, 1993: 1).

The European Union is today the visible evidence of interdependence. The organization has grown as national governments have recognized that they have a "sovereignty deficit." Separately, each lacks the capacity to meet all its responsibilities. This is very obvious in small states. Countries such as Denmark and Ireland have no illusions about how little weight they cast in the balance of power. As a Belgian politician once pointed out, "In Western Europe there are now only two kinds of small countries—those that know it and those that don't know it yet." Within the European Union, each member state participates in all the deliberations of the union's institutions.

Large European states have concluded that being big is not the same as being big enough. The EU offers each big country an opportunity to leverage its influence. France carries more weight if it collaborates with Germany, and Britain can promote London as the financial capital of Europe. Germany's integration in the single market of the EU promotes its economic interest as a major exporter.

ts of membership, remaining outside the union threatens
h government leaflet about entering what was then the
...ained:"Whether we are in the Market or not, Common Mar-
...oing to affect the lives of every family in the country. Inside the
...an play a major part in deciding these policies. Outside, we are on
...i." (quoted in Butler and Kitzinger, 1976: 300)

The European Union is not a state in its own right. The 15 member states—
France, Germany, Italy, Belgium, the Netherlands, Luxembourg, the United Kingdom, Ireland, Denmark, Greece, Spain, Portugal, Austria, Finland, and Sweden—remain independent. In significant policy areas, each state has the right to veto EU
policies. Nor does the EU have a military force or substantial tax revenues; to implement policies it depends almost exclusively upon officials of member states.
Yet treaties bind all EU members to accept collective decisions about a range of
economic and related policies, The decisions of EU institutions are more numerous and impose stronger commitments than do those of the United Nations.
However, the EU does not enjoy the powers of a federal government such as
Switzerland, Belgium, Canada, or the United States (see Sbragia, 1992: 1 ff.).

European institutions are dynamic; they alter by deepening and broadening.
Deepening refers to an increase in the impact of EU policies in member states.
The functions of European institutions have expanded greatly from a narrow
concern with coal and steel through the common market goal of the 1957 Treaty
of Rome that established the European Community to the Single Europe Market
introduced in 1992 (see e.g. Moravcsik, 1991; Garrett, 1992; Cameron, 1992). To
promote a single market requires powers over the movement of goods, services,
labor, and capital, terms of reference that promise further expansion—if member
states approve. The 1992 Maastricht Treaty changed the European Community's
name to the European Union. It also added two new functional pillars to the economic pillar; it proposed that the EU seek to develop a common foreign and security policy, and a common justice and home affairs pillar. The Maastricht Treaty
stated the aim of "creating an ever closer union among the peoples of Europe."

Concurrently, membership of the European Union has *broadened* from the
six founder members—France, Germany, Italy, and the three Benelux countries—
to 15 countries. Outside the former Communist bloc, Switzerland and Norway
are the only European countries that do not belong to the European Union; each
has been accepted for association only to have the move rejected by national
electorates at referendums. Applications from post-Communist states in Central
and Eastern Europe are coming forward, and Turkey, half in Europe and half outside, has been pressing in vain to be considered for membership.

The political institutions of the EU have yet to be changed to match the
deepening of functions and the expansion of membership. The union has powers to place restrictions upon what is done by national governments accountable
to national electorates, but the authorities of the EU are not directly accountable
to a European electorate. This is said to create a "democratic deficit." There is no
agreement between or even within the member states about what ought to be
done. A federalist alternative would be for the union to become a United States of
Europe with a prime minister and cabinet accountable to a directly elected Euro-

pean Parliament. A nationalist alternative, put forward
des patries (Europe of nations), is to remove the imb
ers of the European Union over nationally elected
Treaty called for a special intergovernmental co
problems arising from the increase in EU functions
ical goals among its expanding membership.

In an attempt to bridge the gap between federalist and natio
the Maastricht Treaty endorsed the doctrine of *subsidiarity*—that is, th
which decisions should be taken within Europe ought to vary with the issue.
treaty declares that "decisions are to be taken as close as possible to the citizen."
The Union should act "only if and insofar as the objectives of the proposed action cannot be sufficiently achieved by the member states" and any action taken
"shall not go beyond what is necessary to achieve the objectives of this treaty."
The official explanation of the treaty's definition of subsidiarity is described by a
former president of the European Court of Justice, Lord Mackenzie-Stuart, as "a
disgraceful piece of sloppy draftsmanship, so bad that one is forced to assume it
must be deliberate" (quoted in Adonis and Tyrie, 1993: 3). The judge's explanation
is correct: subsidiarity is acceptable because it is so vague a doctrine that its
meaning in particular cases can only be determined by political bargaining.

The political process in an interdependent Europe is best described as a
game, in which national governments seek to pursue their interests by simultaneously bargaining within a national setting; in a multiplicity of places: with
other member states of the European Union and the European Commission; and
sometimes through such international institutions as the United Nations, or the
International Monetary Fund (cf. Putnam, 1988; Evans et al., 1993). In such a situation it is pointless to argue which "game" is most important. The object is to arrive at outcomes that will be better than what would happen to a country if its
government did not bargain with foreign governments and in intergovernmental
institutions. The best way to secure a majority is to form vertical *and* horizontal
coalitions, consisting of policy makers, parties, and pressure groups linked at national *and* European levels, and occasionally with intercontinental links too.

Institutions provide the arena within which the politics of the European
Union is worked out. EU institutions appear similar in name to those of national
governments, but they are very different in what they can and cannot do in relation to each other and to member states. This is the subject of the first section.
The second describes the limited policy resources of the European Union. For
historical reasons, most of EU revenue is spent on agricultural subsidies. Laws
and regulations are the distinctive resource for extending the impact of the
union. The treaties of the EU are only one form of law; social scientists propound
"laws" of the market, of social development, and of politics. Each has relevance
for interdependence within Europe and is treated in the third section. The EU is
more than a treaty-based organization in search of a constitution; it is a political
project that has aptly been described as a "journey to an unknown destination"
(Shonfield, 1972). Therefore the last section considers conflicting theories and
goals of federalists and nationalists about the potential deepening or broadening
of the European Union.

IONS FOR BARGAINING

uropean Union is not a state in its own right; it lacks its own military force
the revenue-raising powers of a member state. It also has no single capital.
ne European Commission, the central body of the EU, is headquartered in Brussels, but the European Court of Justice sits in Luxembourg, and the Parliament
has its headquarters in Luxembourg and its meeting place in Strasbourg and parliamentary committees also work in Brussels. The official business of the commission is conducted in more than ten languages. Informally, French and English
are the normal languages of communication. The civil service of the European
Union numbers 14,000 permanent officials, less than the number employed by
local government in Amsterdam or Madrid. In relation to its responsibilities and
by comparison to institutions of national governments, the institutions of the EU
are lightweight.

Yet treaties make the EU much more substantial than other well-known international bodies. First, the Rome and Maastricht treaties give it powers to act
and bind member-states; it thus differs from OECD, which is a clearinghouse for
information and advice. Second, policy deliberations in the EU are ongoing. By
contrast, the annual world summit meeting of leaders of seven countries is a
three-day affair of governments who have no treaty obligations to each other.
Third, the EU is responsible for a multiplicity of policies, whereas most intergovernmental agencies have only a single function—for example, NATO is concerned with military defense and the IMF with national finances. (for guides, see
Nugent, 1994; Dinan, 1994).

Councils of National Ministers

Because the European Union consists of states, not people, the key bodies are the
councils in which each member state is represented by a minister of each national government. To prevent any one country dominating council meetings, the
chair rotates every six months from one country to another; so too does the lo-
cation of important meetings. The political heads of member states discuss major
policies of concern to their own governments and to the European Union at the
twice yearly European Council. It also acts as a final court of appeal for politically
sensitive disputes that cannot be settled at lower levels. Before a major decision
is taken—for example, about the single Europe market—it is likely to be the subject of years of discussions and negotiations. Bargaining at the European Council
at Maastricht was necessary to secure unanimous agreement to the Treaty of European Union; these compromises also explain contradictions and vagueness in
the treaty.

Councils of the European Union deal with specific policy areas; membership
varies according to the subject at hand. If the issue is transportation, ministers of
transport will be in attendance, and if agriculture is the topic, ministers of agriculture will attend. About one hundred ministerial councils are held annually. In
the course of a year, the majority of cabinet ministers in national governments attend at least one meeting. Foreign affairs and agriculture are the most frequent
subjects. Before formal meetings, council members engage in bilateral meetings

with their opposite numbers in other countries in efforts to advance their national interest by forming a multinational coalition.

The Council of Ministers can ask the civil service of the European Commission to put forward detailed proposals. The commission's directorates also have the right to initiate proposals. Since the council has the authority to reject or amend laws and regulations proposed by the commission, commission staff must take into account the views of national ministers before putting forward proposals. Much preparatory work for council meetings is done by high-ranking civil servants that each national government sends to meetings of the Committee of Permanent Representatives (COREPER). National officials in COREPER specialize in negotiating bargains between their own government, other national governments, and the staff of the European Commission. When the Council of Ministers meets, it receives proposals that have already been discussed fully between each ministry's representatives and bargained about in the commission's relevant directorate. About three-quarters of the proposals placed on the agenda of the Council of Ministers are approved without discussion.

Voting procedures in council are meant to achieve consensus. Unanimity is required for decisions on new policies about politically sensitive matters such as taxation or the free movement of labor, or to amend a commission proposal against the wishes of the Commission. In 1965 France disrupted work of the community by absenting itself from the council, effectively vetoing all actions. The result was the Luxembourg Compromise of 1966, which held that the council would seek unanimity within a reasonable time on any issue deemed politically sensitive by a national government. A qualified majority is now sufficient to decide lesser issues coming before the council; the majority of matters it deals with are classified as lesser. A qualified majority is usually 70 percent of the votes in council; on minor matters, a simple majority is sufficient.

Votes in council are not awarded on the basis of one country, one vote, or one million citizens, one vote. They are the outcome of political horsetrading balancing the larger and smaller states. The four largest countries—Britain, France, Germany, and Italy—each have 10 votes. The least populous—Denmark, Finland, and Ireland—have 3, and Luxembourg has 2. Germany's 10 votes are five times that of Luxembourg, but Germany's population is more than 100 times larger. If votes were distributed in proportion to population, Germany, as the most populous country, could claim more than a fifth of the total vote in council, and countries with small populations, such as Ireland and Denmark, would have virtually no significance in the calculus of votes. The present distribution of votes and the 70 percent requirement for a qualified majority enable a proposal to be blocked if three large countries oppose it; in practice, proposals are normally not put forward if that is likely to be the case. Smaller countries with only a sixth of the union's population have 30 percent of council votes, sufficient to block a measure requiring approval by a qualified majority.

No member-state wants to be isolated by vetoing a proposal endorsed by the great majority of other members. However, member states are prepared to threaten the use of the veto as a bargaining counter in order to protect special national interests—for example, fishing in Spain or milk production quotas in Italy. The norm for decision making is to avoid votes and seek consensus, a practice familiar in the coalition governments of the great majority of member states of the union. If consensus cannot be found, an issue is usually delayed rather than brought before the council.

Politics unites what national boundaries divide. Within a given policy area, ministers from different countries responsible for the same function share common interests. For example, a scheme to increase university education might be favored by a council composed of education ministers but prove divisive in a national Cabinet including a budget minister trying to keep down government spending. When the council considers employment issues, regardless of country social democratic governments are inclined to favor measures put forward by trade unions, and states with an antisocialist government are inclined to favor policies endorsed by business and industry. When this happens, the council does not divide on national lines but along left versus right lines. The politics of interests normally result in some large and some small countries forming a coalition to cooperate against a competing group of interests from other large and small countries.

The influence of the Council of Ministers varies with the subject (cf. Petersen, 1995). It is highest when the European Union has full powers to act. For example, on trade with the rest of the world as a single market it negotiates on behalf of all member states with the United States, Japan, and other trading blocs. The council's influence is weakest in such fields as foreign policy, a subject that member states prefer to handle nationally and which often reveals disagreements and, in the case of fighting in Bosnia, weakness too.

The Commission

In form, the Commission of the European Union appears like the cabinet of a national government. It is divided into 23 numbered directorates-general (the Brussels term for a department). Many have counterparts in national governments— for example, energy, external relations, and agriculture. Some directorates concern issues that are no more than a subdivision within a national ministry— for example, research or training. A few focus on topics of special concern to the single market—for example, competition policy, or customs union and indirect taxation. There is no directorate general for defense. A comparison of the functional responsibilities of commissioners with national governments emphasizes the commission's greater involvement with details of economic and industrial policy, its lesser concern with social policy, and its low priority for international security issues.

Commissioners come from 15 member states; every country has at least one commissioner and the largest countries have two. Commissioners are not meant to take directions from their national governments, but they are nominated by them. Some are rising political stars who may go to Brussels to advance their national careers; others are pushed out of their national capital to accommodate the ambitions of others; some are washed up politicians who are pensioned off to Brussels; and others have good substantive qualifications. The sharing out of directorates between commissioners is a political juggling act.

The commission differs from a national cabinet because it lacks a prime minister. There is a president of the commission, chosen by a complex bargaining process among member states. The president voices opinions on all matters of European concern, some of which are agreed EU policy, some matters of dispute within the European Council, and a few the personal priority of the president. Jacques Delors, a French Socialist who was president for ten years from 1985, was outstanding in promoting federal policies; his main achievements were the creation of the single market and the Treaty of European Union. He also sought to promote social market policies disliked by free-market parties; in this, he was less successful. His successor as president, Jacques Santer of Luxembourg, was chosen as a compromise candidate not readily identified with any national or political bloc.

Each directorate-general is concerned with formulating and administering policy within a limited functional area. The drafting of proposals for the Council of Ministers is a complex process politically, for the interests of 15 different national governments must be taken into account. It is also complex technically, for an EU decision must take into account the administrative standards and practice of 15 member states. Proposals that ignore national sensitivities and idiosyncrasies of administration may not be approved at council. To coordinate national and European political concerns, commission staff are engaged in continuing dialogue with national government officials. The result is described as bureaucratic interpenetration across national boundaries (cf. Lodge, 1993: 14).

The commission's actions are meant to have a pervasive effect throughout Europe, but it has no administrative institutions or field staff to implement policies on the ground in member states. Only a few measures, such as the disbursement of scientific research grants, are administered directly by Brussels. The policies it adopts are normally implemented by member states. Each national government is responsible for transposing European Union decisions into national legislation in accord with its institutions and practices. The resulting legislation then becomes part of the national legal code, and administered as a national policy. In 1994 the court found 89 instances in which national governments had failed to apply EU law: the countries most often failing to do so were Greece, Ireland, and Italy; the readiest to comply were Denmark and Britain (European Commission, 1995: 440 corrigendum).

Courts to Enunciate the Law

The European Court of Justice (ECJ) has 15 judges, one from each member state. The justices come from two different legal traditions, the Roman law tradition of the judge declaring what the law is, which assumes that the meaning of the law is fixed, whatever the dispute before the court, and the common law conception of the judge applying general principles in changing circumstances (cf. Bengoetxea, 1993).

The court rules on whether the laws and regulations of member states are in conflict with its obligations to the European Union and it interprets ambiguities in EU rules. In case of a conflict between obligations under the EU treaty and national laws and practices, the treaty obligation overrides national law (see Shapiro, 1992a; Snyder, 1990). For example, the British practice of allowing women to claim a retirement pension five years younger than men was challenged by the European Court, and it ruled that this was illegal discrimination.

As a result, the retirement age in Britain is being equalized by raising the age of retirement for women to match that of men.

The European Court of Justice also exerts influence through national courts, which are expected to ask it for a preliminary opinion when a case arises there involving a dispute about the application of an EU law. In doing so, national judges appear to be subordinating their power to that of the European Court. But by making their court the national source of European law, they can enhance their power as against national governments (cf. Garrett, 1995; Weiler, 1993).

The court's influence is limited by what is left out of the treaties that it enforces. For example, the European Union has a ringing general declaration in favor of human rights, but unlike the American Bill of Rights there is no enumeration of specific rights that the court can enforce. The court can interpret the treaty in such ways as to expand the scope for action by the European Union. Weiler (1991: 2437 ff.) describes this as a process of mutation. The court extends its influence through "soft law, rules of conduct which, in principle, have no legally binding force but which nevertheless may have practical effects . . . as national courts are bound to take them into consideration in deciding disputes" (Snyder, 1993: 32).

Parliament: Representation with Little Power

The European Parliament (EP) was initially an assembly of representatives chosen by national parliaments. It was intended to be a consultative body rather than a central institution for making policy or holding the commission accountable. These responsibilities belong to the Council of Ministers. The Parliament has its administrative headquarters in Luxembourg and its plenary sessions are held in Strasbourg on the French side of the Franco-German border. These arrangements satisfy two member states, but cause endless complications for Members of the European Parliament (MEPs) and staffs, and reduce access to EU offices in Brussels.

Since 1979, the European Parliament has been directly elected; an election is held every five years. Its 626 seats are distributed unevenly among the 15 member states. Germany has the most MEPs, because its population since reunification is more than a third bigger than any other country. The four largest member states have more than half the seats in the Parliament. The electoral system differs from country to country in accord with national practice. Even though the Treaty of Maastricht prescribes a uniform procedure for voting by proportional representation, Britain elects its MEPs on the first-past-the-post system, except in Northern Ireland, where MEPs are elected by PR to guarantee at least one seat to a Catholic representative of Irish Nationalists.

Voters respond in a European Parliament election in much the same way as at a national election (see Chapter 7): a social democrat votes for social democratic representatives in the EP, a liberal for a liberal candidate, and religious supporters for Christian Democratic parties. A European Parliament election tends to be a "second order" election, reflecting at the European level whatever happens to be the electorate's mood at the level that remains of primary importance, national politics. Hence, if the government of the day is unpopular for reasons unconnected with European affairs, the EP election will show a swing against it (see Lodge, 1990; Reif, 1985).

As a relatively new Parliament with a high turnover of members, the composition of the European Parliament is more "up-to-date," in the sense that there are fewer veterans than in national Parliaments. When parties make up slates with fewer commitments to holdover members, they appear readier to nominate women candidates. A striking feature of membership of the European Parliament is that the proportion of women is higher from almost every country (Table 13.1). When Finnish parties chose candidates for the first time in 1995, a majority of MEPS were women. In France the use of PR for the European election accounts for the much larger number of women elected. Overall, an average of 31 percent of a country's MEPs are women, compared to 19 percent of members in the national Parliament.

Parties fight European elections under national party labels. The use of proportional representation ensures that every country sends a multiplicity of parties to the European Parliament. Altogether, 78 different parties won seats in the 1994 elections, plus 38 independents from five different countries. Parties competing with each other at the national level do not work as a national group in the European Parliament nor can MEPs be effective without organizing along

TABLE 13.1   WOMEN IN EUROPEAN AND NATIONAL PARLIAMENTS

| | Women as % members | | |
	National	European	Difference
Austria	21	33	+12
Belgium	12	32	+20
Denmark	33	44	+11
Finland	34	62	+28
France	6	30	+24
Germany	26	35	+9
Greece	6	16	+10
Ireland	12	27	+15
Italy	15	13	−2
Luxembourg	20	33	+13
Netherlands	31	32	+1
Portugal	9	8	−1
Spain	16	33	+17
Sweden	40	45	+5
United Kingdom	9	18	+9

Source: National MPs: Inter-Parliamentary Union, *Women in Parliament, 1945–1995* (Geneva: IPU, 1995); Europe: European Parliament database as of February 3, 1995.

TABLE 13.2 PARTIES IN THE EUROPEAN PARLIAMENT

(number of seats)

	Socialist	People	Liberal Democrat	Left	FF*	Democratic Alliance	Green	Radical	Anti-Federalist	Independent
Austria	8	6	1	—	—	—	1	—	—	5
Belgium	6	7	6	—	—	—	2	1	—	3
Denmark	3	3	5	—	—	—	1	—	4	—
Finland	4	4	6	1	—	—	1	—	—	—
France	15	13	1	7	—	14	—	13	13	11
Germany	40	47	—	—	—	—	12	—	—	—
Greece	10	9	—	4	—	2	—	—	—	—
Ireland	1	4	1	—	—	7	2	—	—	—
Italy	18	12	1	5	27	—	4	2	—	18
Luxembourg	2	2	1	—	—	—	1	—	—	—
Netherlands	8	10	10	—	—	—	1	—	2	—
Portugal	10	1	8	3	—	3	—	—	—	—
Spain	22	30	2	9	—	—	—	1	—	—
Sweden	11	6	3	1	—	—	1	—	—	—
United Kingdom	63	19	2	—	—	—	—	—	2	1
Total	221	173	47	30	27	26	26	19	19	38

*A group of Forza Italia MEPs.

Source: European Parliament data base.

party lines. The European Parliament offers incentives to MEPs from different countries to band together in cross-national groups (Table 13.2).

No party group in the European Parliament can claim anything approaching a majority. The largest, the Socialists, has a third of the seats and MEPs from every country. A predominantly Christian group, calling itself the European People's Party, has a quarter of the seats and representatives from every country too. Other groups are formed by a convenient alliance of several national parties wanting to secure the Parliament's subsidies to groups with a stipulated number of MEPs. Cooperation within groups is handicapped by parties with the same name differing in political priorities and interests; in being in government (and thus represented in the Council of Ministers) or in opposition; and by the lack of a common language, as MEPs need only know their national language to win election to the European Parliament.

The European Parliament has limited powers to influence other institutions of the EU. The commission prepares a draft budget for the Council of Ministers and Parliament. The Parliament has the power to reject the budget by a two-thirds vote and has used it (cf. Jacobs and Corbett, 1990). The budget powers of the Parliament enable MEPs to influence "pork barrel" expenditure that is directly and visibly beneficial to their constituents. Parliament's role in legislation is consultative. It receives draft bills that the commission sends to the Council of Ministers. It assigns each bill to a specialist committee, and the full Parliament votes on committee recommendations. These are forwarded to the commission and Council of Ministers for consideration. The Parliament's approval is neither necessary nor final; the council has the final say. The Maastricht Treaty gave the EP the right to veto legislation under restricted circumstance.

In a national government, a cabinet depends upon maintaining the confidence of the national Parliament. This is not the case in the EU; the European Commission's influence depends upon the confidence of the Council of Ministers. Commissioners are nominated by national governments. The members of the European Commission must be approved by the European Parliament as a slate; the slate has never been rejected. The Parliament has the formal power to force the whole commission to resign if it passes a censure motion by a two-thirds majority. It has never used this power. The influence of the European Parliament in the EU is less than that of a national Parliament (cf. Judge et al., 1994).

The inability of the European Parliament to hold the commission accountable is sometimes described as a "democratic deficit." However, this presupposes that the European Union is a state that ought to operate by the same rules as its member states. But the European Union is not (or not yet) a government. It is an institution for coordinating activities of democratically elected national governments, each accountable to its national parliament. Popular influence upon decisions of the union can be exercised through national elections and parliaments. When national governments in the Council of Ministers object to a measure, they are responding to pressures from the national Parliaments and electorate to which they are directly accountable. Critics of the European Union, such as Margaret Thatcher, argue that the union actually creates a democratic deficit, insofar as it has powers to override decisions of a popularly elected national government.

One Union with Many Games and Many Players

To understand how the European Union works in practice, it is important to realize that politicians and institutions within the EU are linked with "games" involving politicians and institutions elsewhere.

What happens in national capitals is important for, even though no one country can command the EU, collectively national governments determine outcomes in the European Council and the Council of Ministers. Furthermore, if decisions of the EU are to affect members, whatever is done in Brussels must stimulate compliance in national capitals. However, this does not mean that the EU is simply a means of adding up what national governments think is in their national interest. Perceptions of national interests are neither fixed nor are they always agreed upon within a nation. Many economic and social issues reveal divisions within countries as much as between them, and a sizable opposition to the line that a country's government of the day takes in EU negotiations. For example, a British social democrat may regard his or her interests better represented in

Brussels by a Swedish social democratic government than by a British Conservative government.

What happens within the institutions of the European Union is important too, for the commission and Parliament can initiate discussions that set the agenda for policy making. The European Court of Justice can go further, mandating national institutions to act in accord with European law.

Transnational pressure groups are an important influence too, for groups can lobby simultaneously in Brussels and in national capitals. For example, universities throughout Europe can lobby for more EU funds to encourage research; trade unions can lobby for stricter social market policies and employers associations can lobby against them; and automobile manufacturers can lobby on behalf of their interests as European producers in competition with Japanese producers. The number of lobbying organizations and lobbyists working in Brussels doubled during the process of preparing for the single market (Andersen and Eliassen, 1993: 38; Mazey and Richardson, 1993).

POLICY RESOURCES: LAWS BEFORE MONEY

The resources of the European Union are very different from those of member states. The EU has a trivial number of employees and spends only about $235 per inhabitant of the member states. Law is the primary resource of the EU. This gives it a substantial influence upon economic activity within the markets of Europe, and enables the European Union to expand its influence into other areas considered part of the "stream of commerce" within the single Europe market.

No Community for Taxing and Spending

If a community of people is defined by the willingness of people to pool their income to meet expenditures, then the 15 member states of the European Union do *not* constitute a community, for the tax revenues of the EU are about 1 percent of the gross national product of member states, and just over 2 percent of total public expenditure of member states. For every deutsche mark, pound, or peseta that the EU collects and spends, national governments spend about 40 times as much.

Yet unlike such institutions as the United Nations, the European Union does have guaranteed sources of income, taxes that national governments collect and forward to Brussels (Figure 13.1). More than half of EU revenue comes from a 1.4 percent share of the value-added tax of national governments. Second in importance are contributions that each national government makes, based on their gross domestic product. Customs duties on industrial imports from outside EU member states and levies from agricultural imports contribute small sums. The total, 67 billion ECU (European currency units) or $87 billion, is substantial in absolute terms but small relative to the resources of member states.

The spending priorities of the European Union are very different from national governments (cf. Figures 13.1 and 11.5, p. 239). Instead of concentrating expenditure on social security, health care, and education, the primary concerns

FIGURE 13.1 EUROPEAN UNION REVENUE AND EXPENDITURE

Revenue: 66 billion ECU ($87 billion)

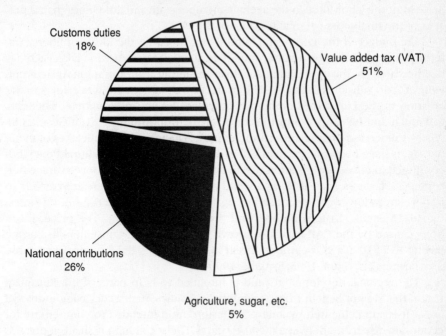

Customs duties 18%

Value added tax (VAT) 51%

National contributions 26%

Agriculture, sugar, etc. 5%

Expenditure

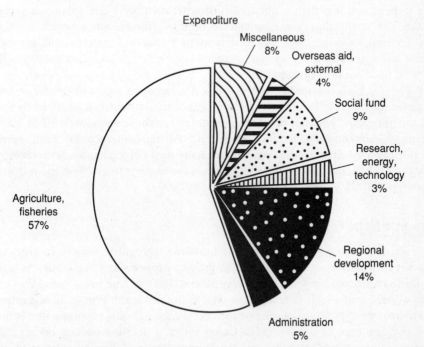

Miscellaneous 8%

Overseas aid, external 4%

Social fund 9%

Research, energy, technology 3%

Agriculture, fisheries 57%

Regional development 14%

Administration 5%

Source: Calculated from European Commission, *General Report of the Activities of the European Union 1994* (Brussels: European Commission, 1995), Chapter VI.2

of member states and their citizens, more than half the EU budget is devoted to agricultural subsidies. This happens even though agriculture accounts for only 8 percent of the labor force in the average member state and little more than 2 percent of the total gross national product of the EU.

The budget of the European Union is not based on the ideals of liberty, fraternity, and peace, but on a butter mountain surrounded by a wine lake. Each has been created by the agricultural surpluses resulting from Common Agricultural Policy (CAP) subsidies of the EU. The protection of agriculture was critical in the creation of the European Community four decades ago, offering major benefits to French and Italian peasants in return for the opportunities given German industry to increase their manufactured exports. The economic structures of member states have been transformed since, but the Common Agricultural Policy has continued in effect, for it is attractive to later entrants with an above-average percentage of farmers, such as Denmark and Ireland. The CAP also creates barriers to imports from lower-cost producers of agricultural products in the United States, Canada, Australia, Eastern Europe, and the developing world. The price distortions caused by the CAP have also grown in significance. Consumers in Europe pay up to a $1000 a year extra each year in higher taxes and food prices to subsidize farmers (cf. Grant, 1995; El-Agraa, 1990).

The regional development fund is intended to help parts of the European Union that do not benefit from agricultural subsidies, such as decaying industrial areas. It is supplemented by a new "cohesion" fund intended to compensate for economic disparities between member states. The social fund is small, about $20 per person, and less than a hundredth of what member states spend on social policy. The proportion of the budget devoted to overseas aid, research, energy and technology is not dissimilar to that spent by national governments, but because national budgets are so much larger, EU spending is "icing" on the funds allocated from national budgets.

The EU budget is redistributive—but not between rich and poor. The big beneficiaries tend to be countries where agricultural products subsidized by the EU are important, whether prosperous countries or those not so well off. In 1993 Denmark, Luxembourg, Ireland, Spain, and Portugal all received back more money from the EU than they paid in. Germany paid twice as much as it received back in EU benefits, and Britain and France were also net losers from the redistribution of money within the EU (Franklin, 1992).

Law as a Major Policy Resource

The states of Europe have always relied on laws to regulate society. To create a market economy, laws were needed to protect property, enforce contracts, and regulate banks and limited liability companies. This was true in countries that espoused free trade, such as England, as well as in France and Prussia, which relied on mercantilist doctrines of the state advancing the national economy. Law is the primary resource of the European Union today. If decision making bodies can agree on a law, treaty commitments create an obligation for member-states to enforce it, even if it contradicts national legislation. Politically, this avoids controversies that arise in levying taxes. It is also harder for member states to quarrel about who gets what, for laws "tend to disguise the winners and losers in politics, as the impacts tend to be played out through the market rather than through taxes and subsidies" (Peters, 1994: 23).

The major legislation of the European Union takes the form of *directives* drafted by the commission and subject to full discussion by the Council of Ministers and the European Parliament before coming into effect. Directives have binding force upon member states; they are implemented by being transposed— that is, they are enacted as national laws by national Parliaments in accord with their own legal procedures. This allows scope for adjustment in implementation, but the commission monitors national legislation to make sure it is in accord with directives. In 1994 there were 33 directives adopted. *Regulations* are prepared by the commission and subject to approval by the Council of Ministers; they come into effect immediately without being transposed into national legislation. Regulations normally refer to issues of narrow concern to a particular industry or business activity. In 1994 there were 3,064 regulations adopted. The use of law as an instrument of public policy varies from policy area to policy area (cf. Pollack, 1994; Bulmer, 1993).

The scope for EU policies is limited by whether member states already have a number of programs in effect in a given area. When this is the case, introducing a uniform policy faces political and practical difficulties, for there is the potential for conflict between EU directives and national laws. Member states do not want to change their established programs simply for the sake of formal uniformity. To make a common market possible, the goal of uniformity has been replaced by that of harmonization, accepting differences between countries that are not in conflict with EU directives or treaties. Harmonization can occur through mutual recognition by all member states of laws of other member states in an area of EU policy. This doctrine was endorsed by the European Court of Justice in the 1979 *Cassis de Dijon* case. A German importer challenged a German law that stated *Cassis* (a medium-strength French drink) could not be sold in Germany because it was too strong to be a wine and too weak to be a spirit. The court held that, subject to a few minimum standards, each member state must accept as lawful in its own territory what is lawful in other states.

The European Union can be more active when member states recognize a comparative advantage in collective action, and the EU has the capacity to act (cf. Scharpf, 1994). For example, environmental pollution is a problem that does not respect national boundaries. In densely populated areas of Europe, pollution can easily be carried across international borders by air currents or by rivers such as the Rhine as they wend their way to the sea. Downstream recipients of pollution need to compel upstream creators of pollution to desist in order to enjoy clean water or air. Another example is the specification of technical standards for commercial products. Multinational corporations prefer a single European standard for products rather than having 15 different national standards for such goods as computers.

In international trade, the European Union has a special authority. It is empowered by treaty to negotiate international trade agreements on behalf of member states, and it wields considerable clout by representing the largest single market in the world. It can use its political clout to promote free trade with countries outside Europe *or* to promote protectionist measures on behalf of European producers, most notably in agriculture. To use the EU to promote protectionism is totally consistent with European traditions of mercantilism. It creates frictions with other continents—for example, the United States and Canada—in agriculture, and with Japan in trade in manufactured products. It also creates tensions within the European Union, for most consumers would benefit from lower food prices brought about by free trade in agriculture.

The Single European Act of 1987 is a monumental example of the impact that law can have on public policy, for it bound member states to accept the free movement of goods, services, capital, and labor. The move to a single market was a massive administrative and political task, involving the adoption of more than 300 harmonized policies by all member states. Regulations concerning such things as customs checks took effect immediately after the single market came into being on January 1, 1993. But other measures designed to end the big discrepancies in prices for such common goods as a Ford automobile are being implemented more slowly. In 1995 the European Commission's annual survey found failures of member states to implement single market laws, to apply them correctly, and to punish offenders. "There is often a clear distinction between an agreement with the Council of Ministers and implementation of that agreement on the ground." France was most often maintaining barriers against free trade. In a warning against confusing the letter of laws laid down in Brussels with what happens in member states, it commented that the single market "could only be carried out to the degree that it was politically acceptable to member states" (Tucker, 1995).

The limits of law are revealed by attempts of the EU to introduce a monetary policy that maintains stable exchange rates between the different currencies of member states. The European Union itself does not issue currency; the ECU (European currency unit) is an accounting device, measuring the average value of national currencies in member states. Differences in national rates of inflation and interest rates cause major fluctuations in the exchange rates of currencies, thus destabilizing trade and forcing governments to act in ways that disrupt national policies. At the initiative of Germany and France, the European Monetary System (EMS) was created in 1979 to protect European countries from big swings in the foreign exchange value of their national currencies (for details, see Artis, 1990). The key currency was not the dollar, but the German deutsche mark, a currency less subject to inflation.

Success in stabilizing exchange rates between countries depends upon the extent to which international money markets regard national government policies as credible in preventing inflation. If national policies are viewed as credible, pressures to alter exchange rates will be slight. For more than a decade, the EMS maintained credibility (Woolley, 1992). However, credibility collapsed spectacularly in 1992, when the British pound was effectively devaluated by almost 15 percent, and the French franc was shortly thereafter devalued against the deutsche mark. Notwithstanding the proclaimed desire of the EU to stabilize currencies, market pressures have caused currencies to continue to fluctuate since.

Low Politics and High Politics: An Economic Giant *AND* a Political Pygmy

The European Union has been described as an economic giant because of the size of its market and the scope of its authority in economic affairs. The impact of the EU on economic activity is real, but its manifestation often focuses upon matters of "low" politics. Regulations concern such matters as the transport of livestock, the labeling of ice cream, and sheepmeat subsidies. Such regulations are not adopted at the whim of bureaucrats, but in response to demands from producers, importers, or other directly affected interest groups, and every member state has at least one ministry concerned with each regulation. However, the issues involved are not headline news; they are discussed in the trade and technical press or on the hog page of a newspaper.

For citizens of member states, policies of national governments remain more important for their everyday concerns than decisions of the European Union. National policies about social security, health care and education, and the local delivery of services as well as law enforcement and refuse collection touch lives directly and in important ways. The activities of the Council of Ministers and the European Commission have an indirect and usually limited impact upon citizens.

The European Union is described as a political pygmy because it lacks authority in "high" politics, such classic concerns of sovereign states as national security and public order. Departments of foreign affairs, defense, justice, and finance are at the center of politics (see Rose, 1982: 157) but not at the center of Brussels politics. Nor is this an accident. National governments have been reluctant to transfer to a supranational body matters of greatest concern to themselves. The Maastricht Treaty introduced two new "pillars" of the Union, a Common Foreign and Security Policy and a Common Policy for Justice and Home Affairs. The limited amount of activity in these areas to date shows the continuing commitment of national government to making their own decisions on such matters as sending troops to Bosnia or deciding who is or is not a citizen.

LAWS OF INTERDEPENDENCE

Laws that affect interdependence go beyond the text of treaties. While "black letter" law is significant, it is a means to political goals that reflect pressures from many directions arising from "laws" of social change and of economics and politics.

At a very high level of abstraction, *laws of social change* predict that industrialization, bureaucratization, secularization, and computerization are everywhere making societies more and more alike (cf. Bell, 1973; Bennett, 1991). Throughout Europe (and in other continents too) people are now educated to think in scientific terms, to work in sophisticated high-tech environments, to enjoy similar leisure pursuits and to expect social benefits delivered by the state. Developments in the mass media, such as television, VCRs, and the Internet, carry knowledge and entertainment across national boundaries as fast as a communications satellite can process it. Fashions spread quickly too. The same consumer goods, whether European, American or Japanese, can be found throughout Europe. The convergence of social norms and behavior among citizens in many states is assumed to make an ever closer European Union inevitable.

While common experiences and attitudes are recognizable across the continent, they have not created a common European society. At most, one might speak of a "secondary community"; that is, people in different countries share some ideas and experiences but not others. Language is an obvious example. English is the common language of Europeans today, but it is a *second* language, not the language spoken in national parliaments or at home. In the member states of the European Union, German is the most frequently spoken home language, and the three Romance languages—French, Italian and Spanish—are the largest linguistic group. Primary attitudes remain distinctive. Even though the EU is removing the legal barriers to the movement of people and services, this does not mean that Italians will want to hire a Dane as their financial advisor, or that there will be a big demand in German schools for hiring teachers from Portugal.

The expansion of the membership of the European Union has actually increased differences among member states. Figure 13.2 compares differences among the original six member states and among the 15 current member states. In GDP per capita, the difference between the richest and poorest country among the original six members—France, Germany, Italy, Belgium, the Netherlands, and Luxembourg—is today only 29 percent, whereas among the 15 current members Luxembourg has a GDP per capita that is more than double that of the least well-off country, Greece. There is also less homogeneity in religion, a historic source of political cleavages. Among the founding members, four countries were Catholic and two mixed. Today, the European Union consists of a secular and Protestant group; countries mixed in their religious composition; and countries historically Catholic.

Geographical distance has also increased greatly. When there were only six member states, Brussels was a morning's train ride or less from five national capitals; only Rome was distant. Today, the most distant capital, Athens, is more than twice as far from Brussels as is Rome, and four other capitals—Helsinki, Stockholm, Madrid, and Lisbon—are also further from Brussels than is Rome. Shared experiences are also reduced by enlargement. This is true in the obvious sense of founding members being much longer in the EU than the nine countries that have joined much later. There is also a distinction between the "new" new members (Austria, Finland, and Sweden) and the "old" new members (Britain, Denmark and Ireland).

In theory, differences can create complementary interests; this is the basis of international trade. Insofar as countries differ, some may be indifferent to issues of particular concern to a few member states, making it easier to concede their demands or to engage in logrolling between states—for example, landlocked Austria can support other countries on an issue involving deep sea fishing, in return for support on a matter of unique concern to it, such as the Danube. However, differences in political traditions, political interests, and goals add to the complexity of policy making. Differences in national wealth make rich countries fearful of being exploited by poorer member states.

Laws of economics have been important in the creation of the single market. Their genesis is in neoclassical economic theory, which postulates that the most efficient and expanding economy is a perfect market in which labor, capital, goods, and services can move freely without governmental restriction, as each

FIGURE 13.2 ENLARGEMENT AND DIVERGENCE IN THE EUROPEAN UNION

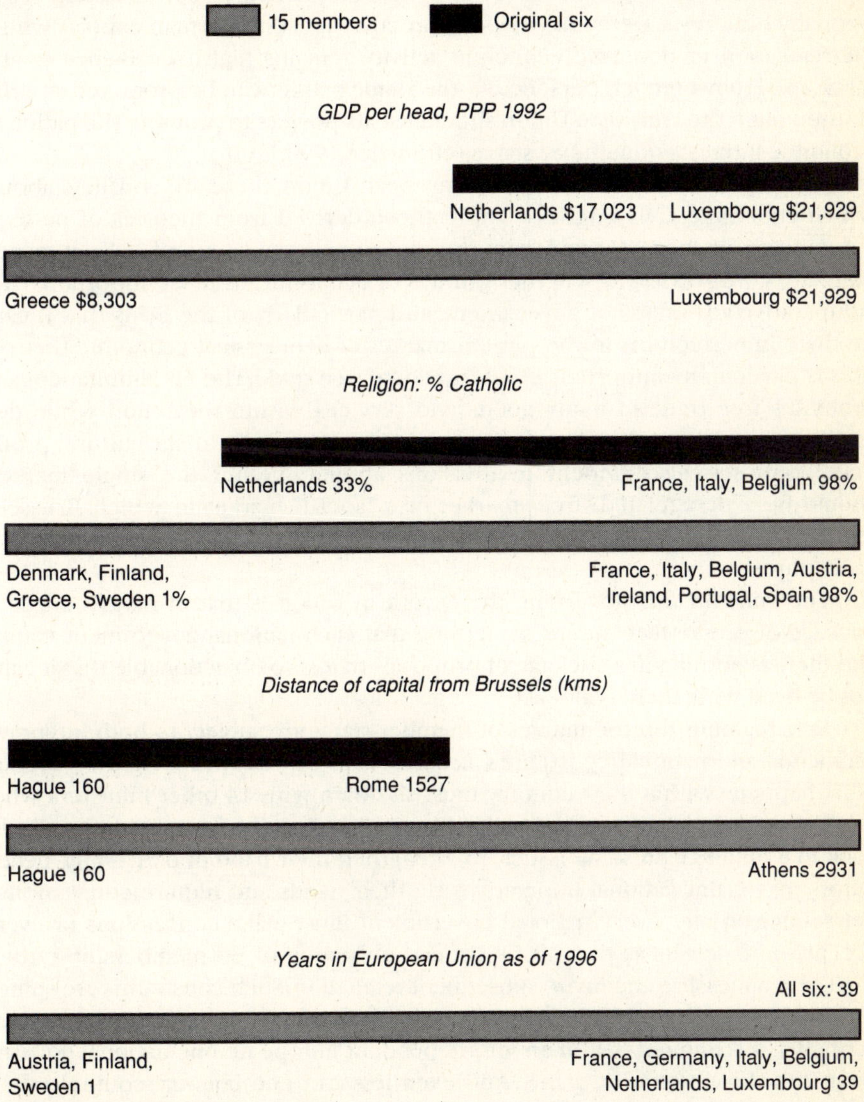

☐ 15 members   ■ Original six

GDP per head, PPP 1992

Netherlands $17,023   Luxembourg $21,929

Greece $8,303   Luxembourg $21,929

Religion: % Catholic

Netherlands 33%   France, Italy, Belgium 98%

Denmark, Finland,
Greece, Sweden 1%   France, Italy, Belgium, Austria,
Ireland, Portugal, Spain 98%

Distance of capital from Brussels (kms)

Hague 160   Rome 1527

Hague 160   Athens 2931

Years in European Union as of 1996

All six: 39

Austria, Finland,
Sweden 1   France, Germany, Italy, Belgium,
Netherlands, Luxembourg 39

Sources: Compiled from *OECD In Figures 1994* (Paris OECD, 1994) and various other sources.

producer and country concentrates on its comparative advantage. In a perfect market, public policies do not subsidize national industries or erect barriers against competition from abroad. The Cecchini Report estimated that a single market would add up to 5 percent of the gross domestic product of the European Union, reduce prices, and create nearly two million new jobs. The United States is sometimes used as an example of the benefits of a single market (cf. Emerson et al., 1988).

From a German perspective, the single market is not so much a triumph of the ideals of Adam Smith as it is of *Ordnungspolitik*—the use of public policy to order economic arrangements, an order that is assumed to be consistent with Germany's interests. Deregulation is espoused as assisting German exports while the regulation of domestic economic activity remains high (see Bieber et al., 1988: 13). From a French perspective, the single market can be promoted as a *dirigiste* policy; the European Union should use its powers to promote the national economic interests of member states (cf. Snyder, 1990: 73 ff.).

In the political economy of the European Union, there are conflicts about which economic laws ought to apply: those derived from theories of perfect competition or those derived from theories of national economics. Even more, there are conflicts about whether politics or economics is most important. The comparative advantage of government, and particularly of the EU is that it can produce imperfections in the perfect market of neoclassical economic theory. This is particularly important in international free trade. The EU simultaneously promotes free trade in many goods and services within the union while defending protectionist barriers to free trade internationally in agricultural products. Politics is also evident in divisions about whether the single market should be a deregulated "free" market or a "social" market in which Brussels regulations impose on employers policies favored by social democrats and trade unions.

The *political law* governing the European Union is that of bargaining. If a package of proposals contains something that each national government wants and there is nothing in a package of proposals that is so objectionable that it cannot be lived with, there is a deal.

In bargaining, representatives of member states are subject to both intergovernmental and national constraints. Leaders who can claim the right to decide what happens within their country must sit down with 14 other ministers who make the same claim—but for a different country. Inevitably, each country finds itself in a minority on some issues. To strengthen their hand in bargaining, negotiators may claim national imperatives tie their hands and require concessions. Yet sooner or later every national government must make concessions or even accept some defeats as part of the general obligation of EU membership rather than veto a measure and invite subsequent retaliation. Such constraints are sometimes described as a limitation upon national sovereignty. They are more aptly described as a statement that in an interdependent Europe no one national government can do whatever it wants. And even less can one country compel other governments to do what it wants. An adept politician can use Brussels to achieve goals that cannot be achieved by one nation acting alone. In some circumstances, a government may even use Brussels as an excuse for adopting policies that may be unpopular nationally.

Because most bargaining about European Union policies is remote from the spotlight of national politics, the former president of the commission, Jacques Delors, has described its policies as arrived at by a process of "benign despotism." However, a fundamental decision, such as the question of whether or not to join the European Union cannot be hidden, and normally creates divisions in national politics. Commitments to closer union in the Maastricht Treaty are also divisive issues in national politics.

In the early 1990s, eight countries held referendums about the European Union (Figure 13.3). In every referendum, national electorates divided. Electorates in Switzerland and Norway rejected proposals by their national governments to join or become associated with the European Union. In Austria, Finland, and Sweden the proposal carried. The Irish gave a two-to-one majority in favor of the Maastricht Treaty, whereas in France it carried by a bare majority. In Denmark the electorate initially voted against the treaty by a narrow margin. After cosmetic amendments, in a second referendum a majority of Danes voted in favor. Even when a referendum was not held, governments faced divisions in their cabinets. In Britain the Conserva-

FIGURE 13.3   REFERENDUM VOTES FOR AND AGAINST THE EUROPEAN UNION

Referendum on Entry or Treaty of Maastricht

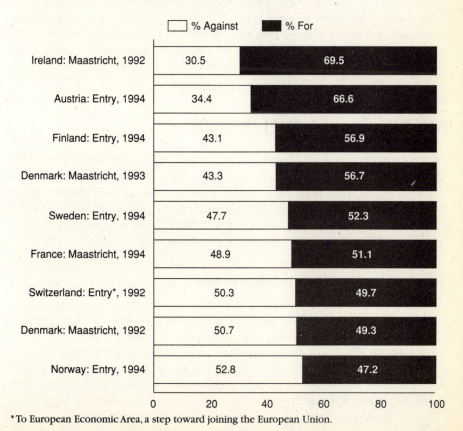

*To European Economic Area, a step toward joining the European Union.

Source: Official national election results.

tive government of John Major suffered the disgrace of losing a key vote in Parliament on Europe, a virtually unheard of setback for a British government.

Membership in the European Union is an "all or nothing" affair for a state. Yet within every member country there are divisions about whether or not steps toward closer union are desirable. In deliberations in the European Council, national leaders are under great cross-pressures. A common instinct of politicians in such circumstances is to blur difference by arriving at agreements that can mean different things to different people. A panel of economists scornfully notes of the Maastricht Treaty that it is "surprisingly unclear and informal, and not resting upon a compelling economic or legal logic" (CEPR, 1993: 13). Its gaps, contradictions, and ambiguities are not accidental but intentional. They allow political differences to be fought about again and again, with each side citing selected chapters from the treaties to justify its position.

Subsidiarity is a good example of the political advantages of ambiguity (see Blichner and Sangolt, 1994). Its inclusion in the Maastricht Treaty was due to some member states wanting not a federalist United States of Europe but a Union that would serve as an instrument for collectively advancing policies that national governments see as in their national interests. Ambiguity is a political asset, allowing policy makers to debate on a case-by-case basis whether a problem should be dealt with at EU or at a national level. If there is a political consensus in the Council of Ministers on a specific issue and support in national Parliaments, then EU action will be endorsed. If there is no political consensus, talk will not lead to EU action. Subsidiarity offers national politicians a means of simultaneously debating what is to be done and who does what.

DYNAMICS OF THE EUROPEAN UNION

While a fuzzy definition of a policy has immediate political advantages, the European Union cannot develop in all directions at once. If this were to happen, it would risk flying apart. Yet there is no agreement, among national leaders, among EU officials, or among social scientists about the future dynamics of a union that is supposed to become closer while it also enlarges, that is to deepen its influence by stretching its consensus-building capacities wider.

Conflicting Theories: How Is the EU to Develop?

The clearest and most ambitious goal is that of federalists: the creation of a United States of Europe, integrating the peoples of Europe into a new multinational state. Like many idealistic goals, it raises the question: How are 15 (or more) member states to become one? The most committed federalists respond with an exhortation: keep moving closer. The EU is compared to a bicycle: It must constantly be going forward if it is not to fall over. Federalists use this analogy to justify a steady stream of proposals to maintain momentum. Opponents accept the metaphor hoping that forward movement to the federal goal can be stopped once and for all. While a clear goal gives purpose to politics and a metaphor adds vividness, neither is a theory about how to get there from here.

Neofunctional theorists see European integration increasing incrementally. They assume that laws of the market will lead to increased economic activity across national boundaries leading to demands for common policies. Increased convergence and communication across national boundaries will make common policies politically more acceptable. This will lead to demands for action by the European Union. A response to an immediate problem can spill over into demands for further actions, when the initial demand can only be achieved if the EU's powers are deepened (Haas, 1964; see also Lindberg and Scheingold, 1970). This theory rejects the idea that progress toward federalism must be steady, but it does predict that the EU will inevitably increase its influence.

History shows that even though the European Union has gone through periods of stagnation, its powers have not contracted. The doctrine of the *acquis communitaire* holds that the EU's powers to act cannot be diminished. Member states dissatisfied with union policies cannot subsequently nullify them. If a national election returns a government that would have vetoed a decision in the Council of Ministers, it will not be reversed; a newly elected national government is bound by the treaty commitments of its predecessor. Countries applying for membership must take the policies and powers of the union as they are; the most they can achieve are special transitional arrangements to ease any difficulties in adapting to EU policies.

Federalist and neofunctionalist theories play down the significance of national interests. State-centered theories describe the European Union as an institutional means by which member states can advance their national interests. General Charles de Gaulle called this a *Europe des patries* (a Europe of nations). A state-centered view accepts that leaps forward, such as the single Europe market, can occur when it is in the interest of independent states to cooperate through the European Union. Such state-centered theories tend to overlook the fact that the European Union is not a temporary alliance, like the coalition formed to fight the war in the Persian Gulf in 1990. An essential feature of the Treaty of Union is that member states are bound to accept its rules when they are inconvenient as well as when they are convenient. Treating the European Union as a league of 15 independent states also ignores the existence of a sixteenth "member," the institutions of the European Union (cf. Weiler, 1991; Moravscik, 1993).

What happens if agreement among member states is not possible? One possibility is that nothing is done; the union maintains established activities but does not deepen. Another alternative is described as a two-speed Europe—countries that want to increase cooperation take the lead, while other member states do not participate. The expansion of the union to 15 members and increasing tensions about the tempo of developments has promoted the two-speed Europe as a compromise that could be accepted by both federalists and nationalists. It is technically feasible to draft laws so that only member states that wish to launch a major initiative, such as monetary union, can do so while others do not. The assumption of a two-speed Europe is that countries that initially do not adopt an

EU policy will sooner or later do so. The tempo of change varies between countries, but the direction remains steady, toward a closer union.

By contrast, in a *variable geometry* Europe member states can head in different directions, some pursuing a federalist goal and others pursuing interests independently. This alternative is also known as Europe *a la carte,* since each government could pick and mix the EU policies it puts into effect. There are precedents for this, since a British Conservative government has opted out of the social charter establishing corporatist-type guidelines for labor-management relations. An *a la carte* Europe is also relevant for defense, since some EU members belong to NATO and others do not. However, the long-term logic of variable geometry is fragmentation. Whereas in a two-speed Europe all countries go in the same direction, in a variable geometry model the more difficult the decisions, the more likely groups of member states are to fly off in different directions.

The evolution of European institutions has combined incremental expansion, as predicted by neofunctionalist theories, and occasional leaps forward, consistent with state-centered theories of the EU as an intergovernmental body serving national interests. Incremental expansion has occurred principally in areas of low politics, such as measures to promote the mobility of students and regulations about safe products, areas where laws and regulations are more important than public expenditure. Occasionally, the coincidence of events and interests among member states leads to a big leap forward, as in the Single European Act of 1987 it has given the Union the authority to regulate the stream of commerce of its member countries, a power that can be extended to influence what have hitherto been regarded as domestic matters, such as whether sugar should be sold by the pound or by the kilogram (cf. Majone, 1991). The 1992 Maastricht Treaty is another leap ahead, prompted by the desire of the German government and its neighbors to integrate a reunified Germany more closely into Brussels institutions rather than risk Germany going it alone in Central and Eastern Europe.

The Problems of Deepening and Broadening

All models of the dynamics of the European Union assume that current member states remain members. No country has ever resigned. Whatever the dissatisfaction of a national government with EU policies, the economic and political costs of withdrawal are considered too high. But a recognition of member states that they must continue to live with each other still leaves open to debate the terms of future relations, in the face of pressures to deepen and to broaden the Union.

The Maastricht Treaty proposes deepening the union on three fronts. It authorized an Economic and Monetary Union (EMU) with an independent central bank issuing a single currency and pursuing anti-inflationary policies independent of member states. A European Monetary Institute has been established in Frankfurt to prepare for it. From the perspective of technocratic economists, EMU is simply another step to maximize economic efficiency. An analysis of the case against a European Central Bank declared, "Arguments that decentralization is morally right even though inefficient are not our concern here" (CEPR, 1993:

11). However, national policy makers cannot ignore political arguments. The creation of a common currency would impose strict limits on a national government's capacity to make taxing and spending decisions, and deprive the governing party of the capacity to change economic policy in accord with the electoral calendar. A common currency would also be a big symbolic step toward a federal Europe. The idea of having Frankfurt rather than Rome fight inflation might appeal to many Italians, but the idea of Paris and Rome influencing the successor of the *Bundesbank* creates anxieties among many Germans.

There are political and technical obstacles to the introduction of a common European currency. Vocal political objections come from Britain, where the national government is hesitant to give a monetary institution in another country control of central instruments of national economic policy. Small countries such as Austria actively endorse the idea of EMU, for they are already forced to follow the course of the deutsche mark, and hope through EMU to gain a seat at the table in Frankfurt where decisions are made. Technical obstacles arise from the fact that a country is not expected to join EMU until its inflation rates, budget deficit, interest rates, and other indicators are converging to the EMU standard. The criteria leave open the level of unemployment and economic growth. In a union of 15 member states, it is unusual for all countries to be similarly successful in achieving any policy goal, especially a goal that is so vulnerable to fluctuations in the international economy.

A second initiative of the Maastricht Treaty is "the eventual framing of a common defense policy which may in time lead to a common defense." In the past, member states have relied for military security upon NATO, in which the United States is preeminent. The war between Serbia, Croatia, and Bosnia has revealed that European countries and the United States cannot always reach agreement about the use of troops in Europe. It has also revealed differences of opinion among member states of the European Union about actions in response to war within Europe. While a common defense policy appears distant, it is a significant goal, for a military force is a fundamental attribute of a sovereign state.

The third initiative advocated by the Maastricht Treaty concerns justice and internal affairs matters, such as citizenship, crime, and drugs. Common citizenship is a logical consequence of the free movement of individuals throughout the single market. An unwanted consequence is the free movement of criminals, drugs, and stolen goods. Furthermore, some countries have had many migrants from extra-European countries—for example, into Britain from the Indian subcontinent and the West Indies, and into France from North Africa. Germany and Austria have common boundaries with a number of post-Communist states, from which could come an influx of illegal migrants from neighboring countries or the former Soviet Union.

Proponents of strengthening the European Union believe that it could increase its appeal to the peoples of Europe by offering citizens a European court to protect individual rights denied nationally. The instrument for doing so is already at hand: the European Convention on Human Rights and the European Court on Human Rights, sponsored by the Council of Europe in Strasbourg. Member states of the European Union are also members of the Council of Europe, and most have recognized the authority of the Human Rights Court to take binding decisions if two-thirds of judges agree. However, the process of bringing cases before this court is cumbersome and slow. The existing court has influence when its findings strengthen the position of national critics of a government's action; it mixes shame and positive encouragement in its efforts to promote human rights (cf. Moravcsik, 1994; Robertson and Merrill, 1993).

The Problems of Broadening

In principle, EU membership is open to any European country willing to abide by its principles, which include democracy. But broadening an institution conceived by six likeminded states into a union with 15 diverse members has caused problems. The shift from unanimous voting to voting by a qualified majority on many issues was adopted. The commitment to treat all national languages equally threatens to turn the headquarters of the European Commission into a Tower of Babel. A further increase in member states will increase strains on institutions.

The collapse of Communism raises the prospect of more than half a dozen states in Central and Eastern Europe joining the European Union in the foreseeable future. However, their circumstances are very different from Norway and Switzerland, the only Western European states now outside the Union. The Czech Republic, Hungary, Poland, Slovakia, Bulgaria, and Romania, followed by Estonia, Latvia, and Lithuania, have each signed association agreements with the EU. Slovenia, the smallest, northernmost and most prosperous successor republic of Yugoslavia, is ready to do so as soon as disputes with Italy are resolved. To become a member, each country must meet four political conditions—establish the rule of law, commitment to democracy, recognize human rights, and protect minorities—and one economic condition, the creation of an internationally viable market economy.

Post-Communist countries are finding it more difficult to construct a market economy than to hold free elections. Because they are disproportionately agricultural, entry of Central and Eastern European countries would pose a fundamental challenge to the Common Agricultural Policy. To pay current levels of subsidies to these countries if they were to become EU members would threaten to break the union's budget. The industrial capacity of Poland is also substantial, especially in industries where production is already in surplus, such as steel, coal, and shipbuilding. A major asset of post-Communist countries, relatively low wages, threatens a flight of capital from high-wage countries or the migration of people from Eastern to Western Europe in search of high wages.

With two dozen member states, the European Union would cover the whole of the European continent. But a union of such magnitude could hardly operate by unanimity. The greater the number of members, the more difficult it is to accommodate the interests of every state on every issue. Broadening increases tensions between richer and poorer countries, bigger and smaller countries, and Northern, Southern, Western, and Eastern European countries. Whereas deepening requires member states to face new problems, broadening forces them to deal with the unknown, new EU members with a Communist past.

chapter **14**

EUROPE IN THE WORLD

The size of the globe is fixed, but the relative importance of countries and of continents is variable. When the modern state developed, Europeans believed that Europe *was* the world, or at least all the world that mattered. In the eighteenth and nineteenth centuries, the major states of Europe projected their power globally by creating empires. The two world wars of this century were stamped Made in Europe. Yet the outcome of World War II created three worlds, the first world of advanced industrial nations; the second world of Communist states; and the third world of developing countries.

In the half-century since 1945, major changes have occurred in the globe. First, almost one hundred new independent states have been created in the wake of the postwar dissolution of empires. Numerically, such states predominate in the United Nations. As part of the same process, European countries have been reducing global interests derived from their imperial past. Second, the collapse of Communist power has ended the Cold War and expanded democratic Europe. NATO still exists but its historic enemy does not. This raises fundamental questions about the requirements for European security and about the global disposition of American military power. Third, national economies have been internationalized; the reduction of trade barriers within and between regions has led to the greater mobility of goods and capital. There is a greater symmetry in economic relations too, as Asian countries such as Japan have become developed, and oil-rich countries play a significant role in the international movement of capital.

Europe's position in the world today is different from a generation ago. When OECD was founded as an organization of advanced industrial nations, 18 of its 20 member states were European; the United States and Canada were the exceptions. Since then, most new members of the OECD—Japan, Australia, New Zealand, and Mexico—have come from outside Europe. The Czech Republic is the first new post-Communist member. No one country or continent can dominate the world economy today. Europe has more people and a larger national product than other countries in OECD, but this is less than half the total of advanced industrial nations. Europe is one of three centers of the international economy, along with North America and Japan.

Modern societies, and evidence of modernization, such as computers and jet airplanes, can be found on every continent. English has emerged as the common language of diplomats and business people, but policies enunciated in English by

TABLE 14.1   CONTRASTS IN MILITARY AND ECONOMIC POWER

		Military		
		Major		**Minor**
			(Examples)	
	Major	United States		Japan, Kuwait
Economic				
	Minor	North Korea		Most EU and UN member states

representatives of Japan and Saudi Arabia are often very different from what native English-speakers would say. Samuel Huntington (1993: 49) concludes: "Western civilization is both Western and modern. Non-Western civilizations have attempted to become modern without becoming Western."

The terms of interdependence are altering. For decades after World War II, the United States was the hegemonic leader on which European nations depended. Europeans described having America as an ally as like being in bed with an elephant. When the elephant rolled over, everyone felt it. American-led alliances are no longer the only groupings of importance in the world. The European Union represents the interests of the largest block of advanced industrial nations on economic issues. OPEC makes an impact as an organization of oil-rich Third World countries.

The end of the Cold War has altered the relative importance of economic and military power. The United States is unique in having global military power and is of major economic importance—but its economy is no longer all important (Kennedy, 1988; Nye, 1990). The great majority of countries, including most states in the European Union, are neither economic nor military powers (Table 14.1). In a world of interdependence, they are a part of a system in which the system is stronger than their state. Even though Japan is very significant in the world economy, because of World War II its constitution and politics keep its military force small. Oil-rich Kuwait is rich but defenseless because it is small, as the invasion by Iraq revealed in 1990. North Korea is insignificant in the world economy, but by attacking South Korea in 1950 it showed that it could start an international war involving the United States and the United Nations, and today it threatens to develop nuclear weapons.

Interdependence creates uncertainties, for there is no agreement within or between European countries about the future course of policy. At world summit meetings the bland pronouncements of leaders of the United States, Canada, Britain, France, Germany, Italy, and Japan mask doubts and disagreements. The first part of this chapter describes how the changing boundaries of Europe are one cause of uncertainty. The second examines how the increasingly global orientation of the United States has reduced the relative significance of its ties with Europe. The conclusion emphasizes that interdependence has created an open Europe in which politics is neither local nor national; it is a "floating crap game" in which national governments find themselves playing for high stakes with ever changing boundaries.

DYNAMIC BOUNDARIES

Whereas post-1945 Europe was limited by the Iron Curtain to half a continent, the boundaries of Europe today are open to the east. This is shown by the movement of the geographical center of population. When the European Community was founded in the 1950s, its notional center of population was actually outside its boundaries, being near Basle, Switzerland. After Britain, Ireland, and Denmark joined, the center of population shifted north and west to Metz in eastern France. After Mediterranean countries joined, the center shifted south and west a little in France to Dijon.

The opening of Europe has shifted its central point east. When Central and Eastern Europe are included in the calculus, the population center of Europe is the old South German city of Ulm, the birthplace of Albert Einstein. Symbolically, Ulm is not on the Rhine, which flows to the North Sea, but on the Danube, which flows through the Balkans to the Black Sea. A circle with Ulm at its center and large enough to include Brussels also includes Prague, Vienna, and Zagreb, the capital of Croatia (Figure 14.1). A circle reaching far enough to include Dublin and Stockholm also brings in the Baltic states, the whole of Eastern Europe, and the Ukraine. A circle big enough to include the most distant capitals of European Union member states, Helsinki, Athens and Lisbon, also includes Saint Petersburg, Istanbul, and North Africa.

Brussels, the political capital of the European Union, is now a "Western" outpost of the continent. There is no desire of aspirants to membership from Central and Eastern Europe to alter this political orientation, for they want to leave behind the problems of their Communist past.

Variable Definitions of Europe

The question—Which countries are now part of Europe?—requires a political not a geographical answer. States of the continent are considered European if they are democratic or aspiring to become democratic and governing according to the rule of law. The commitment to democracy has even been affirmed by the European Bank for Reconstruction and Development (EBRD), which provides economic assistance to post-Communist countries. Its charter commits it to "fundamental principles of multiparty democracy, the rule of law, respect for human rights, and market economies." When economic or military criteria are added (or democracy is removed as a defining attribute), the definition of Europe will alter. Institutionally, European states can be defined by their involvement in one or more of four different organizations: the European Union, the Council of Europe, NATO, or the Organization on Security and Cooperation in Europe (see Table 14.2).

FIGURE 14.1

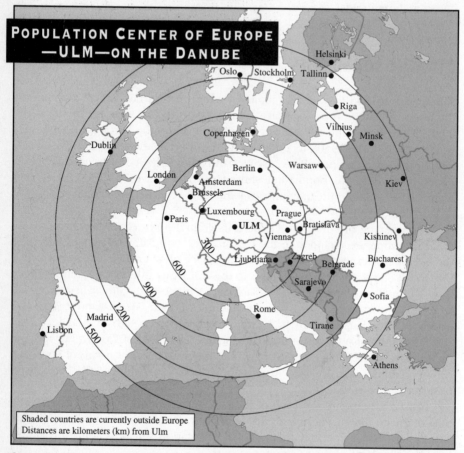

POPULATION CENTER OF EUROPE
—ULM—ON THE DANUBE

Shaded countries are currently outside Europe
Distances are kilometers (km) from Ulm

Source: John Cole and Francis Cole, *The Geography of the European Community* (London: Routledge, 1993), 278.

The *European Union* is a political and an economic organization. In formal terms, a country is a member if it accepts the treaty commitments of the EU; 15 countries have done so to date. In addition, countries can be associated with the EU in the European Economic Area (EEA), which includes Norway, Iceland, and the ministate of Liechtenstein as members. For economic purposes, EEA countries are part of the single market, but they do not participate in the political institutions of the EU.

The 1995 enlargement of the EU increased pressures to deal with post-Communist states, for two new members, Finland and Sweden, are closer to Saint Petersburg than to Brussels, and Vienna is closer to such capital cities as Bratislava, Prague, Budapest, Ljubljana, and Zagreb than to some major cities in Austria. As an open membership organization, the EU is prepared to admit more members—if they are democratic and have a market economy. The European Union has granted associate status to nine post-Communist states, from the Czech Republic to the Baltic states and Bulgaria, and Slovenia is to be added when it settles a dis-

TABLE 14.2 THE FIELD OF EUROPE

	OSCE	Council of Europe	NATO	EU
	X Member		—Not involved	
Core				
Belgium	X	X	X	X
Denmark	X	X	X	X
France	X	X	X	X
Germany	X	X	X	X
Greece	X	X	X	X
Italy	X	X	X	X
Luxembourg	X	X	X	X
Netherlands	X	X	X	X
Portugal	X	X	X	X
Spain	X	X	X	X
United Kingdom	X	X	X	X
Finland	X	X	p	X
Sweden	X	X	p	X
Austria	X	X	p	X
Ireland	X	X	—	X
Norway	X	X	X	e
Switzerland	X	X	—	—
Associates				
Bulgaria	X	X	p	a
Czech Republic	X	X	p	a
Hungary	X	X	p	a
Poland	X	X	p	a
Romania	X	X	p	a
Slovakia	X	X	p	a
Estonia (ex-USSR)	X	X	p	a
Latvia (ex-USSR)	X	X	p	a
Lithuania (ex-USSR)	X	X	p	a
Slovenia (ex-Yugoslavia)	X	X	p	a
Iceland	X	X	X	e
Turkey	X	X	X	—
Cyprus	X	X	—	a
Malta	X	X	—	a
Potential Associates				
Albania	X	g	p	—
Croatia (ex-Yugoslavia)	X	g	—	—
Belarus (ex-USSR)	X	g	p	—

Continued

TABLE 14.2 *Continued*

	OSCE	Council of Europe	NATO	EU
		X Member		—Not involved
Potential Associates				
Moldova (ex-USSR)	X	g	p	—
Russia (ex-USSR)	X	g	p	—
Ukraine (ex-USSR)	X	g	p	—
Within the field				
Armenia (ex-USSR)	X	—	p	—
Azerbaijan (ex-USSR)	X	—	p	—
Georgia (ex-USSR)	X	—	p	—
Kazakhstan (ex-USSR)	X	—	p	—
Kyrgyzstan (ex-USSR)	X	—	p	—
Tajikistan (ex-USSR)	X	—	—	—
Turkmenistan(ex-USSR)	X	—	—	—
Uzbekistan (ex-USSR)	X	—	—	—
Bosnia (ex-Yugoslavia)	—	g	—	—
Macedonia (ex-Yugoslavia)	o	g	—	—
Serbia (ex-Yugoslavia)	—	—	—	—

a: Associate status, not member

e: European Economic Area member with special EU status

g: Guest status

o: Observer status

p: Participant in NATO Partnership for Peace

Source: Compiled by the author. Omitted are ministates such as Andorra, Liechtenstein, Monaco, San Marino, and the Vatican City, and two non-European members of NATO, the United States and Canada.

pute with Italy. The associate agreements are a preliminary step to membership; they make provision for technical assistance, which is particularly important for post-Communist states. A country cannot participate fully in the single European market until it has a market economy. Membership also requires that a country continue to make progress in institutionalizing democratic practices. In addition, before further enlargement, the present 15 members must decide difficult issues about the future of the EU (see Rose, 1995b).

Three other states—Turkey, Malta, and Cyprus—have long had membership applications pending, but no action has been taken. Turkey is particularly significant in defining the boundaries of Europe. The Ottoman Empire was one of the major powers of Europe for centuries; however, it collapsed in World War I. Turkey has intermittently had competitive party politics and elections, but the military has frequently intervened in government, and its treatment of minorities such as Kurds raises problems. Geographically, most of Turkey, including the capital, Ankara, is in the Middle East. Although the state is secular, many citizens are Muslims and there is an active Islamic revivalist movement. The economy of Turkey is a developing market economy with both modern and backward sectors. A population greater than 14 EU member states aggravates its problems. Cyprus, an island now divided by a war involving Turkey and Greek Cypriots is unique because of its division by force. Malta, with a population of 350,000, raises the question of what the EU should do about ministates.

Membership in the *Council of Europe* is evidence of a regime's claim to be democratic. It was founded in 1949 to promote greater cooperation between democratic states of Europe and carries out a limited number of functions on a pan-European basis, including the sponsorship of conventions and agreements dealing with everything from human rights and data protection to measures to reduce hooliganism at European Cup football matches. The criteria for membership are characteristics of a *Rechtsstaat;* member states must "accept the principles of the rule of law and of the enjoyment by all persons within their jurisdiction of human rights and fundamental freedoms." The Council scrutinizes claims of new regimes to be recognized as European democracies. Unlike the United Nations, which has always accepted undemocratic European regimes, the Council of Europe did not admit Communist states. It also did not admit right-wing authoritarian regimes; Spain and Portugal only became members after their dictators fell.

The Council of Europe has expanded its membership selectively since the collapse of Communist regimes (see again Table 14.2). By 1995, it had admitted ten countries from Central and Eastern Europe, starting with Hungary. A number of ex-Communist countries currently are classified as having guest status in the council. Four countries (Russia, Belarus, Moldova, and Ukraine) are from the former Soviet Union, and one is from the former Yugoslavia (Croatia). Eight successor states of the Soviet Union in the Caucuses and Central Asia do not have guest status and Serbia is also in this category. The object of guest status is to encourage new regimes to respect the rule of law so that they may become members subsequently, and to protect the diplomatic and moral authority of the Council by refusing membership to countries that have yet to demonstrate their democratic intent.

A security community is a group of nations that do not fear the outbreak of war between them (cf. Deutsch et al., 1957: 5 ff.). For centuries, Europe was not a security community but an arena of insecurity; states demonstrated insecurity by arming and waging war against each other. Today, the states of the European Union and its associated states plus Switzerland and Norway can certainly be described as a security community. Now that Soviet forces have been withdrawn, West European states no longer fear military attack from post-Communist states of Central and Eastern Europe. Such insecurities as exist in Europe today arise from ethnic tensions, for example, between Hungary and Romania, and from war between successor states of Yugoslavia.

A *military alliance* is defined by an enemy as well as by its membership. During the Cold War, lines were clearly drawn; most European states participated in NATO to provide common defense against a Soviet threat. The Western European Union (WEU) was created as a forum in which most European members of

NATO could discuss issues of common concern while troops remained in the NATO command. Ireland, Sweden, and Switzerland remained neutral by tradition and choice, while Austria and Finland remained neutral because they were subject to pressure from the Soviet Union.

The end of the Cold War has not eliminated the enduring concern of national governments with security, nor has it reduced the commitment of Europeans to some form of collective security. It raises two related questions: Where is the threat to the security of Europe today? Which alliance can best provide security against threats to peace in Europe?

The Russian Federation remains the major military power in the geographical continent of Europe today. The breakup of the Soviet Union has placed two buffer states between Russia and Eastern Europe, Belarus and Ukraine. Today, the only European states with which Russia has a land boundary are Estonia and Finland and, in the Arctic Circle, Norway. The Russian military retains the capacity to wage nuclear war through long-range missiles as well as action on the ground. The Russian assault on Chechnya in December 1994 was a reminder that the collapse of the Soviet Union has not eliminated the willingness of Russia to use force.

The *Organization on Security and Cooperation in Europe (OSCE)* is an association of former or potential adversaries, including countries with nuclear weapons or potential nuclear capabilities. It relies upon diplomacy rather than military force, following Winston Churchill's dictum that "Jaw, jaw is better than war, war." The OSCE has 53 member states, including the United States and Canada. Its large size follows from a policy including all the successor states of the former Soviet Union; successor states of Yugoslavia; and NATO members. Members include countries that regard each other as allies and countries regarded as potential threats to peace or even threats to their own national safety through nuclear accidents. The OSCE also has nonmilitary concerns, such as the promotion of human rights. However, a comparison of membership in the Council of Europe and the OSCE shows that respect for human rights is not a precondition for OSCE membership, nor is abstention from civil war or transborder fighting (cf. Table 14.2).

The logic of drawing potential adversaries closer together explains NATO's partnership for peace program. This creates NATO ties with countries such as Poland, conscripted into the Warsaw Pact by the Soviet Union and now seeking a NATO guarantee of defense against an attack from Russia. At the same time, it also brings into association with NATO successor states of the Soviet Union, including Russia.

Europe on the Move

The boundaries of Europe are dynamic. The boundaries of Europe a century ago covered more than double the area of the post-1945 Europe of democratic nation-states. Many states and principalities within those boundaries have since disappeared. An enumeration of democratic countries of Europe today is a substantially longer list than a decade ago. Today, Europeans can go to Prague or Berlin as easily as in 1913. The difference from the turn of the century is that today these cities are major cities in democratic states.

The multiple boundaries of contemporary Europe are purposeful. The boundaries of the European Union are narrow because it involves a very high degree of political and economic commitment and cooperation. Yet economic boundaries are ambiguous. The EU negotiates as a trading block with other continents, shifting between policies of regional protection and international free trade depending upon the topic at hand. For the purpose of collective defense against a global war breaking out in Europe, the United States remains part of Europe. But for lesser security problems, the United States is free to opt out, and for concerns in other parts of the globe Europeans are free to opt out.

The use of associate status by European organizations is evidence that the boundaries of core institutions such as the European Union are in principle expansive. But there is no timetable for predicting whether expansion occurs before the year 2000 or after. There is even less certainty about how far south and east the European Union will expand in the foreseeable future. The more broadly based Council of Europe even faces the prospect of withdrawing guest status from some countries currently having it, because they default on democratic intentions. Yet in an interdependent continent, the OCSE recognizes that countries outside the pale can still exercise influence if local wars or nuclear accidents spill over their boundaries.

FROM A NORTH ATLANTIC TO A GLOBAL UNITED STATES

The expansion of modern societies to four or more continents has met a very different response in Europe and the United States. In the postwar era European countries have been contracting their global interests and strengthening ties within the continent of Europe. When decisions are made in the European Union, the United States is not a participant; it is on the outside looking in. Concurrently, the United States has grown into a power with global economic and military concerns. For the United States, Europe remains an important region but not the only region of importance. The United States has concerns and commitments in other regions as well—Latin America, the Pacific, the Middle East, Africa and, closer to home, Canada and Mexico—and it need not consult Brussels or national governments in Europe before acting in other continents. Within the United States, big changes in population are leading Americans to pay less attention to Europe and more to other parts of the globe.

America's Multicontinental Interests

Trade illustrates the significance to the United States of many different regions of the world. Whereas intra-European trade is now the norm for member states of the European Union, no one continent is the dominant partner for America's exports or imports. Together, Asia and the Middle East are now the largest single market for America's exports, but they account for less than a third of total exports. Asian manufactured goods and oil from the Middle East make those regions the leading source of America's imports. The Western Hemisphere, led by Canada, accounts for a third of America's imports and exports. The European Union today accounts for 20 percent of American imports and 26 percent of its exports, approximately the same as does Canada (Bureau of the Census, 1994: table 1404).

Europe increases in economic significance for the United States when American investment abroad is the focus, for almost half of the direct investment by American institutions abroad is in Europe. There is more American investment in the United Kingdom than in Canada, more in Germany than Japan, and in France, Italy, and the Netherlands than in Mexico (Bureau of the Census, 1994: table 1316). By investing in factories, retail outlets, and offices that produce goods and services inside the European Union, American multinational firms such as Ford, IBM, McKinsey, and McDonald's can profit from being within a larger market than the United States. Investment in Europe also offers greater security to American investors than do regions such as the Middle East.

As long as NATO continues, the United States has a central role to play in defending half the continent of Europe. But the collapse of the Soviet Union means that threats to European security are more likely to come from "brush fires" that are dangerous to neighbors but are not perceived in the United States as a conflict worth the risk of American lives. Just as political disturbances in Central America are not threats to European interests, so clashes involving small countries in the Balkans or the former Soviet Union are not necessarily threats to American interests. Yet by definition, intraregional conflicts are of concern to neighboring European states.

As long as the United States defines its security role as global, threats from the Middle East, Africa, Central or South America, or Asia can also be of immediate concern in Washington. Insofar as European countries seek to influence what happens outside Europe, this may be done by lobbying in Washington or at the United Nations. But outside Europe, the states of Europe have the option of remaining disengaged from problems that appear difficult to resolve.

Globalization and De-Europeanization of the United States

When European and American leaders invoke a common culture, such remarks are doubly in error. First, they ignore the fact that the population of the United States has always included people with no European heritage, starting with Native American Indians and slaves from Africa. Second, it overlooks the distance between the homelands of different European immigrants—for example, Sweden and Italy. Some were traditionally enemies, such as Ireland and England, or Germany and Poland. Moreover, immigrants such as poor peasants from Southern Italy or refugees from Czarist or Nazi pogroms consciously rejected the poverty and brutality that defined their experience of Europe.

The ancestry of America's population today is heterogeneous in the extreme; the 1990 census coded replies about national origins in more than 600 different categories. A quarter of America's population is definitely non-European, consisting of Native Americans, African-Americans, waves of Hispanic-Americans from Puerto Rico, Mexico and other countries, and Asians (Figure 14.2). The largest category, non-Hispanic whites, consists of people whose ancestors came from many

FIGURE 14.2   DECLINING RELEVANCE OF EUROPEAN ORIGINS IN THE UNITED STATES

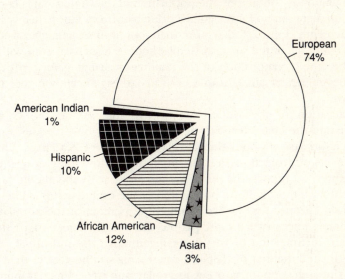

Population 1995: 263 million

European 74%

American Indian 1%

Hispanic 10%

African American 12%

Asian 3%

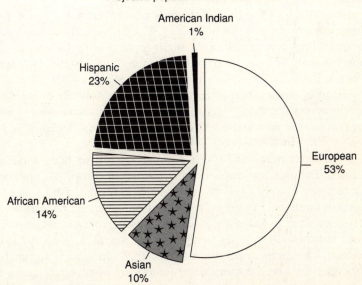

Projected population 2050: 392 million

American Indian 1%

Hispanic 23%

African American 14%

Asian 10%

European 53%

Source: Bureau of the Census, *Statistical Abstract of the United States 1994* (Washington: Government Printing Office, 1994), Table 18. Projection for 2050 is the middle projection of population change. European category includes a small proportion giving ancestry as Canadian, Australian, or other settler country.

different parts of Europe. The great majority left Europe at least a century ago. Ten percent of Americans have so little sense of their ancestors that they reply "don't know" when asked to name their country of origin. The biggest groups, the Germans and Irish, were part of a massive wave of immigration in the 1840s. Where ancestry is distant in time as well as space, people will not know about Europe from first-hand family discussion. Americans are most likely to observe Europe on a package holiday tour.

Since immigration is continuous, the population of the United States continues to change. Immigration no longer comes principally from Europe, as was the case in the nineteenth century. Today more than four-fifths of immigrants come from Hispanic countries of the Western Hemisphere or from Asia. Even without immigration, the ethnic composition of the country is changing, for birth rates among Hispanic-Americans and African Americans are significantly higher than for other groups.

The globalization of the United States will increase in the coming decades. Estimating the characteristics of people not yet born creates a margin of error in a forecast of population developments. The U.S. Census Bureau prepares three sets of projections, a high, medium, and low forecast of future population. Figure 14.2 reports the middle-range forecast. By the middle of the twenty-first century, almost half the population of the United States is likely to have no claim on European roots. Even though 52 percent of the population will have European ancestry, for most people this will be one, two, or three centuries distant in time, and of very little meaning to the individuals concerned. The estimated number of Hispanic-Americans will be greater than the population of the largest country in Europe today, and the estimated number of African-Americans and of Asians will be as large as other large countries in Europe today.

The globalization of the United States is being reinforced by the move of population from frost-belt to sun-belt states. When asked where his or her family comes from, a resident of California might reply Ohio or Oklahoma, if that is as far back as family ties can be traced. The three largest states of America today, California, Texas, and Florida, are all sun-belt states, closer to Central and South American countries than to Europe. California not only borders Mexico but also faces across the Pacific Ocean to Asia. The historic regions of immigration from Europe, the East Coast and the Deep South, are declining in relative size.

The global diversification of America's interests has not been anti-European in intent, just as the growing introversion of politics in Europe has not been anti-American. In times of stress, European countries and the United States tend to see interests in common. In every major European state, the country viewed as most likely to come to its aid in the event of a military attack is not another European power but the United States (see Smith and Wertman, 1992: 29). However, in the absence of a military attack, the attention of Washington is turning to other parts of the globe, while European governments are concentrating more attention upon what is happening in Brussels or Bonn rather than on what is happening in Washington.

POLITICS IN AN OPEN EUROPE

Europeans have never accepted the American political adage, "All politics is local." If that were the case, Europeans would still be living in isolated villages, petty principalities, or prosperous city-states trading independently with the rest of the world, as did Venice or Augsburg, and two world wars would never have happened. World war required centralized modern states mobilizing conscripts from towns and villages to fight and die on foreign soils. An apt description for twentieth-century Europe is "All politics is the politics of the state." The MPs elected by proportional representation do not represent a district but a party. Coalition governments are accountable to a Parliament that represents a variety of cultural and economic interests nationwide.

Porous and Penetrable Boundaries

In a world of interdependence, keeping domestic politics within the boundaries of the state is not as easy as it once was. People who vote for a government are much more concerned with domestic affairs than with European or international affairs. But the definition of what is and is not domestic differs from continent to continent. A survey of television news coverage found that American television concentrated upon America, and the lead story in Japan was about sumo wrestling (Malik and Anderson, 1992). In Europe, the lead news story is usually about Europe, but this can be a nation's prime minister issuing a statement from abroad after a European Union meeting. Once the news is over, Europeans often turn their attention to entertainment programs made abroad or to football matches in which their home team may be playing against another European city in a European Cup competition.

In an open Europe, the boundaries between domestic and foreign affairs are increasingly porous and penetrated. National governments are at the intersection between domestic and European or global pressures—and must juggle all of these. Airports illustrate how the same place can be linked to different parts of the world. London airports now have more flights to other major cities of Europe than to other cities of Britain. National airports also make connections between continents. There are more daily flights from London to New York than between London and such capitals as Madrid or Rome, and more flights to Tokyo than to Bonn.

The growth of multinational corporations shows how interdependence becomes interpenetration. Trade occurs when goods made in one country or continent are sold in another. Interpenetration occurs when goods sold in a country may be made in a factory owned by a foreign company, or assembled nationally from parts made in several different countries. European automobiles illustrate how hard it is becoming to attribute nationality to cars. Today Europe is as big a producer of cars as the United States or Japan. However, the major "European" car manufacturers include Ford and General Motors as well as Volkswagen, Fiat, and Renault. Hardly any of these "American" cars are manufactured in the United States. (Figure 14.3). In the single market the parts that go into a car need not be

FIGURE 14.3 INTERNATIONALIZATION OF EUROPEAN CARS

Ownership of firms producing cars bought in Europe

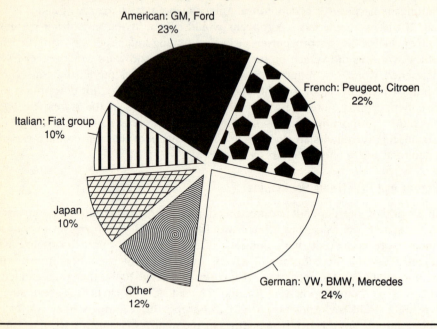

American: GM, Ford
23%

French: Peugeot, Citroen
22%

Italian: Fiat group
10%

Japan
10%

Other
12%

German: VW, BMW, Mercedes
24%

Source: European Automobile Manufacturers Association for Western Europe, 1994.

made in one country. The Ford Motor Company operates factories across Europe: cars that roll off its assembly line near London, Cologne, or Barcelona can have parts from three or four countries and customers in 15 countries.

The more complex the relations in an open Europe, the more important are political resources. Politicians who win national elections must be able to juggle negotiations in Brussels as well as handle personalities and parties that form their governing coalition. Political resources can be created. Political leaders are at the center of intersecting vertical and horizontal networks. In national politics, they are at the top of the political ladder. But they are not alone at the top; lots of horizontal negotiations occur within the cabinet, within the governing party, and with functional interests outside government. In federal countries such as Germany, there are also vertical negotiations with regional and local governments.

In London or Paris, and even more in the capitals of the smaller countries of Europe, there are critical links between national policies and what happens in other countries and in Brussels. External influences present opportunities and impose constraints. A nation's governors must understand the positions and politics of other governments in order to be effective in negotiations with other countries. Incessant talks leave little doubt about what different countries regard as essential and what is bargainable. A study of multilevel diplomacy found that national politicians are now so involved in negotiations with other countries that they are often more likely to misjudge what their own electorates will accept than to misjudge the position of foreign governments (Evans et al., 1993: 400 ff.).

Divisions of national opinion in EU referendums show that agreements that play well around a bargaining table in Maastricht do not always play well in national politics.

The opening of the Berlin Wall in the middle of the night is a dramatic illustration of how quickly changes can sometimes occur in politics. In the multiple games of European politics, success cannot be defined like victory on a battlefield. European leaders have learned the hard way that viewing politics as a zero-sum battle creates more losers than winners. The object is not to win a war but to maintain peace and prosperity.

APPENDIX

Citations in the text refer to a wide variety of books and articles. Refer to these references as well.

An outline of national history. A standard one-volume encyclopedia. For recent political history, see Arthur S. Banks, ed., *Political Handbook of the World* (Binghamton, NY: CSA Publications SUNY, annual).

Locating a country geographically. The significance of distances varies with travel time, which is slight when air journeys are convenient (for example, between national capitals) but can be long if a journey is by rail, road, or water. A standard atlas will identify natural barriers to communication, such as mountains; an airline guide will show which cities are major hubs in air traffic and which are hard to reach.

Parties and elections. For historical developments, see Thomas T. Mackie and Richard Rose, *The International Almanack of Electoral History* (Washington DC: CQ Press, 3rd edition, 1991); for updates, see the final issue of each year's *European Journal of Political Research.*

Economic and social statistics. OECD (Organization for Economic Cooperation and Development) publishes statistics about the economy, employment, and social conditions in many different formats. Its twice a year *Economic Outlook* is a good place to start. For post-Communist countries, the periodic *Transition Reports of the European Bank for Reconstruction and Development* combine analysis and statistics; the April 1995 edition is used for estimates of GDP in the appendix.

Current events. You can read a paper read by Europeans, such as the *Financial Times,* or the weekly *Economist,* which mixes news and opinion. Keesing's *Record of World Events* is up-to-date and well-indexed.

REPUBLIC OF AUSTRIA

Population: 7.8 million. *Area:* 83,853 square miles. It borders Germany, Czech Republic, Slovakia, Hungary, Slovenia, Italy, Switzerland, and Germany. *Capital city:* Vienna, with a population of 1,539,000; second largest city: Graz, 237,000.

National independence: The first Austrian Republic was established in 1918 as a consequence of the break up of the multi-national Habsburg Austro-Hungarian Empire. The country was incorporated in Hitler's Germany in 1938 and became a separate state again in 1945. It was occupied by American, British, French, and Russian troops. Complete independence was not regained until all foreign armies withdrew in 1955.

Constitution: Adopted in 1920. *Head of state:* A ceremonial President, Thomas Klestil, was elected President for a six-year term in 1992. *Head of Government:* the Federal Chancellor (Prime Minister). A federal state divided into nine *Länder;* 77 percent of taxation collected by central government.

Parliament: The National Assembly (*Nationalrat*) has 183 members directly elected for a maximum term of four years; 21 percent are women. The Federal Council (*Bundesrat*) consists of 64 members appointed by the nine Länder.

Ethnic/linguistic composition: Although the great majority of the population is Austrian-born and German-speaking, many families have parents or grandparents born in other parts of the old Austro-Hungarian Empire. The 1991 census classified 7 percent of the resident population as foreigners. *Religion:* Practicing or nominally Catholic or secular.

Member of European Union since 1995. Not a member of NATO.

GDP per capita: $23,495. *GDP per capita PPP adjusted:* $18,096. *Public expenditure in relation to GDP:* 46 percent. *Currency:* schilling. Labor force in services, 57 percent; industry, 36 percent; agriculture, 7 percent.

Competitive nationwide elections first held in 1919; suspended in 1934 when a dictatorship was introduced. Elections held continuously since 1945. Universal male and female suffrage introduced in 1918. *Electoral system:* Proportional representation; a party must win at least one seat in the PR distribution at the *Land* level to benefit from the national distribution of seats. Index of proportionality: 96 percent. Parties winning one percent or more of the vote at the 1995 election:

	% Votes	Seats
Socialists	38.1	71
People's Party	28.3	53
Freedom (Haider) Party	21.9	40
Liberal Forum	5.5	10
Green Alternative	4.8	9
Others	1.4	0

KINGDOM OF BELGIUM

Population: 10.0 million. *Area:* 30,513 square miles. It borders Netherlands, Germany, Luxembourg, France, and the English Channel. *Capital city:* Brussels, with 949,000 people; second largest city: Antwerp, 462,000.

National independence: Belgium was created in 1830 after having previously been under Dutch, French, Spanish, and Austrian rule. Its current eastern boundary with Germany was determined at the end of World War II.

Constitution: The 1831 Constitution established a unitary state, but it has been substantially revised since 1970 to accommodate tensions between Flemish and French speakers, and in 1993 was amended to make Belgium a federal state. *Head of state:* King Albert II. *Head of Government:* Prime Minister. There are three territorial regions—Flanders, Wallonia, and the capital, Brussels.

Parliament: The Chamber of Representatives (*Chambre des Representants* in French; *Kamer des Volksvertegenwoordigers* in Flemish) has 150 members directly elected for a maximum term of four years; 12 percent are women. The upper chamber, the Senate, has 71 members representing territorial and linguistic groups.

Ethnic/linguistic composition: Historically, disagreements about religion between Catholics and anti-clericals were more important than differences of language. Today, language is of greatest political salience. A total of 56 percent of the population is Flemish, speaking a language equivalent to Dutch; 34 percent are French-speaking Walloons, 1 percent German-speakers, and 9 percent resident foreigners. The constitutional reform has also institutionalized Flemish, French, and German communities to deal with education, culture, and linguistic matters.

A founder member of the European Union and of NATO.

GDP per capita: $21,829. *GDP per capita PPP adjusted:* $18,195. *Public expenditure in relation to GDP:* 55 percent. *Currency:* Belgian franc. Labor force in services, 70 percent; industry, 28 percent; agriculture, 3 percent.

Competitive nationwide elections held continuously since 1847. Universal male suffrage introduced in 1893; universal female suffrage in 1948. *Electoral system:* Proportional representation within nine geographical regions. *Index of proportionality:* 92 percent. Parties winning at least one percent of vote at the 1995 election:

	% Votes	Seats
Flemish Christian Democrats	17.2	29
French Christian Democrats	7.7	11
Flemish Socialists	12.6	20
French Socialists	11.9	21
Flemish Liberals	13.1	21
French Liberals	10.3	18
Flemish Block	7.8	11
Flemish Nationalists (Volksunie)	4.7	5
Flemish Greens	4.4	5
French Greens	4.0	7
National Front	2.3	2
Others	4.0	0

REPUBLIC OF BULGARIA

Population: 8.9 million. *Area:* 42,823 square miles. Land borders with Romania, Turkey, Greece, the former Yugoslav republic of Macedonia, and Serbia. Black Sea ports have easy access to ports of the Ukraine. *Capital city:* Sofia, with a population of 1,149,000; the second largest city is Plovdiv, population 397,000.

National independence: The ancient Kingdom of Bulgaria fell under Turkish rule in 1396. It gained autonomy in 1878 and independence in 1908. Bulgaria was on the losing side in both world wars. Its current boundaries date from the end of World War II. The monarchy was abolished and a Communist regime established under the leadership of Georgi Dimitrov. Todor Zhivkov, in power from 1954 until 1989, was staunchly loyal to Moscow and there was little evidence of internal dissent. In November 1989, street demonstrations in Sofia were followed by the legalization of opposition political parties and the formation of a new government.

Constitution: Adopted in 1991. *Head of state:* Zhelyu Zhelev was elected President in 1990 and re-elected in 1992 for a five-year term. *Head of Government:* the Prime Minister. A unitary state. The single-chamber Parliament, the National Assembly (*Narodno Sobranie*) has 240 members directly elected for a maximum term of four years; 13 percent are women.

Ethnic/linguistic composition: The 1992 census recorded Bulgarians as 86 percent of the population, Turks 10 percent, and gypsies 4 percent. The Bulgarian religion is Orthodox, but church attendance is limited. Turks have a Moslem heritage.

Recognized as having associate status in relation to the European Union.

GDP per capita PPP adjusted: $3,730 as estimated by EBRD [European Bank for Reconstruction and Development], 1993. *Inflation rate, 1994:* 122 percent. *Currency:* lev.

Competitive nationwide elections first held in 1990 with universal male and female suffrage. The Socialist Party, a renamed and reorganized party of Communists, won the largest share of the vote and seats. *Electoral System:* Proportional representation, a party must win at least four percent of the vote nationwide to qualify for seats. *Index of proportionality:* 85 percent. Parties winning at least one percent of vote at the 1994 election:

	% Votes	Seats
Socialists	43.5	125
Union of Democratic Forces	24.2	69
People's Union, Agrarians	6.5	18
Movement Rights, Freedom (Turks)	5.4	15
Bulgarian Business Bloc	4.7	13
Democratic Alternative	3.8	0
New Choice Alliance	1.5	0
Bulgarian Communists	1.5	0
Patriotic Union	1.4	0
Kingdom of Bulgarians	1.4	0
Others	6.1	0

CZECH REPUBLIC

Population: 10.3 million. *Area:* 30,450 miles. Land borders with Germany, Poland, Slovakia, and Austria. The present boundaries date from the division of Czechoslovakia in January 1993. It includes Bohemia and Moravia—the territories of the old Czech kings. From 1620 to 1918 the land was ruled by the Habsburg monarchy in Vienna. The capital city, Prague, has a population of 1,220,000; Brno, the chief city in Moravia, is second largest, with a population of 391,000.

National Independence: Czechoslovakia's national independence was proclaimed at the end of World War I. Czech lands had a large German-speaking minority. Between the wars Czechoslovakia had a democratically-elected government. The Munich agreement of 1938 ceded Czech territory to Germany. In March 1939 Hitler's army occupied the country, and Czech lands became incorporated into Germany. At the end of World War II, the Soviet Army occupied Czechoslovakia. Territories lost at Munich were returned to Czechoslovakia; the eastern portion of Slovakia was added to the Soviet Union. By 1948 the Communist takeover was complete. In the 1968 "Prague spring" the government announced reforms reducing the Communist monopoly of power; these were crushed in August 1968 by an invasion led by Soviet troops. In November 1989 street demonstrations in Prague were followed by the abolition of the Communist monopoly of power. A new government was formed in November 1990.

The negotiation of a democratic constitution for the federal Czechoslovak Republic produced demands by Slovak nationalists unacceptable to Czech parties. The result was a "velvet divorce"; on January 1, 1993 the Czech Republic and Slovakia became separate independent states.

Constitution: Adopted in 1993. *Head of state:* The President, Vaclav Havel, a playwright, was elected by Parliament to a five-year term in 1992. *Head of Government:* the Prime Minister. A unitary state. The lower house of the Parliament, the Chamber of Deputies (*Snemovna Poslancu*) has 200 members elected for a maximum term of four years; 10 percent are women.

Ethnic/linguistic composition: The population is 81 percent Czech, 13 percent Moravian, 3 percent Slovak, and the remainder immigrants and gypsies. At the end of World War II, the German minority moved to Germany. The language is Czech and is written in the Roman alphabet. Roman Catholicism is the traditional religion of Czechs, but anti-clerical political groups have always been strong.

Recognized as having associate status in relation to the European Union. Along with Hungary, Poland, and Slovakia, the Czech Republic forms the Visegrad bloc of cooperating countries in Central Europe.

GDP per capita PPP adjusted as estimated by EBRD (European Bank for Reconstruction and Development) 1993: $7,700. *Inflation rate, 1994:* 11 percent. *Currency:* koruna.

Competitive nationwide elections were first held in Czechoslovakia in 1920 with universal suffrage for men and women; elections were suspended by annexation to Germany and unfree under Communist rule. Elections to the Czech

National Assembly are held by proportional representation; a party needs five percent of the vote to qualify for a share of seats. *Index of Proportionality:* 80 percent. Parties winning one percent or more of the vote at the 1992 election are:

	% Votes	Seats
Civic Dem.–Christian Dem. parties	29.7	76
Left bloc	14.5	35
Social Democrats	6.5	16
Liberal Social Union	6.5	16
Chr. Dem. Union–People's	6.3	15
Republicans	6.0	14
Civic Democratic Alliance/Forum	5.9	14
Self-Govt. Moravia & Silesia	5.9	14
Others	18.7	0

KINGDOM OF DENMARK

Population: 5.1 million. *Area:* 16,629 square miles. It borders Germany by land, and has sea links with Sweden, Norway, and Britain. *Capital city:* Copenhagen has 1,346,000 residents in its metropolitan area; the second largest city is Aarhus, with 274,000 people.

National independence: Initial state formation occurred in the tenth century. In 1814 Denmark granted Norway to the Kingdom of Sweden and some territory in Northern Germany to Prussia. Its present boundaries reflect the loss of Schleswig-Holstein in a war with Prussia and Austria in 1864.

Constitution: Denmark became a constitutional monarchy in 1948; the current constitution was adopted in 1953. *Head of state:* Queen Margrethe II. *Head of Government:* Prime Minister. A unitary state.

Parliament: A single chamber, the *Folketing,* elected for a maximum of four years with 175 members, plus two each from the Faroe Islands and Greenland; 33 percent of MPs are women.

Ethnic/linguistic composition: Overwhelmingly Danish, with 95 percent of the population born in Denmark. The population is nominally Lutheran but only a small percentage regularly attend church.

A founder member of NATO and a member of the European Union since 1973.

GDP per capita: $27,551. *GDP per capita PPP adjusted:* $17,813. *Public expenditure in relation to GDP:* 57 percent. *Currency:* krone. Labor force in services, 67 percent; industry, 28 percent; agriculture, 6 percent.

Competitive nationwide elections held continuously since 1901. Universal suffrage for men and women introduced in 1915. *Electoral system:* Proportional representation; minimum of 2 percent of votes normally required to qualify for seats. Index of proportionality, 99 percent. Parties winning at least one percent of vote at the 1994 election:

	% Votes	Seats
Social Democrats	34.6	62
Liberals	23.3	42
Conservatives	15.0	27
Socialist People's	7.3	13
Progress	6.4	11
Radical	4.6	8
Red–Green unity list	3.1	6
Center Democrats	2.8	5
Christian People's	1.8	0
Others	1.0	1

REPUBLIC OF FINLAND

Population: 5.1 million. *Area:* 130,119 square miles. It borders Russia, Sweden, and Norway by land, and Estonia is across a narrow stretch of the Baltic Sea. *Capital city:* Helsinki, with a population of 820,000 in its metropolitan area; the second largest city is Espoo, with 182,000.

National independence: The territory constituting Finland was initially part of the Kingdom of Sweden; in 1809 it became a Grand Duchy under the rule of the Russian Czar. Finns declared independence in 1917 and a peace treaty was signed with the Soviet Union in 1920. The Soviet Union invaded Finland in 1939 and about 12 percent of its territory was ceded to the Soviet Union in 1947.

Constitution: The current constitution was adopted in 1919. *Head of state:* a President with some political responsibilities. Martii Ahtisaari was popularly elected to a six-year term in 1994. *Head of Government:* Prime Minister. A unitary state; central government collects 93 percent of tax revenue. *Parliament:* A single chamber, the *Eduskunta* , elected for a maximum of four years with 200 members; 34 percent are women.

Ethnic/linguistic composition: The population is 92 percent Finnish, 6 percent Swedish, and 2 percent others. The society is nominally Lutheran but only a small percentage regularly attend church.

A member of the European Union since 1995. Under terms of a 1948 Treaty of Friendship with the Soviet Union, Finland has been non-aligned militarily and was subject to Soviet influence,

GDP per capita: $21,058. *GDP per capita PPP adjusted:* $14,545. *Public expenditure in relation to GDP:* 56 percent. *Currency:* markka. Labor force in services, 63 percent; industry, 28 percent; agriculture, 9 percent.

Competitive nationwide elections introduced in 1907, and universal suffrage for both men and women granted at that time. *Electoral system:* Proportional representation. Index of proportionality, 93 percent. Parties winning at least one percent of vote at the 1994 election:

	% Votes	Seats
Social Democrats	28.3	63
Center	19.8	44
National Coalition	17.9	39
Left-Wing Alliance	11.2	22
Swedish People's Party	5.4	12
Greens	6.5	9
Christian League	3.0	7
Progressive Finns	2.8	2
Rural	1.3	1
Alliance for Free Finland	1.0	0
Other	2.3	1

REPUBLIC OF FRANCE

Population: 56.6 million. *Area:* 211,026 square miles. It borders Belgium, Luxembourg, Germany, Switzerland, Italy, Spain, and the English Channel and the Mediterranean. Paris is the capital with 9.4 million people in the metropolitan area. Lyon and Marseille each have more than 1.2 million people in their metropolitan areas.

　National independence: A kingdom since the tenth century. Current boundaries the result of resolution of Franco-German disputes after World War II.

　Constitution: A republic proclaimed in 1792, three years after the French Revolution. The current constitution was adopted in 1958 after a bloodless seizure of power by General Charles de Gaulle. *Head of state:* President with political responsibilities; Jacques Chirac popularly elected to a seven-year term in 1995. The Prime Minister is head of government, responsible to both the President and the Parliament. A unitary state; central government collects 90 percent of total tax revenue.

　Parliament: The National Assembly (*Assemblée Nationale*) is directly elected for a maximum term of five years with 555 members plus 22 from overseas territories; 6 percent are women. The Senate has 321 members chosen by electoral colleges of local governments.

　Ethnic/linguistic composition: France has always had many immigrants; the 1991 census showed 9 percent of the population was not born in France. Portuguese, Algerians, and Moroccans are each about one percent of the French population. The French language has been a major force for assimilation; in Alsace, German also has official recognition, and the Breton language is sometimes used in Brittany. Since the revolution there have been major political divisions between anti-clerical republicans and committed Catholics. Immigration from North Africa has made Islam an issue.

A founder member of the European Union and of NATO. In 1966 President de Gaulle withdrew French forces from NATO and closed its bases in France. France has its own nuclear weapons.

GDP per capita: $23,006. *GDP per capita PPP adjusted:* $18,590. *Public expenditure in relation to GDP:* 48 percent. *Currency:* Franc. Labour force employed in services, 66 percent; industry, 29 percent; agriculture, 5 percent.

Competitive elections introduced in 1849 with adult male suffrage. The rise of Napoleon III disrupted elections. The modern pattern of party competition became visible by the 1910 election. Universal suffrage for women was adopted in 1944.

Electing the President: The two candidates with the largest share of the vote in the first ballot face each other in a second round run-off election held two weeks later. In the 1995 Presidential election the two Gaullist candidates opposed each other in the first round, thus making it an intra-party primary as well as a national ballot. The results were:

Ballots: % vote	1st	2nd
L. Jospin, Socialist	23.3	47.4
Jacques Chirac, Gaullist Rally	20.9	52.6
Edouard Balladur, Gaullist Rally	18.6	—
Jean-Marie LePen, National Front	15.0	—
Robert Hue, Communist	8.6	—
Arlette Laguiller, Workers Struggle	5.3	—
Philippe de Villiers, Anti-European Union	4.7	—
Dominique Voynet, Green	3.3	—
Jacques Cheminade, New Solidarity	0.3	—

Electing the National Assembly: Members are chosen in single-member districts. If no candidate wins more than half the vote in the first round, a second ballot is held; candidates who received at least an eighth of the vote in the first round are eligible to stand and a simple plurality is sufficient to win. The system favors coalitions and loose party alignments. The system makes it difficult for extremists to win seats, whether Communists or anti-immigrant National Front candidates. The Index of Proportionality is 59 percent. The 1993 National Assembly result was:

	% Votes: 1st round	Seats: 2nd round
Gaullist Rally for Republic	20.2	257
Union French Democracy	19.4	215
Socialists	19.2	57
Anti-immigrant National Front	12.7	0
Diverse Greens	10.6	0
Communists	9.1	23
Conservatives	4.3	19
Other left	2.4	6
Others	2.1	0

FEDERAL REPUBLIC OF GERMANY

Population: 80.3 million. *Area:* 137,854 square miles. It borders Poland, the Czech Republic, Austria, Switzerland, France, Luxembourg, Belgium, the Netherlands, Denmark, and the North and Baltic seas. Capital city since 1949, Bonn (population, 297,000). The capital is to move to Berlin (population, 3,454,000), the former capital of an undivided Germany. The second largest city is Hamburg, with 1,675,000 people.

National independence: The German-speaking peoples of Central Europe have never formed a single state; German is today an official language of five European countries. Major steps to create a state occurred in the mid-nineteenth century under the expansionist leadership of the Prussian Crown. After the defeat of the German Empire in World War I, the first German Republic was created under the Weimar constitution. Adolf Hitler replaced this with a Nazi regime in 1933; it collapsed in 1945. Two Germanies were created, the democratic Federal Republic and the German Democratic Republic under Communist control. The two were re-united in 1990 following the opening of the Berlin Wall in 1989.

Constitution: The 1949 Basic Law. *Head of state:* A President chosen by an electoral college consisting of representatives of the upper house of Parliament and the *Länder. Head of Government:* the Federal Chancellor (that is, Prime Minister). A federal state with 16 constituent *Länder* , 11 from the old Republic and 5 new members from the former East Germany. The federal government collects 71 percent of tax revenue.

Parliament: The lower house, the Federal Assembly (*Bundestag*) has 672 directly elected members; 26 percent are women. The upper house, the Federal Council (*Bundesrat*) consists of representatives chosen by the *Länder.*

Ethnic/linguistic composition: In citizenship, homogeneously German, but economic boom attracted millions of foreign "guest workers" and persons claiming German ethnic origin have come from Eastern Europe. There are 6.9 million resident foreigners, including almost 2mn Turks and 1mn Yugoslavs. The population is divided between Protestants, Catholics, and secular groups, with major differences in religious composition between regions of Germany.

A founder member of the European Union and admitted to NATO in 1955 as part of the build-up of defense against Soviet troops on Germany's eastern and southern borders.

GDP per capita: $27,592. *GDP per capita PPP adjusted:* $20,435. *Public expenditure in relation to GDP:* 44 percent. *Currency:* Deutsche Mark. Labor force in services, 59 percent; industry, 38 percent; agriculture, 3 percent.

Competitive nationwide elections first held in 1871, but suspended by Hitler, and unfree uncompetitive elections held in the Germany Democratic Republic during its life. Continuous free elections in the Federal Republic since 1949. Universal suffrage for men and women introduced in 1918.

Electoral system: Half the *Bundestag* members are elected by first-past-the-post in single-member districts; the other half elected by proportional representation, subject to the requirement that a party wins three single-member seats or 5 percent of the vote nationwide. *Index of Proportionality:* 97 percent. Parties winning more than one percent of the vote at the 1994 election:

	% Votes	Seats
Christian Democrats*	41.5	294
Social Democrats	36.4	252
Free Democrats	6.9	47
Greens	7.3	49
Party of Democratic Socialism**	4.4	30
Others	3.5	0

*Includes the Christian Social Union in Bavaria.

**A party of ex-Communists contesting single-member seats only in East Germany.

REPUBLIC OF GREECE

Population: 10.4 million. *Area:* 50,944 square miles. It borders Albania, the former Yugoslav republic of Macedonia, Bulgaria, Turkey, the Aegean sea, and, across the Adriatic sea, Italy. *Capital city:* Athens, with 3,072,000 in its metropolitan area; second largest city, Thessaloniki, 383,000.

National independence: An uprising against the Ottoman Empire in 1821 led to international recognition of independence under a monarchy in 1830. After World War I, Greece received a major influx of Greeks fleeing from the territory of the Republic of Turkey, established after the collapse of the Ottoman Empire. Cyprus, an independent island state with Greek and Turkish inhabitants, remains a point of conflict between the two countries. There are also border disputes with the neighboring former Yugoslav republic of Macedonia.

Constitution: Adopted in 1975 after the collapse of military rule introduced in 1967 and a 1974 referendum voting to replace the monarchy with a republic. *Head of state:* A President chosen by Parliament. *Head of Government:* Prime Minister. A unitary state; central government collects 98 percent of tax revenue. *Parliament:* A single chamber, the *Vouli,* directly elected with 300 members; 6 percent are women.

Ethnic/linguistic composition: Overwhelmingly Greek, with a Turkish minority in its northeastern corner. In religion, Greek Orthodox or secular.

A member of the European Union since 1981 and of NATO since 1952.

GDP per capita: $7,562. *GDP per capita PPP adjusted:* $8,303. *Public expenditure in relation to GDP:* 47 percent. *Currency:* drachma. Labour force in services, 50 percent; industry, 28 percent; agriculture, 22 percent.

While universal male suffrage was introduced in the mid-nineteenth century, there were no national parties and significant intimidation and corruption during elections. Free competitive elections were held in 1926 and thence until a military dictatorship took power in 1936. Elections were re-introduced in 1946, with the Communist Party outlawed because of its role in the Greek civil war. No elections held between 1964 and 1974 because of military rule. Universal female suffrage in 1952.

Electoral system: Proportional representation, with 3 percent of the total vote normally required to qualify for a share of 288 seats. Leading parties name an additional 12 members. *Index of Proportionality:* 90 percent. Parties gaining more than one percent of the vote in 1994:

	% Vote	Seats
Socialists	46.9	170
New Democracy	39.3	111
Political Spring	4.9	10
Coalition of the Left	2.9	0
Communist Party	4.5	9
Others	1.5	0

HUNGARIAN REPUBLIC

Population: 10.4 million. *Area:* 35,919 square miles. Land borders with Slovakia, Ukraine, Romania, Serbia, Croatia, Slovenia, and Austria. The capital city, Budapest, has 1,954,000 inhabitants; the second city is Debrecen with 216,000.

National independence: The Kingdom of Hungary is a thousand years old. It was under Ottoman rule from 1526 until 1686, and then part of the Habsburg empire until 1918. In the 1920 Trianon Treaty, Hungary lost the bulk of its non-Hungarian population and territories, and some Hungarians were incorporated in the neighboring states of Romania, Czechoslovakia, and Yugoslavia. Between the wars it had an authoritarian regime headed by Admiral Miklos Horthy. Hungary sided with Germany in World War II and temporarily expanded its territory. At the end of the war its boundaries reverted to those of 1920. Soviet military occupation was followed by a Communist seizure of power, complete by 1949. In 1956 an anti-Soviet uprising was crushed by Soviet troops. From the early 1960s the Communist regime began to experiment with "market" socialism and reduced repression. In 1989 Communists initiated liberalization prior to the fall of the Berlin Wall.

Constitution: Adopted in 1989. *Head of state:* The President, Arpad Goncz, was elected by Parliament to a four-year term in 1994. *Head of Government:* the Prime Minister. The post has rotated between anti-Communists and ex-Communists. A unitary state. The single chamber National Assembly (*Orzaggyules*) has 386 members, including eight reserved for representatives of ethnic minorities; 11 percent are women. The Assembly is elected by universal male and female suffrage for a four-year term.

Ethnic/linguistic composition: The population is largely Hungarian, but there are ethnic minorities from neighboring countries and gypsies. About three-quarters of the population is nominally Catholic; there is a large Protestant minority and many Hungarians are secular.

Recognized as having associate status in relation to the European Union. One of four Visegrad countries.

GDP per capita PPP adjusted as estimated by EBRD (European Bank for Reconstruction and Development) in 1993: $6,280. *Inflation rate, 1994:* 21 percent. *Currency:* forint.

Hungary has occasionally held free elections since the turn of the century. In November 1945 a free election gave the Communist Party only 17 percent of the

vote, and 22 percent in 1947, before the Communists seized power and eliminated competition. The first free post-Communist election was held in 1990.

Each elector casts two ballots, one for a party list and the other for one candidate for a single-member seat. A total of 176 single-member seats are elected in a
two-round first past the post ballot; 152 seats are filled by regional proportional
representation; and 58 seats at the national level compensating parties that have
failed to win seats at lower levels in proportion to votes. *Index of Proportionality:*
78 percent. Parties winning one percent or more of the vote at the 1994 election:

	% Votes	Seats
Socialists	33.0	209
Alliance of Free Democrats	19.8	70
Hungarian Democratic Forum	11.7	37
Independent Smallholders	8.9	26
Christian Democrats	7.1	22
Alliance of Young Democrats	7.0	20
Hungarian Workers' Party	3.2	0
Republicans	2.5	0
Agrarians	2.1	1
Justice and Life (Csurka party)	1.6	0
Social Democrats	1.0	0
Others	2.1	1

REPUBLIC OF IRELAND

Population: 3.5 million. *Area:* 27,136 square miles. It has a land border with the
Northern Ireland portion of the United Kingdom; the Irish sea is its border with
England and Wales. *Capital city:* Dublin, with a metropolitan population of
915,000; second largest city, Cork, with 174,000.

National independence: Until 1921 the whole of the island of Ireland was
governed as a part of the United Kingdom under the British Crown. An uprising
against the Crown in 1916 led to a Peace Treaty in 1921 that divided the island between six predominantly Protestant counties of Ulster remaining in the United
Kingdom as Northern Ireland and 26 counties forming the Irish Free State. This
was followed by a civil war about partition. The Irish Constitution claims the territory of Northern Ireland as part of the Republic, although it rejects the Irish Republican Army's (IRA) use of physical force to secure unity. Since 1969, as a result
of violence in Northern Ireland between Catholic Republicans and British Protestants, the Republic and the British government have increasingly cooperated. In
1994 this led to a suspension of violence by the IRA and Protestant paramilitaries.

Constitution: In 1937 a new constitution was adopted, making Ireland a Republic; major clauses are subject to amendment by referendum. The country remained neutral in World War II and withdrew from the British Commonwealth in
1949. A unitary state; 96 percent of tax revenue collected centrally. *Head of state:*

A popularly elected President. *Head of Government:* Prime Minister (in Gaelic, *Taoiseach*). *Parliament (Oireachtas):* An elected lower chamber (the *Dail*) with 166 members; 12 percent are women. There is a 60 member Senate chosen by a mixture of means to represent various vocational and corporate interests.

Ethnic/linguistic composition: Overwhelmingly Irish and practicing Catholic. Protestants constitute about 5 percent of the population. Irish is an official language along with English, but it is the first language of only a small percentage of the population.

A member of the European Union since 1973; not a member of NATO.

GDP per capita: $13,729. *GDP per capita PPP adjusted:* $12,391. *Public expenditure in relation to GDP:* 42 percent. *Currency:* Irish pound (punt). Labor force in services, 57 percent; industry, 29 percent; agriculture, 14 percent.

The Irish franchise law was the same as Britain's prior to independence. Universal male suffrage was introduced in 1918, and women were granted the right to vote in 1928. Free competitive elections have been held as long as in Britain, and since the foundation of the independent state. *Electoral system:* Single transferable vote (STV) proportional representation. *Index of Proportionality:* 94 percent. Parties gaining more than one percent of the vote in the 1992 election:

	% Vote	Seats
Fianna Fail	39.1	68
Fine Gael	24.5	45
Irish Labour	19.3	33
Progressive Democrats	4.7	10
Democratic Left	2.8	4
Sinn Fein	1.6	0
Greens	1.4	1
Others	6.6	5

REPUBLIC OF ITALY

Population: 56.1 million. *Area:* 116,303 square miles. It has land borders with Switzerland, Austria, Slovenia, France, and Switzerland, and Montenegro, Albania, and Greece are across the Adriatic sea. Capital city: Rome, population 2,723,000; second largest city, Milan, population 1,358,000.

National independence: The nation-state of Italy was created as a state in 1861 from a mixture of principalities, foreign domains, and papal territories. It was a Kingdom under the House of Savoy. Benito Mussolini created a Fascist dictatorship in 1922, and was deposed in 1943. The Republic was created in 1946 after a referendum rejected the monarchy. The current state boundaries were created after World War II.

Constitution: The current constitution was adopted in 1948. Since 1992 scandals involving corruption and the mafia have led to the indictment of many leading politicians, including ex-Prime Ministers. A decentralized unitary state subdivided into fifteen regions and five special autonomous regions, provinces and municipalities. Central government collects 97 percent of tax revenue. *Head of State:* A President chosen by Parliament for a seven-year term, since 1992 Oscar Scalfaro. *Head of Government:* known as the President of the Council of Ministers or Prime Minister. *Parliament:* A directly elected Chamber of Deputies (*Camera dei Deputati*) with 630 members; 15 percent are women. The Senate has 315 members chosen by a mixture of means, including direct election.

Ethnic/linguistic composition: Overwhelmingly Italian, with special rights for a small German-speaking population in the area bordering Austria. In religion the population divides between practicing Catholics and anti-clericals.

A member of the European Union and of NATO since their foundation.

GDP per capita: $21,122. *GDP per capita PPP adjusted:* $17,482. *Public expenditure in relation to GDP:* 51 percent. *Currency:* Lira. Labour force in services, 60 percent; industry, 32 percent; agriculture, 8 percent.

Competitive elections contested between nationwide groups were achieved by 1895. Universal male suffrage was introduced in 1919, but free elections were suspended under fascism. Universal female suffrage was introduced before the return of free competitive elections in 1946. For most of the postwar period elections have been solely by proportional representation.

Following a 1991 referendum, a new election law was introduced providing for the election of three-quarters of MPs by simple plurality vote in single-member districts, and one-quarter by proportional representation, with a threshold requiring 4 percent of the vote. In 1994 the Index of Proportionality was 85 percent overall and 78 percent for the single-member seats elected by first past the post. Corruption scandals, the break up of the Catholic-led Christian Democratic Party and of the Communist Party, and the new electoral system have effectively created a new party system in Italy. Parties and alliances of parties gaining more than one percent of the vote in the 1994 election:

	% Vote	Seats
Freedom Alliance	(42.9)	(366)
Forza Italia/Go Italy	21.0	
National Alliance	13.5	
Northern League	8.4	
Pact for Italy (ex-Christian Democrats)	(15.7)	(46)
Popular Party	11.1	
Segni group	4.6	
Progressive Alliance	(34.4)	(213)
Democratic Left	20.4	
Communists	6.0	
Greens	2.7	
Socialists	2.2	
Anti-Mafia/La Rete	1.9	
Democratic Alliance	1.2	
Others	(7.0)	(5)

GRAND DUCHY OF LUXEMBOURG

Population: 384,000. *Area:* 998 square miles. Land boundaries with Belgium, the Netherlands, Germany, and France. *Capital city:* Luxembourg, with 75,800 inhabitants; the second largest city is Esch-Alzette, with 24,000. The small state is divided into four regions.

National independence: The Grand Duchy was formed in 1815 under the King of the Netherlands; independence dates from 1890, when a different King was installed. Current boundaries date from the cession of a French-speaking territory to Belgium in 1839.

Constitution: Adopted in 1868, and subsequently much amended. *Head of state:* Grand Duke Jean. *Head of Government:* Prime Minister. A unitary state; central government collects 88 percent of revenue. *Parliament:* A single chamber, the Chamber of Deputies, with 60 members elected for a maximum term of five years; 20 percent of MPs are women

Ethnic/linguistic composition: The official languages are French and German; most of the citizenry speaks French, German, and Letzebuergesch, a dialect of Germanic origin. As the home of a variety of intergovernmental European Union institutions, 31 percent of the country's residents are foreign.

A founder member of NATO and of the European Union.

GDP per capita: $27,073. *GDP per capita PPP adjusted:* $21,929. *Public expenditure in relation to GDP:* 45 pecent. *Currency:* Luxembourg franc; the Belgian franc is also legal tender. Labor force in services, 66 percent; industry, 31 percent; agriculture, 3 percent.

Competitive elections were introduced in 1868, and universal suffrage for men and women introduced in 1918. *Electoral system:* a modified form of proportional representation in which each elector has as many votes as there are seats in the region in which he or she lives. *Index of proportionality:* 92 percent. Parties winning one percent of vote at the 1994 election:

	% Votes	Seats
Christian Social	30.3	21
Socialist	25.4	17
Democrats	19.3	12
Greens	9.9	5
Action for Democracy, Pensioners	9.0	5
Anti-immigrant Party	2.6	0
Others	3.4	0

KINGDOM OF NETHERLANDS

Population: 13.1 million. *Area:* 13,103 square miles. It borders Germany and Belgium by land, and is across the North Sea from Britain. The capital, the Hague, has

695,000 inhabitants; it is the third largest metropolitan area after Amsterdam, population 1.1 million, and Rotterdam, with 1,074,000.

National independence: The Netherlands achieved independence from foreign kings in the seventeenth century. Its current boundaries were defined after the creation of Belgium.

Constitution: Adopted in 1814, and amended subsequently. *Head of state:* Queen Beatrix. *Head of Government:* Prime Minister. A unitary state; central government collects 96 percent of tax revenue. *Parliament* (the *Staten Generaal*) consists of a lower house (the *Tweede Kamer*) of 150 members popularly elected for a four-year term, and an upper house (*Eerste Kamer*) of 75 members selected by provincial councils; 31 percent of MPs are women.

Ethnic/linguistic composition: The official language is Dutch and the population overwhelmingly Dutch. Society is divided along religious lines between Protestants, Catholics, and secular groups, each actively linked to political and social institutions.

A founder member of NATO and of the European Union.

GDP per capita: $21,102. *GDP per capita PPP adjusted:* $17,023. *Public expenditure in relation to GDP:* 55 percent. *Currency:* Guilder. Labor force in services, 71 percent; industry, 25 percent; agriculture, 4 percent.

Competitive nationwide elections have been held continuously since 1888. Universal suffrage for men was introduced in 1917 and for women in 1919. The electoral system is a pure form of proportional representation in which each party nominates a list of candidates to compete for a share of the vote nationally; only two-thirds of one percent of the vote is required to win a seat in Parliament. *Index of proportionality:* 97 percent. Parties winning one percent of vote at the 1994 election:

	% Votes	Seats
Christian Democratic Appeal	22.2	34
Labour Party	24.0	37
Liberal Party	20.0	31
Democrats '66	15.5	24
General Union of Elderly	3.6	6
Green Left	3.5	5
Anti-immigrant Centre Democrats	2.5	3
Reformed Church Political Fed'n	1.8	3
Reformed Church Party	1.7	2
Reformed Church Political Union	1.3	2
Socialists	1.3	2
Radical 55+ Pensioners' Union	0.9	1
Others	1.6	0

KINGDOM OF NORWAY

Population: 4.3 million. *Area:* 149,282 square miles. It borders Sweden and Finland by land, and Denmark and Britain are accessible by sea. Oslo is the capital, with 459,000 inhabitants. The second largest city is Bergen, population 213,000.

National independence: Norway was a territory under the Swedish crown until 1905, when it became an independent state with its current boundaries.

Constitution: Adopted in 1814. *Head of state:* King Harald V. *Head of Government:* Prime Minister. A unitary state; central government collects 80 percent of tax revenue. Parliament (*Storting*) is a popularly elected chamber of 165 members elected for a four-year term. The members then divide into two separate houses, a lower house (*Odelsting*) with three-quarters of the members, and an upper house (*Lagting*) with one-quarter. Of the total, 39 percent are women.

Ethnic/linguistic composition: An ethnically homogeneous country. The nominal religion of the country is Lutheran but church attendance is very low.

A founder member of NATO. Membership in the European Union has twice been rejected by national referendums.

GDP per capita: $26,343. *GDP per capita PPP adjusted:* $17,756. *Public expenditure in relation to GDP:* 53 percent. *Currency:* krone. Labor force in services, 71 percent; industry, 23 percent; agriculture, 6 percent.

Competitive nationwide elections have been held continuously since 1888. Universal suffrage for men was introduced in 1917 and for women in 1919. The electoral system is a pure form of proportional representation in which each party nominates a list of candidates to compete for a share of the vote nationally; only two-thirds of one percent of the vote is required to win a seat in Parliament. *Index of proportionality:* 94 percent. Parties winning one percent of vote at the 1993 election:

	Votes	**Seats**
Labour	36.9	67
Conservatives	17.0	28
Centre	16.7	32
Christian People's	7.9	13
Left Socialist	7.9	13
Progress	6.3	10
Liberals	3.6	1
Communist Workers	1.1	1
Pensioners	1.1	0
Others	1.5	0

POLISH REPUBLIC

Population: 37.8 million. *Area:* 120,725 square miles. It has land borders with Belarus, Ukraine, Slovakia, the Czech Republic, Germany, the Kaliningrad extension of the Russian Federation, and Lithuania. It also has ports that face toward Sweden. The current boundaries were defined after World War II, when the Soviet Union annexed territories to the east and awarded Poland territories formerly part of Eastern Germany and Prussia. The capital city, Warsaw, has a population of 2,416,000; the second largest city is Lodz, population 852,000.

National independence: Although Poland existed as a kingdom by the eleventh century, its territories have usually been under foreign rule and were often partitioned among neighboring Kingdoms of the Russian Czar, the Habsburgs, and Prussia. It became an independent republic in 1918. In 1926 a dictatorship was introduced under the control of Marshal Jozef Pilsudski. Following the Nazi-Soviet Pact of August 1939, Poland was invaded by Germany and the Soviet Union. Soviet occupation at the end of the war supported a Communist regime under the control of Moscow. Strikes and protests intermittently gave public demonstration to resentment of that regime. In 1980 a nationwide union was organized, Solidarity, headed by Lech Walesa. Martial law was declared in 1981. The Communist regime agreed to reform measures in 1989 and in January 1990 the Communist Party formally disbanded.

Constitution: A 1952 document has been greatly amended, especially by the 1992 "little" Constitution. *Head of state:* A President, popularly elected by a majority in a two-ballot vote. Lech Walesa was elected in 1990 for a five-year term and re-elected in 1995. *Head of Government:* the Prime Minister. The post has rotated between anti-Communists and ex-Communists. A unitary state. The lower house of the Parliament, the *Sejm,* has 460 members elected by universal male and female suffrage for four years; 13 percent are women. The upper house, the Senate, has 100 members chosen by simple majority vote in each province.

Ethnic/linguistic composition: World War II and the Holocaust have resulted in the Polish population being ethnically extremely homogeneous. The population is Catholic, and there is a high level of church attendance.

Recognized as having associate status in relation to the European Union. One of four Visegrad countries.

GDP per capita PPP adjusted as estimated by EBRD (European Bank for Reconstruction and Development) in 1993: $5,010. *Inflation rate, 1994:* 30 percent. *Currency:* zloty.

Poland briefly had elections after World War I, and in 1989 held a parliamentary election in which a majority of seats in the *Sejm* were reserved for the Communist Party; Solidarity won every seat freely contested. The first free post-Communist elections were held in 1990. Members of the *Sejm* are elected by a combination of regional and national list proportional representation. Except for ethnic minority parties, 5 percent of the national vote is required to qualify for proportional representation seats, and an electoral coalition requires 7 percent of the vote. *Index of Proportionality:* 66 percent. Parties winning one percent or more of the vote at the 1993 election are:

	% Votes	Seats
Democratic Left	20.4	171
Polish Peasant Party	15.4	132
Democratic Union	10.6	74
Union of Labour (coalition)	7.3	41
Catholic Fatherland coalition	6.4	0
Independent Poland: KPN	5.8	22
Nonparty Bloc for Reforms: BBWR	5.4	16
Solidarity	4.9	0
Centre Alliance	4.4	0
Liberal Democrats	4.0	0
Real Politics Union	3.2	0
Self-Defense	2.8	0
Party X	2.8	0
Coalition for the Republic	2.8	0
Agrarian Alliance	2.4	0
German minority	0.7	4
Others	0.7	0

The President is popularly elected by a two-ballot system. If no candidate secures more than half the votes cast on the first ballot, the top two candidates face each other in the second election. In the 1995 Presidential election the results were:

Ballots: % vote	1st	2nd
Alexander Kwasniewski, Democratic Left (ex-Communist)	35.1	51.7
Lech Walesa, ex-Solidarity leader	33.1	48.3
Jacek Kuron, ex-dissident	9.2	—
Jan Olszewski, ex-Prime Minister	6.9	—
Waldemar Pawlak, Peasant Party	4.3	—
Tadeusz Zielinski	3.5	—
Hanna Gronkiewicz-Waltz, Conservative	2.8	—
Six others	5.1	—

REPUBLIC OF PORTUGAL

Population: 9.8 million. *Area:* 35,553 square miles. It borders Spain by land and its position on the Atlantic in the southwest corner of Europe makes it relatively close to Brazil. The capital, Lisbon, has a population of 2,048,000; the second city, Oporto, has a population of 358,000.

National independence: Portugal has been an independent state almost continuously since the twelfth century; mountains and ocean have given it a well-defined boundary. For most of this period it was a monarchy. A republic was proclaimed in 1910; it was overthrown by a military coup in 1926. In 1933 the head of government, Antonio Salazar, introduced a fascist type of constitutional dictatorship. This regime was overthrown in 1974, leading to the introduction of a freely elected government.

Constitution: Adopted in 1976. *Head of state:* A President, popularly elected for a five-year term, with significant executive authority. On 14 January 1996 Jorge Sampaio, a Socialist, was elected President for a five-year term with 54 percent of the vote in a straight fight with former Social Democratic Prime Minister Cavalco Silva. Mario Soares was elected in 1986 and re-elected in 1991. *Head of Government:* Prime Minister. A unitary state; central government collects 95 percent of tax revenue. A single-chamber Parliament (*Assembleia da Republica*) with 230 members is popularly elected for a four-year term. Nine percent of MPs are women.

Ethnic/linguistic composition: Portugal is ethnically homogeneous and Portuguese the only language in use. The nominal religion is Catholicism, but church attendance is limited.

Portugal was a founder member of NATO and joined the European Union in 1986.

GDP per capita: $8,551. *GDP per capita PPP adjusted:* $9,786. *Public expenditure in relation to GDP:* 39 percent. *Currency:* escudo. Labor force in services, 55 percent; industry, 33 percent; agriculture, 12 percent.

Prior to the collapse of the Salazar regime, there was no tradition of free competitive elections. The first free elections for Parliament afterwards were held in 1975, with all men entitled to vote; universal suffrage for women was introduced in 1976. The electoral system for Parliament is proportional representation; the President must have an absolute majority of votes cast, and this is assured through a run-off second ballot with only the two leading contenders on the first round. *Index of Proportionality:* 92 percent. Parties winning one percent of vote at the 1995 election:

	% Votes	Seats
Socialists	44.5	112
Social Democrats	34.7	88
Center Social Democrats	9.2	15
Communist-led Democratic Union	8.7	15
Others	2.9	0

ROMANIA

Population: 22.7 million. *Area:* 91,699 square miles. It has land borders with Ukraine, Moldova, Bulgaria, Serbia, and Hungary. It also has ports on the Black Sea. Although the Romanian people have occupied their territories since Roman times, many different ethnic groups have also lived there, and lands were contested between the Ottoman Empire, Russia, and other authorities. After World War I, Romania annexed Bessarabia from Russia, Bukovina from Austria, and Transylvania and the Banat from Hungary. In World War II it lost territories back to the Soviet Union and Bulgaria. The capital is Bucharest, with a population of 2,350,000. The second largest city is the seaport of Constanta, population 381,000.

National independence: In 1881 Romania was proclaimed an independent kingdom. It was governed by a series of more or less authoritarian leaders, sometimes with the facade of elections. Romania sided with Nazi Germany against the Soviet Union. Soviet occupation at the end of the war was followed by the creation of a Communist regime. In 1947 the King was forced to abdicate and a Republic proclaimed. In 1965 Nicolae Ceausescu became Communist leader; internally, he established an extremely repressive regime while externally cultivating friendly relations with Western nations. In December 1989 a bloody confrontation between police and crowds of ethnic Hungarians in Timisoara was followed by disturbances elsewhere and the army turned against Ceausescu, who was tried along with his wife on charges of genocide and embezzlement and summarily executed. A new regime was introduced under the National Salvation Front.

Constitution: A new constitution was written and approved by referendum in 1991. *Head of state:* A President with extensive powers is popularly elected by a majority in a two-ballot vote. In 1992 Ion Iliescu was elected for a four-year term. *Head of Government:* the Prime Minister. A unitary state. The lower house of the Parliament, the Chamber of Deputies (*Camera Deputatilor*) has 341 members elected for a four-year term, including thirteen seats allocated to non-Hungarian ethnic minorities; 4 percent of members are women. The upper house, the Senate, has 143 elected members.

Ethnic/linguistic composition: Romanians are the dominant ethnic group, about 88 percent of the population; Romanian is the national language. Hungarians, principally in Transylvania, are about 8 percent of the population. The remainder is divided among Gypsies and other ethnic groups, including Germans. The Romanian Orthodox Church is by far the largest church.

Recognized as having associate status in relation to the European Union.

GDP per capita PPP adjusted as estimated by EBRD (European Bank for Reconstruction and Development) in 1993: $2,910. Inflation rate, 1994: 62 percent. Currency: leu.

The first post-Communist elections were held in May 1990. In the Presidential vote, Ion Iliescu, a Communist who had broken with Ceauşescu and led the uprising against him, was elected President with 85 percent of the vote. The National Salvation Front won nine times as many votes and seats as the second party. In autumn 1992, a second round of elections was held. The Presidential election was held on a non-party basis. The results were:

Ballots: % vote	1st	2nd
Ion Iliescu	47.3	61.4
Emil Constantinescu	31.2	38.6
Gheorghe Funar	10.9	—
Caius Dragomir	4.8	—
Ioan Manzalu	3.1	—
Mircea Druc	2.7	—

The Chamber of Deputies is elected by proportional representation, with a 3 percent threshold necessary to qualify for seat distribution. *Index of Proportionality:* 81 percent. Parties winning more than one percent of the vote in 1992 were:

	% Votes	Seats
Democratic National Salvation Front*	27.7	117
Democratic Convention of Romania	20.0	82
National Salvation Front: Democrats	10.2	43
Romanian National Unity	7.7	30
Hungarian Democratic Union of Romania	7.5	27
Greater Romania Party	3.9	16
Socialist Labour	3.0	13
Agrarian Democrats	2.9	0
Non-Hungarian minorities	0.9	13
Others	16.1	0

*In 1993 became the principal part of a merged Party of Social Democracy in Romania.

SLOVAK REPUBLIC

Population: 5.3 million. *Area:* 18,933 miles. Land borders with Czech Republic, Poland, Ukraine, Hungary, and Austria. The present boundaries date from the division of Czechoslovakia in January 1993. The capital city, Bratislava, has a population of 440,000; Kosice is the second largest city with a population of 238,000.

National independence: The territory has long been populated by people of Slovak nationality; from the tenth century to 1918 it was usually under the rule of Hungary. The national independence of Czechoslovakia was proclaimed at the end of World War I (see also, Czech Republic). Between World War I and II, Slovaks were a minority in Czechoslovakia, and some parties demanded autonomy from Prague. The Munich agreement of 1938 ceded Slovak territory to Poland and Hungary. Following the German occupation of Czechoslovakia in March 1939, Slovakia became a nominally independent state with a priest, Father Josef Tiso, as dictator; it sided with Germany in World War II. At the end of the war, Slovakia once more became part of Czechoslovakia under Communist domination. In 1969 the state became federal, thus laying the institutional foundations for separate governments in Slovakia and the Czech Republic. In autumn 1989, protests against Communist rule took on a nationalist as well as an anti-Communist tinge in Slovakia.

The negotiation of a new democratic constitution for the federal Czechoslovak Republic produced demands by Slovak nationalists unacceptable to Czech parties. The result was a "velvet divorce"; on January 1, 1993, the Czech Republic and Slovakia became separate independent states.

Constitution: Adopted in 1993. *Head of state:* The President, Mihal Kovac, elected by Parliament for a five-year term. *Head of Government:* the Prime Minister. The post has intermittently been held by Vladimir Meciar, a former Communist accused of using strong-arm methods but who has left office after losing a vote of confidence in Parliament. A unitary state. The single chamber National Council (*Narodna Rada Slovensky Repubiky*) has 150 members elected by universal male and female suffrage for a four-year term; 15 percent are women.

Ethnic/linguistic composition: The population is .86 percent Slovak, 11 percent Hungarian, and the remainder is divided among Ruthenes, Ukrainians and Gypsies. The language is Slovak. Slovakia is Catholic in practice as well as in nominal allegiance.

Recognized as having associate status in relation to the European Union. One of four Visegrad countries.

GDP per capita PPP adjusted as estimated by EBRD (European Bank for Reconstruction and Development) in 1993: $6,450. Inflation rate, 1994: 12 percent. *Currency:* koruna.

Competitive nationwide elections were first held in Czechoslovakia in 1920 with universal suffrage for men and women; elections were suspended by annexation to Germany in 1939, and unfree under Communist rule. Elections to the Slovak National Assembly are held by proportional representation for a four-year term. A party needs 5 percent of the vote to qualify for seats. Index of Proportionality: 87 percent. Parties winning one percent or more of the vote at the 1994 election are:

	% Votes	Seats
Movement for a Democratic Slovakia	35.0	61
Common Choice	10.4	18
Hungarian coalition	10.2	17
Christian Democrats	10.1	17
Democratic Union of Slovakia	8.6	15
Slovak Workers	7.3	13
Slovak National Party	5.4	9
Democratic Party	3.4	0
Communist Party of Slovakia	2.7	0
Christian Social Union	2.1	0
New Slovakia	1.3	0
Party against Corruption	1.3	0
Movement Prosperous Czechoslovakia	1.1	0
Others	1.1	0

KINGDOM OF SPAIN

Population: 39.0 million. *Area:* 194,896 square miles. Land boundaries with France and Portugal, and coastal boundaries on the Mediterranean Sea and the Atlantic Ocean. Madrid is the capital with a population of 2,909,000; the second largest city is Barcelona, with 1,625,000.

National independence: Spain was united as a Kingdom in 1492, expanded into a global empire and then became relatively impoverished. Spain was briefly a Republic in 1873–74 and again in 1931. A bloody civil war commenced in 1936 between the republican and left-wing forces and conservative and fascist forces led by General Francisco Franco. Franco won, and ruled without elections until his death in 1975.

Constitution: A democratic constitution was approved by popular referendum in 1978. *Head of state:* King Juan Carlos I, who took the oath of office following the death of General Franco, and played an important mediating role in the transition to democracy. *Head of Government:* Prime Minister. Under pressure from ethnic and separatist groups in the Basque country, Catalonia and Andalusia, the unitary state has devolved substantial powers to autonomous regions. Central government collects 87 percent of tax revenue. The Parliament (*Las Cortes Generales*) has a lower chamber (*Congreso de los Diputados*) of 350 members elected for a four-year term; 16 percent are women. The Senate has 256 members, four-fifths directly elected from provinces and the remainder nominated by legislatures.

Ethnic/linguistic composition: The Constitution designates Castilian Spanish as the official language of the state, while also recognizing "all other Spanish languages" as official within regions where different versions of this Romance language are spoken. Catalan is spoken by two-thirds in the region of Catalonia; Galician, a language similar to Portuguese, is spoken by nine-tenths in that region; and the ancient Basque language, which is not a Romance language, is spoken by one-quarter of the population in that region. Language is used to support claims for distinctive political institutions, and in the Basque country an armed group, ETA, uses violence in pursuit of independence. The country is Catholic but divides between practicing Catholics and anti-clericals.

Spain was admitted to NATO in 1982 and joined the European Union in 1986.

GDP per capita: $14,708. *GDP per capita PPP adjusted:* $12,853. *Public expenditure as share of GDP:* 39 percent *Currency:* Peseta. Labor force in services, 58 percent; industry, 32 percent; agriculture, 10 percent.

Although Spain had intermittently held elections prior to the Second Republic, the first nationwide competitive election occurred in 1931 with universal suffrage for both men and women. Free parliamentary elections resumed in 1977. The electoral system for Parliament is proportional representation. *Index of proportionality:* 88 percent. Parties winning one percent of vote at the 1993 election:

	% Votes	Seats
Socialists	38.8	159
Popular Party	34.8	141
Communists and United Left	9.6	18
Convergence and Unity	4.9	17
Democratic and Social Centre	1.8	0
Greens	1.1	0
Basque Nationalists	1.2	5
Basque Extremists	0.9	2
Basque Solidarity	0.5	1
Canary Islands group	0.9	4
Catalan Republican Left	0.8	1
Aragonese Regionalists	0.6	1
Valencian Union	0.5	1
Others	3.6	0

KINGDOM OF SWEDEN

Population: 8.6 million. *Area:* 173,000 square miles. It borders Finland and Norway by land and its long coastline gives it proximity by water to the Baltic states, Germany and Denmark. The capital city of Stockholm is also the largest city, with 1,057,000 people. Second in population is Gothenburg, 466,000.

National independence: Since the tenth century. Its current borders were established in 1905, when union with Norway ended.

Constitution: In 1975, replacing the 1809 version. *Head of state:* King Carl XVI Gustaf. *Head of Government:* Prime Minister. *Parliament:* A single chamber, the *Riksdag;* 349 members, of which 40 percent are women. Three-year fixed term. Unitary state; 69 percent of taxation collected centrally.

Ethnic/linguistic composition: 94 percent Swedish; 6 percent resident aliens, of which the largest group are Finns. Most Swedes are nominally Lutheran but not regular church attenders.

Member of European Union since 1995. Not a member of NATO.

GDP per capita: $28,489. *GDP per capita PPP adjusted:* $16,590 *Public expenditure as share of GDP:* 60 percent. *Currency:* krona. Labor force in services, 70 percent; industry, 27 percent; agriculture, 3 percent.

Competitive nationwide elections continuously since 1887. Universal male suffrage since 1907; female suffrage, since 1919. Proportional representation electoral system; minimum of 4 percent of vote for allocation of seats. *Index of proportionality:* 98 percent. Parties winning at least one percent of vote at 1994 election:

	% Votes	Seats
Social Democrats	45.3	161
Moderates	22.4	80
Centre Party, agrarian	7.7	27
Liberal People's Party	7.2	26
Left Party	6.2	22
Greens	5.0	18
Christian Democrats	4.1	15
New Democracy	1.2	0
Others	0.9	0

CONFEDERATION OF SWITZERLAND

Population: 6.9 million. *Area:* 15,943 square miles. It borders Germany, Austria, Italy, and France. The capital city is Berne, with a metropolitan population of 299,000. The largest city is Zurich, population of 941,000 followed by Geneva with 394,000 and Basel with 360,000.

National independence: Territories now part of Switzerland began to join together in a mutual defense league in 1291. At the end of the Napoleonic Wars the neutrality of territories within the current state was recognized by their principal powerful neighbors. In 1848 a federal government was established.

Constitution: 1874. *Head of state and of government:* The office rotates annually between members of the Federal Council, which constitutes the Cabinet of Switzerland. A distinctive feature of the Council is that it is a long-standing coalition of leaders of the four largest parties in Parliament.

Parliament: The lower house, the National Council, consists of 200 members elected for a four-year term; 18 percent of members are women. The Council of State has 46 members, two selected by each canton. A federal state divided into 23 cantons, each of which has substantial powers; the federal government collects 63 percent of tax revenue.

Ethnic/linguistic composition: Switzerland has four official languages, 64 percent give German as their first language, 19 percent French, 8 percent Italian, and one percent Romansch, with 9 percent having other languages as their original tongue. Of the total population, 15 percent are resident foreigners. Religious differences cut across linguistic lines, dividing Catholics and Protestants, and believers and secular and anti-clerical groups.

Switzerland is a nation that has maintained neutrality among its warring neighbors. It is not a member of the United Nations, although some UN offices are in the country. In 1992 a national referendum rejected measures bringing the country into association with the European Union.

GDP per capita: $34,962. *GDP per capita PPP adjusted:* $22,268. *Public expenditure as share of GDP:* 35 percent. *Currency:* Swiss franc. Labor force in services, 60 percent; industry, 34 percent; agriculture, 6 percent.

Since 1848 all Swiss males have had the right to vote; the secret ballot was introduced in 1872. Women gained the right to vote in 1971. Competitive elections have been held on a nationwide basis since 1896. The electoral system in use is proportional representation at the cantonal level. *Index of Proportionality:* 91 percent. Parties winning one percent of vote at the 1995 election:

	% Votes	Seats
Social Democrats	21.8	54
Radical Democrats	20.2	45
Christian Democrats	17.0	34
Swiss People's	14.9	29
Greens	5.0	9
Liberals	2.7	7
Motorists' Party	4.0	7
League of Independents	1.8	3
Anti-Immigrant Swiss Democrats	3.1	3
Evangelical Party	1.8	2
Workers' Party	1.2	3
Ticino League	1.1	1
Other	5.4	3

UNITED KINGDOM

Population: 57.6 million. *Area:* 94,249 square miles. Its only land boundary is with the Republic of Ireland. The English Channel, by sea and by tunnel, provides a link with France and Belgium; historically, sea lanes were used to form an intercontinental empire. The capital, London, has a population of 6.7 million in its metropolitan area. Glasgow is the largest city in Scotland, Cardiff the largest city in Wales and Belfast the largest city in Northern Ireland.

National independence: The United Kingdom was formed in stages by the expansion of the territory of the English Crown. The conquest of Ireland began in the twelfth century, Wales was joined in the late fifteenth century, and Scotland between 1603 and 1707. All four territories became part of a single United Kingdom Parliament in 1801. The bulk of Ireland seceded in 1921. The current boundaries of the United Kingdom of Great Britain and Northern Ireland, consisting of one and one-sixth islands, date from 1921.

Constitution: There is no single written constitutional document setting out binding rules for the institutions of governance. The oldest, Magna Carta (the Great Charter), dates from 1215. As long as it has the support of a majority in Parliament, the government of the day can depart from customs and conventions. *Head of state:* Queen Elizabeth II. *Head of Government:* Prime Minister. *Parliament:* The House of Commons consists of 651 MPs elected for a maximum term of five years; 9 percent are women. The House of Lords consists of hereditary peers plus lords given a peerage for life, and a small number of *ex officio* bishops and judges. The United Kingdom it a unitary state; 95 percent of tax revenue is collected centrally. There are some distinctive administrative arrangements for public policy in Scotland, Wales, and Northern Ireland.

Ethnic/linguistic composition: The population of England is five-sixths of the United Kingdom; Scotland has 5.0 million, Wales 2.8 million, and Northern Ireland 1.6 million. A minority in Wales speak the Welsh language as well as English, and a small fraction of Scots speak Gaelic. In Northern Ireland divisions between a majority of Protestants and a Catholic minority are politically fundamental. Immigration from Commonwealth countries makes the United Kingdom, and particularly England, a multi-racial society, with approximately 840,000 Indians, 500,000 Caribbeans, 640,000 from Pakistan or Bangladesh, and 390,000 Africans and other blacks.

The United Kingdom was a founder member of NATO and joined the European Union in 1973.

GDP per capita: $18,027. *GDP per capita PPP adjusted:* $16,340. *Public expenditure as share of GDP:* 40 percent. *Currency:* Pound. Labor force in services, 71 percent; industry, 27 percent; agriculture, 2 percent.

Elections have been held in England since medieval times, but the modern form of nationwide elections between competing parties did not develop until 1885. Universal male suffrage was introduced in 1918; women were granted the right to vote on the same basis as men in 1928. MPs are elected by the simple plurality first-past-the-post system. *Index of Proportionality:* 83 percent. Parties winning one percent or more of vote at the 1992 election:

	% Votes	Seats
Conservatives	41.9	336
Labour	34.4	271
Liberal Democrats	17.8	20
Ulster Unionists & Loyalists	1.2	13
Irish Nationalists	0.8	4
Scottish Nationalists	1.9	3
Plaid Cymru (Welsh Nationalists)	0.5	4
Other	1.5	0

BIBLIOGRAPHY

Aberbach, Joel D., Putnam, Robert D., and Rockman, Bert A. 1981. *Bureaucrats and Politicians in Western Democracies.* Cambridge: Harvard University Press.

Abramson, Paul, and Inglehart, Ronald. 1992. "Generational Replacement and Value Change in Eight West European Societies." *British Journal of Political Science* 22, no. 2: 183-228.

Adam, Jan. 1991. "Social Contract." In J. Adam, ed., *Economic Reform and Welfare Services in the USSR, Poland and Hungary,* 1-25. Basingstoke, England: Macmillan.

Adonis, Andrew, and Tyrie, Andrew. 1993. *Subsidiarity: No Panacea.* London: European Policy Forum.

Agh, Attila. 1993. "Europeanization through Privatization and Pluralization in Hungary," *Journal of Public Policy,* 13, no. 1: 1-35.

Agh, Attila, ed. 1994. *The Emergence of East Central European Parliaments.* Budapest: Hungarian Centre of Democracy Studies.

Alba, Carlos R. 1980. "The Organization of Authoritarian Leadership: Franco Spain." In R. Rose and E. Suleiman, eds., *Presidents and Prime Ministers,* 256-283. Washington: American Enterprise Institute.

Allardt, Erik. 1986. "The Civic Conception of the Welfare State in Scandinavia." In R. Rose and R. Shiratori, eds., *The Welfare State East and West,* 107-125. New York: Oxford University Press.

Almond, Gabriel A., Flanagan, S. C., and Mundt, R. J., eds. 1973. *Crisis, Choice, and Change.* Boston: Little, Brown.

Almond, Gabriel A. and Verba, Sidney. 1963. *The Civic Culture.* Princeton: Princeton University Press.

Andersen, Svein S., and Eliassen, Kjell A. 1993. *Making Policy in Europe: The Europeiafication of National Policy-Making.* Thousand Oaks, CA: Sage Publications.

Anderson, Charles W. 1970. *The Political Economy of Modern Spain.* Madison: University of Wisconsin Press.

Anderson, Eugene N., and Anderson, Pauline R. 1967. *Political Institutions and Social Change in Continental Europe in the Nineteenth Century.* Berkeley: University of California Press.

Andeweg, Rudy B. 1991. "The Dutch Prime Minister: Not Just Chairman, Not Yet Chief? *West European Politics* 14, no. 2: 116-133.

Andorka, Rudolf. 1993. "Regime Transitions in Hungary in the 20th Century." *Governance* 6, no. 3: 358-371.

Arendt, Hannah. 1958. *The Origins of Totalitarianism,* 2nd ed. New York: Meridian.

Arthur, W. B. 1988. "Self-Reinforcing Mechanisms in Economics." In P. W. Anderson, K. J. Arrow and D. Pines, eds., *The Economy as an Evolving Complex System,* vol. 5, 9–32. Santa Fe, NM: Santa Fe Institute Studies in the Sciences of Complexity/Addison-Wesley Publishing.

Artis, M. J., 1990. "The European Monetary System." In A. M. El-Agraa, ed., *Economics of the European Community,* 3rd ed., 304–324. New York: Phillip Allan.

Ashford, Sheena, and Timms, Noel. 1992. *What Europe Thinks: A Study of Western European Values.* Aldershot, England: Dartmouth.

Aslund, Anders. 1990. "How Small Is the Soviet National Economy?" In H. S. Rowen and Charles Wolf Jr., eds., *The Impoverished Superpower: Perestroika and the Soviet Military Burden,* 13–61. San Francisco: ICS Press.

Aucoin, Peter. 1990. "Administrative Reform in Public Management," *Governance,* 3, 115–37.

Bagehot, Walter. 1867/1928. *The English Constitution.* London: Oxford University Press/World's Classics edition.

Baker, Kendall, Dalton, Russell, and Hildebrandt, Kai. 1981. *Germany Transformed: Political Culture and the New Politics.* Cambridge: Harvard University Press.

Baldwin, Peter. 1990. *The Politics of Social Solidarity: Class Bases of the European Welfare State, 1875–1975.* New York: Cambridge University Press.

Banting, Keith G., and Simeon, Richard, eds. 1985. *Redesigning the State: The Politics of Constitutional Change.* Toronto: University of Toronto Press.

Barnes, Samuel H., and Kaase, Max, eds. 1979. *Political Action: Mass Participation in Five Western Democracies.* Beverly Hills: Sage Publications.

Bartolini, Stefano, and Mair, Peter. 1990. *Identity, Competition and Electoral Availability: The Stabilization of European Electorates 1885–1985.* New York: Cambridge University Press.

Baylis, Thomas A. 1989. *Governing by Committee: Collegial Leadership in Advanced Societies.* Albany: State University of New York Press.

Baylis, Thomas A. 1994. *Presidents vs. Prime Ministers: Shaping Executive Authority in Eastern Europe.* Glasgow: University of Strathclyde Studies in Public Policy No. 238.

Beetham, David, ed. 1994. *Defining and Measuring Democracy.* Thousand Oaks, CA.: Sage Publications.

Bell, Daniel. 1973. *The Coming of Post-Industrial Society.* New York: Basic Books.

Bendix, Reinhard, and Rokkan, Stein. 1964. "The Extension of National Citizenship to the Lower Classes." In R. Bendix, *Nation-building and Citizenship,* 74–100. New York: John Wiley.

Bengoetxea, Joxerramon. 1993. *The Legal Reasoning of the European Court of Justice: Towards a European Jurisprudence.* Oxford: Clarendon Press.

Bennett, Colin. 1991. "What Is Policy Convergence and What Causes It?" *British Journal of Political Science* 21, no. 2: 215–234.

Bentley, A. F., 1949. *The Process of Government.* Evanston: Principia Press of Illinois.

Berglund, Sten, and Dellenbrant, Jan Ake, eds. 1994. *The New Democracies in Eastern Europe: Party Systems and Political Cleavages,* 2nd ed. Aldershot, England: Edward Elgar.

Berlin, Isaiah. 1969. "Two Concepts of Liberty." In Isaiah Berlin *Four Essays on Liberty.* Oxford: Oxford University Press, 118–172.

Beyme, Klaus von. 1980. *Challenge to Power: Trade Unions and Industrial Relations in Capitalist Countries.* Beverly Hills: Sage Publications.

Beyme, Klaus von. 1983. "Coalition Government in Western Germany." In V. Bogdanor, q.v., 16-37.

Beyme, Klaus von. 1993. "Regime Transition and Recruitment of Elites in Eastern Europe." *Governance* 6, no. 3: 409-425.

Bieber, R., Dehousse, R., Pinder, J., and Weiler, J., eds. 1988. *1992: One European Market?* Baden-Baden, Germany: Nomos for the European University Institute.

Black, A. 1984. *Guilds and Civil Society in European Political Thought from the Twelfth Century to the Present.* London: Methuen.

Blais, Andre. 1991. "The Debate over Electoral Systems." *International Political Science Review* 12, no. 2: 239-260.

Blichner, Lars C., and Sangolt, Linda. 1994. "The Concept of Subsidiarity and the Debate on European Cooperation: Pitfalls and Possibilities." *Governance* 7, no. 3: 284-306.

Blondel, Jean, and Mueller-Rommel, F., eds. 1985. *Cabinets in Western Europe.* Beverly Hills: Sage Publications.

Blondel, Jean, and Thiebault, Jean-Louis, eds. 1991. *The Profession of Government Minister in Western Europe.* London: Macmillan.

Bogdanor, Vernon, ed. 1983. *Coalition Government in Western Europe.* London: Heinemann Educational Books.

Bogdanor, Vernon, ed. 1985. *Representatives of the People? Parliaments and Constituents in Western Democracies.* Aldershot, England: Gower Books.

Bogdanor, Vernon, ed. 1988. *Constitutions in Democratic Politics.* Aldershot, England: Gower.

Bogdanor, Vernon. 1990. "Founding Elections and Regime Change." *Electoral Studies* 9, no. 4: 288-294.

Bonime-Blanc, Andrea. 1987. *Spain's Transition to Democracy: The Politics of Constitution-making.* Boulder: Westview Press.

Bremmer, Ian, and Taras, Ray, eds. 1993. *Nations and Politics in the Soviet Successor States.* Cambridge, England: Cambridge University Press.

Breslauer, George W. 1978. "On the Adaptability of Soviet Welfare-State Authoritarianism." In Karl W. Ryavec, ed. *Soviet Society and the Communist Party,* 3-25. Amherst: University of Massachusetts Press.

Brittan, Samuel. 1975. "The Economic Consequences of Democracy," *British Journal of Political Science,* 5, no. 2: 129-159.

Brubaker, Rogers. 1994. *Citizenship and Nationhood in France and Germany.* Cambridge: Harvard University Press.

Bryce, James. 1921. *Modern Democracies.* London: Macmillan.

Budge, Ian, and Keman, Hans. 1990. *Parties and Democracy: Coalition Formation and Government Functioning in Twenty States.* Oxford: Oxford University Press.

Budge, Ian, Robertson, David, and Hearl, Derek, eds. 1987. *Ideology, Strategy and Party Change: Spatial Analyses of Post-War Election Programmes in 19 Democracies.* New York: Cambridge University Press.

Bugajski, Janusz. 1994. *Ethnic Politics in Eastern Europe.* Armonk, NY: M. E. Sharpe.

Bulmer, Simon J. 1993. "The Governance of the European Union: A New Institutional Approach." *Journal of Public Policy* 13, no. 4: 351–380.

Bulpitt, Jim. 1983. *Territory and Power in the United Kingdom: An Interpretation.* Manchester, England: Manchester University Press.

Bureau of the Census, 1994. *Statistical Abstract of the United States 1994.* Washington: Government Printing Office.

Burgess, Michael, and Gagnon, A. G., eds. 1993. *Comparative Federalism and Federation.* Hemel Hampstead, England: Harvester Wheatsheaf.

Burk, Kathleen, and Cairncross, Alec. 1992. *Goodbye, Great Britain: The 1976 IMF Crisis.* New Haven: Yale University Press.

Burley, Anne-Marie, and Mattli, Walter. 1993. "Europe Before the Court: A Political Theory of Legal Integration." *International Organization* 47, no. 1: 41–74.

Butler, David, Adonis, Andrew, and Travers, Tony. 1994. *Failure in British Government: The Politics of the Poll Tax.* Oxford: Oxford University Press.

Butler, David, and Kitzinger, Uwe. 1976. *The 1975 Referendum.* London: Macmillan.

Butler, David, and Ranney, Austin, eds. 1994. *Referendums Around the World: The Growing Use of Direct Democracy.* London: Macmillan.

Butorova, Zora, and Butora, Martin. 1995. "Political Parties, Value Orientations, and Slovakia's Road to Independence." In Gordon Wightman, ed., *Party Formation in East-Central Europe,* 107–133. Aldershot, England: Edward Elgar.

Cain, Bruce, Ferejohn, John, and Fiorina, Morris. 1987. *The Personal Vote.* Cambridge: Harvard University Press.

Cameron, David. 1992. "The 1992 Initiative: Causes and Consequences." In Sbragia, q.v., 23–74.

Carnaghan, Ellen. 1994. *Alienation, Apathy or Ambivalence? Don't Knows and Democracy in Russia.* Glasgow: University of Strathclyde Studies in Public Policy No. 237.

Cassese, Sabino. 1984. "The Higher Civil Service in Italy." In E. Suleiman, ed., *Bureaucrats and Policymaking,* 35–71. New York: Holmes and Meier.

Cassese, Sabino. 1990. "Toward a European Model of Public Administration." In D. S. Clark, ed., *Comparative and Private International Law,* 353–367. Berlin: Duncker and Humblot.

Cassese, Sabino, and Torchia, Luisa. 1993. "The Meso Level in Italy." In L. J. Sharpe, q.v., 1993., 91–116.

Castles, Francis G. 1986. "Whatever Happened to the Communist Welfare State?" *Studies in Comparative Communism* 19, nos. 3/4: 213–226.

Cawson, Alan. 1986. *Corporatism and Political Theory.* Oxford: Blackwell.

CEPR (Centre for Economic Policy and Research). 1993. *Making Sense of Subsidiarity.* London: CEPR Report Monitoring European Integration 4.

Chapman, Brian. 1970. *Police State.* London: Pall Mall.

Chester, D. N. 1981. *The English Administrative System, 1780–1870.* Oxford: Clarendon Press.

Chubb, Basil. 1982. *The Government and Politics of Ireland,* 2nd ed. New York: Longman.

Chubb, Basil. 1991. *The Politics of the Irish Constitution.* Dublin: Institute of Public Administration.

Clark, John, and Wildavsky, Aaron. 1990. *The Moral Collapse of Communism: Poland as a Cautionary Tale.* San Francisco: Institute of Contemporary Studies Press.

Cole, John, and Cole, Francis. 1993. *The Geography of the European Community.* New York: Routledge.

Conquest, Robert. 1990. *The Great Terror: A Reassessment.* London: Hutchinson.

Converse, P. E., and Dupeux, G. 1966. "Politicization of the Electorate in France and the United States." In A. Campbell et al., *Elections and the Political Order,* 269-291. New York: Wiley.

Cook, Linda J. 1993. *The Soviet Social Contract and Why It Failed.* Cambridge: Harvard University Press.

Cotta, Maurizio. 1994. "Building Party Systems after the Dictatorship." In G. Pridham and T. Vanhanen, eds. *Democratization in Eastern Europe,* 99-127. New York: Routledge.

Crewe, Ivor, and Searing, Donald. 1988. "Ideological Change in the British Conservative Party." *American Political Science Review* 82, no. 2: 361-384.

Cuchillo, Montserrat. 1993. "The Autonomous Communities as the Spanish Meso." In L. J. Sharpe, 1993, q.v., 210-237.

Daalder, Hans. 1966. "Parties, Elites and Political Developments in Western Europe." In Joseph LaPalombara and Myron Weiner, eds., *Political Parties and Political Development,* 43-78. Princeton: Princeton University Press.

Daalder, Hans. 1992. "A Crisis of Party?" *Scandinavian Political Studies* 15, no. 4: 269-288.

Dahl, Robert A. 1956. *A Preface to Democratic Theory.* Chicago: University of Chicago Press.

Dahl, Robert A. 1970. *After the Revolution?* New Haven: Yale University Press.

Dahl, Robert A. 1971. *Polyarchy: Participation and Opposition.* New Haven: Yale University Press.

Dahl, Robert A. 1994. "A Democratic Dilemma: System Effectiveness Versus Citizen Participation." *Political Science Quarterly* 109, no. 1: 23-34.

Dalton, Russell J. 1988. *Citizen Politics in Western Democracies.* Chatham, NJ: Chatham House.

Dalton, Russell. 1993. *Politics in Germany,* 2nd ed. New York: HarperCollins.

Dalton, Russell J. 1994. "Communists and Democrats: Democratic Attitudes in the Two Germanies." *British Journal of Political Science* 24, no. 4: 469-494.

Dalton, Russell J., Flanagan, Scott C., and Beck, Paul Allen, eds. 1984. *Electoral Change in Advanced Industrial Societies.* Princeton: Princeton University Press.

Dalton, Russell J., and Kuechler, Manfred, eds. 1990. *Challenging the Political Order.* Oxford: Polity Press.

Davies, Bleddyn. 1968. *Social Needs and Resources in Local Government.* London: Michael Joseph.

Davis, S. R. 1978. *The Federal Principle.* Berkeley: University of California Press.

Deacon, Bob. 1993. "Developments in East European Social Policy." In C. Jones, ed., *New Perspectives on the Welfare State in Europe,* 177-197. Boston: Routledge.

Dente, Bruno, and Kjellberg, Francesco, ed. 1988. *The Dynamics of Institutional Change: Local Government Reorganization in Western Democracies.* Newbury Park, CA: Sage Publications.

D'Entreves, A. P. 1967. *The Notion of the State.* Oxford: Clarendon Press.

Derlien, Hans-Ulrich. 1993. "German Unification and Bureaucratic Transformation." *International Political Science Review* 14, no. 4: 319-334.

Derlien, Hans-Ulrich, and Szablowski, George J., eds. 1993. "Regime Transitions, Elites and Bureaucracies in Eastern Europe." *Governance* 6, no. 3 (special issue): 303–453.

Deutsch, Karl W. 1963. *The Nerves of Government.* New York: Free Press.

Deutsch, Karl W., et al. 1957. *Political Community in the North Atlantic Area.* Princeton: Princeton University Press.

Dewachter, Wilfried. 1987. "Changes in a *Particratie*: The Belgian Party System from 1944 to 1986." In Hans Daalder, ed., *Party Systems in Denmark, Austria, Switzerland, the Netherlands, and Belgium,* 285–363. London: Frances Pinter.

Diamondouros, Nikoforos, and Gunther, Richard, eds. *Democratic Politics in the New Southern Europe.* Baltimore: Johns Hopkins University Press.

Dietz, Mary G. 1994. "'The Slow Boring of Hard Boards': Methodical Thinking and the Work of Politics." *American Political Science Review* 88, no. 4: 873–886.

Dinan, Desmond. 1994. *Ever Closer Union?* London: Macmillan.

Dix, Robert H. 1994. "History and Democracy Revisited." *Comparative Politics* 27, no. 1: 91–106.

Dogan, Mattei, and Pelassy, Dominique. 1990. *How to Compare Nations,* 2nd ed. Chatham, NJ: Chatham House.

Doukas, George. 1993. "Party Elites and Democratization in Greece." *Parliamentary Affairs* 46, no. 4: 506–516.

Duchacek, Ivo D. 1973. *Power Maps: Comparative Politics of Constitutions.* Santa Barbara, CA.: American Bibliographical Center—Clio Press.

Dunsire, Andrew, and Hood, Christopher. 1989. *Cutback Management in Public Bureaucracies.* New York: Cambridge University Press.

Dyson, Kenneth H. F. 1980. *The State Tradition in Western Europe.* Oxford: Martin Robertson.

East European Constitutional Review. 1994. "Forum: The Evolving Presidency in Eastern Europe." 2, no. 4/3,1: (double issue) 36–106.

Easton, David. 1965. *A Systems Analysis of Political Life.* New York: Wiley.

Ehrmann, Henry W. 1976. *Comparative Legal Cultures.* Englewood Cliffs, NJ: Prentice-Hall.

Ekiert, Grzegorz. 1991. "Democratization Processes in East Central Europe," *British Journal of Political Science* 21, no. 3: 285–313.

El-Agraa, A. M., ed. 1990. "The Common Agricultural Policy." In A. M. El-Agraa, ed., *Economics of the European Community,* 3rd ed., 187–217. New York: Phillip Allan.

Elster, Jon. 1991. "Constitutionalism in Eastern Europe: An Introduction." *University of Chicago Law Review* 58, no. 2: 447–482.

Elster, Jon. 1992. "On Majoritarianism and Rights." *East European Constitutional Review* 1, no. 3: 19–24.

Emerson, Michael, Aujean, M., Catinat, M., Goybet, P. and Jacquemin, A. 1988. *The Economics of 1992.* Cambridge: MIT Press.

Emmons, Terence. 1983. *The Formation of Political Parties and the First National Elections in Russia.* Cambridge: Harvard University Press.

Engelmann, Frederick C. 1966. "Austria: the Pooling of Opposition." In R. A. Dahl, ed., *Political Oppositions in Western Democracies,* 260–283. New Haven: Yale University Press.

Esping-Andersen, Gosta. 1990. *The Three Worlds of Welfare Capitalism.* Princeton: Princeton University Press.

Esping-Andersen, Gosta. 1994. *After the Golden Age: The Future of the Welfare State in the New Global Order.* Geneva: UNRISD (United Nations Research Institute for Social Development) Occasional Paper No. 7.

Ester, Peter, Halman, Loek, Moor, Ruud de. 1993. *The Individualizing Society: Value Change in Europe and North America.* Tilburg, Netherlands: Tilburg University Press.

Eulau, Heinz, and Lewis-Beck, Michael S., eds. 1985. *Economic Conditions and Electoral Outcomes: The United States and Western Europe.* New York: Agathon Press.

Eurobarometer. 1993. *Central and Eastern Eurobarometer,* No. 3. Brussels: European Commission.

European Commission. 1995. *General Report of the Activities of the European Union 1994.* Brussels: European Commission.

Evans, Geoffrey, and Whitefield, Stephen. 1993. "Identifying the Bases of Party Competition in Eastern Europe." *British Journal of Political Science* 23, no. 4: 521–548.

Evans, Peter B., Jacobson, Harold K., and Putnam, Robert D., eds. 1993. *Double-Edged Diplomacy: International Bargaining and Domestic Politics.* Berkeley: University of California Press.

Eyal, Jonathan. 1993. "Romania." In Stephen Whitefield, ed., *The New Institutional Architecture of Eastern Europe,* 121–12. London: Macmillan.

Featherstone, K., and Katsoudas, D. 1987. *Political Change in Greece Before and After the Colonels.* London: Croom Helm.

Fernandez, Susan Aguilar. 1994. "Convergence in Economic Policy? The Resilience of National Institutional Designs in Spain and Germany." *Journal of Public Policy* 14, no. 1: 39–56.

Finer, S. E., Bogdanor, Vernon, and Rudden, Bernard. 1995. *Comparing Constitutions.* Oxford: Clarendon Press.

Fiorina, Morris P. 1981. *Retrospective Voting in American National Elections.* New Haven: Yale University Press.

Fleron, Frederic J. Jr., and Hoffmann, Erik P., eds. 1993. *Post-Communist Studies and Political Science.* Boulder: Westview Press.

Flora, Peter. 1983. *State, Economy and Society in Western Europe, 1815–1975,* vol. I, *The Growth of Mass Democracies and Welfare States.* Chicago: St. James Press.

Flora, Peter, and Alber, Jens. 1981. "Modernization, Democratization, and the Development of Welfare States in Western Europe." In P. Flora and A. J. Heidenheimer, eds., *The Development of Welfare States in Europe and America,* 37–80. New Brunswick, NJ: Transaction Publishers.

Flora, Peter, and Heidenheimer, A. J., eds. 1981. *The Development of Welfare States in Europe and America.* New Brunswick, NJ: Transaction Publishers.

Flora, Peter, Kraus, Franz, and Pfenning, Winfried. 1987. *State, Economy and Society in Western Europe, 1815–1975,* vol. 2. Chicago: St. James Press.

Franklin, Michael. 1992. *The EC Budget.* London: Royal Institute of International Affairs Fiscal Studies.

Franklin, S. H. 1969. *The European Peasantry.* London: Methuen.

Freddi, Giorgio. 1986. "Bureaucratic Rationalities and the Prospect for Party Government." In F. G. Castles and Rudolf Wildenmann, eds., *Visions and Realities of Party Government,* 143–178. Berlin: Walter de Gruyter.

Freedom House. 1994. "1994 Freedom Around the World." *Freedom Review* 25, no. 1: 5–41.

Freeman, Richard, Swedenborg, B., and Topel, R. 1995. *Economic Troubles in Sweden's Welfare State.* Stockholm: Centre for Business and Policy Studies/ National Bureau of Economic Research Project, No. 69.

Friedrich, C. J. and Brzezinski, Z. 1967. *Totalitarian Dictatorship and Autocracy.* New York: Praeger.

Furtak, Robert K., ed. 1990. *Elections in Socialist States.* Hemel Hempstead, England: Harvester Wheatsheaf.

Gallagher, Tom. 1983. *Portugal: A Twentieth Century Interpretation.* Manchester: Manchester University Press.

Garber, Larry, and Bjornlund, Eric, eds. 1992. *The New Democratic Frontier.* Washington: National Democratic Institute for International Affairs.

Garrett, Geoffrey. 1992. "International Cooperation and Institutional Choice: the European Community's Internal Market." *International Organization* 46, no. 2: 535–560.

Garrett, Geoffrey. 1995. "The Politics of Legal Integration in the European Union." *International Organization* 49, no. 1: 170–181.

Garton-Ash, Tim. 1990. "Eastern Europe: Aprés le Deluge, Nous." *New York Review of Books* 37, no. 13 (August 16): 51–57.

Gastil, Raymond D. 1987. *Freedom in the World: Political Rights and Civil Liberties.* New York: Greenwood Press.

Giedion, Sigfried. 1967. *Space Time and Architecture: the Growth of a New Tradition,* 5th ed. Cambridge: Harvard University Press.

Godt, P. 1989. "Health Care." In P. Godt, ed., *Policymaking in France,* 191–210. London: Pinter.

Goetz, Klaus H., and Cullen, Peter J., eds. 1995. *Constitutional Policy in Unified Germany.* London: Frank Cass.

Golay, John F. 1958. *The Founding of the Federal Republic of Germany.* Chicago: University of Chicago Press.

Goodin, R. E., and LeGrand, Julian. 1987. *Not Only the Poor: The Middle Classes and the Welfare State.* London: George Allen and Unwin.

Goodman, John B. 1992. *Monetary Sovereignty: The Politics of Central Banking in Western Europe.* Ithaca: Cornell University Press.

Gordon, Margaret S. 1988. *Social Security Policies in Industrial Countries: A Comparative Analysis.* New York: Cambridge University Press.

Gowers, Andrew, and Buchan, David. 1993. "Balladur Criticises Low-Wage Rivalry Faced by EU." *Financial Times* (December 31).

Graham, George J. Jr. 1984. "Consensus." In Giovanni Sartori, ed., *Social Science Concepts: A Systematic Analysis,* 89–124. Beverly Hills: Sage Publications.

Graham, Lawrence S. 1992. "Redefining the Portuguese Transition to Democracy." In J. Higley and R. Gunther, eds., *Elites and Democratic Consolidation in Latin America and Southern Europe,* 282–299. New York: Cambridge University Press.

Grant, Wyn. 1989. *Pressure Groups, Politics and Democracy in Britain.* New York: Philip Allan.

Grant, Wyn. 1995. "The Limits of Common Agricultural Policy Reform and the Option of Denationalization." *European Public Policy* 2, no. 1: 1–18.

Gregory, Paul R. 1987. "Productivity, Slack, and Time Theft in the Soviet Economy." In James R. Millar, ed., *Politics, Work and Daily Life in the USSR,* 241–275. New York: Cambridge University Press.

Grossman, Gregory. 1977. "The Second Economy of the USSR." *Problems of Communism* 26, no. 5: 25–40.

Gunlicks, Arthur B., ed. 1981. *Local Government Reform and Reorganization: An International Perspective.* Port Washington, NY: Kennikat Press.

Gunther, Richard. 1992. "Spain: the Very Model of the Modern Elite Settlement." In J. Higley and R. Gunther, eds., *Elites and Democratic Consolidation in Latin America and Southern Europe.* 38–80. New York: Cambridge University Press.

Gunther, Richard, and Montero, Jose Ramon. In press. "The Anchors of Partisanship: A Comparative Analysis of Voting Behavior in Four Southern European Democracies." In N. Diamandouros and R. Gunther, eds., *Democratic Politics in the New Southern Europe.*

Gunther, Richard, Sani, Giacomo, and Shabad, Goldie. 1988. *Spain after Franco: the Making of a Competitive Party System,* rev. ed. Berkeley: University of California Press.

Guyomarch, A. 1990. "Adversary Politics, Civil Liberties, and Law and Order." In P. Hall, J. Hayward, and H. Machin, eds., *Developments in French Politics.* London: Macmillan.

Haas, E. B. 1964. *Beyond the Nation-State: Functionalism and International Organization.* Stanford: Stanford University Press.

Hadfield, B., ed. 1992. *Northern Ireland: Politics and the Constitution.* Buckingham, England: Open University Press.

Hall, Peter A., ed. 1989. *The Political Power of Economic Ideas.* Princeton: Princeton University Press.

Hamilton, Stephen F. 1990. *Apprenticeship for Adulthood.* New York: Free Press.

Hankiss, Elemer. 1990. *East European Alternatives.* Oxford: Clarendon Press.

Hanson, Philip. 1986. "The Serendipitious Soviet Achievement of Full Employment: Labor Shortage and Labor Hoarding in the Soviet Economy." In David Lane, ed., *Labor and Employment in the USSR,* 83–111. New York: New York University Press.

Harries, Owen. 1993. "The Collapse of 'the West.'" *Foreign Affairs* 72, no. 4: 41–53.

Hartz, Louis. 1955. *The Liberal Tradition in America.* New York: Harcourt, Brace.

Hayward, Jack, 1983. *Governing France: The One and Indivisible Republic.* London: Weidenfeld and Nicolson, 2nd ed.

Hayward, Jack, ed. 1993. *DeGaulle to Mitterrand: Presidential Power in France.* London: Hurst.

Headey, Bruce W. 1974. *British Cabinet Ministers: the Roles of Politicians in Executive Office.* London: George Allen and Unwin.

Health Affairs. "Pursuit of Health Systems Reform." 10, no. 3 (special issue): 4–268.

Heclo, Hugh. 1981. "Toward a New Welfare State?" In P. Flora and A. J. Heidenheimer, eds., *The Development of Welfare States in Europe and America,* 383–406. New Brunswick, NJ: Transaction.

Heidenheimer, Arnold. 1986. "Politics, Policy and *Policey* as Concepts in English and Continental Languages." *Review of Politics* 48, no. 1: 3–30.

Heidenheimer, Arnold, Heclo, Hugh, and Adams, Carolyn Teich. 1990. *Comparative Public Policy,* 3rd ed. New York: St. Martin's Press.

Hermet, Guy. 1988. "Emerging from Dictatorship: The Role of the Constitution in Spain (1978) and Portugal (1976)." In V. Bogdanor, ed., q.v., 257–273.

Hermet, Guy, Rouquie, Alain, and Rose, Richard, eds. 1978. *Elections Without Choice.* London: Macmillan.

Higley, John, and Gunther, Richard, eds. 1992. *Elites and Democratic Consolidation in Latin America and Southern Europe.* New York: Cambridge University Press.

Hine, David. 1993. *Governing Italy: The Politics of Bargained Pluralism.* New York: Oxford University Press.

Hine, David, and Finocchi, Renato. 1991. "The Italian Prime Minister." *West European Politics* 14, no. 2: 79–96.

Hoffman, Stanley. 1959. "The French Constitution of 1958." *American Political Science Review* 53, no. 2, 332–357.

Holmes, Stephen. 1993. "Back to the Drawing Board." *East European Constitutional Review* 2, no. 1: 21–25.

Holmes, Stephen. 1995. "Conceptions of Democracy in the Draft Constitutions of Post-Communist Countries." In Beverly Crawford, ed., *Markets, States and Democracy,* 71–81. Boulder, CO: Westview Press.

Holzmann, Robert, Gacs, Janos, and Winckler, George, eds. 1995. *Output Decline in Eastern Europe.* Dordrecht, Netherlands: Kluwer.

Hood, Christopher, and Schuppert, G. F., eds. 1988. *Delivering Public Services in Western Europe.* London: Sage Publications.

Howard, A. E. Dick, ed. 1993. *Constitution Making in Eastern Europe.* Baltimore: Woodrow Wilson Center Press/ Johns Hopkins University Press.

Humana, Charles. 1986. *World Human Rights Guide.* London: Hutchinson.

Huntington, Samuel P. 1991. *The Third Wave: Democratization in the Late Twentieth Century.* Norman: University of Oklahoma Press.

Huntington, Samuel P. 1993. "The Clash of Civilizations?" *Foreign Affairs* 72, no. 3: 22–49.

Husbands, Christopher T. 1981. "Contemporary Right-Wing Extremism in Western European Democracies." *European Journal of Political Research* 9, no. 1: 75–100.

Ignazi, Piero. 1992. "The Silent Counter-Revolution: Hypotheses on the Emergence of Extreme Right-Wing Parties in Europe." *European Journal of Political Research* 22: 3–34.

Inglehart, Ronald. 1977. *The Silent Revolution: Changing Values and Political Styles Among Western Publics.* Princeton: Princeton University Press.

Inglehart, Ronald. 1990. *Culture Shift in Advanced Industrial Society.* Princeton: Princeton University Press.

Inkeles, Alex, ed. 1991. *On Measuring Democracy: Its Consequences and Concomitants.* New Brunswick, NJ: Transaction Publishers.

Institute for Public Policy Research. 1991. *The Constitution of the United Kingdom.* London: IPPR.

Inter-Parliamentary Union. 1986. *Parliaments of the World,* 2 vols., 2nd ed. Aldershot, England: Gower.

Jacobs, Francis, and Corbett, Richard, with Michael Shackleton. 1990. *The European Parliament.* Boulder, CO.: Westview Press.

Janos, A. 1991. "Social Science, Communism and the Dynamics of Political Change." *World Politics* 44: 81–112.

Jasiewicz, Krzystof. 1994. "Poland." *European Journal of Political Research* 26, no. 3/4: 397–408.

Jordan, A. Grant, and Schubert, K. 1992. "A Preliminary Ordering of Policy Network Labels." *European Journal of Political Research* 21 no. 1: 7–28.

Jowell, Jeffrey, and Oliver, Dawn, eds. 1994. *The Changing Constitution,* 3rd ed. Oxford: Oxford University Press.

Jowitt, Kenneth. 1992. *New World Disorder: The Leninist Extinction.* Berkeley: University of California Press.

Judge, David, Earnshaw, David, and Cowan, Ngaire. 1994. "Ripples or Waves: The European Parliament in the European Community Policy Process." *Journal of European Public Policy* 1, no. 1: 27–52.

Karasimeonov, Georgi. 1995. "Differentiation Postponed: Party Pluralism in Bulgaria." In G. Wightman, ed., *Party Formation in East-Central Europe,* 154–178. Aldershot, England: Edward Elgar.

Katsenelinboigen, Aaron. 1977. "Colored Markets in the Soviet Union." *Soviet Studies* 29, no. 1: 62–85.

Katz, Richard, and Mair, Peter. 1995. "Changing Models of Party Organization and Party Democracy: The Emergence of the Cartel Party." *Party Politics* 1, no. 1.

Katzenstein, Peter J. 1985. *Small States in World Markets.* Ithaca: Cornell University Press.

Kavanagh, Dennis A. 1973. "Crisis Management and Incremental Adaptation in British Politics: The 1931 Crisis of the British Party System." In Almond, Gabriel A., Flanagan, S. C. and Mundt, R. J., eds., *Crisis, Choice, and Change,* 152–223. Boston: Little, Brown.

Kavanagh, Dennis, 1974. *Crisis, Charisma and British Political Leadership.* London: Sage Papers in Contemporary Political Sociology 06-001.

Kavanagh, Dennis. 1990. *Thatcherism and British Politics: The End of Consensus?* 2nd ed. Oxford: Oxford University Press.

Keeler, John T. S. 1987. *The Politics of Neocorporatism in France.* New York: Oxford University Press.

Keeler, John T. S., 1993. "Executive Power and Policy-Making Patterns in France: Gauging the Impact of Fifth Republic Institutions." *West European Politics* 16, no. 4: 518–544.

Kennedy, Paul. 1988. *The Rise and Fall of the Great Powers.* London: Unwin Hyman.

Keohane, Robert O. 1984. *After Hegemony: Cooperation and Discord in the World Political Economy.* Princeton: Princeton University Press.

Keohane, Robert O., and Nye, Joseph. 1977. *Power and Interdependence,* 2nd ed. Boston: Little, Brown.

Kerr, Henry. 1987. "The Swiss Party System: Steadfast and Changing." In Hans Daalder, ed., *Party Systems in Denmark, Austria, Switzerland, the Netherlands and Belgium,* 107–192. London: Frances Pinter.

Kirchheimer, Otto. 1966. "The Transformation of the West European Party Systems." In J. LaPalombara and M. Weiner, eds., *Political Parties and Political Development,* 177–200. Princeton: Princeton University Press.

Kirchner, Emil, ed. 1988. *Liberal Parties in Western Europe.* New York: Cambridge University Press.

Kitschelt, Herbert. 1992. "The Formation of Party Systems in East Central Europe." *Politics and Society* 20, no. 1: 7–50.

Kitschelt, Herbert. 1994. *The Transformation of European Social Democracy.* New York: Cambridge University Press.

Kitschelt, Herbert. 1995. *Party Systems in East Central Europe: Consolidation or Fluidity?* Glasgow: University of Strathclyde Studies in Public Policy No. 241.

Klingemann, Hans-Dieter. 1979. "The Background of Ideological Conceptualization." In Samuel H. Barnes and Max Kaase, eds., *Political Action: Mass Participation in Five Western Democracies,* 255–278. Beverly Hills: Sage Publications.

Klingemann, Hans-Dieter. 1995. Party Positions and Voter Orientations." In Hans-Dieter Klingemann and Dieter Fuchs, eds., *Citizens and the State,* 183–205. Oxford: Oxford University Press.

Klingemann, Hans-Dieter, and Wattenberg, Martin P. 1992. "Decaying Versus Developing Party Systems." *British Journal of Political Science* 22, no. 2: 131–150.

Knutsen, Oddbjorn. 1995. "The Impact of Old Politics and New Politics Value Orientations on Party Choice: A Comparative Study." *Journal of Public Policy* 15, no. 1, 1–63.

Koenig, Klaus. "Bureaucratic Integration by Elite Transfer: The Case of the Former GDR." *Governance* 6, no. 3: 386–396.

Koestler, Arthur, 1940. *Darkness at Noon.* London: Jonathan Cape.

Kohli, Martin, Rein, Martin, Guillemard, Anne-Marie, and van Gunsteren, Herman, eds. 1991. *Time for Retirement.* New York: Cambridge University Press.

Kommers, Donald. 1989. *The Constitutional Jurisprudence of the Federal Republic of Germany.* Durham, NC: Duke University Press.

Kommers, Donald. 1994. "The Federal Constitutional Court in the German Political System." *Comparative Political Studies* 26, no. 4 470–491.

Kornai, Janos. 1990. *Vision and Reality, Market and State.* London: Harvester/Wheatsheaf.

Kornai, Janos. 1992. *The Socialist Economy: The Political Economy of Communism.* Princeton: Princeton University Press.

Kostelecky, Tomas. 1995. "Changing Party Allegiances in a Changing Party System." In G. Wightman, ed., *Party Formation in East-Central Europe,* 79–106. New York: Routledge.

Koutsoukis, Kleomenis S. 1994. "Cabinet Decision-Making in the Hellenic Republic, 1974–1992." In Michael Laver and Kenneth A. Shepsle, eds., *Cabinet Ministers and Parliamentary Government,* 270–282 New York: Cambridge University Press.

Kurzer, Paulette. 1993. *Business and Banking: Political Change and Economic Integration In Western Europe.* Ithaca: Cornell University Press.

Kuusela, Kimmo. 1994. "The Founding Electoral Systems in Eastern Europe, 1989–91." In Geoffrey Pridham and Tatu Vanhanen, eds., *Democratization in Eastern Europe,* 128–150. New York: Routledge.

Laasko, M., and Taagepera, R. 1979. "Effective Number of Parties: A Measure with Applications to West Europe," *Comparative Political Studies* 12: 3–27.

Laitin, David D. 1991. "The National Uprisings in the Soviet Union." *World Politics,* 44, no. 1: 139–177.

Landfried, Christine. 1994. "The Judicialization of Politics in Germany," *International Political Science Review* 15, no. 2: 113–124.

Lane, Jan-Erik, and Ersson, Svante O. *Politics and Society in Western Europe.* Newbury Park, CA.: Sage Publications.

Lane, Jan-Erik, McKay, David, and Newton, Kenneth, eds. 1991. *Political Data Handbook: OECD Countries.* Oxford: Oxford University Press.

LaPalombara, Joseph. 1987. *Democracy Italian Style.* New Haven: Yale University Press.

Larsson, Torbjörn. 1994. "Cabinet Ministers and Parliamentary Government in Sweden." In Michael Laver and Kenneth A. Shepsle, eds., *Cabinet Ministers and Parliamentary Government,* 169–186. New York: Cambridge University Press.

Laver, Michael, and Schofield, Norman. 1990. *Multiparty Government: The Logic of Coalition in Europe.* Oxford: Oxford University Press.

Laver, Michael, and Shepsle, Kenneth A., eds. 1994. *Cabinet Ministers and Parliamentary Government.* New York: Cambridge University Press.

Lehmbruch, Gerhard, and Schmitter, Philippe C., ed. 1982. *Patterns of Corporatist Policymaking.* Beverly Hills: Sage Publications.

LeMay, G. L. 1955. *British Government, 1914–1953: Select Documents.* London: Methuen.

Lewis-Beck, Michael, 1988. *Economics and Elections: The Major Western Democracies.* Ann Arbor: University of Michigan Press.

Lewis-Beck, Michael, Norpoth, H., and Lafay, J-D., eds. 1991. *Economics and Politics: The Calculus of Support.* University of Michigan Press.

Liebert, Ulrike, and Cotta, Maurizio, eds. 1992. *Parliament and Democratic Consolidation in Southern Europe.* London: Pinter Publishers.

Lijphart, Arend. 1975. *The Politics of Accommodation: Pluralism and Democracy in the Netherlands,* 2nd ed. Berkeley: University of California Press.

Lijphart, Arend. 1984. *Democracies: Patterns of Majoritarian and Consensus Government in Twenty-One Countries.* New Haven: Yale University Press.

Lijphart, Arend, ed. 1992. *Parliamentary Versus Presidential Government.* Oxford: Oxford University Press.

Lijphart, Arend. 1994. "Democracies: Forms, Performance, and Constitutional Engineering." *European Journal of Political Research* 25, no. 1: 1–17.

Lijphart, Arend, and Crepaz, M. M. L. 1991. "Corporatism and Consensus Democracy in Eighteen Countries." *British Journal of Political Science* 21, no. 2: 235–246.

Lindberg, Leon, and Scheingold, S. A. 1970. *Europe's Would-Be Polity: Patterns of Change in the European Community.* Englewood Cliffs, NJ: Prentice-Hall.

Linder, W. 1994. *Swiss Democracy: Possible Solutions to Conflict in Multicultural Societies.* London: Macmillan.

Linz, Juan J. 1975. "Totalitarian and Authoritarian Regimes." In Fred I. Greenstein and Nelson W. Polsby, eds., *Handbook of Political Science,* vol. 3, 175–411. Reading, MA: Addison-Wesley.

Linz, Juan J. 1990. "The Perils of Presidentialism." *Journal of Democracy* 1, no. 1: 51–70.

Linz, Juan J. 1993. "State Building and Nation Building." *European Review* 1, no. 4: 355–369.

Lipset, S. M. 1960. *Political Man.* New York: Doubleday.

Lipset, S.M., and Bence, Gyorgy. 1994. "Anticipations of the Failure of Communism." *Theory and Society* 23, no. 2: 169–210.

Lipset, S. M., and Rokkan, Stein. 1967. "Introduction." In S. M. Lipset and Stein Rokkan, eds., *Party Systems and Voter Alignments,* 1–64. New York: Free Press.

Lodge, Juliet, ed. 1990. *The 1989 Election of the European Parliament.* Basingstoke, England: Macmillan.

Lodge, Juliet. 1993. "EC Policymaking: Institutional Dynamics." In Lodge, ed., *The European Community and the Challenge of the Future*, 2nd ed., 1–36. London: Pinter.

Loewenberg, Gerhard. 1968. "The Remaking of the German Party System." *Polity* 1, no. 1: 87–113.

Lomax, Bill. 1995. "Impediments to Democratization in Post-Communist East-Central Europe." In Gordon Wightman, ed., *Party Formation in East-Central Europe*, 179–201. Aldershot, England: Edward Elgar.

Lorwin, Val R. 1966. "Belgium: Religion, Class, and Language in National Politics." In R.A. Dahl, ed., *Political Oppositions in Western Democracies*, 147–187. New Haven: Yale University Press.

McAllister, Ian. 1982. "United Kingdom Nationalist Parties; One Nationalism or Three?" In P. Madgwick and R. Rose, eds., *The Territorial Dimension in United Kingdom Politics*, 202–223. London: Macmillan.

McGregor, James. 1993. "How Electoral Laws Shape Eastern Europe's Parliaments." *RFE/RL Research Report* 2, no. 4 (January 22): 11–18.

McGregor, James. 1994. "The Presidency in East Central Europe." *RFE/RL Research Report* 3, no. 2: 23–31.

McKenzie, Robert T., and Silver, Allan. 1968. *Angels in Marble*. London: Heinemann.

Mackie, Thomas T. 1991. "General Elections in Western Nations During 1990." *European Journal of Political Research* 21: 318–332.

Mackie, T. T., and Hogwood, B. W., eds. 1985. *Unlocking the Cabinet: Cabinet Structures in Comparative Perspective*. Beverly Hills: Sage Publications.

Mackie, T. T., and Rose, Richard. 1991. *The International Almanac of Electoral History*, 3rd ed. Washington: CQ Press.

Machin, Howard. 1977. *The Prefect in French Administration*. London: Croom Helm.

Majone, Giandomenico. 1991. "Cross-National Sources of Regulatory Policymaking in Europe and the United States." *Journal of Public Policy* 11, no. 1: 79–106.

Majone, Giandomenico. 1994. "Paradoxes of Privatization and Deregulation." *Journal of European Public Policy*, 1, no. 1: 53–69.

Malik, Rex, and Anderson, Karen. 1992. "The Global News Agenda Survey." *Intermedia*, International Institute of Communications, London 20, no. 1: 8–70.

Maloney, W. A., Jordan, Grant, and McLaughlin, A. M. 1994. "Interest Groups and Public Policy: The Insider/Outside Model Revisited." *Journal of Public Policy* 14, no. 3: 17–38.

Marer, Paul, Arvay, Janos, O'Connor, John, Schrenk, Martin, and Swanson, Daniel. 1992. *Historically Planned Economies: A Guide to the Data*. Washington: World Bank.

Marin, Bernd. 1987. "From Consociationalism to Technocorporatism: The Austrian Case as a Model-Generator?" In Ilja Scholten, ed., *Political Stability and Neo-Corporatism*, 39–69. Beverly Hills: Sage Publications.

Markus, Gyorgy G. 1991. "Parties, Camps and Cleavages in Postcommunist Hungary." In *Viertaljahresberichte: Probleme der Internationalen Zusammenarbeit*, 245–254. Bonn: J. H. W. Dietz Nachfolger.

Marshall, Geoffrey. 1984. *Constitutional Conventions: The Rules and Forms of Political Accountability*. Oxford: Clarendon Press.

Marshall, T. H. 1950. *Citizenship and Social Class*. Cambridge: Cambridge University Press.

Mayntz, Renate. 1980. "Executive Leadership in Germany." In R. Rose and E. Suleiman, eds., *Presidents and Prime Ministers*, 139–170. Washington: American Enterprise Institute.

Mayntz, Renate. 1984. "German Federal Bureaucrats: A Functional Elite between Politics and Administration." In E. Suleiman, ed., *Bureaucrats and Policymaking,* 174-205. New York: Holmes and Meier.

Mazey, Sonia, and Richardson, J., ed. 1993. *Lobbying in the European Community.* Oxford: Oxford University Press.

Meinecke, F. 1957. *Machiavellism: The Doctrine of Raison d'Etat and Its Place in Modern History,* ed. Werner Stark. London: Routledge and Kegan Paul.

Meny, Yves. 1990. *Government and Politics in Western Europe.* Oxford: Oxford University Press.

Merkl, Peter H. 1963. *The Origin of the West German Republic.* New York: Oxford University Press.

Metcalfe, Les. 1993. "Conviction Politics and Dynamic Conservatism: Mrs. Thatcher's Managerial Revolution." *International Political Science Review* 14 no. 4: 351-372.

Meyer, Henry Cord. 1955. *Mitteleuropa in German Thought and Action, 1815-1945.* The Hague, Netherlands: Martinus Nijhoff.

Milward, Alan S. 1984. *The Reconstruction of Western Europe, 1945-51.* London: Methuen.

Milward, Alan S. 1992. *The European Rescue of the Nation-State.* New York: Routledge.

Mishler, William, and Rose, Richard. 1994. "Support for Parliaments and Regimes in the Transition Toward Democracy in Eastern Europe." *Legislative Studies Quarterly* 19, no. 1: 5-32.

Mishler, William, and Rose, Richard. 1995. "Trajectories of Fear and Hope: Support for Democracy in Post-Communist Europe." *Comparative Politics Studies* 28, no. 4: 553-581.

Mitchell, B. R. 1975. *European Historical Statistics, 1750-1970.* London: Macmillan.

Moran, Michael, and Prosser, Tony, eds. 1994. *Privatization and Regulatory Change in Europe.* Philadelphia: Open University Press.

Moravcsik, Andrew. 1991. "Negotiating the Single European Act: National Interests and Conventional Statecraft in the European Community." *International Organization* 45, no. 1: 19-56.

Moravcsik, Andrew. 1993. "Preferences and Power in the European Community: A Liberal Intergovernmentalist Approach." *Journal of Common Market Studies* 31, no. 4: 473-524.

Moravcsik, Andrew. 1994. "Lessons from the European Human Rights Regime." In *Advancing Democracy and Human Rights in the Americas: What Role for the OAS?* 35-58. Washington: Inter-American Dialogue.

Molle, Willem. 1994. *The Economics of European Integration.* 2nd ed. Aldershot, England: Dartmouth.

Mueller-Rommel, Ferdinand. 1989. *New Politics in Western Europe: The Rise of Green Parties and Alternative Lists.* Boulder, CO: Westview Press.

Mueller-Rommel, Ferdinand, and Pridham, Geoffrey, eds. 1991. *Small Parties in Western Europe.* Newbury Park, CA: Sage Publications.

Nelson, Daniel C. 1990. "Romania." *Electoral Studies* 9, no. 4: 355-366.

Nettl, J. P. 1968. "The State as a Conceptual Variable." *World Politics* 20, no. 4: 559-592.

New Democracies Barometer. *Comparative Nationwide Sample Surveys of Bulgaria, Czech Republic, Slovakia, Hungary, Poland, Romania, Slovenia, Croatia, Belarus and Ukraine* (Annual). Vienna: Paul Lazarsfeld Society.

Niskanen, William. 1971. *Representative Government and Bureaucracy.* Chicago: Aldine.

Noelle-Neumann, Elisabeth. 1993. *The Spiral of Silence,* 2nd ed. Chicago: University of Chicago Press.

Nordlinger, Eric A. 1981. *On the Autonomy of the Democratic State.* Cambridge: Harvard University Press.

Norton, Philip, ed. 1990. *Legislatures.* Oxford: Oxford University Press.

Nugent, Neill. 1994. *The Government and Politics of the European Union,* 3rd ed. London: Macmillan.

Nye, Joseph S. 1990. *Bound to Lead: The Changing Nature of American Power.* New York: Basic Books.

O'Brien, Patrick. 1978. "Constitutional Totalitarianism." *Survey* 23, no. 3: 70–80.

O'Donnell, Guillermo. 1994. "Delegative Democracy." *Journal of Democracy* 5, no. 1, 55–69.

O'Donnell, Guillermo, and Schmitter, P. C. 1986. *Transitions from Authoritarian Rule: Tentative Conclusions About Uncertain Democracies.* Baltimore: Johns Hopkins University Press.

O'Donnell, G., Schmitter, P. C., and Whitehead, Laurence, eds. 1986. *Transitions from Authoritarian Rule: Latin America.* Baltimore: Johns Hopkins University Press.

OECD. 1993. *Education at a Glance: OECD Indicators.* Paris: OECD Center for Educational Research and Innovation.

Olsen, Johan P. 1980. "Governing Norway: Segmentation, Anticipation, and Consensus Formation." In R. Rose and E. Suleiman, eds. *Presidents and Prime Ministers,* 203–255. Washington: American Enterprise Institute.

Olson, David M. 1993. "Political Parties and Party Systems in Regime Transformation." *American Review of Politics* 14 (winter): 619–658.

Olson, David M. 1993a. "Dissolution of the State: Political Parties and the 1992 Election in Czechoslovakia." *Communist and Post-Communist Studies* 26, no. 3: 301–314.

Olson, David M. 1994. *Democratic Legislative Institutions: A Comparative View.* Armonk, NY: M. E. Sharpe.

Olson, David M. In press. "The Parliaments of New Democracies: The Experience of Central Europe." In George Kurian, ed., *World Encyclopedia of Parliaments and Legislatures.* Washington, DC: CQ Press

Olson, David, and Mezey, Michael, eds. 1991. *Legislatures in the Policy Process.* New York: Cambridge University Press.

Page, Edward C. 1992. *Localism and Centralism in Europe: The Political and Legal Bases of Local Self-Government.* New York: Oxford University Press.

Page, Edward C. 1992a. *Political Authority and Bureaucratic Power: A Comparative Analysis,* 2nd ed. London: Harvester Wheatsheaf.

Page, Edward C., and Goldsmith, Michael J., ed. 1987. *Central and Local Government Relations: A Comparative Analysis of West European Unitary States.* Newbury Park, CA.: Sage Publications.

Palma, Giuseppe di. 1977. *Surviving Without Governing: Italian Parties in Parliament.* Berkeley: University of California Press.

Palma, Giuseppe di. 1990. *To Craft Democracies: An Essay on Democratic Transitions.* Berkeley: University of California Press.

Papadakis, Elim, and Bean, Clive. 1993. "Popular Support for the Welfare State." *Journal of Public Policy* 13, no. 4: 227-254.

Parris, Henry. 1969. *Constitutional Bureaucracy.* London: George Allen and Unwin.

Parry, Geraint, Moyser, George, and Day, Neil. 1992. *Political Participation and Democracy in Britain.* New York: Cambridge University Press.

Parry, Richard. 1981. "Territory and Public Employment." *Journal of Public Policy* 1, no. 2: 221-250.

Pasquino, Gianfranco. 1986. "The Demise of the First Fascist Regime and Italy's Transition to Democracy: 1943-1948." In G. O'Donnell, P. C. Schmitter and L. Whitehead, eds. *Transitions from Authoritarian Rule: Southern Europe,* 45-70. Baltimore: Johns Hopkins University Press.

Pedersen, Mogens N. 1979. "Electoral Volatility in Western Europe, 1948-1977." *European Journal of Political Research* 7, no. 1: 1-26.

Pempel, T. J., ed. 1990. *Uncommon Democracies: The One-Party Dominant Regimes.* Ithaca, NY: Cornell University Press.

Perez Diaz, Victor. 1993. *The Return of Civil Society: The Emergence of Democracy in Spain.* Cambridge.: Harvard University Press.

Peters, B. Guy. 1991. *European Politics Reconsidered.* New York: Holmes and Meier.

Peters, B. Guy. 1991a. *The Politics of Taxation.* Oxford: Basil Blackwell.

Peters, B. Guy. 1994. "Agenda-setting in the European Community." *Journal of European Public Policy* 1, no. 1: 9-26.

Peterson, John. 1995. "Decision-making in the European Union: Towards a Framework for Analysis." *Journal of European Public Policy* 2, no. 1: 69-93.

Pierre, Jon. 1993. "Legitimacy, Institutional Change and the Politics of Public Administration in Sweden." *International Political Science Review* 14, no. 4: 387-402.

Plasser, Fritz, and Ulram, Peter. 1993. "Zum Stand der Demokratisierung in Ost-Mitteleuropa." *Transformation oder Stagnation?* Vienna: Zentrum fuer Angewandte Politikforschung.

Pollack, Mark A. 1994. "Creeping Competence: The Expanding Agenda of the European Community." *Journal of Public Policy* 13, no. 2: 95-146.

Pravda, Alex. 1978. "Elections in Communist Party States." In Guy Hermet, Alain Rouquie, and Richard Rose, eds., *Elections Without Choice,* 169-195. London: Macmillan.

Pravda, Alex. 1986. "Elections In Communist Party States." In Steven White and D. Nelson, eds., *Communist Political Systems: A Reader.* London: Macmillan.

Pridham, Geoffrey, ed. 1984. *The New Mediterranean Democracies: Regime Transition in Spain, Greece and Portugal.* London: Frank Cass.

Pridham, Geoffrey. 1990. "Political Actors, Linkages and Interactions: Democratic Consolidation in Southern Europe." *West European Politics* 13, no. 4: 103-117.

Pryor, Frederic L. 1992. *The Red and the Green.* Princeton: Princeton University Press.

Przeworski, Adam. 1991. *Democracy and the Market.* New York: Cambridge University Press.

Putnam, Robert D. 1988. "Diplomacy and Domestic Politics: The Logic of Two-Level Games." *International Organization* 42: 427-460.

Putnam, Robert D. 1993. *Making Democracy Work,* with Robert Leonardi and Raffaella Y. Nanetti. Princeton: Princeton University Press.

Rady, Martyn. 1994. "The 1994 Hungarian Election." *Representation* 32, no. 119: 69–72.

Ramaswamy, Ramana. 1993. *The Structural Crisis in the Swedish Economy: The Role of Labor Markets.* Washington: International Monetary Fund Papers on Policy Analysis and Assessment, No. 93/18.

Ranelagh, John, 1991. *Thatcher's People.* London: HarperCollins.

Rapaczynski, Andrzej. 1993. "Constitutional Politics in Poland." In A. E. Dick Howard, ed., *Constitution Making in Eastern Europe,* 93–132. Baltimore: Johns Hopkins University Press.

Reif, Karlheinz, ed. 1985. *Ten European Elections.* Aldershot, England: Gower.

Rhodes, R. A. W. 1992. "Intergovernmental Relations: Unitary Systems." In Mary Hawksworth and Maurice Kogan, eds., *Encyclopedia of Government and Politics,* vol. 1, 316–335. New York: Routledge.

Ricketts, Martin, and Shoesmith, Edward. 1990. *British Economic Opinion: A Survey of a Thousand Economists.* London: Institute of Economic Affairs.

Roach, J., and Thomaneck, J., eds. 1985. *Police and Public Order in Europe.* London: Croom Helm.

Robertson, A. H., and Merrill, J. G. 1993. *Human Rights in Europe: A Study of the European Convention on Human Rights.* Manchester, England: Manchester University Press.

Roeder, Philip G. 1993. *Red Sunset: The Failure of Soviet Politics.* Princeton: Princeton University Press.

Rokkan, Stein. 1970. *Citizens, Elections, and Parties.* New York: David McKay.

Rose, Richard, forthcoming. "The Art of Writing about Politics." In Hans Daalder, ed., *The Intellectual Autobiography of Comparative European Politics.* London: Frances Pinter.

Rose, Richard. 1976. "On the Priorities of Government." *European Journal of Political Research* 4, no. 3: 247–89.

Rose, Richard. 1976a. "On the Priorities of Citizenship in the Deep South and Northern Ireland." *Journal of Politics* 38, no. 2: 247–291.

Rose, Richard. 1982. "Is the United Kingdom a State? Northern Ireland as a Test Case." In P. Madgwick and R. Rose, eds., *The Territorial Dimension in United Kingdom Politics,* 100–136. London: Macmillan.

Rose, Richard. 1982a. *The Territorial Dimension in Politics: Understanding the United Kingdom.* Chatham, NJ: Chatham House.

Rose, Richard. 1983. "Electoral Systems and Constitutions." In Vernon Bogdanor and D. E. Butler, eds., *Democracy and Elections,* 20–45. New York: Cambridge University Press.

Rose, Richard. 1984. *Understanding Big Government.* Newbury Park, CA: Sage Publications.

Rose, Richard. 1985. "From Government at the Centre to Government Nationwide." In Y. Meny and V. Wright, eds., *Centre-Periphery Relations in Western Europe,* 13–32. London: George Allen and Unwin.

Rose, Richard. 1985a. *Public Employment in Western Nations.* New York: Cambridge University Press.

Rose, Richard. 1985b. "The Program Approach to the Growth of Government." *British Journal of Political Science* 15, no. 1: 1–28.

Rose, Richard. 1986. "Law as a Resource of Public Policy." *Parliamentary Affairs,* 39, no. 3: 297–314.

Rose, Richard. 1986a. "The State's Contribution to the Welfare Mix in Britain." In R. Rose and R. Shiratori, eds., *The Welfare State East and West,* 80–106. New York: Oxford University Press.

Rose, Richard. 1987. *Ministers and Ministries: A Functional Analysis.* Oxford: Clarendon Press.

Rose, Richard. 1987a. "Steering the Ship of State: One Tiller but Two Pairs of Hands." *British Journal of Political Science* 17, no. 4: 409–433.

Rose, Richard. 1988. "Loyalty, Voice, or Exit? Margaret Thatcher's Challenge to the Civil Service." In T. Ellwein, J. J. Hesse, R. Mayntz and F. W. Scharpf, eds., *Jahrbuch zur Staats- und Verwaltungswissenschaft,* 189–218. Baden-Baden, Germany: Nomos.

Rose, Richard. 1989. "How Exceptional Is the American Political Economy?" *Political Science Quarterly* 104, no. 1: 91–115.

Rose, Richard. 1989a. "Privatization as a Problem of Satisficing and Dissatisficing," *American Review of Public Administration* 19, no. 2: 97–118.

Rose, Richard. 1989b. *Politics in England,* 5th ed. New York: HarperCollins,

Rose, Richard. 1989c. *Ordinary People in Public Policy.* Newbury Park, CA: Sage Publications.

Rose, Richard. 1990. "Charging for Public Services: A Practical Paradigm." *Public Administration* 68, no. 3: 297–313.

Rose, Richard, 1991. "Comparing Forms of Comparative Analysis." *Political Studies* 39, no. 3: 446–462.

Rose, Richard. 1991a. "Prime Ministers in Parliamentary Democracies." *West European Politics* 14, no. 2: 9–24.

Rose, Richard. 1991b. *The Postmodern President,* 2nd ed. Chatham, NJ: Chatham House.

Rose, Richard. 1992. "Escaping Absolute Dissatisfaction: A Trial and Error Model of Change in Eastern Europe." *Journal of Theoretical Politics* 4, no. 4: 371–393.

Rose, Richard. 1992a. "Toward a Civil Economy." *Journal of Democracy* 3, no. 2: 13–26.

Rose, Richard. 1993. *Lesson-Drawing in Public Policy: A Guide to Learning Across Time and Space.* Chatham, N.J.: Chatham House.

Rose, Richard. 1993a. "Bringing Freedom Back In." In Catherine Jones, ed., *New Perspectives on the Welfare State in Europe,* 221–241. New York: Routledge.

Rose, Richard. 1993b. "Contradictions between Micro and Macro-Economic Goals in Post-Communist Societies." *Europe-Asian Studies (formerly, Soviet Studies)* 45, no. 3: 419–444.

Rose, Richard. 1994. *Comparing Welfare Across Time and Space.* Vienna: European Centre for Social Welfare Policy and Research, European Centre Eurosocial Report 49.

Rose, Richard. 1995. "Freedom as a Fundamental Value," *International Social Science Journal,* no. 145, 457–471.

Rose, Richard. 1995a. "Adaptation, Resilience and Destitution: Alternative Responses to Transition in the Ukraine." *Problems of Post-Communism* 42, no. 6 November/December 52–61.

Rose, Richard. 1995b. "Democracy and Enlarging the European Union Eastwards." *Journal of Common Market Studies,* 33, no. 3: 427–450.

Rose, Richard. 1996. "Ex-Communists in Post-Communist Societies." *Political Quarterly,* January.

Rose, Richard, and Davies, Phillip. 1994. *Inheritance in Public Policy: Change Without Choice in Britain.* New Haven and London: Yale University Press.

Rose, Richard, and Garvin, Tom. 1983. "The Public Policy Effects of Independence: Ireland as a Test Case." *European Journal of Political Research* 11, no. 2: 377–397.

Rose, Richard, and Haerpfer, Christian. 1994. *New Democracies Barometer III: Learning from What Is Happening.* Glasgow: University of Strathclyde Studies in Public Policy No. 230.

Rose, Richard and Karran, Terrence. 1987. *Taxation by Political Inertia.* London: George Allen and Unwin.

Rose, Richard, and Kavanagh, Dennis. 1976. "The Monarchy in Contemporary Political Culture." *Comparative Politics* 8, no. 3: 548–576.

Rose, Richard, and McAllister, Ian. 1996. "Is Money the Measure of Welfare in Russia?" *Review Income and Wealth* 42, no. 1 March.

Rose, Richard, and Mackie, Thomas T. 1983. "Incumbency in Government: Asset or Liability?" In H. Daalder and P. Mair, eds. *Western European Party Systems,* 115–137. Beverly Hills: Sage Publications.

Rose, Richard, and Mackie, Thomas T. 1988. "Do Parties Persist or Fail? The Big Trade-Off Facing Organizations." In Kay Lawson and Peter Merkl, eds., *When Parties Fail,* 533–558. Princeton: Princeton University Press.

Rose, Richard, and Makkai, Toni. 1995. "Consensus or Dissensus About Welfare in Post-Communist Societies." *European Journal of Political Research* 28, no. 2: 203–224.

Rose, Richard, and Maley, William. 1994. "Conflict or Compromise in the Baltic States?" *RFE/RL Research Report,* 3, no. 28: 26–35.

Rose, Richard, and Mishler, William. 1994. "Mass Reaction to Regime Change in Eastern Europe: Polarization or Leaders and Laggards?" *British Journal of Political Science* 24, no. 2: 159–182.

Rose, Richard, and Mishler, William. 1996. "Representation and Leadership in Post-Communist Political Systems." *Journal of Communist Studies and Transition Politics,* 12, no. 2.

Rose, Richard, and Mishler, William. 1995. *What Are the Alternatives to Democracy in Post-Communist Societies?* Glasgow: University of Strathclyde Studies in Public Policy No. 248.

Rose, Richard, and Page, Edward C. 1996. "German Responses to Regime Change: Culture, Economy or Context?" *West European Politics,* 19.

Rose, Richard, and Peters, B. Guy. 1978. *Can Government Go Bankrupt?* New York: Basic Books.

Rose, Richard, and Tikhomirov, Evgeny. 1993. "Who Grows Food in Russia and Eastern Europe?" *Post-Soviet Geography* 34, no. 2: 111–126.

Rose, Richard and Urwin, Derek W., 1970, "Persistence and Change in Western Party Systems since 1945," *Political Studies,* 18, no. 3: 287–319.

Rose, Richard, and Urwin, Derek W. 1975. *Regional Differentiation and Political Unity in Western Nations.* Beverly Hills: Sage Contemporary Political Sociology Series 06-007.

Rothstein, Bo. 1993. "The Crisis of the Swedish Social Democrats and the Future of the Universal Welfare State." *Governance* 6, no. 2: 492–517.

Rouban, Luc, ed. 1993. "Public Administration and Political Change." *International Political Science Review* 14, no. 4: 315–422.

Rule, Wilma. 1987. "Electoral Systems, Contextual Factors and Women's Opportunity for Election to Parliament in 23 Democracies." *Western Political Quarterly* 40: 477–498.

Rustow, Dankwart A. 1955. *The Politics of Compromise: A Study of Parties and Cabinet Government in Sweden.* Princeton: Princeton University Press.

Rustow, D.A. 1970. "Transitions to Democracy." *Comparative Politics* 2: 337–363.

Sachs, Jeffrey. 1993. *Poland's Jump to the Market Economy.* Cambridge: MIT Press.

Saltman, Richard B. 1988. *International Handbook of Healthcare Systems.* New York: Greenwood.

Sartori, Giovanni. 1976. *Parties and Party Systems.* New York: Cambridge University Press.

Sartori, Giovanni, ed. 1984. *Social Science Concepts.* Beverly Hills: Sage Publications.

Sartori, Giovanni. 1987. *The Theory of Democracy Revisited.* Chatham, NJ: Chatham House.

Sartori, Giovanni. 1993. "Totalitarianism, Model Mania and Learning from Error." *Journal of Theoretical Politics* 5, no. 1: 5–22.

Sartori, Giovanni, 1994. *Comparative Constitutional Engineering.* Basingstoke, England: Macmillan.

Sbragia, Alberta, ed. 1992. *Euro-Politics: Institutions and Policymaking in the "New" European Community.* Washington: Brookings Institution.

Scharpf, Friz W. 1994. "Community and Autonomy: Multi-Level Policymaking in the European Union." *Journal of European Public Policy* 1, no. 2: 219–242.

Schattschneider, E. E. 1961. *The Semi-Sovereign People.* New York: Holt, Rinehart.

Schmidhauser, John. 1992. "Courts." In Mary Hawkesworth and Maurice Kogan, eds., *Encyclopedia of Government and Politics,* vol. 1, 293–303. New York: Routledge.

Schmidt, Manfred. 1983. "Two Logics of Coalition Policy: The West German Case." In V. Bogdanor, q.v., 38–58.

Schmidt, Vivien. 1990. *Democratizing France.* New York: Cambridge University Press.

Schmitt, Hermann, and Mannheimer, Renato, eds. 1991. "The European Elections of June, 1989." *European Journal of Political Research* 19, no. 1.

Schmitter, Philippe C. 1974. "Still the Century of Corporatism?" *Review of Politics* 36: 85–131.

Schmitter, Philippe C., and Karl, Terry Lynn. 1991. "What Democracy Is . . . and Is Not." *Journal of Democracy* 2, no. 2, 75–88.

Schmitter, C., and Lehmbruch, G., eds. 1980. *Trends Toward Corporatist Intermediation.* London: Sage Publications.

Schumpeter, Joseph A. 1946. "The American Economic in the Interwar Period." *American Economic Review* 36 (supplement): 1–10.

Schumpeter, Joseph A. 1952. *Capitalism, Socialism and Democracy,* 4th ed. London: George Allen and Unwin.

Schwartz, Herman. 1993. "The New Courts: An Overview." *East European Constitutional Review,* 2, no. 2: 28–32.

Shafir, Martin. 1992. "Romania's Elections: Why the Democratic Convention Lost." *RFE/RL Research Report* 1, no. 43 (October, 30): 1–5.

Shapiro, Martin. 1992. "The European Court of Justice." In A. Sbragia, q.v., 123–151.

Shapiro, Martin, and Stone, Alec, eds. 1994. "The New Constitutional Politics of Europe." *Comparative Political Studies* 26, no. 4: 397–561.

Share, Donald. 1985. "Two Transitions: Democratization and the Evolution of the Spanish Socialist Left." *West European Politics* 8, no. 1: 82–103.

Sharpe, L. J., ed. 1993. *The Rise of Meso Government in Europe.* Newbury Park, CA.: Sage Publications.

Shils, Edward A. 1956. *The Torment of Secrecy.* London: Heinemann.

Shin, Doh Chull. 1994. "On the Third Wave of Democratization." *World Politics* 47, no. 1: 135–170.

Shlapentokh, Vladimir. 1989. *Public and Private Life of the Soviet People: Changing Values in Post-Stalin Russia.* New York: Oxford University Press.

Shonfield, Andrew. 1972. *Europe: Journey to an Unknown Destination.* Baltimore: Penguin Books.

Shugart, Matthew Soberg, and Carey, John M. 1992. *Presidents and Assemblies: Constitutional Design and Electoral Dynamics.* New York: Cambridge University Press.

Sicherl, Pavle. 1992. "Integrating Comparisons Across Time and Space: Methodology and Applications to Disparities Within Yugoslavia." *Journal of Public Policy* 12, no. 4: 377–404.

Sivard, Ruth Leger. 1993. *World Military and Social Expenditures 1993,* 15th ed. Washington: World Priorities.

Smith, Gordon K. 1991. "The Resources of a German Chancellor." *West European Politics* 13, no. 2: 48–61.

Smith, Steven K., and Wertman, Douglas A. 1992. *US-West European Relations during the Reagan Years: The Perspectives of West European Politics.* London: Macmillan.

Snyder, Francis. 1990. *New Directions in Community Law.* London: Weidenfeld and Nicolson.

Snyder, Francis. 1993. "The Effectiveness of European Community Law: Institutions, Processes, Tools and Techniques." *Modern Law Review* 56, no. 1: 19–54.

Staniszkis, Jadwiga. 1984. *Poland's Self-Limiting Revolution.* Princeton: Princeton University Press.

Stanley, Harold W., and Niemi, Richard G. 1994. *Vital Statistics on American Politics,* 4th ed. Washington: CQ Press.

Steiner, Juerg, and Dorff, Robert H. 1980. "Decision by Interpretation," *British Journal of Political Science* 10, no. 1: 1–13.

Stepan, Alfred, and Skach, Cindy. 1993. "Constitutional Frameworks and Democratic Consolidation." *World Politics* 46, no. 1: 1–22.

Stewart, William H. 1982. "Metaphors, Models and the Development of Federal Theory." *Publius* 12: 5–24.

Stokes, Donald E. 1963. "Spatial Models of Party Competition." *American Political Science Review* 57: 368–377.

Stone, Alec. 1992. *The Birth of Judicial Politics in France.* New York: Oxford University Press.

Streeck, Wolfgang, and Schmitter, Philippe C., eds. 1985. *Private Interest Government.* Beverly Hills: Sage Publications.

Strom, Kaare. 1990. *Minority Government and Majority Rule.* New York: Cambridge University Press.

Suleiman, Ezra, ed., 1984. *Bureaucrats and Policymaking.* New York: Holmes and Meier.

Summers, Lawrence. 1992. "The Next Decade in Central and Eastern Europe." In C. Clague and G. C. Rausser, eds., *The Emergence of Market Economies in Eastern Europe.* 25-34. Cambridge, MA: Blackwell.

Szablowski, George. 1993. "Governing and Competing Elites in Poland." *Governance,* 6, no. 3, 341-357.

Szablowski, George, and Derlien, Hans-Ulrich. 1993. "East European Transitions, Elites, Bureaucracies and the European Community." *Governance* 6, no. 3: 304-323.

Szporluk, Roman. 1991. "The Soviet West—or Far Eastern Europe?" *East European Politics and Society* 5, no. 3: 466-482.

Taagepera, R., and Shugart, M. S. 1989. *Seats and Votes: The Effects and Determinants of Electoral Systems.* New Haven: Yale University Press.

Tanzi, Vito, ed. 1992. *Fiscal Policies in Economies in Transition.* Washington: International Monetary Fund.

Tarrow, Sidney. 1977. *Between Center and Periphery: Grassroots Politicians in Italy and France.* New Haven: Yale University Press.

Therborn, Goran. 1995. *European Modernity and Beyond.* Thousand Oaks, CA: Sage Publications.

Thomas, J. J. 1992. *Informal Economic Activity.* New York: Harvester Wheatsheaf.

Thompson, Sir George. 1961. *The Inspiration of Science.* London: Oxford University Press.

Tilly, Charles, ed. 1975. *The Formation of National States in Western Europe.* Princeton: Princeton University Press.

Titmuss, Richard. 1958. *Essays on "The Welfare State."* London: George Allen and Unwin.

Tucker, Emma. 1995. "Serious Problems Hinder the EU's Single Market." *Financial Times* (June 16, 1995).

Turpin, Colin. 1985. *British Government and the Constitution: Text, Cases and Materials.* London: Weidenfeld and Nicolson.

UNICEF. 1994. *Crisis in Mortality, Health and Nutrition.* Florence, Italy: International Child Development Centre Regional Monitoring Report No. 2.

Urwin, Derek W. 1974. "Germany: Continuity and Change in Electoral Politics." In R. Rose, ed., *Electoral Behavior,* 109-170. New York: Free Press.

Urwin, Derek W. 1980. *From Ploughshare to Ballotbox: The Politics of Agrarian Defence in Europe.* Oslo: Universitetsforlaget.

Urwin, Derek W. 1989. *Western Europe since 1945,* 4th ed. New York: Longman.

Vallinder, Torbjorn, ed. 1994. "The Judicialization of Politics." *International Political Science Review* 15, no. 2: 91-198.

Vanhanen, Tatu. 1990. *The Process of Democratization: a Comparative Study of 147 States, 1980-88.* New York: Crane Russak.

van Waarden, F. 1992. "New Dimensions and Types of Policy Networks." *European Journal of Political Research* 21, no. 1: 29-52.

Vickers, John, and Yarrow, George. 1988. *Privatization: An Economic Analysis.* Cambridge: MIT Press.

Vinton, Louisa. 1992. "Poland's Little Constitution Clarifies Walesa's Powers." *RFE/RL Research Report* (September 4).

Vinton, Louisa. 1993. "Poland Goes Left." *RFE/RL Research Report* 2, no. 40 (October 8): 21–23.

Vogel, David. 1986. *National Styles of Regulation: Environmental Policy in Great Britain and the United States.* Ithaca: Cornell University Press.

Volcansek, Mary L., ed. 1992. *Judicial Politics and Policymaking in Western Europe.* London: Frank Cass.

Walker, Jack L. 1991. *Mobilizing Interest Groups in America.* Ann Arbor: University of Michigan Press.

Wallace, Claire, and Palyanitsya, Andrii. 1995. "East-West Migration in the Czech Republic." *Journal of Public Policy* 15, no. 1: 89–109.

Wallace, Helen, Wallace, William and Webb, Carole, eds. 1983. *Policymaking in the European Community,* 2nd ed. New York: Wiley.

Waller, Michael. 1994. "Groups, Parties and Political Change in Eastern Europe from 1977." In G. Pridham and T. Vanhanen, eds., *Democratization in Eastern Europe,* 63–98. New York: Routledge.

Waller, Michael. 1995. "Starting-up Problems: Communists, Social Democrats, and Greens." In G. Wightman, ed., *Party Formation in East-Central Europe,* 217–237. Aldershot, England: Edward Elgar.

Waltman, Jerold, and Holland, Kenneth, eds. 1988. *The Political Role of Law Courts in Modern Democracies.* London: Macmillan.

Warwick, Paul V. 1994. *Government Survival in Parliamentary Democracies.* New York: Cambridge University Press.

Waters, Sarah. 1994. "'Tangentopoli' and the Emergence of a New Political Order in Italy." *West European Politics* 17, no. 1: 169–182.

Weaver, R. Kent, and Rockman, Bert A., eds. 1993. *Do Institutions Matter? Government Capabilities in the United States and Abroad.* Washington: Brookings Institution.

Webb, W. L. 1992. "The Polish General Election of 1991." *Electoral Studies* 11, no. 2: 166–170.

Weber, Eugen. 1979. *Peasants into Frenchmen: The Modernization of Rural France, 1870–1914.* London: Chatto and Windus.

Weber, Max. 1972. *Wirtschaft und Gesellschaft,* 5th ed. Tübingen, Germany: J. C. B. Mohr.

Wedel, Janine R. 1986 *The Private Poland.* New York: Facts on File.

Wedel, Janine R., ed. 1992. *The Unplanned Society: Poland During and After Communism.* New York: Columbia University Press.

Weil, Frederick D. 1987. "Cohorts Regimes, and the Legitimation of Democracy: West Germany Since 1945." *American Sociological Review* 52: 308–324.

Weil, Frederick D. 1989. "The Sources and Structure of Legitimation in Western Democracies." *American Sociological Review* 54: 682–706.

Weiler, Joseph. 1991. "The Transformation of Europe." *Yale Law Journal* 100, no. 8: 2403–2483.

Weiler, Joseph. 1993. "Journey to an Unknown Destination: The European Court of Justice in the Arena of Political Integration." *Journal of Common Market Studies* 31, no. 4: 417–446.

Weiner, Myron, and Ozbudun, Ergun, eds. 1987. *Competitive Elections in Developing Countries.* Durham, NC: Duke University Press.

Welsh, Helga A. 1994. "Political Transition Processes in Central and Eastern Europe," *Comparative Politics* 26, no. 4: 379-394.

Westney, Eleanor. 1987. *Innovation and Imitation: The Transfer of Western Organizational Patterns to Meiji Japan.* Cambridge: Harvard University Press.

White, Stephen L., ed. 1990. "Elections in Eastern Europe." *Electoral Studies* 9, no. 4: 277-366.

White, Stephen L., and McAllister, Ian. 1994. *Communists After Communism.* Glasgow: University of Strathclyde Studies in Public Policy No. 221.

White, Stephen, McAllister, Ian, and Rose, Richard. 1996. *How Russia Votes.* Chatham, NJ: Chatham House.

Wightman, Gordon, ed. 1995. *Party Formation in East-Central Europe.* Aldershot, England: Edward Elgar.

Williamson, Peter J. 1989. *Corporatism in Perspective: An Introductory Guide to Corporatist Theory.* Beverly Hills, CA.: Sage Publications.

Wilsford, David. 1994. "Path Dependency, or Why History Makes It Difficult but Not Impossible to Reform Health Care Systems in a Big Way," *Journal of Public Policy* 14, no. 3: 251-284.

Winiecki, Jan. 1988. "Four Kinds of Fallacies in Comparing Market-Type and Soviet-Type Economies: Issues and Outcomes." *Banca Nazionale del Lavoro Quarterly Review.* no. 164: 79-103.

Winiecki, Jan. 1988a. *The Distorted World of Soviet-Type Economics.* London: Routledge.

Wittfogel, Karl. 1957. *Oriental Despotism: A Comparative Study of Total Power.* New Haven: Yale University Press.

Woldendorp, Jaap, Keman, Hans, and Budge, Ian, eds. 1993. "Party Government in 20 Democracies." a special issue of *European Journal of Political Research* 24, 1.

Wolff, Larry. 1994. *Inventing Eastern Europe: The Map of Civilization on the Mind of the Enlightenment.* Stanford: Stanford University Press.

Wolinetz, Steven B. 1991. "Party System Change: The Catch-all Thesis Revisited." *West European Politics.* 14, no. 1: 113-128.

Woolley, John T. 1992. "Policy Credibility and European Monetary Institutions." In A. Sbragia, q.v., 157-190.

Young, Hugo. 1990. *One of Us.* London: Pan Books.

Z. 1990. "To the Stalin Mausoleum." *Daedalus* 119, 1, 295-344.

Zaslavsky, V., and Brym, Robert. 1978. "The Functions of Elections in the USSR." *Soviet Studies* 30: 362-371.

INDEX